# Diploma Case Study Book

## Analysis and Decision

## 2002–2003

GW01035933

# Diploma Case Study Book

## Analysis and Decision

# 2002–2003

Ashok Ranchhod

BUTTERWORTH
HEINEMANN

OXFORD   AMSTERDAM   BOSTON   LONDON   NEW YORK   PARIS
SAN DIEGO   SAN FRANCISCO   SINGAPORE   SYDNEY   TOKYO

Butterworth-Heinemann
An imprint of Elsevier Science
Linacre House, Jordan Hill, Oxford OX2 8DP
225 Wildwood Avenue, Woburn MA 01801-2041

First published 2002

Copyright © 2002, Ashok Ranchhod. All rights reserved

The right of Ashok Ranchhod to be identified as the author of this work
has been asserted in accordance with the Copyright, Designs and
Patents Act 1988

No part of this publication may be reproduced in any material form (including
photocopying or storing in any medium by electronic means and whether
or not transiently or incidentally to some other use of this publication) without
the written permission of the copyright holder except in accordance with the
provisions of the Copyright, Designs and Patents Act 1988 or under the terms of
a licence issued by the Copyright Licensing Agency Ltd, 90 Tottenham Court Road,
London, England W1T 4LP. Applications for the copyright holder's written
permission to reproduce any part of this publication should be addressed
to the publisher

**British Library Cataloguing in Publication Data**
A catalogue record for this book is available from the British Library

ISBN 0 7506 5711 1

For information on all Butterworth-Heinemann publications
visit our website at www.bh.com

Typeset by Integra Software Services Pvt. Ltd, Pondicherry, India
www.integra-india.com
Printed and bound in Italy

# Contents

## A message from the author

For some time now, the Chartered Institute of Marketing Diploma has been stressing the strategic aspects of marketing at the Diploma level. This has led to a considerable development of the four Diploma papers. The Analysis and Decision Paper encompasses the multidisciplinary nature of marketing, drawing on a range of concepts studied at the Certificate, Advanced Diploma and Diploma levels of the Chartered Institute of Marketing. Considerable skills in marketing as well as depth of knowledge in marketing are required. This version updates some of the ideas introduced last year. There are two new units. One discusses some of the contemporary aspects of marketing and the other shows a worked case.

*Professor Ashok Ranchhod 2002*

CIM Senior Examiner, Analysis and Decision

## An introduction from the academic development advisor

This year has seen the continuation of our commitment to ensure that the CIM Coursebooks are kept up to date and relevant for the forthcoming session. This is deemed as essential as the dynamics of the global market are forever changing, often in a way most unexpected and indeed not anticipated – as no doubt you will have all experienced, especially in the wake of September 11th.

Over the past few years there have been a series of syllabus changes initiated by the Chartered Institute of Marketing to ensure that their qualifications continue to be relevant and of significant consequence in the world of marketing, both within industry and academia. As a result Butterworth-Heinemann and I are continuing to rigorously revise and update the Coursebook series in order to make sure that every title is the best possible study aid and accurately reflects the latest CIM syllabus.

The ongoing updates and revisions to the series include both restructuring and the inclusion of many new mini cases and examples to support the learning and assessment process. The authors are accomplished writers and have been commissioned both for their CIM course teaching and examining experience and their wide general knowledge of the latest marketing thinking.

We are certain that the coursebooks will be highly beneficial to your study, providing you with structure, direction, relevant examples and assessment opportunities that will enable you to focus on acquiring the broad range of theory and concepts required to underpin the examination and continuous assessment process.

The editorial team and authors wish you every success as you embark upon your studies.

*Karen Beamish*

Academic Development Advisor

## How to use these coursebooks

Everyone who has contributed to this series has been careful to structure the books with the exams in mind. Each unit, therefore, covers an essential part of the syllabus. You need to work through the complete coursebook systematically to ensure that you have covered everything you need to know.

This coursebook is divided into units each containing a selection of the following standard elements:

- **Objectives** tell you what part of the syllabus you will be covering and what you will be expected to know, having read the unit.
- **Questions** are designed to give you practice – they will be similar to those you get in the exam.
- **Answers** give you a suggested format for answering exam questions. *Remember* there is no such thing as a model answer – you should use these examples only as guidelines.
- **Exam hints** are tips from the senior examiner or examiner which are designed to help you avoid common mistakes made by previous candidates.
- **Study tips** give you guidance on improving your knowledge base.
- **Contemporary issues** is a section looking specifically at some of the current issues in marketing.
- **Summaries** cover what you should have picked up from reading the unit.

As this paper has no specific syllabus the key issues surrounding the development and execution of the Case Study are discussed. The interlink between the various other areas of the CIM syllabi are stressed. In order to get the best out of this text you should also refresh your current knowledge of the other Diploma subjects.

## About MarketingOnline

With this year's coursebooks Butterworth-Heinemann is offering readers free access to MarketingOnline (www.marketingonline.co.uk), our premier online support engine for the CIM marketing courses. On this site you can benefit from:

- Tutorials on key topics every two weeks during the term, comprehensive revision support material and access to revision days from Tactics – the highly acclaimed independent trainer for CIM courses.
- Fully customizable electronic versions of the coursebooks – annotate, cut and paste sections of text to create your own tailored learning notes.
- Access to the e-Library – electronic versions of eight classic BH marketing texts to enrich and extend your knowledge.
- Instant access to specimen papers and answers, as well as other extra material and weblinks related to the coursebooks.
- Capacity to search the coursebook online for instant access to definitions and key concepts.

---

### Logging on

Before you can access MarketingOnline you will first need to get a password. Please go to www.marketingonline.co.uk where you will find registration instructions for coursebook purchasers. Once you have got your password, you will need to log on using the onscreen instructions. This will give you access to the various functions outlined below.

---

## Using MarketingOnline

MarketingOnline is broadly divided into six sections which can each be accessed from the front page after you have logged on to the system:

1  **The coursebooks**: buttons corresponding to the three levels of CIM marketing qualification are situated on the home page. Select your level and you will be presented with the four coursebook titles for each module of that level. Click on the desired coursebook to access the full online text (divided up by chapter). On each page of text you have the option to add an electronic bookmark or annotation by following the onscreen instructions. You can also freely cut and paste text into a blank word document to create your own learning notes.

2  **The e-Library**: click on the 'BH Library' button on the front page to access the eight titles in the e-Library. Again you can annotate, bookmark and copy text as you see fit.

3  **Revision material**: click on the 'Revision material' link and select the appropriate CIM level and coursebook to access revision material.

4  **Useful links**: click on 'Useful links' to access a list of links to other sites of interest for further reading and research.

5  **Glossary**: click on the 'Glossary' button to access our online dictionary of marketing terms.

6  **Discussion**: click on the 'Discussion' button to access our various online noticeboards. All users can access and put up entries on our public noticeboard using onscreen instructions. If your college has registered as a MarketingOnline user you may also have access to your own 'Tutor Group Discussion' where you can interact with your fellow students and tutors.

If you have specific queries about using MarketingOnline then you should consult our fully searchable FAQ section – again, this is accessible through the appropriate link on the front page of the site. Please also note that a **full user guide** can be downloaded by clicking on the link on the opening page of the website.

# Part 1: Approaching the Analysis and Decision Paper

## Introduction

The Analysis and Decision paper is generally the final paper that students studying for CIM qualifications undertake. It requires students to have a good knowledge of all the subjects covered at all levels. It is particularly important that candidates have a good knowledge of subject areas at Advanced Diploma and Diploma levels. For this reason, there is no specific syllabus for this paper. The new Planning and Control syllabus gives a good insight into the key areas of marketing and offers a basis for strategic analysis and implementation. This type of knowledge is required to tackle the A & D paper. Together with this it is highly important that students have an equally strong grasp of Integrated Marketing Communications and International Strategy at the Diploma level. The paper requires the application of all the marketing knowledge and experience that students would have gained over several years.

As the title of the paper 'Analysis and Decision' suggests, good analytical and implementation skills within a marketing context are required. Marketers always need to have good analytical capabilities in order to develop marketing strategies. Once these strategies have been developed, clear and sensible decisions need to be made. Candidates need to be conversant with all aspects of marketing, especially contemporary issues. Cases are by their very nature set in different sectors, have different contexts and require knowledge from different areas of marketing. Marketing problems are rarely neatly packaged. Candidates, therefore, have to have the capability to draw from their wealth of experience and knowledge and also to demonstrate flexibility and creativity by being able to tackle problems in a variety of contexts set in a variety of sectors in different areas of the globe. As we enter the new millennium, marketing is undergoing many changes and marketers need to be able to develop a range of skills. These skills are tested in this module through the outcomes that are outlined below.

## The changing focus of the paper

- Marketing as a subject area is undergoing major changes. These changes are taking place as a result of dramatic shifts in technology demographics, globalization, systems of production, logistics and ecological issues. The papers, therefore are designed to reflect more of these contemporary issues in addition to the knowledge base mentioned above.
- The case studies will also be designed to develop strategic marketing issues which can be operationalized and implemented within realistic constraints. It is often forgotten that marketing is not just about positioning and growth, but also about effectiveness within given constraints within most organizations. These constraints mean that strategies have to be sensibly evaluated and chosen with hard decisions being made. When particular strategies are chosen, it is clear that the constraints could be many and varied. Constraints, for instance, could be financial, organizational (both employee and culture related), marketing (image, size of markets, branding, distribution systems, networks) and if, the organization is a division of a larger entity, headquarter imposed constraints.

### Globalization

- The rapid changes in technology are far reaching as they are changing the normal paradigms of marketing. The four Ps cannot now be discussed with certainty. The nature and direction of marketing strategies, necessarily have to take into account the massive

*Impact of www* computing power available and the new developments on the Web. Many multi-nationals have operated globally for decades, but technology is changing the patterns of production and consumption.

- For instance, global brands are available anywhere and production facilities may be located in a myriad of different countries (Philips, December, 1998 case). For smaller companies, locked into local markets, the Internet holds the promises and pitfalls of operating in a global arena.
- The introduction of the euro means that pan-European marketing strategies have to be thought through in a different manner. The changing nature and the growth of South Asian markets has an enormous impact on the marketing strategies of organizations (*see* the Biocatalysts case study). The nature and strength of the American market is often forgotten (Acclaim case). The case studies will reflect these changes and will embrace many different sectors of industry.

## Organizational issues

- When developing marketing strategies it is important that the culture and nature of the organization is taken into account. Marketing strategies often succeed and fail as a result of inappropriate personnel, inappropriate structures or climates within organizations. Success or failure of strategies can be defined by utilizing a number of different performance measures such as market share growth, return on investment, brand awareness and sales growth among others. Organizations are therefore always striving to create the appropriate structures and develop appropriate cultures to meet the demands of the market place.
- The customer is king and marketing strategists have to place the level of market orientation at the centre of their thinking.

## Sustainability

- With the growing problems related to the general environmental deterioration and the increasing concern over climatic changes, the issues surrounding sustainability are of critical importance to marketers. Marketing literature has for long been concerned with growth and market share. It is important that issues surrounding the constraints imposed by the environment are taken into account. The world is facing an enormous challenge in terms of the availability of resources and the needs of the population.

## Constraints

- In some respects a challenge posed to marketing strategists is the need to consider constraints and responsibility. Constraints can be financial (Biocatalysts case) or related to the human resource capabilities of an organization. In many instances constraints can be imposed by the external environment and these are particularly important for the growth of a company's markets (Acclaim case study).

## Financial Issues

- Financial issues will always play a key role in developing strategies. A good knowledge of basic financial statements such as P & L accounts, Balance Sheets and Cashflow statements is required.

## Knowledge of Contemporary Marketing Issues

- Each case is different and will therefore test some knowledge of contemporary issues. Students therefore need to be encouraged to read journal articles pertaining to the case study.

## Application of previous knowledge

- The need to apply models for analysis will continue. However, a more critical approach in applying these techniques will be needed. The paper will reflect the need for both academic and practical knowledge as true marketers need to have experience in both areas for developing sensible strategies.

## Issues of Implementation and Control

- An awareness of the clear decision-making and implementation strategies will be tested. As will be strategic positioning, innovation and branding in the context of implementation and control.

## Links with other papers

This paper deliberately has no syllabus. The paper is the culmination of all the knowledge gained at the Advanced Certificate and Diploma levels. The foundations laid by the Marketing Communications Strategy, International Marketing Strategy and Planning and Control Syllabi underpin the Analysis and Decision Paper. In addition to this, the Planning and Control syllabus offers the fundamental underpinning knowledge needed to undertake strategic analysis. In tutoring and preparing students for this paper, tutors need to be aware of the linkages with other areas and they need to be able to draw from a variety of literature sources in order to enhance and improve their Analytic- and Decision-making skills.

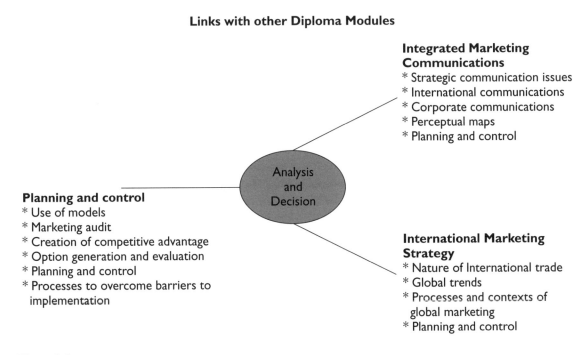

**Links with other Diploma Modules**

*Figure 1.1*

## Outcomes

As this paper has no syllabus and expects to draw on material from all the other syllabi on the CIM Certificate, Advanced Certificate and Diploma stages, the emphasis is on outcomes. These outcomes are listed and explained below.

- Demonstrate an in-depth understanding of the strategic marketing planning process and develop a creative and innovative strategic marketing plan.

*The links with the Planning and Control paper are fairly clear. This outcome tests the level of creativity that you have reached in marketing as well as your ability to direct others, as a result of the development of a marketing plan.*

- Critically evaluate case studies using a wide variety of marketing techniques, concepts and models and an understanding of contemporary marketing issues.

*Case analysis will require knowledge from a range of previous sources such as finance, international marketing and communication. This outcome relates to the necessary skills all marketers should possess – financial management skills and information management skills. Marketing needs individuals who can create information from data and then relate this to contemporary marketing theory and strategies.*

- Critically evaluate various options available within given constraints and justify any decisions taken.

*It is important that students are able to effectively analyse sensible options and to work within given financial, marketing, personnel and possibly ecological constraints. This is a key skill that marketers need to develop. Without good evaluative skills, clear and sensible marketing strategies cannot be devised.*

- Understand and apply competitive positioning strategies within a given case study.

*Competitive positioning is part of the Planning and Control syllabus and to some extent also the communications and international syllabi. It is important that students can use the key matrices as well as perceptual maps. This aspect of marketing tests your analytical skills. Information needs to be analysed and then collated critically into marketing models.*

- Demonstrate the ability to analyse numerical data and management information and utilize this to make decisions about key underlying issues within the case study.

*This is one area where students seem to under-perform. Often there is a range of marketing and financial information which needs to be analysed PRIOR to developing possible options. Students need to be aware or need to refresh their knowledge of the Advanced Certificate Module: Management Information for Marketing Decisions.*

- Synthesize various strands of knowledge from the different Diploma subjects effectively in the context of the Case Study Examination.

*The Case requires candidates to be aware that every case is different and that every case requires a kaleidoscopic knowledge from other areas of the CIM marketing modules. It is also important that this knowledge is used WITHIN the required context of the case. This outcome is related to developing creativity and an ability to synthesize knowledge from various sources in a coherent manner, so that it can be applied to the problem in question.*

- Apply both practical and academic marketing knowledge within a given Case Study.

*Many candidates usually just pick out theoretical models; often without properly applying them to the case. It is important that the theory is applicable. At the same time the ability to apply the theory, with examples, shows an insight into the practical applications. This may be easier for candidates with some practical experience of marketing.*

- Comprehend and resolve a wide variety of marketing problems.

*As each case is different, there will be a variety of industries and a variety of problems that will need addressing. Practice on previous cases therefore is quite important.*

- Comprehend cultural issues in developing and implementing strategies.

*An understanding of the cultural framework within which plans should be formulated is important, if given strategies are to succeed.*

- Develop appropriate control aspects and contingency plans.

  *This goes back to the first point made about planning. No plan or programme of action for a company is complete without understanding that control measures are important. At the same time contingency plans should also be considered. This outcome, again, tests your ability to be directive.*

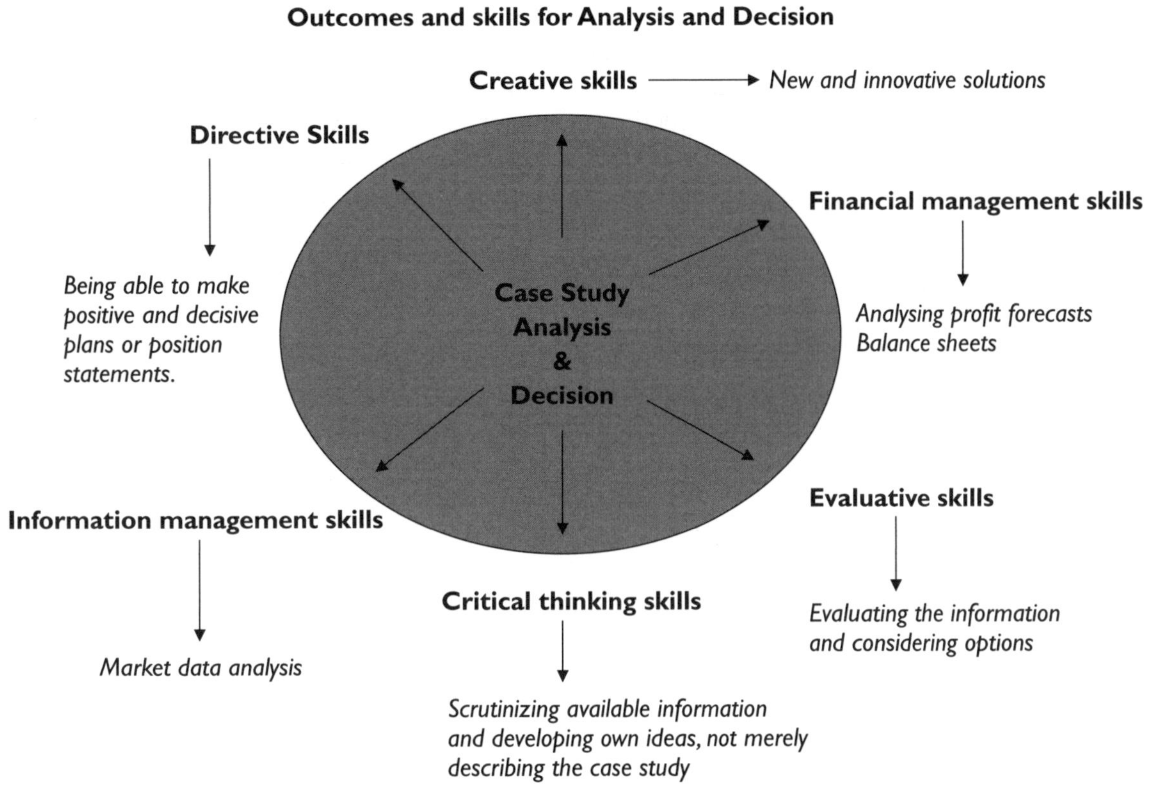

**Outcomes and skills for Analysis and Decision**

**Creative skills** ⟶ *New and innovative solutions*

**Directive Skills**

*Being able to make positive and decisive plans or position statements.*

**Case Study Analysis & Decision**

**Financial management skills**

*Analysing profit forecasts Balance sheets*

**Information management skills**

*Market data analysis*

**Critical thinking skills**

*Scrutinizing available information and developing own ideas, not merely describing the case study*

**Evaluative skills**

*Evaluating the information and considering options*

*Figure 1.2*

## Summary

This chapter gives you an idea of the issues the Analysis and Decision Paper covers. It also shows that learning outcomes are more important than specific syllabus regurgitation. In order to reach the desired outcomes, students need to be able to critically assess and absorb the key concepts in the other areas of the Diploma and their applications to real marketing problems. When studying previous cases students should attempt to list the key outcomes that they have achieved, together with some of the key skills that they have used in order to reach a satisfactory level of competence.

## A brief overview

A case study is an account of the major events taking place in a business within an industry sector over a number of years. A case usually features many of the key events in that it chronicles the events that have been dealt with and have to be dealt with by marketing managers. Issues pertaining to the competitive environment, changes in the business definition and the main areas of the served market segments have to be dealt with by marketing managers.

Cases give students a chance to understand some of the problems faced by organizations and be able to analyse them in detail.

Cases allow students to utilize their understanding of key concepts. Their meaning is made clearer when applied to case studies. Theory and concepts help to analyse a company's situation. Analysing a case requires great powers of deduction. Facts and figures are often hidden in the different areas of the case. The conceptual tools help to probe the case and gather evidence of events. In the real world, it is important to understand that there are no right answers. For most companies strategic marketing management is difficult. Developing strategies is generally an uncertain game, making it more important to develop a careful diagnosis. All that managers can do is to make the best guess.

As different individuals have differing ideas, case studies provide students with the opportunity to participate in class and to learn from others. Tutors often act as facilitators in this process of enquiry and analysis. In actual businesses this is exactly the way decisions are made. It is important therefore, that students can analyse the situation and be confident of their solutions.

## Analysing a case study

The CIM Diploma paper is rightly called Analysis and Decision. One of the purposes of the Case Study is to let you analyse the situation that the company finds itself in. In doing this you will need to apply many of the key concepts that you would have learnt in the other modules. A case study has to be read several times before a clear idea of the key issues can be established. This enables you to establish a picture of the environment in which the company is operating as well as the company's position within it. Eventually based on this analysis you will make a series of decisions to take the company forward into the future. A detailed and effective analysis of a case should include the following:

   a. The key historical events that have contributed to the development of the company
   b. A PESTLE analysis, which looks at Political, Economic, Social, Technological, Legal and Environmental issues surrounding the case
   c. A SWOT analysis and its evaluation
   d. Product market analyses and the links to strategic marketing
   e. Any constraints that the company faces from a resource point of view. These could be human, financial, technical or environmental
   f. Any structural features or control systems.
   g. A list of key issues that emanate from the above.

# The analyses

## The key historical events that have contributed to the development of the company

Cases often contain a history of the company. It is important to analyse this history and to list the key critical events that helped to shape the company's development. At the same time an analysis of the history will also offer insights into the evolution of a particular industry as in the case of Acclaim Incorporated. Historical analysis and charting can help in understanding product market decisions and any development and diversification decisions that have been made by the company.

## A PESTLE analysis, which looks at Political, Economic, Social, Technological, Legal and Environmental issues surrounding the case

Cases will contain some or all of the key PESTLE factors. This type of analysis allows you to understand the macroenvironment facing the industry sector that the company is immersed in. The Porter five forces framework allows a structured analysis of the environment and the competitive pressures on companies within the industry sector. The PESTLE factors also help to highlight key trends within the markets. Amongst others, these could be demographic profile trends (important in the Clerical Medical case), sociological issues (on GM Foods in Biocatalysts), branding trends in different markets (Philips case). Some of the technological factors may show up the lifecycle stages and any special factors affecting the model (Acclaim case). Analysing each of the factors gives some idea of the opportunities and threats facing a company.

## A SWOT analysis and its evaluation

In addition to the PESTLE analysis, a review of the company strengths and weaknesses is required. This is an internal audit of the company allowing you to examine each function in which the company is currently strong or weak. Companies could have a weakness in their branding strategies or new product development, yet may have current products which are well positioned in the market. Is a company in an overall strong position? Can it operate profitably in its current market sectors? How can the company minimize the threats to its position and expand on its opportunities? Can the company turn its weaknesses into strengths? A good SWOT analysis helps you to understand, in a clear and succinct manner, how the company is positioned. As part of this analysis, you may want to use the Porter five forces framework.

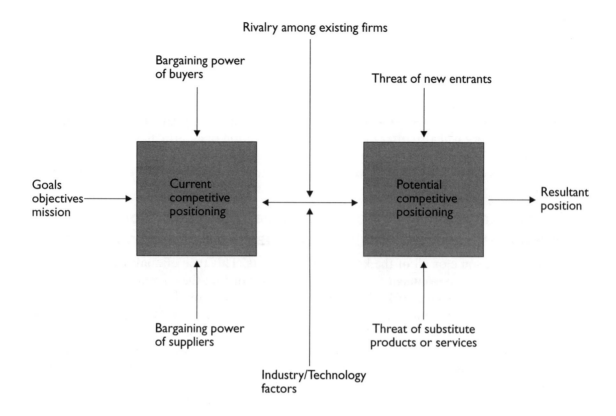

**Figure 2.1** *Porter framework*

## Product market analyses and the links to strategic marketing

Following on from the SWOT analysis, an analysis of the products and the markets within which the products and services are sold should be undertaken. This type of analysis will require you to be familiar with the various portfolio models such as the GE Matrix, the BCG matrix, the Ansoff matrix and various other relevant matrices. Below are examples of the expanded Ansoff Matrix (Figure 2.2) and Figure 2.3 shows the Directional Policy Matrix.

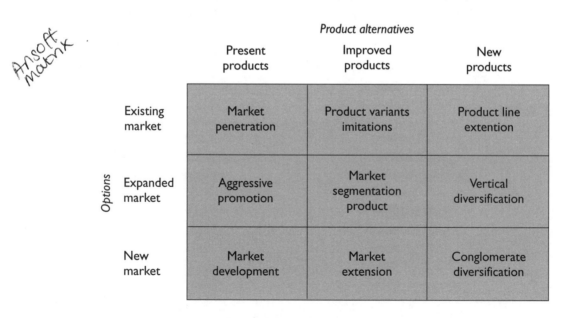

**Figure 2.2** *Growth vector analyses*

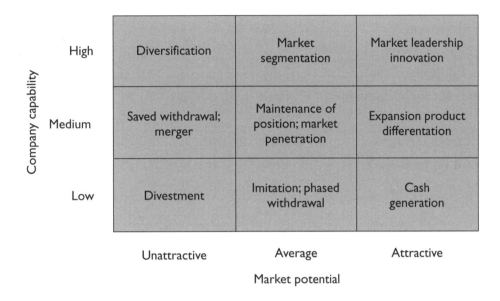

|  | Unattractive | Average | Attractive |
|---|---|---|---|
| High | Diversification | Market segmentation | Market leadership innovation |
| Medium | Saved withdrawal; merger | Maintenance of position; market penetration | Expansion product differentation |
| Low | Divestment | Imitation; phased withdrawal | Cash generation |

Company capability (vertical axis) — Market potential (horizontal axis)

**Figure 2.3** *Directional policy matrix*

In addition to these you may wish to utilize perceptual maps and consider product positioning from a competitive point of view. Linked to the product/market analysis should be a review of any gaps that the organization faces. These gaps could be:

- Product line gap: *Closing this gap entails completion of a product line, either in width or in depth, by introducing new or improved products*
- Distribution gap: *This gap can be reduced by expanding the coverage, intensity, and exposure of distribution*
- Usage gap: *To increase usage a firm needs to induce current non-users to try the product and encourage current users to increase their usage*
- Competitive gap: *This gap can be closed by making inroads into the market position of direct competitors as well as those who market substitute products*
- Internationalization gap: *This gap can be shortened through exporting, joint venture arrangements and strategic alliances*
- Communications gap: *This gap can be shortened through advertising strategies, PR, or proactive use of the Web.*

## SPACE analysis

All these analyses can be tied together by using SPACE analysis as discussed by the BCG group. SPACE stands for Strategic Position and Action Evaluation. This analysis is based on the following:

a.  The company's Financial Strength (FS)
b.  The Company's Competitive Advantage (CA)
c.  The Industry strength (The strength of the industry sector in which the company operates (IS))
d.  The stability of the environment in which the company operates (ES).

This analysis is based on your ability to analyse key aspects of the case study, pertaining to the company. The analysis depends on answering a range of questions and then taking an average.

Step one analysing each aspect as shown above.

## Financial Strength (FS)

*Factors determining financial strength*

| | | | | | | | | | |
|---|---|---|---|---|---|---|---|---|---|
| Return on investment | Low | 0 | 1 | 2 | 3 | 4 | 5 | 6 | High |
| Leverage (Debt to equity ratio) | Low | 0 | 1 | 2 | 3 | 4 | 5 | 6 | High |
| Liquidity (cash held) | Low | 0 | 1 | 2 | 3 | 4 | 5 | 6 | High |
| Capital required/capital available | High | 0 | 1 | 2 | 3 | 4 | 5 | 6 | Low |
| Cash flow | Weak | 0 | 1 | 2 | 3 | 4 | 5 | 6 | Strong |
| Ease of exit from the market | Difficult | 0 | 1 | 2 | 3 | 4 | 5 | 6 | Easy |
| Risk involved in the business | Low | 0 | 1 | 2 | 3 | 4 | 5 | 6 | High |
| Other (your own factor) | Low | 0 | 1 | 2 | 3 | 4 | 5 | 6 | High |

*Average:*

*Critical factors and your assessment of this area of the organization*

## Competitive Advantage (CA)

*Factors determining competitive advantage*

| | | | | | | | | | |
|---|---|---|---|---|---|---|---|---|---|
| Market share | Low | 0 | 1 | 2 | 3 | 4 | 5 | 6 | High |
| Product/Service quality (compared to competitors) | Low | 0 | 1 | 2 | 3 | 4 | 5 | 6 | High |
| Product life cycles stages (for range of products/services) | Similar | 0 | 1 | 2 | 3 | 4 | 5 | 6 | Different |
| Product/service replacement cycle | Variable | 0 | 1 | 2 | 3 | 4 | 5 | 6 | Fixed |
| Customer loyalty | Low | 0 | 1 | 2 | 3 | 4 | 5 | 6 | High |
| General utilization of capacity by the competition | Low | 0 | 1 | 2 | 3 | 4 | 5 | 6 | High |
| Technological knowledge and competence | Low | 0 | 1 | 2 | 3 | 4 | 5 | 6 | High |
| The degree of vertical integration of the company | Low | 0 | 1 | 2 | 3 | 4 | 5 | 6 | High |
| Other (your own factor) | Low | 0 | 1 | 2 | 3 | 4 | 5 | 6 | High |

*Average −6 =*

*Suppose the total score comes to 36. This divided by 8 factors = 4.5 take away 6 = −1.5 (So you will get a negative score for this factor)*

*Critical factors and your assessment of this area of the organization*

## Industry Strength (IS)

*Factors determining industry strength*

| | | 0 | 1 | 2 | 3 | 4 | 5 | 6 | |
|---|---|---|---|---|---|---|---|---|---|
| Growth potential | Low | 0 | 1 | 2 | 3 | 4 | 5 | 6 | High |
| Profit potential | Low | 0 | 1 | 2 | 3 | 4 | 5 | 6 | High |
| Financial stability (within the sector) | Low | 0 | 1 | 2 | 3 | 4 | 5 | 6 | High |
| Technological know how (needed to operate within the sector) | Simple | 0 | 1 | 2 | 3 | 4 | 5 | 6 | Complex |
| Resource utilization (generally within the sector) | Poor | 0 | 1 | 2 | 3 | 4 | 5 | 6 | Good |
| Capital intensity (requisite capital for operating in the sector) | High | 0 | 1 | 2 | 3 | 4 | 5 | 6 | Low |
| Ease of entry into the market | Easy | 0 | 1 | 2 | 3 | 4 | 5 | 6 | Difficult |
| Level of productivity and capacity utilization | Low | 0 | 1 | 2 | 3 | 4 | 5 | 6 | High |
| Other (your choice of factor) | Low | 0 | 1 | 2 | 3 | 4 | 5 | 6 | High |

*Average:*

*Critical factors determining industry strength:*

## Environmental stability (ES)

*Factors determining environmental stability*

| | | 0 | 1 | 2 | 3 | 4 | 5 | 6 | |
|---|---|---|---|---|---|---|---|---|---|
| Technological Changes | Many | 0 | 1 | 2 | 3 | 4 | 5 | 6 | Few |
| Rate of Inflation | High | 0 | 1 | 2 | 3 | 4 | 5 | 6 | Low |
| Variability of demand | High | 0 | 1 | 2 | 3 | 4 | 5 | 6 | Low |
| Price range of competing products | Wide | 0 | 1 | 2 | 3 | 4 | 5 | 6 | Narrow |
| Barriers to entry into the market | Few | 0 | 1 | 2 | 3 | 4 | 5 | 6 | Many |
| Competitive pressure | High | 0 | 1 | 2 | 3 | 4 | 5 | 6 | Low |
| Price elasticity of demand | Elastic | 0 | 1 | 2 | 3 | 4 | 5 | 6 | Inelastic |

Other (a factor of your own choice)

*Average $-6 =$*

*Again for this assessment, suppose the average is 40. this divided by 8 = 5 Then 5 − 6 = −1 (A negative figure)*

*The key critical factors that determine Environmental Stability.*

Your analysis should then be plotted on the following axes in order to determine the strategic position of the company under question.

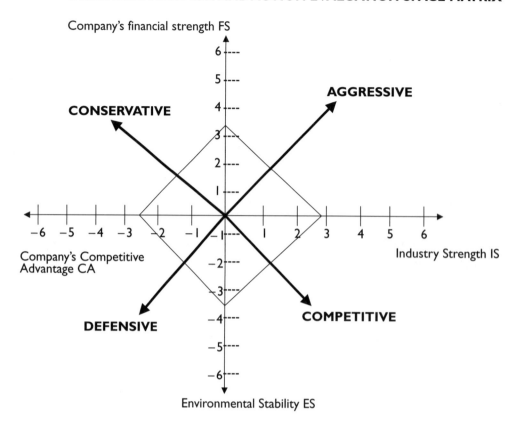

**STRATEGIC POSITION AND ACTION EVALUATION SPACE MATRIX**

*Figure 2.4*

Once this analysis is done, you can plot the actual position of the company by just getting two points (one for the X axis and one for the Y axis). This can be easily obtained by adding CA and IS (you will either get a negative point or a positive point) and adding FS and ES (you will either get a negative point or a positive point). These two points will then determine the overall quadrant in which the company will fall.

The implications for falling within particular sectors are these: (always remember that this exercise should be quite objective and be based on as much real information that you can obtain as possible. Like any other real life analysis you may also have to make certain assumptions.)

(For all the examples it is assumed that the company positions are in the middle of each quadrant)

a.  *Aggressive posture*: In this quadrant, a company is set within an attractive industry which faces little environmental turbulence. The company enjoys a good competitive advantage which it can protect with good financial strength. As this sector is attractive, it is likely to attract new entrants. The company needs to protect its position through acquisitions, by increasing market share or by extending its lead in specific products and services in which it is the market leader. Companies in this sector have the potential to be cost leaders if they are in an FMCG market.

b.  *Competitive posture*: In this quadrant, the industry is attractive and the company enjoys competitive advantage within a turbulent environment. The company needs to acquire financial strength. It needs to do this in order to improve its marketing and improve its product lines. It may also need to reduce costs and protect competitive advantage in a declining market. In such a quadrant, a company may need to look for cash resources either through merger or through being acquired. Companies in this area need to differentiate their product offerings and utilize their marketing skills as much as possible.

c. *Conservative posture*: If a company is positioned within this quadrant, it has a focus on financial stability within a stable market. The chances are that the growth is fairly low. Under such circumstances, a company will need to become competitive in its product or service offering. It may also need to consider investing its cash in entering new attractive markets or offering new competitive products. It may also need to consider pruning its product lines. Companies located in this sector would benefit from a more focused product or service. They may be able to do well in niche markets, organized along geographic lines, product lines or along buyer groups.

d. *Defensive posture*: A company set within this quadrant lacks a competitive product or service. It also has low financial strength and is situated in an unattractive industry sector. Competitiveness is crucial and the company will have to consider retrenchment by pruning its product lines, reducing costs dramatically, cutting capacity and slowing down on any investment. Companies located within this sector are often ripe for turnaround strategies. They can also be relatively defenseless, making them easy targets for takeovers. Product strategies probably need to consider 'harvesting' cash cows.

Note: It is important to realize that the SPACE analysis should be used *judiciously* as it may only be *appropriate* for many private sector companies. It may be *inappropriate* for public sector or non-profit sector analysis. Parts of the analysis could be modified for use in different sectors. This, however, will need sound knowledge, creativity and an ability to sensibly translate the basic premise of SPACE to a new sector.

## Any constraints that the company faces from a resource point of view. These could be market, human, financial, technical or environmental

Companies face a variety of constraints when developing their strategies. These constraints could be market constraints (size and growth potential of a market), financial constraints (the ability to finance marketing campaigns, foster new product development, cashflow, ability to raise money, etc.), technical (the ability to develop new products, to market products, manage information systems, Web capability) and finally environmental (these could be pollution management capability, or public concerns as in the case of GM Foods in Biocatalysts).

## Any structural features or control systems

Analyses should include an understanding of the present structural pattern of the organization and the way in which this contributes to or detracts from developing its marketing strategies. For instance, is there a defined marketing structure? Are there systems for monitoring marketing effectiveness or orientation? Are the systems rigid or flexible?

# Key issues

As a result of these analyses, you should be able to list a number of key issues which are facing the company described in the case study. These key issues form a valuable resource when answering the questions set in the examination.

These type of analyses can then be linked to any *strategic plan* that you may have considered developing.

A generalized approach to formulating a Strategic Plan would probably contain the following:

1. Statement of the problem

   *This will contain a situation analysis of the company, its problem areas and its general capability.*

2. Analysis of Data

- Industry

    *This would cover an analysis of the growth potential, SWOT, market structure and competitive pressures.*

- Product/Service analysis

    *This would consider areas such as market share, pricing, promotion, new product development, distribution, branding and level of market orientation of the company.*

- Financial Analysis

    *The financial performance of a company gives guidelines on its profitability, return on investment, shareholder value, liquidity, inventory levels and possible resource requirements for growth. (See section on Financial Analysis)*

- Management

    *If organization charts are available, any gaps in the marketing structure should be ascertained. Also, issues such as mission, values and objectives should be taken into account.*

3. Generation of options and an evaluation of these

    *In this section, the options regarding entry into different product/market sectors, strategic alliances, branding strategies, R & D development, internationalization, joint ventures, diversification, vertical or horizontal integration.*

4. Recommendations (Decisions) and strategies

    *This should be the crucial element of the plan, encompassing key decisions that may be taken, giving reasons for choosing these, understanding the possible reactions to these by competitors and the justifications for these. Resource implications also need to be considered. Clear and decisive objectives must be set.*

5. Implementation, contingency and control

    *This section should look at how easily the recommendations could be adopted, taking into account resource allocation, cost implications, budgets and timetables. This section should also envisage contingency requirements in case of difficulties regarding implementation strategies. When considering implementation, it is also important to develop monitoring systems for ascertaining the success of the recommended strategies.*

## Summary

When evaluating a case, it is important to be systematic. Analyse the case in a logical fashion, beginning with the identification of operating and financial strengths and weaknesses and environmental opportunities and threats. Move on to assess the value of a company's current strategies only when you are fully conversant with the SWOT analysis of the company. Ask yourself whether the company's current strategies make sense, given its SWOT analysis. If they do not, what changes need to be made? What are your recommendations? Above all, link any strategic recommendations you may make to the SWOT and GAP analyses. State explicitly how the strategies you identify take advantage of the company's strengths to exploit environmental opportunities, how they rectify the company's weaknesses, and how they counter any of the threats from the PESTLE factors. It is also important that you consider the strategic options that may be available to the organization. Some of the options may not be feasible, suitable or acceptable in the light of the points you will have covered above. Make sure that you outline the strategies that need to be adopted to implement any recommendations that you make. Many company strategies fail as a result of poor implementation or unrealistic expectations of market growth and demand. You therefore have to be aware that your recommendations are sensible and fit the existing resource base and capability of the firm.

# Unit 3
# Contemporary issues in marketing

## Introduction

This unit has been designed to give you small pieces of discourse on some of the contemporary issues in marketing. We do not mean this to act as a substitute for books or articles that are written in the various topic areas. If anything, you should consider this section as a catalyst for you to explore marketing issues in depth and look for any contemporary issues pertaining to the case that you are currently analysing.

## E-Marketing

### Internet Marketing

The growth of the Internet shows no signs of abating and has profound implications for businesses in Europe. On the one hand there is a move towards monetary union in order to unify markets in Europe on the other hand there is also a global pull on organizations largely driven by the Internet. The Internet is still largely American led with Canada and the UK hard on its heels. A large proportion of the business done on the web is in America, mainly because it is the most connected network but this is now changing with more and more servers being set up in Europe and indeed worldwide. E-Commerce knows no boundaries and UK companies will need to be able to undertake communication and transactions, with ease, initially at the European level, but also at the global level. Familarization with the Euro and trading in the Euro, should be an advantage for companies ready to embrace the Internet.

### *Issues to consider*

The last three to four years have seen an explosive growth of the number of people using the Internet. The projected world-wide usage for 2000 is estimated to be around 140 million with over 100 million being based in the USA (Commercenet, 1999), though in a rapidly growing medium figures can be somewhat suspect. The use of the Internet has become increasingly popular in the last five years, especially in the industrialized countries, in which the cost of accessing and building an Internet site is relatively low. The Internet has many potential uses, depending on the objectives and capabilities of the user. It can be a:

- Source of information
- Communication tool
- Distribution channel for products and services.

The new developments in the field of multimedia software have increased the range of information than can be transmitted, which can now be expressed in the form of printed text, image, sound, or a combination of all these.

With Europe being the second largest economic zone in the world, it is important for UK companies to provide websites which can accommodate cultural and language issues.

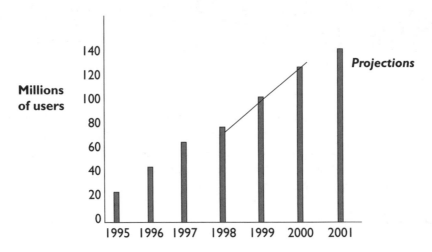

**Internet Population**

*Figure 3.1*

## *Opportunities*

Taking into consideration the advantages of speed, interaction and flexibility, it is easy to understand why the Internet is considered as a revolutionary tool for the development of commercial transactions. Many innovative companies have made attempts to transfer a part of their marketing activities on the Internet, in order to benefit from the advantages offered by this unique system of communication.

## The strategic Advantages of effective internet marketing

- Ease of communications and via the Web and E-mail use
- Improved corporate logistics
- Cost savings on advertising and transactions
- Chance to improve the corporate image
- Chance to improve visibility globally and develop niche strategies
- Improvements in the management of the value chain
- World wide market research
- Price transparency
- Enhanced support for intermediaries or their elimination.

Business on the Web transfers more of the selling function to the customer, through online ordering and the use of fill-out forms, thus helping to bring transactions to a faster conclusion. This permits a third benefit in the form of capture-of-customer information. Obviously the use of these techniques requires reliable electronic hardware support systems such as Hi Fi systems, computers, video recorders etc. Current statistics (Commercenet, 1999), seem to contradict Figure 3.2. The statistics actually show that car and car parts account for over 18 million transactions with books, computers, clothing, CDs and videos a distant second at around 12 million transactions.

**Where online scores**

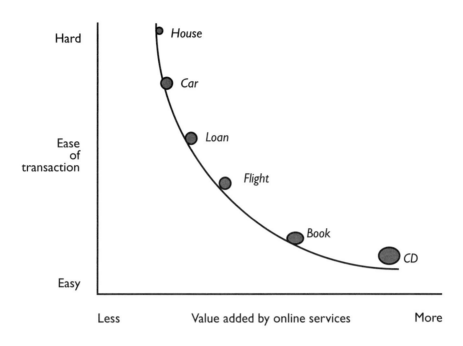

*Figure 3.2*

However, not all the products are equally fit for electronic commerce and much will depend on the online selling efficiency for different products. The consumers' familiarity with a certain product or service will also influence the frequency and the volume of online transactions.

Despite the existing problems related with the ease of access and overall security of electronic transactions, predictions for growth are extremely optimistic. The range and the volume of products sold online is likely to go into hypergrowth in the future, expanding the size and the value of the electronic market.

*Table 3.1* *Projected size of E-commerce Market by 2000*

| Market Size, Characteristics | Estimate |
| --- | --- |
| Total value of all Internet-based purchases | $4.5 to $6 billion |
| Total value of all purchases per average buyer | $600 to $800 |
| Value of average Internet purchase transaction | $25 to $35 |
| Total Internet-based purchase transactions | $130 to $200 million |
| Percentage of purchases for online products | 60–70% |
| Percentage of purchases for delivered goods | 30–40% |

*Source:* Cameron, D. Electronic Commerce: The New Business Platform for the Internet, 1997

Forrester Research on the Internet predict that the business-to-business trading volumes are likely to reach $1 to $3 trillion globally by the year 2003.

*Table 3.2 Online Shopping Revenue by Market Segment (millions)*

|  | 1996 | 1997 | 1998 | 1999 | 2000 |
|---|---|---|---|---|---|
| **Computer products** | $140 | $323 | $701 | $1228 | $2105 |
| **Travel** | $126 | $276 | $572 | $961 | $1579 |
| **Entertainment** | $85 | $194 | $420 | $733 | $1250 |
| **Apparel** | $46 | $89 | $163 | $234 | $322 |
| **Gifts and Flowers** | $45 | $103 | $222 | $386 | $658 |
| **Food and drink** | $39 | $78 | $149 | $227 | $336 |
| **Other** | $37 | $75 | $144 | $221 | $329 |
| **Total** | $518 | $1138 | $2371 | $3990 | $6579 |

*Source:* Cameron, D. Electronic Commerce: The New Business Platform for the Internet, 1997

For the purposes of Case Study analysis you should look through previous papers and see where Internet marketing and e-commerce issues crop up. For instance, they are in the following current cases:

    a.   Malaysian Airlines
    b.   Clerical Medical
    c.   Pirelli
    d.   Daugavpils.

# Green Marketing

Social responsibility in marketing refers to marketers selecting activities, and conducting them, in such a way that promote public good and have a positive effect on society. Socially responsible marketing embraces both environmental stewardship and cause marketing. The former refers to a company acting to protect the natural environment in the process of carrying out its business. This is manifested through green marketing.

> Green marketing is a strategic option that seeks to create a differential positioning in the market by taking up environmental stewardship.

Today's consumer is increasingly concerned with issues relating to the environment. Air pollution, water pollution and the depletion of the earth's ozone layer are some of the serious environmental concerns that have a bearing, at least partially, on many consumers' purchase decisions. This is borne out by numerous opinion polls and consumer research. Consumers, as citizens of the world, are using their purchasing power to pressurize the culprits and reward those companies that are perceived to be green. Groups such as Green Peace, Friends of the Earth and Consumers' Association spearhead the pressure. This is impacting upon the operations of heavy industries, chemical processing plants, as well as on the utilities such as water companies. Additionally, producers are having to offer more environmentally friendly products in the form of emission control in cars, recyclable packaging, ozone friendly sprays and so on.

Obviously, consumers are aware that still much needs to be done if the environmental threats facing the earth are to be countered effectively. Air and water pollution have to be reduced significantly, forests managed more effectively and waste reduced substantially. So, consumer pressure will continue.

*The pressure is not just from consumers. Encouraged by them, governments are also taking action to promote environmental issues and green marketing through legislation, while the EU is attempting to harmonize such legislation amongst the member states. EU's efforts cover: agriculture, energy, industry, tourism and transport. Regular world summits are held on the issue of the environment although, arguably, more rhetoric than real action is achieved as a result.*

Progress is, however, slow. Companies carry on with their harmful practices, and governmental dedication to green issues is varied around the world, from Germany and northern Europe where governments have a better record than most, to other parts of the world where ignorance, lack of political will or bowing to commercial pressure has frustrated progress.

The forces for environmentalism should not be considered merely as threats, but also as opportunities. Forward thinking companies such as Volkswagen and Procter and Gamble already take green issues seriously in their product development. Indeed, the modern organization will look upon environmentalism and green marketing as an opportunity to position itself favourably in the minds of consumers, and at the same time make a positive impact on the environment. There is economic benefit as well as other possible benefits such as public good will, better corporate image and perception, by customers, of a trustworthy brand which can be enjoyed as a result of genuine attempt at becoming a green company.

---

### Tutorial discussion questions

1. What actions can a company such as Marks and Spencer take in order to position themselves as green marketers? How would this benefit them? What arguments would you put forward to the Managing Directors to convince them that green marketing would be a viable option for Marks and Spencer?
2. What are the problems of adopting and operating a green strategy for an organization engaged in international marketing? How would you attempt to solve those problems?

---

# Relationship Marketing

In recent years, Relationship Marketing (RM) has gained enormous popularity amongst academics and practitioners of marketing. This popularity has been gained at the expense of, so called, traditional or transactional marketing which has been taught and practised for the past fifty years or so, and is based primarily on the management of the 4Ps. RM attempts to gain customer loyalty, by focusing on building long-term relationships with customers, placing importance on a customer's life-time value to the company rather than the profit achieved in a single transaction. Furthermore, RM emphasises share of customer rather than market share, which is often a yardstick for success in transactional marketing.

Various researchers have found that it is cheaper to keep existing customers than to acquire new ones, and that normally the longer a relationship lasts the more profitable it is for a company. Technological developments make it possible, more than ever before, to build accurate and up to date databases on customers, make it possible to determine their purchase requirements and profile accurately. As a result customized offerings could be made to each customer, and in the process added value is created.

RM, if successful, creates a confidence by the customer in the supplier (and vice versa) helping to build trust and, hence, loyalty particularly in situations where there is customer perceived risk in the purchase. Successful RM requires an integrated approach, involving all the stakeholders of a company, change of organizational culture in favour of RM and adherence to TQM. The latter goes hand in hand with RM and is essential to a customer and quality orientated marketing operation.

Christopher et al. distinguish RM and transactional marketing in the following manner:

*Transaction Marketing*

- Focus on single sale
- Orientation on product features
- Short time-scale
- Little emphasis on customer service
- Limited customer commitment
- Moderate customer contact
- Quality is primarily a concern of production.

*Relationship Marketing*

- Focus on customer retention
- Orientation on product benefits
- Long time-scale
- High customer service emphasis
- High customer commitment
- High customer contact
- Quality is the concern of all.

(Christopher, M., Payne, A., Ballantyne, D. (1991) Relationship Marketing – Bringing quality, customer service, and marketing together)

Payne, et al, suggest that the process of RM involves attempts at moving customers up *the relationship marketing ladder of loyalty,* illustrated below:

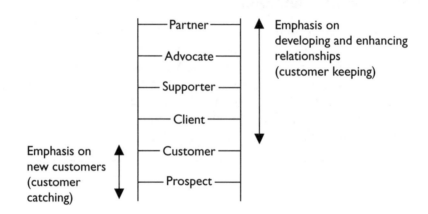

**Figure 3.3** *The relationship marketing ladder of loyalty*

(Payne, A., Christopher, M., Clark, M., Peck, H. (1997) Relationship Marketing for Competitive Advantage-Winning and Keeping Customers)

Kotler proposes that there are three levels of benefits that a company can offer to its customers in attempting to build a relationship with them:

**Financial** – These are based on financial benefits offered by companies in the form of frequency marketing programmes and club marketing programmes. These benefits are usually in the form of reward or incentives to frequent buyers.

**Social** – These are benefits that customers are offered by the company through individualized and customized relations and treating customers as clients.

**Structural** – These are benefits offered by the existence of structural ties between the supplier and the customer where the supplier offers equipment, computer linkages and advice to help customers manage their orders, inventory, etc.

(Based on Kotler, P. (2000) Marketing Management – The Millennium Edition)

Obviously, the existence of social and structural ties and a genuine belief in relationship marketing as a philosophy of business are more likely to help create mutually profitable long-term relationships.

In addition to this, technology is rapidly changing the way in which relationships are managed. Customers are able to contact companies through various channels and these need to be understood and managed by an organization. These are shown in the figure below;

**Creating a relationship web**

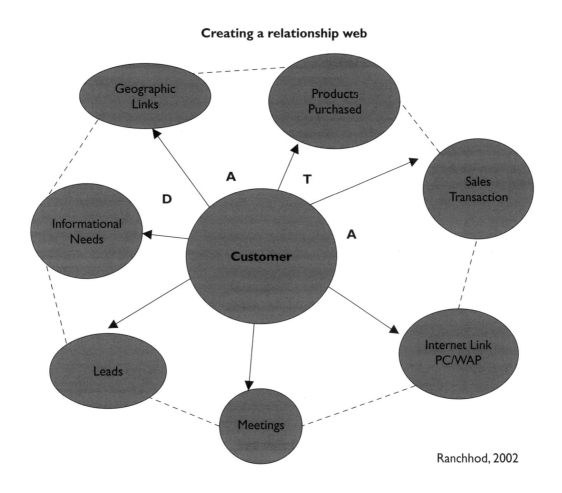

Ranchhod, 2002

*Figure 3.4*

---

**Tutorial discussion question**

Which types of markets, and which business sectors, are more suited to Relationship Marketing? Why?

---

Note the importance of relationship marketing strategies for Clerical Medical.

## Stakeholders and Marketing

Organizational stakeholders are many and varied in nature. Stakeholders are any groups of individuals that are in some way either affected by a company's actions, or in turn, can affect a company's actions. In many ways understanding stakeholder's interests and concerns and translating them into effective marketing strategies and company positioning within a market-place is one of the great challenges facing organizations in the 21st century. It is no longer enough to just consider products segments and markets. It is necessary to consider not only customer – company interactions, but also company – shareholder, company – community, company – environment and a host of the other interactions. Consumers are getting more intelligent and may want to consider not only the products on offer, but also a company's record on ethical issues and even its image within the marketplace. Stakeholders have the power and influence to determine the success or failure of particular marketing strategies adopted by an organization. The diagram below illustrates the complex nature of stakeholders and how they interact with organizations.

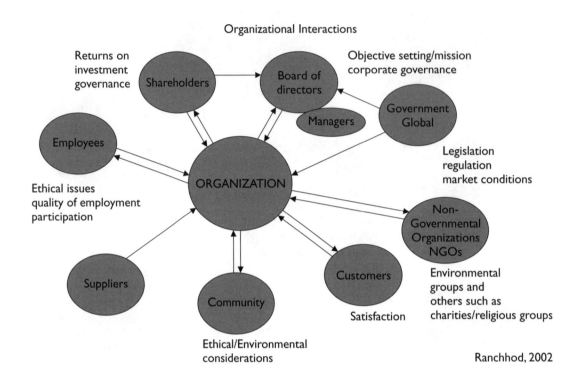

*Figure 3.5*

As an exercise, consider the Daugavpils case study and look at the impact various stakeholders would have on the success or failure of their marketing strategies.

# Branding

> 'A brand is a name, term, sign, symbol, or design, or a combination of them, intended to identify the goods or services of one seller and to differentiate them from those of competitors'

Definitions of branding, invariably, do not portray the true nature of branding. A sign, symbol or design does not turn a product into a brand. The essential attribute of a brand is the successful matching of both the physical and psychological needs of the target market with the total product offering under a brand name. Branding gives a personality to a product that has no identity and associates it with certain core values and images, and in doing so turns the brand into an aggregate of meanings to the customer. This, in turn, helps with the satisfaction of physical as well as emotional needs. Branding is a central issue in marketing strategy, and a major tool in differentiation and creating competitive advantage. In this respect branding and Relationship Marketing (RM) can be used jointly to great advantage.

*Importance of Branding*

Ever-increasing competition and the ease with which physical attributes and USPs are copied are the main reasons for the importance of branding and emotional bonding with customers. Branding, as with RM, is essentially a means of gaining customer loyalty through building trust and confidence. Trust and confidence help reduce the perceived risk associated with a purchase, and help gain customer commitment and loyalty. A brand that enjoys the trust of its target markets will benefit from added value. Branding used in conjunction with RM can create and enhance this added value, and help reduce brand promiscuity that has become apparent in some consumer markets. Hence, it is imperative that issues relating to quality and consistency are taken seriously, and that changes in branding strategy, and positioning are not taken lightly. The issue of quality, consistency and customer care and everything else that goes to make up the augmented product is even more important in the service sector where production and consumption often occur simultaneously. Trust is also a component of brand equity.

> Trust exists 'when one partner has confidence in an exchange partner's reliability and integrity'

Brands, which carry high degree of recognition, trust and customer loyalty, command high levels of brand equity, which is an asset to for owners. Brand equity, or the value of a brand, is measured in different ways by different people. Some put an emphasis on the financial aspects, others on brand awareness and response. The trend is, however, to base brand equity on brand recognition and loyalty, perceived quality, patents and trade marks, and the quality of the channels of distribution.

> 'Brand equity consists of the differential attributes underpinning a brand which give increased value to the firm's balance sheet'
>
> de Chernatony, L., McDonald, M. (1998) Creating Powerful Brands in Consumer, Service and Industrial Markets

*Benefits of Successful Brands.*

Successful brands, with high equities, are beneficial to their owners in several ways. They are:

- Enable charging of higher prices than competitors do for products which are very similar in quality
- Enable the owner to stay out of price wars (at least to some degree)
- Help to reduce marketing costs
- Help with brand extensions
- Help with planning and forecasting due to having a loyal customer base.

The diagram below illustrates the various aspects that should be considered when evaluating a brand.

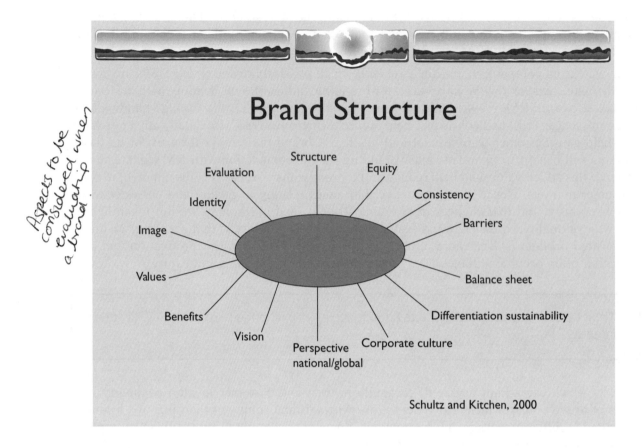

*Aspects to be considered when evaluating a brand.*

# Brand Structure

Structure
Evaluation
Equity
Identity
Consistency
Image
Barriers
Values
Balance sheet
Benefits
Differentiation sustainability
Vision
Corporate culture
Perspective national/global

Schultz and Kitchen, 2000

*Figure 3.6*

## Factors affecting a brand position

There are several issues, which need to be considered seriously with regard to branding. These are briefly listed here.

1.  Branding is a very costly business, which requires long term commitment. Does the company have the resources to cope? Does the company need to brand at all?
2.  Correct segmentation and targeting.
3.  Proper marketing research to identify customers' physical and emotional needs.
4.  Matching of the target market's physical and emotional needs with the total brand offering based on systematic product development, choice of brand personality, images and core values supported by total quality management.
5.  The selection of an appropriate brand name is crucial particularly in an increasingly global competition. The company must choose between **individual names** for its products, **family names** (blanket or separate), or a **combination of a trade name and product name.**
6.  The adoption of an appropriate overall branding strategy after due consideration given to:
    *   Line extension strategy
    *   Brand extension strategy
    *   Multi-brand strategy
    *   Co-branding strategy.
7.  Correct positioning of the brand, with repositioning only if necessary and with careful planning.
8.  Integrated and consistent marketing communications, modified and changed only after careful consideration and under special circumstances.
9.  Constant monitoring and evaluation.

According to Intrabrand/Citibank, the world's most valuable brands are:

| Brand | Country | Industry |
|---|---|---|
| Coca-Cola | US | Food |
| Microsoft | US | Software |
| IBM | US | Technology |
| Intel | US | Technology |
| General Electric | US | Electronics |
| Ford | US | Automobiles |
| Disney | US | Media |

## Tutorial discussion question

How can a British financial services company wishing to expand into the EU create trust amongst its new target market? List and explain the short-term and long-term strategies and practices that the company can adopt to achieve this aim.

# Globalization

Globalization refers to the trend towards uniformity in demand for products, supply of standardized products, and the application by corporations of identical or very similar marketing strategies around the world.

*Technology, Levitt wrote in 1983, was driving the world 'towards a converging commonality' through 'proletarianized communication, transport, and travel' and making 'isolated places and improvished people eager for modernity's allurements'. He argued that consequently there were emerging global markets for standardized products and that 'Gone are accustomed differences in national or regional preference.' He predicted the end of the multinational corporations and their replacement by global corporations making standardized offerings everywhere, and digressing from that strategy only after all possibilities to retain it had been explored.*

Levitt's paper ignited a debate with supporters and opponents at opposite ends, but today even Levitt agrees that his vision was rather too optimistic. There are certainly forces of convergence at work, but cultural, legal and economic differences amongst nations still exist acting as barrier to globalization and standardization of products and marketing strategies. Globalization is certainly taking place, particularly in such sectors as pop music, fashion and IT although the pace of change is not as fast as Levitt predicted. Also there is some evidence of the forces of divergence too, for example a return to Muslim fundamentalism in the Middle East and North Africa.

In recent years the debate seems to have settled with a reasonable degree of consensus that while for many reasons, and in many cases, globalization, i.e. standardization may be an attractive option for companies there ought to be some modifications allowed, at least, to the marketing mix depending on the country of operation. Encouraged by the writings of such authors as Kenichi Ohmae there seems to be a general agreement, though not a universal one, that the best policy is 'Think global, Act local'. Strictly speaking there are few, if any, corporations that are truly global.

The term global company is often wrongly used to refer to a company engaged in international operations. A global company is one that does not distinguish between domestic and international operations, applies the same marketing strategy and positioning in all countries of operation, but may adapt its marketing mix to a degree in each market, for example, Coca-Cola, McDonalds, Kodak.

A multinational company is one with operations and subsidiaries in more than one country, treating each country as unique in terms of its marketing strategy and mix, e.g. ICI, Unilever.

## Drivers of globalization

Based on Doole and Lowe in International Marketing Strategy (1999) the move towards globalization can be identified in terms of:

**Globalization of Market Access**   There is increasing access to previously inaccessible markets, e.g. China and Eastern Europe even-though local problems have meant that MNEs have found it necessary to form partnerships with local firms and individuals. There is increasing regionalization taking place, helped by the growth of trading blocks reducing inter-country barriers and enabling the operation of more standardized pan-regional marketing programmes.

**Globalization of market opportunities**   Continued deregulation in a number of industrial sectors is resulting in the disappearance of the traditional demarcation lines between the constituent parts of the industry, e.g. the demarcation between banking, insurance, pensions and so on within the financial services sector.

**Globalization of industry standards**   There is increasing adoption of technical operating standards around the world, e.g. ISO 9000, and particularly within trading blocks as a requirement of harmonization regulations

**Globalization of sourcing**   Globalization of sourcing refers to obtaining raw materials and components from world-wide locations. It is used to reduce both costs and the level of risk involved as well as to increase reliability and quality of needed supplies. Sourcing can be a basis for competitive advantage. Increasingly corporations source materials, components and services globally and in doing so benefit from:

*Cheaper labour rates*
*Better or more uniform quality*
*Better access to the best technology, innovation and ideas*
*Access to local markets*
*Economies of scale in terms of location of manufacturing and distribution for an entire region*
*Lower taxes and duties*
*Potentially lower logistics costs due to more effective use of IT in transportation and warehousing*
*More consistent supply in the quality of foodstuffs as a result of arranging supplies from countries with different growing seasons.*

*Benefits*

**Globalization of core products and services**   In most cases now, the competition is not at the core but at the augmented product level, hence making it easier to opt for standardization at the former level.

**Globalization of technology**   Convergence in terms of technology is strongly evident around the world and witnessed particularly in information technology, entertainment and consumer electronics. This convergence is being fuelled by the products of a small number of global players, e.g. IBM and Microsoft in computer software.

**Globalization of customer requirements**   Convergence of requirements is taking place in certain segments of the world markets, e.g. teenage music and fashion, also in business support services such as law firms and consultants. The teenage market is of great importance to international marketers. A Western traveller in many parts of the world is often surprised at the highly noticeable large proportion of young people in the streets. In fact, in many parts of the world more than half the population is under 20 years old. Hence globalization of youth markets would serve global companies well.

**Globalization of competition**   Industry giants are replicating the same fight in each corner of the world. The increasing pace of competition fuelled by technological advancement means that customers' expectations are increasing too. Innovative products at decreasing prices are constantly replacing established ones. Many companies are finding that in order to recoup product development costs, survive and prosper they need to think in terms of global marketing.

**Globalization of cooperation**   The requirement by global operations for huge investment is leading to alliances between corporations and members of a supply chain.

**Globalization of distribution**   Increasing concentration of the supply chain on fewer and more powerful members, as well as changes in technology is revolutionizing the whole process of transaction.

**Globalization of technology**   Major advancements in telecommunications and information technology such as satellite TV and the Internet are making it essential to develop a consistent global corporate identity and brand image, as well as improving dialogue between customers and suppliers.

**Globalization of strategy, business programmes and processes**   The globalization effects pose challenges to corporations to aim for improved operational efficiency and market effectiveness.

## Barriers to globalization

The process of globalization is not a smooth one and the following factors act as barriers to standardization, reducing the speed of change:

**Economic factors**   Differences in GDP and income per capita, levels of economic development and infrastructure amongst countries and regions of the world still very much exist making it difficult to standardize marketing programmes and mixes globally.

**Cultural differences**   Cultural differences are still in great evidence in many respects and affecting consumer tastes, attitudes to ownership and the use to which products are put. Cultural differences around the world mean that even if products could be standardized, very often communication has to be adapted to promote different physical and psychological benefits of the product. A stockbroker in London buying a Range Rover will often be seeking to satisfy, at least partially, different practical and psychological needs than a farmer buying the same product in Zimbabwe.

**Political differences**   The end of communism in Eastern Europe, and the liberalization of the Chinese attitude to trade, may have reduced the extent of ideological differences in the world, but differences still exist, as do politically unstable governments, making too risky to include some countries and regions under a global strategy umbrella.

**Laws and regulations**   Despite the trend towards harmonization within trading blocks there are still huge differences in laws and regulations amongst countries and act as barriers towards standardization of products, price control and credit availability, as well as media restrictions and promotion.

Even within the European Union and after so many years of attempting to harmonize laws there are many differences in most areas of legislation. For example, the electrical voltage and the number of pins on electrical equipment, what can be claimed in advertisements, etc.

Because of the above difficulties it is felt by some that of globalization is a long way off, and that at best it is happening within the advanced economies leaving the rest of the world even further behind.

Globalization necessitates a serious attempt by companies to identify appropriate competitive strategies. This will normally mean deciding between cost leadership, product differentiation and market focus. However, prior to that, the company will have to consider seriously the decision to go global. While there are many advantages associated with a global strategy there are also many situations where differentiation could be more advantageous to a company. Hence, multinational operation must not always be considered as inferior to global operation. To be successful in global marketing the following must be considered as a minimum requirement:

Proper consideration ought to given to the question of whether to operate as a global company based on a realistic assessment of:

   a. Internal factors such as corporate objectives, nature of products, human, physical and financial resources
   b. External factors in terms of market opportunities, level of risk and nature of competition
   c. The existence a management force that is truly cosmopolitan in attitude, and knowledgeable about world cultures and social trends, history and politics. A successful global manager needs to be someone more than just a domestic salesman with a new title
   d. A geocentric management orientation which values local people's contribution to the company's operations
   e. Identification of homogeneous international demand segments.
      **Ethnocentric orientation–Views** foreign markets as an extension of the domestic markets, and the domestic marketing programmes are assumed to represent the 'best' practice and applied, more or less, unchanged in foreign markets.
      **Polycentric orientation–Views** each country of operations as unique in terms of its characteristics, and a different set of objectives, strategy and marketing mix formula is applied to each one.
      **Regiocentric orientation–Treat** each region where the company operates as unique requiring integrated regional objectives and strategies.
      **Geocentric orientation–Views** the world as potentially a single market with the company attempting to develop integrated global objectives and strategies.

Many companies are now even 'born global', in the sense that in order to reach markets, they have to launch themselves globally in order to have a critical mass for their products or services. Companies within the IT sector and within the Biotechnology sector are particularly global in nature.

Consider the Pirelli case study and look at the factors driving globalization.

## Summary

This unit offers you some insights into the current contemporary issues in marketing. The topics are by no means exhaustive and you should always be reading current articles and books to increase your knowledge of current developments.

# Unit 4
# Financial analysis and marketing measures

## Introduction

Cases are based on real companies which have financial reporting systems. Usually, for the purposes of disseminating information to shareholders and stakeholders, companies produce annual accounts explaining financial flows, profits and losses and balance sheets. Many accounts also contain information on market shares, geographical segmentation and regional segmentation. Recently there has been considerable interest generated in understanding the use of particular sets of data pertaining to marketing. These can be measurement of brand equity, customer satisfaction, loyalty/retention, share of voice and marketing spend. Some of these measures are shown in the table below. Interestingly not many companies actually utilize the full range of marketing metrics for measuring their marketing performance. Often we are only left with the age-old financial measures. These measures do help in understanding the position of a company. Quite often they are used by senior managers to gauge trends, especially if data for previous years is available in the same format. In most cases, the analyses are based on financial ratios. These accounting ratios are used in the interpretation of financial statements. Usually, these ratios are at their most useful when compared to ratios for different time periods. This can be helpful in identifying trends and understanding strengths and weaknesses. If for instance, inventory levels are high in a balance sheet, does it imply that there is a peak, where the company is anticipating a surge in demand for products, or does it imply falling sales? The section below, outlines the key ratios that are useful for analysing company performance. In addition to this, companies have to be able to understand measures that are about marketing performance. Some of these measures may link up to financial performance and indeed may be key to the success or failure of a company's marketing strategy. Such measures could be customer satisfaction, information dissemination capability within an organization, IT sophistication, market share, customer retention amongst others.

## Profit ratios

Profit ratios measure the management's overall effectiveness in generating profits from the available resources. If a company is highly efficient in its markets, then, it should exhibit a high level of profitability. It is useful to compare a company's profitability against that of its major competitors in its industry. Such a comparison tells whether the company is operating more or less efficiently than its rivals. Over a period of time any changes in profit ratios will indicate whether a company is improving its performance or not.

1. *Gross profit margin* The gross profit margin is obtained by deducting variable production expenses from the general sales. The amount remaining can then be allocated to cover general and administrative expenses and other operating costs. It is defined as follows:

$$\text{Gross Profit Margin} = \frac{\text{Sales Revenue} - \text{Cost of Goods Sold}}{\text{Sales Revenue}}$$

2. *Net profit margin* This is based on the net profits obtained after taxes, loan interest and administration expenses have been paid. This net income is then divided by the sales revenue to obtain the net profit margin. Net profits are important because companies need to make profits to survive and also invest in the future to develop and grow markets.

$$\text{Net Profit Margin} = \frac{\text{Net Income}}{\text{Sales Revenue}}$$

3. *Return on total asset*  This ratio measures the profit earned on the employment of assets. It is defined as follows:

$$\text{Return on Total Assets} = \frac{\text{Net Income}}{\text{Total Assets}}$$

4. *Net income* is the profit after preferred dividends (those set by contract) have been paid. Total assets include both current and fixed assets.

5. *Return on shareholders' equity*  This ratio measures the percentage of profit earned on the shares held within the company. Companies attractive to shareholders are those that can maximize this ratio. The greater the return, the greater the amount of money that can be distributed to individual shareholders. It is defined as follows:

$$\text{Return on Shareholders' equity} = \frac{\text{Profits after taxes}}{\text{Total equity}}$$

6. *Liquidity*  The amount of liquidity refers to ready cash that may be available to a company, for immediate use. The lower the liquidity, the greater the danger of a company, not being able to meet its immediate cash commitments or tactical marketing requirements.

   a.
   $$\text{Current Ratio} = \frac{\text{Current Assets}}{\text{Current liabilities}}$$

   b.
   $$\text{Quick ratio} = \frac{\text{Total assets}}{\text{Total liabilities}}$$

   c.
   $$\text{Inventory to net working capital} = \frac{\text{Inventory}}{\text{Current assets} - \text{current liabilities}}$$

7. *Leverage*  If a company has borrowed little money, then it is possible for it to increase the amount of money it can raise in the marketplace, either through loans or share issues. The money can enable further investments in marketing or new product development.

   a.
   $$\text{Debt to assets ratio} = \frac{\text{Total debt}}{\text{Total assets}}$$

   b.
   $$\text{Debt to equity ratio} = \frac{\text{Total debt}}{\text{Total equity}}$$

   c.
   $$\text{Long term debt to equity ratio} = \frac{\text{Long term debt}}{\text{Total equity}}$$

8. *Activity* This reflects the efficiency with which the company is dealing in the market place. High inventory levels could signify flagging sales, indicating poor distribution, lack of advertising or sales efforts.

a.
$$\text{Inventory turnover} = \frac{\text{Sales}}{\text{Inventory}}$$

b.
$$\text{Fixed Asset turnover} = \frac{\text{Sales}}{\text{Fixed Assets}}$$

c.
$$\text{Average Collection Period} = \frac{\text{Accounts receivable}}{\text{Average daily sales}}$$

## Marketing Metrics

These will vary from one company to another. The key points to consider are:

a. Who are the main users of company reports, and how important are they as data sources?

Shareholders will be interested in profitability and long-term growth. On the other hand directors and employees will be interested in issues such as market share, growth in the client base, profitability per customer, distribution costs, customer satisfaction etc. Thus information usage is very dependent on the functions within an organization. For instance in the Malaysian Airline case, apart from general financial analysis, marketing directors would be interested in:

1. Brand awareness, brand recall amongst the general population
2. Advertising spend and effectiveness
3. Malaysian Airlines' market share for key routes
4. Customer satisfaction levels
5. Growth in yield depending on the customer mix (i.e. business class, economy class, first class).

b. Thus you should be asking questions like – How well are these needs being met through current company reports?

Which marketing metrics should be considered, in order to meet these needs?

These metrics are now considered as a necessary adjunct to normal financial measures because:

1. There has been a change from seller to buyer power
2. Over the last two decades, there has been a transition from manufacturing to service industries, and indeed information led industry structures, needing more developed measures
3. Rate and speed of change
4. Increasing emphasis on customer relationship marketing
5. Dynamic changes in distribution channels
6. New approaches to corporate performance measurement
7. Progress in valuing brands.

The table below gives you some idea of some of the new measures that could be adopted in assessing marketing performance.

*Marketing metrics for possible use in company reporting*

| Market data | Market size | Market trend |
| --- | --- | --- |
| Relative Market Performance | • Unit volume trend<br>• Market share (volume)<br>• Market share by mix by major market segment (value) | • Relative price levels and trends<br>• Sales by major brand (value)<br>• Major brand trends (value) channel (value) |
| Customer Performance | • Number of customers<br>• Customer loyalty<br>• Customer complaints<br>• Relative quality<br>• Relative value | • Customer service levels<br>• Customer satisfaction<br>• Consumption per capita (value)<br>• Would recommend company or brands to friend |
| Innovation | • Activity calendar (past year)<br>• New product/service review<br>• New products/services launched in past 5 years as % of this year's sales | • Statement of future opportunities and objectives<br>• Partnerships, acquisitions, licenses |
| Efficiency | • Capacity utilization<br>• R & D productivity | • Awards |
| People and Competency | • % employee turnover<br>• % employees participating in share purchase or profit sharing | • Training activities, and training spend<br>• Spend as % of sales<br>• Employee satisfaction<br>• Intellectual property |
| Investment | • R & D priorities and spend as % of sales<br>• Capital expenditure activity and spend as % of sales<br>• Advertising spend as % of sales | • Total marketing spend as % of sales<br>• Technical support to customers |
| Branding | • Preference<br>• Purchase intent<br>• Brand value<br>• Brand strength | • Awareness<br>• Image<br>• Perceived differential<br>• Brand positioning |
| Distribution | • Level<br>• Trend | • Channel mix<br>• Channel trend |

# Summary

All the above ratios are useful in analysing a company's performance. Companies may be better or poorer than the average performers in the sector. You may also feel that the analyses yield results that may be unusual or present opportunities for improving the company's position in the marketplace. These should be taken into account when establishing future strategies and objectives. In addition to these, marketers have recently been seriously considering additional measurements to understand marketing success. These are known as Marketing Metrics. Examples of these are shown in Figures 2.2 and 2.3. It should be realized that measuring marketing performance is a complex process and is likely to vary from company to company and sector to sector. Service sector measurements will be different from product sector measurements. You will therefore have to look at the relevant measures on a case to case basis.

This case study has been chosen to illustrate the way in which a case could be possibly tackled. When tackling any case, it is important to have a sensible system where you undertake the following tasks:

- a. General analysis, where you undertake a SWOT analysis and then proceed to using analytical tools such as portfolio analysis, Porter analysis and gap analysis
- b. It is also useful to undertake financial analysis as and when necessary. In this particular case financial analysis can only be undertaken on distribution of funds
- c. Choose options for the development of markets and evaluate them
- d. Develop strategies for the chosen option (s). Plan tactics for the short-term to implement the strategies
- e. Consider contingency plans and monitoring the plan.

In developing a strategic marketing plan therefore, the following should be considered:

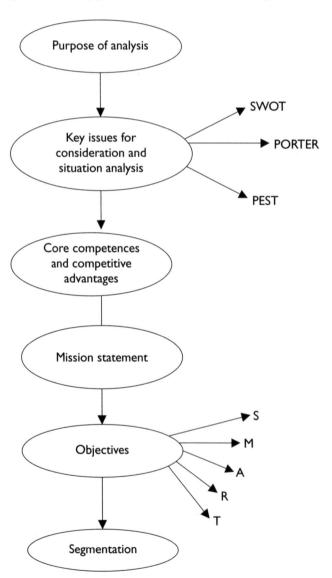

*Figure 5.1*

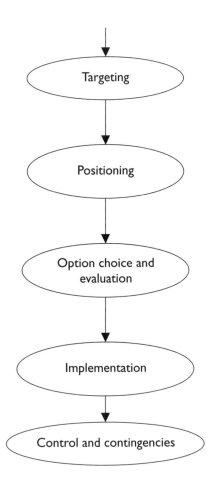

*Figure 5.1.* *(continued)*

1. **Purpose**: This report proposes a three years strategic marketing plan for the City of Daugaupils which aims to capitalize on the opportunities presented by HRH Prince of Wales visit.

2. **Summary of situational analysis:**

- Strengths    Beautiful, historic location
  Good sports facilities
  Good rail, road, river transportation
  Skilled, cheap, available labour
  Factories available, close to raw materials.
- Weaknesses    No clear strategy
  Poor financial position
  Poor reputation in Riga (among citizens – 75% want to leave)
  High unemployment, deteriorating health
  Poor quality airport.
- Opportunities    PR/profile of media coverage as a result of HRH's visit; Links to UK
  Globalization (companies investing here)
  Cross border travel; tourism
  Latvia to double its military spend by 2003 to join NATO – requiring manufacturing and engineering spend
  Use of charismatic mayor, with good contacts, to generate PR and profile.

- Threats  Global recession reducing overseas investment of companies
  Reduced air travel/tourism due to terrorism
  Risk of civil unrest due to unemployment
  Increasing isolation/curtailment of spending by Riga.

*Key issues to address are:*

- Develop and implement overall strategy
- Improve short-term financial position
- Generate investment form longer term growth
- Reduce unemployment
- Ensure the opportunities presented by the one off visit by HRH are maximized; profile raised; contacts/relationships established
- Meet the conflicting demands/communications needs of stakeholders.

3. **Competitive advantage:** The city is weak in many factors but the available advantages are:

- Low cost, available workforce
- Skills – engineering, sports
- Factories/sports facilities – only speedway in Baltics
- Alliance with twinned towns
- Beautiful location, transport infrastructure.

However, awareness of the above is minimal even in Latvia, never mind in the wider EU. The HRH visit presents a tremendous opportunity to overcome this deficiency.

4. **Mission statement:** To be recognized as a highly rated City for both manufacturing excellence at low cost and as an attractive sports/sightseeing tourist destination.

5. **Objectives:** These are in an adapted Balances Score-Card format to avoid over focus on one area.

| **Objectives** | **To be measured by** |
|---|---|
| *Financial* | *Audit of City Hall records* |
| 1. Increase the number of companies manufacturing in the city by: <br>    • 2 in 2002 <br>    • 3 in each of 2003 and 2004 <br> 2. Increase tourist volumes from 16.3k in 1998 to: <br>    • 20k in 2002 <br>    • 30k p.a. by 2004 <br> 3. Improve the access by air by end 2004. | Tourist board figures <br> (NB. identify if more up to date figures than 1998 are available as 16.3k may have fallen) <br> • Funds secured in 2002 <br> • Airlines agree to connect to 5 more EU cities <br> • Airport development commenced 2003/complete 2004 |

| | |
|---|---|
| *Profile/Reputation* | *Audit of press cuttings and news coverage* |
| 1. Increase the positive news coverage featuring the mayor to<br>   • 25 national/international news features p.a<br>   • 3 TV interviews p.a.<br>2. Ensure the HRH visit shows the City in a positive light and is covered by all major global TV stations.<br>3. Increase the tourism visitors who revisit within 1 year from 20% in 2000 to 30% by 2004. | Audit of news coverage<br>Hotel and train records plus satisfaction surveys. In due course, customer relationship marketing system tracking. |
| *Citizens of Daugaupils* | *City statistics – count all unemployment* |
| 1. Reduce unemployment from 28% to 20% by 2004.<br>2. Increase satisfaction levels<br>   • reduce the 75% who wish to leave by 50% by 2004. | Quality research from 40 citizens (major cultural groups) to identify issues.<br>Quantitative research every 2 years 1000 citizens. |

6. **Segmentation:** Segmentation is the process of dividing a varied and differing group of buyers into smaller groups, within which broadly similar patterns of buyers needs exist. The following matrix shows tourists and businesses. The internal segment of employees, citizens of Daugaupils and Riga are considered in Section 7.

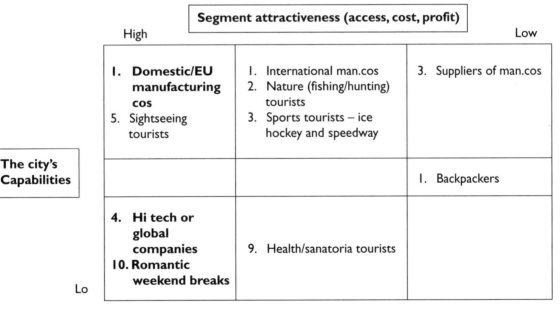

*Figure 5.2*

*Justification*

- Businesses
  1. Fit with your capabilities. Will generate jobs/income and bring western practices.
  2. Competition is greater; difficult to access

3. Profitability is lower – reduced ability to invest/pay tax
4. You've not got the infrastructure.

- Tourists
    1. Affluent, longer visits, spend in hotels/restaurants
    2. Stay 3–4 days, reduced spend in B&B's/camping
    3. Spend on good/access to venues/merchandise but only short stays
    4. You need to modernize buildings, competition from other cities, positive perception difficult to achieve regarding disease
    5. Limited spending; tacky perception
    6. Too much competition from Vienna, Prague, Copenhagen.

7. **Targeting:** Targeting is required to determine the segments on which the City has an advantage over competitors. The following are the key segments to target in the short term.

    - National and International Journalists – using the mayors contacts and charisma; plus the contacts of Nigel Seymour-Dale and the UK Embassy regarding the HRH visit
    - Employees in City Hall
    - Citizens of Daugaupils – opinion leaders/formers; middle class (who can help or hinder reform); unemployed
    - Influences – Riga; consulates; twinned towns; tourist offices
    - Sightseeing and nature tourists – living within 150km ( rail/road); twinned cities with connecting flights; nature – male groups aged 40 + ; father and sons; sightseeing – older couples (aged 50 + )
    - Domestic/EU manufacturing business:

        i. companies expanding/doing business with one of the three neighbouring countries

        ii. segment by: sic code; number of employees; turnover.

8. **Positioning:** Positioning is the attempt by marketers to give a product or service a distinctive identity or image, giving perceived benefits over competitive products/services. The following maps show how you should position the City to avoid head-on (expensive) competition.

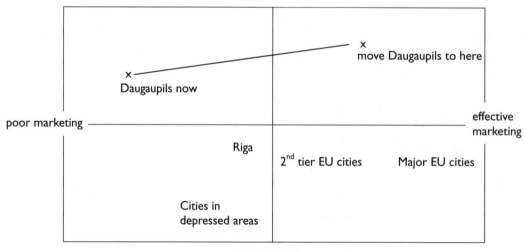

*Figure 5.3*

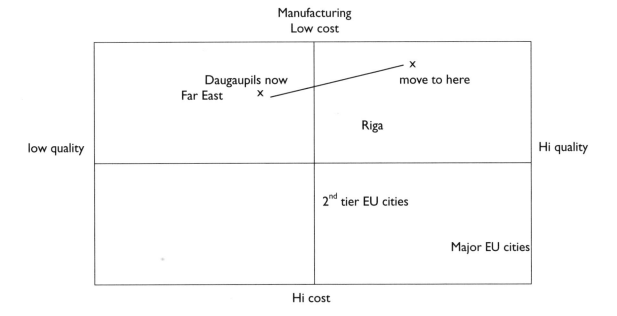

*Figure 5.4*

9. **Strategic options:** You should adopt a low cost, narrow focus strategy (as opposed to a differentiated, mass market focus) because:

   - It requires significant budget to differentiate and make people aware of this via promotion
   - It uses your competencies – a low cost, skilled workforce
   - Narrowly focusing on nature, sports and sightseeing tourism requires minimal investment. You do not have the 'mass market' glamour/reputation of many other tourist destinations or the funds to build this.

Spending on other areas should be curtailed wherever possible (e.g. culture/theatre/exhibition)

The strategies to focus on are:-

*Existing markets*

| **Market Penetration** | **Product Development** |
|---|---|
| *Segments* | *Segments* |
| • Domestic/EU man.cos | • Employees and citizens (ie. change focus) |
| • sight/nature tourists | • Sports tourism – need to attract top games |

*Tactics*

- Liaise with existing businesses, incentives to recruit, lobby twinned towns, PR and use Ashworth/Voogel score; build relations with UK Embassy
- Given interest in architecture; ensure HRM tours the churches/monuments; establish if Harry can accompany him – waterski-ing/fishing/media coverage; re-contact previous visitors, lobby tourist offices, PR with Nat Geographic articles, build website

*Tactics*

- Internal marketing, appoint web team
- PR and newsletters, charitable giving, satisfaction research
- Lobby twinned towns and mayors contacts to arrange top sports matches

*New markets*

**Market Development**

Segments – International manufacturing cos – long term

Tactics

- Build airport, lobby airlines
- Uplift PR
- Arrange trade delegations

**Diversification**

None – Too risky

10. **Implementation:** The communications strategies to follow are:

- Profile – PR, relationship building
- Push – Personal selling/lobbying, direct mail, email
- Pull – Website and limited advertising (limited budget).

The web will support the profile/push strategy and will primarily be used by journalists/tour operators initially, as we do not have the budget to advertise/direct mail tourists directly to generate web traffic.

A high level timing plan is:-

**Branding/positioning**                                    **2002    2003    2004**

Update logo; build web site

PR – Mayor

PR – Lobby journalists regarding HRH visit

Advertising (limited)

**Employees of City Hall**

Internal marketing plan

Regular updates

Satisfaction research

**Citizens of Daugaupils**

PR – Local journalists/TV

Newsletters regarding ST disease

Satisfaction research

Accelerate English teaching (with George Soros Open School support)

Arrange gap year student placements with companies around
Salford University

**Key influences**

Lobby UK Embassy regarding closer working relationship/
tourist
offices/business contacts

Lobby Riga and EU via LRDA for funding – airport/military spend

Lobby tour operators/airlines

Lobby Riga for world champ leg

**Previous visitors**

Recontact regarding HRH visit

Build database/personalize contacts

Regular newsletters

**Attract new tourists**

Maximize PR of HRH visit-sights and fishing

Exhibit at International Travel Market in Earls Court 11/02

Arrange sports events – EU and twinned cities

**Attract new businesses/create jobs**

Tax benefits for existing cos to expand

PR using Ashworth and Voogd score

Trade delegations via EU contacts

**Budget**

| | 2002 | 2003 | 2004 |
|---|---|---|---|
| • Profile | 60% | 60% | 50% |
| • Push | 30% | 30% | 30% |
| • Pull | 10% | 10% | 20% |

11. **Control:** The control measures are outlined at section 5 with the objectives. The following should also be introduced:

    • Monthly review of spend and income vs budget to produce a variance analysis
    • Quarterly project progress reports.

    The controls should be used to ensure that plans are refined if some objectives are not being met.

    An example of a contingency plan would be to focus more efforts on nature/sightseeing tourism if a nearby city retaliated with a significant sports promotion which impacts on your visitor numbers.

    This type of strategic planning exercise helps with the understanding of the case and can also help to generate ideas. In addition to this exercise, it is important to consider some other key contemporary issues such as:

    a. Branding and communication possibilities
    b. The international dimensions of the case.

# Branding

A brand is defined as the name, symbol, words or design used to identify the products or services of a producer and differentiate these from those of competitor products in the eyes of the customer.

Branding benefits to the City would include:

- Adds a $3^{rd}$ dimension to price/quality – differentiates in customers eyes
- Competitive advantage – hard to copy
- Earns customer trust which can exclude competitors (it is 5 times cheaper to retain existing businesses/tourists than win new ones).

Branding benefits to consumer include:

- Reduces risk – a known quantity/quality
- Reduces the burden of decision making
- Can provide psychological reassurance/reward ('lets go back to that lovely City again – we deserve it').

## Current Position

Brand equity is comprised of – awareness, perceived quality, identity and loyalty. However, your City has a distinct market position but a weak brand – there is very low awareness; where there is awareness the perception is poor; there is no common identity or values among the citizens and only 20% of visitors return.

To maximize brand impact the following points need addressing:

- Clarity – there is limited perception of the brand by consumers who are unaware of the city's distinguishing features – suggesting that a significant communications/ repositioning programme is required.
- Credibility – this needs to be properly conveyed by formally adopting an unofficial title of 'Capital of the land of the blue lakes'
- Competitiveness – this edge needs to be retained by using the coat of arms (regarding history/heritage) but this could be modernized
- Consistency – the city council needs to display the same, new logo on all three entrances to the city, on literature, the updated website, City Hall vehicles etc.

Given the current very poor perception of the citizens of Daugaupils (75% want to leave) and Riga, creating a distinctive brand image is a significant challenge which requires a long term, sustained strategy. It is vital that maximum profile and PR is obtained from the HRH visit as this is likely to be the only newsworthy occurrence where you can grab the attention of the world's media (in particular the EU media). However, once the HRH visit has passed it is still vital that contacts and relationships are maintained/enhanced, and the charismatic mayor should be used for this.

It is recommended that the City should aspire to the following brand values:

- Values which are common to all segments, which should remain consistent through all brand deployment are:
  1. Nice environment to live, visit or work – the capital of the land of the blue lakes
  2. Easy to get good transportation
  3. Professional
  4. Growing/successful area.

- The differences for each segment, which should be reflected in the communications for that particular segment (and need to be consistently displayed) are:

|  | CITIZENS | MAN. CO'S | TOURISTS |
|---|---|---|---|
| PERSONALITY | Proud | Reliability | Mystical |
| VALUES | Honest | Expert | Tranquil |
| EMOTIONAL | Belonging/valued | Reassurance | Enjoyment |
| RATIONAL | Multi-cultural harmony | East : West Gateway | Options at your fingertips |
| FUNCTIONAL | Hardworking | Low cost workforce | Natural Beauty |

These key points of branding should be considered for further development.

You should also consider the potential impact of the Internet for international marketing. For this purpose, I have actually chosen a good answer from a distinction level candidate.

# Internet Implications

1. **Purpose:** This section outlines how the Internet could be used as part of a strategy to attract international investment and tourism to the region.
2. **E-marketing:** E-marketing is the way marketers increase sales or build brand awareness via the Internet, be it over the target markets' PC, TV or mobile phone.
   Benefits include:
   - Global audience.
   - Increased speed/greater responsiveness
   - Medium for getting feedback from customers/market research
   - Low cost – less need to print brochures, type letters, answer phones
   - Improve your image with Riga – embracing 21$^{st}$ century technology, not backward and poor.
   - As this enables customers to shop around for the lowest price, it could benefit you given your low cost strategy positioning
   - Direct contact with customers can allow better relationship management and reduce the time and cost of finding and maintaining intermediary networks such as tour operators. However, this cutting out of the middleman has very important implications for pricing and branding and should only be considered later in the plan period
   - Able to build a database and use this for personalized communications with networks – such as twinned towns, tour operators.
3. **Planning:** As with all marketing and communications, you must ensure that you know your customers that you add value in your contacts and that you differentiate from your competitors. You need to decide:
   - Who you wish to communicate with
   - Why
   - What messages to convey
   - When.

   before you start building/implementing new web sites.
   For example, the Internet can be used for any (or all) of the following:
   - Relationship management with existing tourists or tour operators/twinned towns
   - Finding/accessing new markets
   - Selling on-line
   - Knowledge management – feedback from customers, sharing of information, best practices with twinned cities
   - Internal communications and training.

4. **Potential Issues:** It is important that the Internet is put in context – while its usage is growing and will continue to do so, it still only accounts for a minority of overall sales. It is not the answer to all your problems, especially given the lack of budget to promote the site/make your customers aware of it. In the short term, the more important part of the plan is to ensure the PR, profile raising, personal lobbying by key managers is effectively implemented.

Internet issues that need to be addressed are:

- Change City Hall from a command led to a marketing led culture
- Plan thoroughly (as section 3 above)
- Resource up – design, keep it updated, speed of answering emails. Ensure the service is at a high level so that people enjoy dealing with the City. For example use the 'Intelligent Autoresponder' to emails that Blackstar.com use (a DVD site) – which immediately sends an email back stating 'Thank you for your email, there are currently 51 emails ahead of yours waiting an answer so we should be able to respond in 1 hour and 10 minutes'
- Use it to enhance brand image – this needs to be consistent/integrated with all other marketing communications (PR) key account management.
- Set objectives (see later) and monitor their achievement/the effectiveness.

The following research by IBM/Interbrand regarding the key drivers of brand effectiveness on the Internet should be reviewed (and the WTO web guidelines) when building your web site and functionality.

- Accessibility
- Navigability
- Customer Service – NB. DHL research states that 20% of goods bought over the Internet arrive late.
- Technical performance – NB. quick download times (do not have large pictures) to avoid dissatisfying customers as did BOO.Com.
- Content – keep it relevant, updated, personalised.
- Consistency of branding.

5. **Potential uses:** The following should be developed:

- Internally within City Hall – Internet to share brand values, progress reports on plans (good news) updates, mayor's Q&A, share best practice, increase understanding and motivation, ensure shared vision. Need to encourage usage (eg. rewards, stop paper copies). These staff, are the ones who will deal with your external customers so a high quality, professional and consistent approach is vital
- Internet site for potential tourists – small photos of beautiful areas, links to fishing/sports sites, hotels/train timetables etc. NB. There is a limited pull ability of the web when awareness is low. As it is easy and cheap to register many domain names (to increase the chances of a customer coming across your site) you should register a number of names and register these with all the major search engines (Yahoo, Google etc). Examples of domain names are: Fishinginpeace.com; SpeedwayBaltic.com.
- Password protected Extranet site for:
  1. Tour operators – to check hotel availability, flight times, book hotels/flights, check statements/invoices
  2. Existing companies – for tax forms, policies, queries etc.
- E-mail – The e-mail addresses of all website visitors (and visitors in person to the regions – via hotel/train booking forms etc) should be requested. These details, as well as brief personal details (on interests, hobbies, name, address) etc. should be used to build a customer relationship database. This needs to be kept updated

and used to personalize communications with previous (and potential future) visitors. For example, a newsletter could be emailed every 6 months outlining forthcoming sports events/fishing season; for previous visitors – invite feedback on how the City can be improved (perhaps offer a free trip/holiday prize draw as an incentive to participate). You need to give customers the ability to stop receiving this if they wish.

Given the current financial and social position of the citizens of Daugaupils, the Internet is not a viable means of communicating with them. This will have to rely on the traditional forms of PR, news broadcasting, newsletters.

6. **Objectives and measures:** Objectives need to be set for each key target segment.

For example:

| OBJECTIVE | MEASURE |
|---|---|
| 30% of visitors to return within 1 year | CRM systems, email, satisfaction surveys. |
| Obtain a 0.5% click through rate from intro to our sites. | Web tracking systems. |
| Increase the website access to sales conversion rate to 20% per 5 tour operators per year. | Web tracking, key account manager feedback. |
| Obtian feedback from 5% of customers emailed with the newsletter. | Ratio of emails sent to responses received. |

## Conclusion

The Internet will have an initially small, but increasingly growing and important role to play in your future profile, sales and customer relationship/serving strategy.

## Examination approaches

The examiners, when looking at answers to examination questions based on the case study, look to:

### Analytical and critical thinking

The style of the case study has changed over the last two years and the two previous case studies are indicative of this change. The examination paper generally has three questions. Strategic planning, analytical and decision making skills will always be tested.

Candidates should be able to analyse each case and comprehend the other areas of the diploma syllabi from where they may need to draw their underpinning knowledge. Although candidates need to demonstrate their underpinning knowledge in the context of the Case Study, it is important that they show some creative flair and innovation in their answers.

The examiners are looking for the candidates to demonstrate analytical ability, interpretive skills, insight, innovation and creativity in answering questions. They are also looking for candidates to take clear and sensible decisions within the context of the case study. A critical awareness of the specific issues involved, relevant theoretical underpinning, attention to detail, coherence and justification of strategies adopted will also be assessed.

### Decision making

The title of the paper – 'Analysis and Decision' implies that the candidates are competent enough to analyse problems within a marketing context and subsequently take appropriate *decisions* to implement marketing strategies for an organization. In order to achieve competence in this area prospective candidates will need to be conversant with all aspects of marketing, as strategic marketing problems do not come in neat packages. A comprehensive grasp of the basic subjects at the Certificate and Advanced Certificate level together with the key subjects of International Marketing and Marketing Communications is needed. The Planning and Control Paper is an integral part of the preparation. Decisions made have to reflect the fact that candidates have thoroughly understood the key marketing issues impinging on the case. They have to make decisions which are realistic and justifiable and above all actionable within the given constraints.

### Judging between courses of action

When analysing a case study, it would be surprising if only one course of action was possible. Often there are several alternatives to a problem and a company has to weigh up the chances of success and pursue a particular course of action. As an examination candidate, you are expected to pursue courses of action which are possible, realistic and sustainable. The examiners are not looking for right or wrong answers, they are searching for solutions that will work within the given scenario of the case study.

### Handling assumptions and inferences

All cases are based on real life information that may have gaps within it. No company works in a perfect environment or with perfect information. This would not only be impossible, but would be outside the capability of any human being. The result is that we all create an image of the way in which a company is operating. In creating that image and understanding it, there may be gaps that need filling. These can be done by the projection of trends (e.g. Acclaim and the Games Market), or by making certain assumptions about market demand or product suitability. In most cases students will need to make certain assumptions. As long as these are not wildly off the mark and help to augment the case and your arguments, they are perfectly acceptable. In some cases candidates may wish to point out that further market research is necessary (e.g. the food enzymes market in Europe for Biocatalysts).

## Presenting a point of view

All cases are about presenting a point of view. Examiners expect student answers to vary. It is therefore important, when preparing for the case, that you do not get hung up on thinking that your friend or colleague has the right answer. If you have analysed the case thoroughly and you feel that you have a clear view of the strategies that should be adopted by the company then you should put these forward. At all times you should consider the detail, coherence and strategic aspects of arguments, justifying them fully.

## Relating theory to practice and vice versa

In order to be a good practising marketing manager, you need to be able to seamlessly knit marketing theory to practical solutions. I see this as a symbiotic process. Too often we see managers who only emphasize the practical aspects and by doing that, deny their companies the benefit of marketing frameworks and any new knowledge that may be available. By the same token, simply propounding theoretical frameworks, with little or no thought given to the practical application of these frameworks to real problems is also unacceptable. In order to formulate sensible solutions to cases you will need to be knowledgeable about both practical marketing aspects and theoretical issues and contemporary marketing thinking.

# How to pass the Case Study paper

In general, candidates are expected to allocate some study time at a centre in order to prepare for the case study. The notional study time is 45 hours over a period of ten to twelve weeks. Roughly half of this time should be allocated for work on previous cases and the rest for developing analyses and scenarios for the new case and preparing for the examination that candidates will be sitting.

## The paper

The Analysis and Decision paper is the culmination of all the marketing subjects covered at all levels, but especially the Diploma and the Advanced Diploma. For this reason, there is no specific syllabus for this paper. The new Planning and Control syllabus now gives a clear strategic focus. This type of expertise will be needed to tackle the Case Study paper. It is also clear that it will not be possible to tackle the Case Study without a clear grasp of the fundamentals of Marketing Communications and International Marketing. In this sense, for all students the Case Study is a culmination of the application of all the marketing knowledge that you have gained over several years.

## Open Book Examination

For the vast majority of the students, the Analysis and Decision paper is an open book examination. This means that candidates are allowed to take whatever written material they wish into an examination. In general most candidates take books, reports and details of their own analyses. Used judiciously, this material can be useful for referencing when answering questions. As an *aide-mémoire*, taking in certain books can be helpful, however there are also potential dangers. Many candidates think that even with poor preparation, they can do well as this is an open book examination and they can utilize theory from textbooks. Often too much time is spent 'looking' for certain bits of information. This means that valuable writing and thinking time is lost.

*Another temptation that candidates sometimes succumb to is pre-prepared answers which they may have produced in syndicates. It is important to note that all examiners are trained to spot these and these types of answers are failed. In situations like these candidates often try to twist the questions to suit their answers and therefore soon become unstuck.*

It is highly important, therefore, that a considerable amount of time is spent on developing tables, undertaking detailed analyses, producing diagrams and assembling this information in a folder. This is helpful for quick referencing during the examination. It also leaves candidates free to think about which bits of information may be useful to use in framing answers.

## Closed Book Examinations (Pilot Centres)

In June 2000, several centres in the UK undertook a pilot study where candidates were asked to sit closed book examinations. However, they were allowed to attach six pages of analyses as appendices to their answers (minimum font size: 11). In their written answers on the day they were allowed to cross-refer to the appendices. The marks for the analyses were allocated in the following manner:

Marks for analysis:                           15

Marks for the application of the analysis:    15

*(On the day of the examination)*

This methodology has been introduced in order to:

   a.  Reward students for work done in the four weeks between the release of the case and the day of the examination.
   b.  Enable students to concentrate on the case and utilize the analyses effectively in their answers.

So far we have found that the students have responded well to the challenge and the level of depth in the answers appears to be good.

# Notes to candidates

These notes are modified from time to time, depending on the context within which the cases are set. The following is an example of what was used in the June 2000 case study.

---

**Extended knowledge**

**Notes to candidates, June 2000**

The examiners will be marking your scripts on the basis of questions put to you in the examination room. Candidates are advised to pay particular attention to the *mark allocation on the examination paper and budget their time accordingly.*

Your role is outlined in the candidates' brief and you will be required to recommend clear courses of action.

You WILL NOT be awarded marks merely for analysis. This should have been undertaken before the examination day in preparation for meeting the tasks which will be specified in the examination paper.

Candidates are advised not to waste valuable time collecting unnecessary data. The cases are based upon real world situations. No useful purpose will therefore be served by contacting companies in this industry and candidates are *strictly instructed not to do so* as it would simply cause unnecessary confusion.

---

As in real life, anomalies will be found in this Case situation. Please simply state assumptions where necessary when answering questions. The CIM is not in a position to answer queries on Case data. Candidates are tested on their overall understanding of the Case and in key issues, not on minor details. There are no catch questions or hidden agendas. In addition, for this particular Case, the CIM is not prepared to answer any financial queries.

**Additional information will be introduced in the examination paper itself which candidates must take into account when answering the questions set.**

Acquaint yourself thoroughly with the Case Study and be prepared to follow closely the instructions given to you on the examination day. To answer examination questions effectively, candidates must adopt a report format.

The copying of pre-prepared 'group' answers written by consultants/tutors is strictly forbidden and will be penalized by failure. The questions will demand analysis in the examination itself and individually composed answers are required to pass.

From case to case, there may be minor modifications to the candidates' notes depending on the type and style of case.

# The Candidate's Brief

This brief is an integral part of the Case Study. It gives some idea of the role you are expected to play in solving the case study. The candidate's brief gives individuals a position either as an external consultant or an internal manager. On the day of the examination they are expected to answer the questions set from the point of view of the role that has been allocated.

Below are two examples.

## Insight

### Candidate's Brief Clerical Medical Case, June 2000

You are Mr. Don Sherwood, a Marketing Consultant who has had considerable experience in analysing different industry sectors for a number of companies with a view to helping them to perform competitively. For this assignment, the Clerical Medical Investment Group Limited has invited you to undertake an internal and external analysis of their current situation.

You have consulted widely within the industry and within the Group. The insurance and pensions industry is quite complex, yet you have managed to find some useful information on consumer profiles and the competitive positions of the various players in the sector.

As a result of your efforts you have built up an interesting profile of the industry and Clerical Medical's position within it. At a future meeting to be set on the 16th of June 2000, you are to present your findings to the Marketing Director, Mr. James Broadbent, in order to help him to develop future plans for the organization.

**Insight**

**Candidate's Brief Philips Case Study**

You are James Lee, a Marketing Consultant with a great deal of experience in advising companies to develop marketing communications strategies. You have been engaged by Jacques Dupetite, the Marketing Director of Philips, based in the Netherlands. Philips is a large multinational company which began its operations in the Netherlands. It straddles many product/market sectors and its brand identity has become somewhat diffuse.

You have collected together a lot of information on Philips, including several global market research reports relating to Philips' new approach to marketing. You have spent several days with the Marketing Director who is particularly interested in developing a coherent brand image for the company in all its global markets. The client is willing to release a very large budget in order to further this aim.

You are to prepare a report of your initial recommendations for the main board of Philips, which will include the Electronics Brand Director from the UK. The report will be presented on 11 December 1998.

## The use of additional information

On the day of the examination you will be given two sets of information. One is the additional information pertaining to the case. As the senior examiner, I feel that candidates should be able to cope with the introduction of a small amount of new information on the day. This would be the case in real life situations too. The other, is the set of questions set with regards to the case study.

The additional information is something that you should take into consideration when answering the questions set as its is likely to have some bearing on the market conditions or on some areas of the case. The additional information will not invalidate all the work that has been undertaken over the four weeks. The additional information is introduced to test the ability of candidates to be flexible in their thinking and to test the ability to assimilate and effectively incorporate new material into the development of their strategies.

# Gauging performance

To perform well on the paper, candidates will have to exhibit the following:
* A need to concentrate on the strategic aspects of marketing underpinned by the necessary detail
* The ability to identify 'gaps' in the Case Study and to outline the assumptions made
* The ability to critically apply relevant models for case analysis
* The ability to draw and synthesize from any of the diploma subject areas as relevant
* Concentration on the question set rather than the pre-prepared answer
* The ability to answer in the report format with comprehensive sentences rather than providing simplistic lists
* The judicious use of diagrams for illustrative purposes
* The ability to draw disparate links together and give coherent answers
* The use of interesting and useful articles from journals in their answers
* Innovation and creativity in answering the questions
* Demonstration of practical applications of marketing knowledge

- Sensible use of time and an ability to plan the answers within the set time
- A good understanding of the case study set.

The best way to prepare for the case would entail the following considerations:

- Practice on previous examination papers
- Reading and digesting the senior examiner's report
- Reading, books, newspapers, relevant marketing and academic journals
- For each examination case ascertaining the relevant knowledge base that will be required
- Being flexible and critical when using analytical models instead of being prescriptive.

In addition to the above, candidates should also be prepared to undertake the following:

- The use of relevant models for the sector in which the case study is based
- The use of each candidate's practical and business experience using any illustrative examples
- The use of diagrams
- A thorough marketing and financial analysis of each case study within the given context of the Case Study
- An awareness and application of strategic marketing plans
- Revisiting relevant syllabi from the Diploma and Advanced Diploma within the given context of the Case Study.

## Summary

When working on the case and in the examination, do not repeat in summary form large pieces of factual information from the case. The examiners are fully aware of the case. It is better to use the information in the case to illustrate your statements, to defend your arguments, or to make salient points. Beyond the brief introduction to the company, you must avoid being descriptive; instead, you must be analytical.

You will need to ensure that the sections and subsections of your discussion flow logically and smoothly from one to the next. Try to build on what has gone before so that each analysis builds on the previous one. A piecemeal approach to analysis results in fragmented writing lacking coherence. This is because the parts do not flow from one to the next, and this becomes apparent to the examiners. Sometimes this happens when intensive group and individual approaches are put together.

It is important to write in a report format using clear English, avoiding grammatical and spelling errors. Clarity of approach and the judicious use of diagrams helps examiners to follow your arguments easily.

Finally:

- Practice on previous cases and to see how you would have approached the case differently from the specimen answers given
- Read and digest senior examiner's reports
- Read books, newspapers and relevant marketing and academic journals.

Be flexible and critical when utilizing analytical models and steer away from being prescriptive in your approach. More practice will result in better insights and help you with being creative and innovative when framing your answers.

*The units that follow give you an indication of the way that students have approached examinations. This has been done through the usage of specimen answers with comments from the Senior Examiner. You should attempt to analyse these answers and look for areas of improvement that would be possible within the examination time frame.*

## Candidate's Brief

You are an internationally renowned Marketing Consultant specializing in the development and implementation of strategic marketing policies. You have been engaged by Mr Margrave, the Managing Director of Pirelli Cables.

The case is based around Pirelli General plc and is mainly concerned with the growth and development of the cables section of Pirelli. You have been asked to look at the company's current position in the cable market, together with the international implications of deregulation in the electricity markets. The Pirelli brand name is well known internationally. You have collected together a lot of information on Pirelli, including the development of its e-commerce strategies. You have spent several days with the Marketing Director as well as the Managing Director.

The clients are interested in releasing a sensible budget in order to develop their marketing strategies.

You are to prepare a report of your initial recommendations for the main board of Pirelli General on 8th December, 2000.

---

### Important Notice

This Case material is based on an actual organization and existing market conditions.

Candidates are strictly instructed NOT TO CONTACT Pirelli or any other companies in the industry. Additional information will be provided at the time of the examination. Further copies may be obtained from The Chartered Institute of Marketing, Moor Hall, Cookham, Maidenhead, Berkshire, SL6 9QH, UK.

---

© The Chartered Institute of Marketing

## Pirelli

### Introduction

Pirelli is a well known international company with a brand name that is instantly recognizable. However, the brand conjures up visions of tyres and famous calendars. Yet little is generally known of the vast empire that is the global company Pirelli, which straddles a range of industries. This case will outline the general areas in which Pirelli operate and will then concentrate on a particular sector, the cable sector. Pirelli was founded by Giovanni Batlista Pirelli in 1872 in Milan, Italy. It concentrated on the production of general rubber products. In 1880, it started its first cable production operation in order to meet demands for insulated telegraph wire.

As car production began in earnest in the 1900s, Pirelli embarked upon tyre production. By this time Pirelli had manufacturing plants in most European countries, and also in Brazil, which provided much of the rubber supply needed for tyre manufacturing. In the 1950s, Pirelli expanded globally and began to diversify into other spheres; for instance producing cables in Canada and Mexico and diversified products (rubber goods, plastics, textiles etc.) in France. Pirelli also established two holding companies, one in Italy and one in Switzerland. The Italian holding company controlled Tyres and Diversified Products in Italy, France and Belgium. The companies operating in Argentina, Brazil, Canada, Mexico, Spain and the UK on the other hand were controlled by the Swiss holding company. Markets were mainly national and were under the firm and direct control of the local companies. Product and process knowledge was developed centrally in Milan and transferred to units in other parts of Italy and abroad. In the 1960s, the company continued to expand abroad and established itself in Germany, Greece, Turkey and Peru, at the same time cultivating the idea of far-reaching co-operation among major rubber manufacturers. During this period the company lost the lead in tyre production as it was slow to move production from "conventional" to "radial" tyres (with the cross-plying of rubber for a better grip), and as a result lost market share to increasingly tougher competitors such as Michelin, Goodyear and Continental. At the same time, most of Italy was entering a difficult period of industrial relations with many left-wing factions springing up which were difficult to control. This political and social turmoil continued for several years, well into the 1970s.

In the 1970s, the company embarked on a series of joint ventures with Dunlop (a UK based rubber manufacturer) of equal shareholding. This period also saw the first major upheaval in the normal business model in western countries as a result of the oil crisis. Raw material prices rose dramatically and profits fell. At the same time, the social turmoil in Italy added to Pirelli's problems. To find its way out of these problems, Pirelli drew up a restructuring and recovery plan. In order to lessen its dependency on rubber, it followed the classic Ansoff model of trying to diversify into non-rubber and/or rubber related products (e.g. major engineering works within the sphere of Diversified Products) while abandoning the manufacture of low value-added products en route.

During this decade the joint venture with Dunlop, which had lasted 10 years, came to an end. In revising its international strategy, Pirelli gave up its diversification projects and began again, to concentrate on its more traditional areas of activity. A growing global economic recovery meant that Pirelli had to start thinking in terms of supply systems not just products, as markets were not as local as they once were. As a result, the controlling and operating structures were changed. In 1982, Pirelli S.p.A. in Milan and Societe International Pirelli in Bale, became purely financial holding companies. Pirelli Societe Generale S.A., Bale, came into being and was entrusted with the operating management of all Pirelli companies worldwide.

Three sectors, Cable, Tyres and Diversified Products, were formed and the concept of a "business" that moves outside the boundaries of local markets, in order to exploit all existing synergy's, in terms of manufacture, marketing and development began to take shape. This meant that each sector could grow outside the national framework on an international platform with synergies in production and manufacturing as appropriate.

A number of major acquisitions were completed in the 1980s, once again in the pursuit of a greater presence in international markets:

- Trefimetaux and Filergie in France (Cables).
- Armstrong in the USA (Tyres).
- Metzeler in Germany (Tyres and Diversified Products).

In 1988, the controlling structure was further simplified with Societe Internationale Pirelli becoming the major shareholder of Pirelli S.p.A. The latter took over the worldwide operating management responsibility previously entrusted to P.S.G. In 1989, ownership of the various tyre operations around the world was transferred to Pirelli Tyre Holding N.V. in the Netherlands; subsequently, approximately 25% of this company's share capital was floated on the market. Ownership of cable operations worldwide was transferred to Pirelli Cavi S.p.A., fully owned by Pirelli S.p.A.

The 1990s began with a recession and consequently there was a fall in demand for vehicles and industrial machinery, followed by a slow-down in the investment of public funds in areas such as telecommunications and energy (cables). Pirelli was restructured once again and the Diversified Products Sector was sold off. Three key strategies were followed:

a. To develop economic competitiveness (in terms of capability to reduce costs and consequently the breakeven point).
b. To develop technological competitiveness (in terms of capability to innovate products and manufacturing processes better and quicker than the competition).

c. To enhance customer service competitiveness (in terms of capability to offer the right product, at the right time and in the right place).

As a result of the stages of historical development that Pirelli has gone through, it is now present in all continents, with manufacturing facilities, research centres and sales and marketing companies. The company has expanded its presence in Eastern Europe, South East Asia and South America. Pirelli now has 70 factories in 16 countries, with over 36,200 employees, (see Appendix 1. for the Group Operating Structure and the Corporate Functions).

## Pirelli Cables and Systems

The cable sector first began life in 1906 with the development of a submarine power cable. This was followed by the development of the "Emmanueli", the first oil filled High Tension (HT) power cable. In 1932, the first submarine telephone cable was laid. The 1950s saw the development of the coaxial telephone cables. In the 1970s, the first fibre optic cable installations were carried out together with the development of very high-voltage power cables. The company then entered into optical fibre production and fibre optic submarine cable production. The 1990s saw the development of specialized cables, rapid R&D and the development of Superconductor cables. Details of the key areas in which Pirelli operates are shown in Figure 1. Figure 2 shows some of the key ways in which cables are utilized on land.

Thus Pirelli produce:

- Power transmission cables for all the voltages currently in use.
- Conventional and fibre optic telecommunications cables.
- Cables for the building trade and general industry as well as for special applications.

The cable sector also provides a "turnkey" service for its customers.

As a true technological partner to its customers around the globe, Pirelli offers the market a series of integrated components (products, systems, installations and overall engineering projects), particularly in telecommunications and power transmission, (see Appendix 1).

In the telecommunications area, optical technologies are growing fast with production aimed in that direction. Pirelli is at the forefront of photonics.

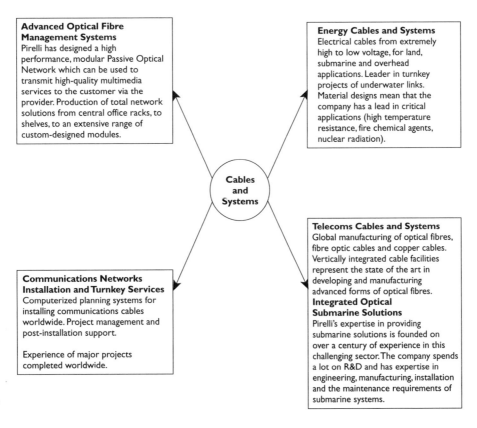

*Figure 1*

Pirelli was the first to commercialize optical amplifiers on a large scale in 1993 in the USA. In 1995, in order to gain recognition in the field of supplying systems, the cable sector set up a joint venture with Quante, a German company active in the sector of electronic equipment and components for telephone networks. This company, Pirelli-Quante, researches, develops, produces and markets integrated telecommunications systems on a worldwide scale.

In the case of supertension cables, the primary objective is to increase the power conveyed. In recent years, Pirelli has been engaged in the development of cables based on a new generation of superconducting materials. This research has taken place in the USA.

For submarine connections, Pirelli has developed high-voltage cables suitable for laying at depths of up to 2,000 metres.

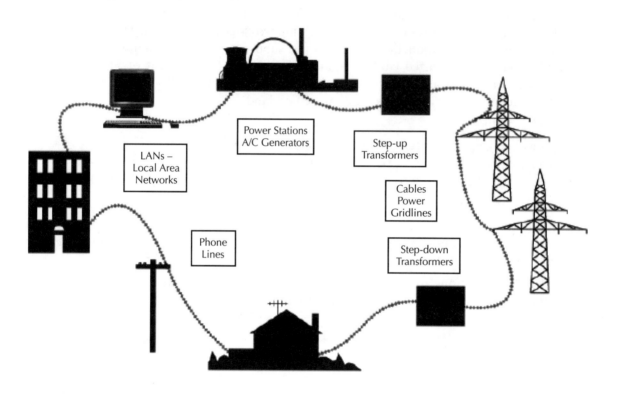

*Figure 2*

## The Market

The world cable market is quite fragmented, comprising of an assembly of national markets, each one with its own peculiar characteristics and standards. Cable Sector companies as a result still mainly work for local power and telecommunications customers, exporting only a modest proportion of their products. However, significant developments are taking place, particularly in Europe where markets are opening up with deregulation and the breaking up of monopolies. New operators from the Eastern European sector are speedily entering the market with price and service playing increasingly important roles. At the same time, the distributors and wholesalers are rebadging cables produced in Eastern Europe.

Figure 3 shows the distribution of centres Pirelli has around the world. It is also the world's largest cable manufacturer. The next section looks at the issues surrounding the UK cable market in the utility sector. The UK issues are a pointer to the possible changes in the international market.

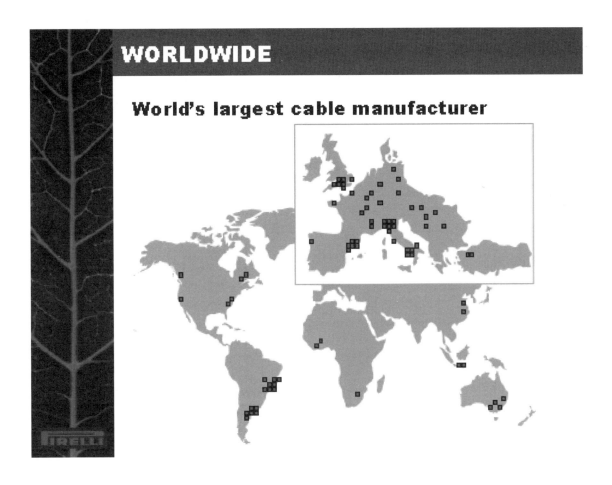

**WORLDWIDE**

**World's largest cable manufacturer**

*Figure 3*

## Issues Surrounding Outsourcing by Utility Companies in the UK

Utility companies, owing to deregulation, are under pressure to re-evaluate their approach to business processes, in order to become more efficient and profitable. One of the key areas they are considering is outsourcing non-core functions. From research carried out by Datamonitor it appears that:

- 72% of utility companies would consider outsourcing at least one aspect of their sales and marketing operations.
- 58% of utilities already outsource their metering businesses.
- 38% of utilities are now sourcing at least one aspect of their IT functions from third parties.
- 87% of utility companies state they would consider entering into a contract with an external company to manage their call centres.

Figure 4 shows the key areas that could be considered for outsourcing, with expected cost saving and operational improvement. The plots show that expected cost savings from the outsourcing of networks and facilities could be up to 15%. This offers good opportunities to a company such as Pirelli. Major systems contracts can last for seven years or more (see discussion on the HTS cable system for Detroit). Under these circumstances, the financial commitments are great and unclear or unstable contracts can be disastrous to both parties (outsourcer and supplier). It is important, under these circumstances, for there to be clearly defined contracts with inbuilt flexibility, but well-defined and measurable performance criteria. These contracts also require good planning, realistic goals and excellent communications. It is also important that the staff involved are committed and can maintain good customer relationships.

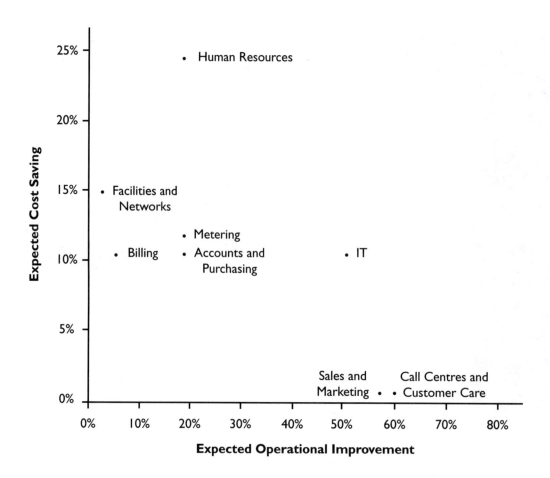

*Figure 4*

Following privatization of the utilities in the UK, a number of regulatory authorities were established to enforce the public interest. Ofgem (Office of Gas and Electricity Markets) was established to regulate the gas supply and electricity industries. Ofgem believes in promoting competition in electricity connections by addressing the factors affecting its development. It acts in the best interest of the consumer. The reasons for this are:

a.  Ofgem received over 100 submissions in response to its December 1998 consultation document. Many submissions expressed concern about the pricing and quality of service provided by the Public Energy Suppliers (PES) connections, advocating the removal of all obstacles preventing third parties from carrying out connection functions.

b.  Third parties interested in providing connections indicate that competition could deliver significant benefits to customers.

c.  Liberalizing the electricity connections market is a necessary step towards the greater co-ordination of gas and electricity regimes.

The 1998 consultation document set out five main areas of concern:

•  The PESs distinguish between "contestable" and "non-contestable" work. This runs the risk that PESs could stifle competition by unduly restricting the scope for contestable work or by rebalancing charges between the contestable and non-contestable elements, (see Appendix 2).

•  Concern was expressed that some PESs were unduly restrictive in approving contractors, although there are arrangements allowing other PESs to carry out work in each PES area.

•  Concern was expressed that delay by the PESs in providing information, or the prospect of delay, could cause a customer to decide to have the connection installed by the PES rather than a third party.

- Some customers said that the terms offered by PESs for connection were unduly onerous. In particular, they said that PESs' connection charges had increased significantly, particularly in relation to streetlighting. Some customers suggested that third party contractors were subjected to pressure from PESs, aimed at dissuading them from competing against the host PES.

To this end, Ofgem are proposing the possible demarcations for contestable and non-contestable work so that progress can be made. The proposals (not fully detailed here) mean that options open up for companies such as Pirelli to offer network solutions. The PESs on the other hand are concerned about safety standards and wish to see a single, industry-wide, national accredited registration scheme.

## Issues in the UK Market

There are five major suppliers in the marketplace:

- AEI.
- Draka.
- Wessel.
- BICC.
- Pirelli.

Pirelli has now purchased the higher end of the general cable capability, along with that supplying the utilities. Draka have bought the lower end of the general manufacturing capability. Draka have also bought Delta Cables and Pirelli has bought certain cable plants from Seimens.

All the manufacturers operate in the general market with the larger players such as Pirelli, Alcatel and BICC operating in both the general and utility markets. There is over-capacity in the market. Profitability has fallen and there is continuing rationalization in the market. There are considerable competitive pressures from low-cost imports which now represent 40% of the market in the UK.

## Market Segments

The market consists of the following segments:

### The Utilities Market

This market needs cables which can carry up to 400kV (KiloVolts). The two main buyers are the National Grid Company (NGC), requiring cables with a transmission capability between 275kV and 400kV, and the Regional Electricity Companies (RECs), which require cables with a transmission capability lying between 1kV and 132kV for distribution to customer homes and businesses. (See Appendix 3.).

The NGC is supplied exclusively by Pirelli and BICC, and the RECs are supplied by Pirelli, BICC and Alcatel respectively.

In previous years, in the utilities market, the electricity boards had highly segmented structures with different departments responsible for different functions of system design, specification and project management.

In recent years, privatization and deregulation have meant that considerable delayering has occurred in order to meet profit targets. In order to progress the cost-cutting, it is likely that installation will pass onto sub-contractors with design and specification being undertaken by the manufacturers.

This means that the traditional routes to market are under threat, with a question mark over who may win the competition for business in the future – the manufacturers or the major contractors. There is no reason why the major contractors cannot design as well as source cables from differing manufacturers based on quality and price. Many skilled, highly qualified and experienced ex-electricity board engineers have formed their own companies or have been enticed to work for contractors, broadening their skills capacity and offering to the RECs.

However, in the area of supertension cables for carrying power, RECs tend to buy the complete system only from manufacturers such as Pirelli, as they have the capability to manage the risks involved with such projects.

The market changes therefore mean that the RECs will be looking for the best possible products and services their money can buy. It also means that companies supplying products will need to be more proactive in offering a range of services, and not just specific products. Market relationships are likely to be important in the future.

As RECs become more cost conscious, logistics play an increasingly important role, as the companies no longer carry stocks of cable of different length at different locations. Most RECs are likely to demand various sizes of cables on a just-in-time delivery basis.

### Pirelli's Position

Within the utilities market, Pirelli is the dominant manufacturer, having reached this position initially through product differentiation and relationship building with the key technical people responsible for specifying products. However, the traditional structures are now changing and the technical people are in decline, with service quality in key areas such as manufacturing and logistics becoming more important. Within the utilities market there is a great deal of mobility with key staff moving on and power relationships continually changing. Stock management is increasingly important, placing a new burden on manufacturers such as Pirelli. At the same time new technology and skills are required to service the customer. The manufacturers are also now competing with big contractors, who may have headhunted skilled staff from the RECs. The contractors are also more willing to source cables from cheaper sources such as Poland with ISO 9002 certification. Price and service are fast becoming the most important issues in marketing within the utilities sector. The cables section in the UK operates as Pirelli General plc. The company accounts and businesses are shown in Appendix 6.

### The General Market

This market consists of cables of 11kV and under, used in buildings and building projects. The cables are building wire, low-voltage and medium-voltage cables. The market consists of:

- Distributors.
- Wholesalers.
- Merchants (DIY Stores).
- Contractors, large and small (installers).
- OEMs (Original Equipment Manufacturers).

The bulk of the products sold within this market are commodity products, with a few manufacturers establishing product differentiation and thus charging a price premium. Building wires offer the greatest scope, as enhanced safety features are likely to have the biggest impact. Pirelli has managed to differentiate itself by launching low smoke and fire resistant products within the Afumex brand and the LSOH brand (low smoke, zero halogen).

### Distribution

Currently the distribution model is the one depicted in Figure 5. It is clear that both push and pull strategies are in operation. The difficulties lie in defining a pull strategy which rests on product differentiation and branding. The company strategy needs to consider building on product benefits, in an attempt to move away from a commoditised environment.

*The essential difference between a distributor and a wholesaler is that distributors will typically break bulk, i.e. they will purchase the larger items such as large reels of cable, which they will then cut to order. Wholesalers will only purchase items that they can sell on as they are.*

As Figure 5 shows, the manufacturers, such as Pirelli, are to a greater or lesser degree cut-off from the end-users by the distributors and wholesalers. The distributors and wholesalers wield enormous power, as they control the range of products and prices offered to the end-users. The distributors have managed to extract extra discounts from the manufacturers, and at the same time have not necessarily passed on the savings to the end-user. This creates an impression amongst the consumers that the manufacturer is responsible for the high product prices. Distributors are mainly interested in maximising returns, thereby commoditising the products and not enhancing brand values and perceptions. For distributors it is better to sell a currently available product which can give the highest margin, irrespective of origin or provenance. Opportunities therefore exist for manufacturers to attempt to shift the balance of power with the distributors, though this may not be easy.

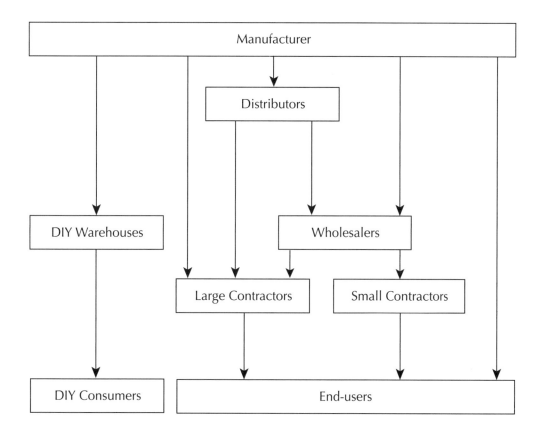

*Figure 5*

The contractors could then benefit from good service agreements, project management and flexibility in terms of delivery. Currently there are 100 large contractors with a combined turnover of £5 billion.

## UK Electricity Supply Segments

The UK Electricity Supply industry can be segmented into four distinct areas:

- Generation: the producing of electricity.
- Transmission: bulk transport through EHV network.
- Distribution: transport at successively reducing voltages in HV/MV and LV network to supply points (domestic and industrial).
- Electricity Supply: buying and selling of electricity – a commodity trading activity.

The last two segments have historically been combined in individual utility businesses but have increasingly been separated out, influenced by regulatory pressures. The supply segment, being a trading activity, does not directly involve cable, (see Appendix 3 for details of the electricity makers in the UK).

The annual value of each segment of the market is very much dependent on the level of project work in Generation and Transmission, but during 1998 it may be estimated as follows:

- Generation – £10 million (Project dependent – includes General Market cables – BS6724 and Fire Performance cables).
- Transmission – £75 million (Potentially ranges from £20 million to £150 million).
- Distribution – £75 million.

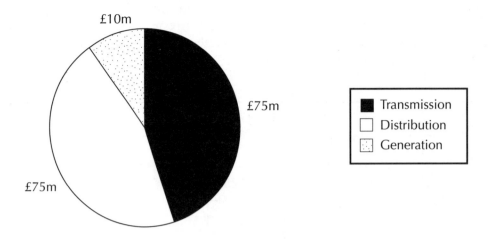

*Figure 6*

## Industry Map

The customers in the distribution segment of the utilities market are the RECs and certain contractors. The routes of supply and installation for LV (Low Voltage), MV (Medium Voltage) and 132kV cables are diagrammatically detailed below:

### For LV/MV Cables

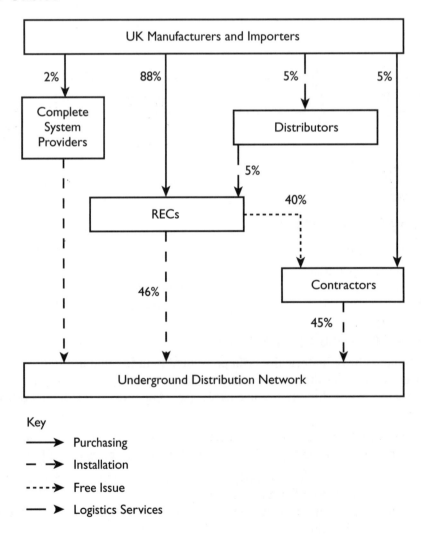

*Figure 7*

## For 132kV

- Manufacturers provide cable and installation system: 90%.
- Some cable installed by contractors: 10%.
- RECs do not install 132kV systems in-house.
- No distributors are involved in the chain.

## Influences on Regional Electricity Companies (RECs)

a. **Ofgem**

RECs need to make money for their shareholders and at the same time be fair to the consumers that purchase the product. Ofgem determines price levels and oversees that fairness is operating. Some of the performance indicators are:

- The number of interruptions in supply (per 100 customers).
- Number of supply minutes lost by customers (per customers).
- Percentage of interruptions not restored within 3 hours.
- Percentage of interruptions not restored within 24 hours.

These are all important factors which relate to network maintenance and enhancement.

b. **Shareholders**

There is pressure to improve profitability for the major shareholders. Initially the profitability was poor (early 1990s) at around 5-10%. Subsequent rationalization of operations, efficiency improvements and cost reduction activities have improved returns to around 40%. Table 1 shows this.

*Table 1*

| RECs | Distribution Turnover (£m) | Distribution Profit (£m) | Supply Turnover (£m) | Supply Profit (£m) |
|---|---|---|---|---|
| London Electricity | 336 | 125 | 1265 | 7.1 |
| Midlands Electricity | 345 | 142 | 1141 | 19 |
| Northern Electric | 218 | 73 | 825 | 22 |
| SEEBOARD | 270 | 135 | 960 | 41.8 |
| SWEB | 231 | 105 | 787 | 6.7 |
| Yorkshire Electricity | 307 | 140 | 1182 | 19.3 |
| East Midlands Electricity | 340 | 131 | 1121 | 4.5 |
| Scottish Power/Manweb | 549 | 265 | 1722 | 65 |
| NORWEB | 342 | 154 | 1097 | 28 |
| SWALEC | 185 | 81 | 507 | 17.9 |
| Southern Electric | 387 | 170 | 1511 | 35 |
| Scottish Hydro-Electric | 156 | 70 | 439 | −3.2 |

*\* No results published for Eastern Electricity. Table from ESI Handbook 1999.*

c. **Mergers and Acquisitions, (see Table 2)**

This activity has been accelerated by the opportunity to make money out of the industry. This has led to changes of ownership and consolidation within the industry. Some companies have diversified into other utilities (Welsh Water's purchase of SWALEC), others have integrated vertically (to combine generation, distribution and supply), and another group has integrated horizontally (as Southern Electric and Scottish Hydro-Electric). The mergers and acquisition activity is likely to shrink the number of key players who are operating. International influences, though not yet strong, could play a significant role. The American utility companies are interested in acquisitions, as are new European network owners such as EdF (French utility company). In the end this may result in greater standardization of technologies.

**Table 2** *Ownership of RECs*

| RECs | New Owners | Bid Price (£ billion) | Completion Date of Acquisition |
|---|---|---|---|
| Eastern Group | Texas Utilities (US) | 4.4 | May 1998 |
| London Electricity | EdF (France) | 1.92 | April 1999 |
| Midlands Electricity* | Avon Energy Partners (US) | 1.73 | June 1996 |
| Northern Electric | CalEnergy (US) | 0.78 | Dec 1996 |
| SEEBOARD | Central & Southwest Co. (US) | 1.6 | Jan 1996 |
| SWEB | Southern Co. jointly with PP&L Resources (US) | 1.1 | Sept 1995 |
| Yorkshire Electricity | American Electric Power and Public Service Co. of Colorado (US) | 1.5 | April 1997 |
| East Midlands Electricity | PowerGen (UK) | 1.9 | July 1998 |
| Manweb | Scottish Power (UK) | 1.2 | Oct 1995 |
| NORWEB | North West Water (UK) | 1.79 | Nov 1995 |
| SWALEC | Welsh Water – now Hyder Group (UK) | 0.88 | June 1996 |
| Southern Electric | Merger with Scottish Hydro-Electric to form Scottish & Southern Energy (UK) | – | Sept 1998 |

*Table current at May 1999.*

## Technological Trends

### Cost Reduction

New cables systems can help with cost reduction and this is an important factor for RECs.

### Reliability

There are many old cables which are reaching the end of their lives. RECs are very interested in developing good network and systems management.

### Systems Approach

Changes in cable technology means that retraining of staff is required. In a competitive environment RECs may be amenable to a supplier who can help with design specifications as well as the hardware.

## Competitors

The UK Utilities are currently supplied by manufacturers from both the UK and Europe, with the purchasing functions of each REC having actively sought to increase competition for tenders by approving European manufacturers over the past 5–6 years.

Current competitors include BICC, AEI, Alcatel, Fulgor & ABB. However, other manufacturers such as Ericssons, NKT, Reka, Datwyler & Studer have all supplied or attempted to gain a share of the UK market. (See Appendix 4 for Marketing Share by Product Sector).

Some international competitors have set up or utilized UK distributors such as DATE, Kelverdeck or NOSKAB to stock, cut and deliver their products to utilities, but the larger manufacturers have supplied direct to the REC.

Current market shares 1998/1999:

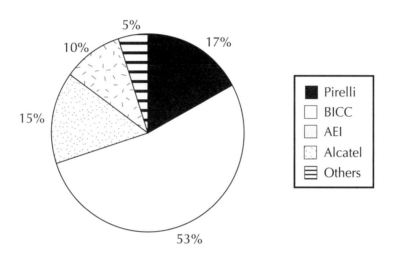

**Figure 8** *Market share by Competitor*

### AEI Cables

This is part of the TT Group and focuses mainly on the UK market. The company follows an aggressive pricing policy to gain market share, which currently stands at 15% of the utilities market. The company supplies overhead lines, cable compounds, cable accessories and has a wide range of general market products including fire performance cables.

### Alcatel

The company's market share in the utilities market is low as it has no manufacturing presence in the UK. Cables are supplied from Norway or Germany.

### ABB Kabel

The company supplies cables from various locations including Eire and Scandinavia. They tend to offer complete projects. (Not shown in pie chart).

### BICC

The European Commission recently approved plans for Pirelli to buy the Italian and British production plants of cable manufacturer BICC General. BICC General is part of General Cable Corporation of the United States. Taking an unusual stance, after an in-depth probe, the EU's antitrust watchdog waved the deal through without imposing any conditions.

'The commission concluded that power cable markets are in the process of becoming European, thanks in particular to the gradual liberalization of the electricity sector and that Pirelli will face sufficient competition, including from alternative service providers.'

'It will also have to count with the strong bargaining power of powerful energy utilities,' it added.

'The concentration will not lead to the creation or strengthening of any dominant position, either single or collective, in respect of the markets for the provision of power cables of low/ medium and high/extra-high-voltage to the utilities,' it concluded.

BICC General will retain its plants in Spain and Portugal.

BICC is technically sound and supplies to the utilities market and does not have a spread of products. It has a technical lead and produces low-cost cables.

## Others

The 'others' tend to be smaller manufacturers in Europe. The greatest threat to Pirelli are contractors who 'rebadge' products emanating from Eastern Europe or Korea. These cables are produced at low cost with international quality approved stamps. In the longer run there may well be threats from countries like India, where there is a developed electricity market with a substantial number of cable manufacturers operating. Many of these companies are now actively promoting their products and services on the Internet.

## E-Strategies

It is clear that for major manufacturers such as Pirelli, considerable leverage could be gained in the marketplace through the development of e-commerce on a global basis. On March 20, 2000, the Board of Pirelli SpA examined and endorsed the new e-Pirelli Project, a radical transformation of the Group. Two thousand billion Lira have been allocated to the project over a period of two years (2000–2002). The Pirelli cables division has been instrumental in the fast diffusion of the World Wide Web, through the development of extremely high transmission capacity optical components and systems. Pirelli's strategy, in turn, is based on becoming an e-company, utilizing the speed and flexibility of the network to develop innovative business practices. Over a period of years, the company has spent money to create one of the most advanced networks in Europe, winning the Gartner Group's prestigious EIT award for Excellence in Information Technology. The company is intent on transforming all company processes and to operating as a leader in the world of high technology and the new e-economy.

The e-Pirelli Project is expected to grow in the following directions:

1. The development and enhancement of Pirelli optical components and systems activities linked to e-technology. Also through spin-offs and the creation of strategic alliances and technological partnerships with primary companies.
2. Developing the full use of online technology in the group's core activities (tyres, cables and systems), from purchasing through to finished product sales.
3. Developing and initiating a series of new entrepreneurial activities, i.e. network linked start-ups.

The e-Pirelli Project rests its foundations on a network that now links over 14,000 workstations in 35 countries. It is expected that within 24 months the new e-Pirelli network will offer surfing opportunities worldwide to a population of 90 million people, including employees, suppliers, dealers and consumers.

## Cables E-commerce

An online order management system for general market cables (which represent roughly 25% of the sector's total sales) has already been successfully started up in some of the major European countries by Pirelli. This is a first step towards covering the entire sector. The projected e-commerce share of the general market in Italy by the end of 2000 is 65%, with the entire

European sector sales reaching 40% by the end of the year, with sales of over 400 million Euro. The online sales system, therefore, is destined to expand fast, embracing every segment of the Cables and Systems Sector. Pirelli cables has developed both Intranet and Extranet strategies. The Extranet brings together Pirelli's internal communities and the external communities that operate together on a Business to Business (B2B) basis. The company feels that this way of using the net gives more surprising and immediate results in terms of efficiency and innovation. Cable@Pirelli is exactly that: an Extranet site with restricted access, protected by special security systems. Access to Cable@Pirelli is given exclusively to Pirelli's distributors.

Web-based Business to Business (B2B) projects have been started by Pirelli Cables and Systems to develop and sustain a strategic change in the traditional way of doing business. A change in vision is anticipated. B2B solutions applied to the general market, utilities, contractors and Original Equipment Manufacturer (OEMs) give each party a chance to reach their different strategic aims, by providing better service provisions, cost reduction and contribution to customer satisfaction. The B2B links offer better customer attention and at the same time decreasing costs, which were often difficult before as there had to be a trade off between the two.

The particular benefits offered by the B2B projects are:

a. Simplification of the order management process of the general market to enhance the level of service and reduce costs.
b. Improving the order entry process, in terms of order tracking, after-sales support and providing many different e-Services for the distributors.
c. Global network available to Pirelli's distributors in many countries around the world such as Italy, Hungary, UK, Austria, Spain, Brazil, Argentina, USA, Canada and Australia.
d. A 24 hour (seven days a week) service so that order requests can be made at any time, at any place.
e. Ease of process information update through web solutions.
f. Reduction of transaction costs as less administration and paper is needed.
g. Distributors can leaf through the catalogue on the Web and forward their orders online, using a standard form, checking the state of progress of the order and obtaining information on the delivery. A method which allows price discounts and personalized promotions to be included.

The e-Solution method is now being used intensively in Italy (during the pilot), with over 50% of the orders being made online.

**Sample of Services Provided by the Cable@Pirelli Solution**

| Service | Functionality |
| --- | --- |
| Personal Data | Personal Data |
| | Account Position |
| Order | Order Entry |
| | Order Upload/Download |
| | Order Tracking |
| | Historical Order and Analysis |
| After Sales | Claim Entry |
| | Claim Analysis |
| Delivery | Delivery Tracking |
| | Delivery Download |

## Research and Development (R&D)

The company has integrated global R&D centres, which will now be linked through the Intranet and the e-Pirelli project. Over £300 million is committed to R&D projects, with new products being produced in order to provide better and more effective solutions to customer needs.

Currently Pirelli is working on a new technology capable of significantly upgrading the transmission capability of a standard single mode fibre, thereby achieving higher transmission capacity in an optical network with the same number of channels. The technology allows the application of broadband fibre gratings to extend the transmission capacity of single mode fibre, which represents more than 90% of the world's installed base for fibre optic networks. These gratings automatically correct the dispersion that occurs when high-speed optical pulses are transmitted over long distances through fibre. This is an extremely important piece of research which offers telecom carriers a new range of technology options for high capacity networks, allowing the currently installed fibre network base to be used for newer state-of-the-art systems. This has important implications for creating the information services and communications network of tomorrow. The AT&T laboratories in New Jersey, USA, are leaders in the development of technologies and standards for audio, speech, video and image compression; electronic commerce and digital copyright management; search and directory services; speech processing and coding of all sorts; network architecture, design, engineering and operations; and other areas critical to the advancement of new communications, Internet included. These new breakthroughs have been achieved largely as a result of Pirelli's know-how in the field of photonics. In keeping up with the developments, Pirelli funds research at many leading institutions throughout the world, in order to keep ahead in the area of telecommunications.

On conventional cables, the continuous emphasis on R&D has resulted in the production of a range of Fire Resistant cables known as the Afumex brand (Low Smoke Zero Halogen Cable Family) with a Drylam sheathing system which has a chemical and moisture barrier for cables installed in critical environments.

Pireflex, launched on the French market in June 1996, was produced as a result of a comprehensive market study. The research indicated that there was an opportunity for a cable that could effectively meet the requirements of every niche in the power transmission market. The R&D department created a watertight, flexible and resistant (to heat and nuclear reaction) cable – the Pireflex. This cable covers a range of applications from handling and mobile equipment, to stage and audio visual equipment and submersible apparatus. Total watertightness is Pireflex's strongest feature. This enables the sales teams to sell these cables on genuine product advantage and not just on pricing. A comprehensive communications package consisting of direct marketing campaigns, leaflets and posters has been developed to launch Pireflex and support sales activity. Sold to wholesalers, major installers and OEMs, Pireflex is already a commercial success in France and will soon be marketed to Germany and Belgium.

In 1999, the US Department of Energy (DOE) announced the award of a contract that will result in the world's first high-temperature superconductor (HTS) power cable to deliver electricity in a utility network. The cable is being manufactured and installed by Pirelli Cables and Systems using HTS wire, produced by American Superconductor Corporation. Another corporation will develop the cooling system for the cable, and a company called EPRI will partially fund and help to manage the project. The cable is being installed in downtown Detroit to support the revitalization of the older urban area in a non-intrusive environmentally friendly way. The existing cable is being retrofitted with the 400-foot HTS cable in existing conduits, avoiding the disruption and damage caused by additional digging. The cable system will carry three times the power carried by conventional copper cables. However, because HTS cable has far lower electrical resistance, only about 250 pounds of it are needed to replace more than nine tons of copper wire. The situation is very similar to fibre optic cables replacing copper communication cables. The DOE believes that superconducting technology offers the potential to save the USA more than $6 billion annually, by stemming the losses during delivery. Such a technological advance also offers the hope of efficient and effective electricity delivery to a diversity of suppliers, including hydro-electric suppliers, smaller electricity generators and wind power generators.

## Ecological Issues

Pirelli have branched out into a new brand known as the Ecology low-voltage cables. These new lines of products totally eliminate lead from insulation and coating compounds. This new range is eco-compatible and an important step forward in the direction of environmental protection and recyclability. Consumers are also concerned about magnetic radiation from overhead cables, leading to diseases such as leukemia. There are also concerns on a global basis about electricity generation and groups like Friends of the Earth and the World Wildlife Fund are beginning to have an impact on setting up buyers from companies that generate electricity in a non-polluting manner (see Appendix 5).

## Utility Competition

The deregulation of the electricity and gas retail market over the last two years has undoubtedly revolutionized the utilities sector. National Power, which has a 2.8% market share of domestic gas, has forged ahead with a branding campaign for nPower. In December 1999, Virgin hired Jon Kinsey, British Gas Trading marketing chief, as Virgin Home Services managing director. He will head the Virgin operation which is expected to target the utilities market and offer everything from phone to electricity and water to gas services. Virgin's entry will serve to show how few real brands exist in the utilities sector. Prior to deregulation, utilities did not need to build brands because consumers had little choice about where they bought their gas or electricity from. The challenge is to create a known and trusted brand in an industry where the interest is low. Research shows that by September 1999, about 10% of all residential electricity customers had changed suppliers. Branding is playing an important role. A recent UK survey revealed that the brand identity of the electricity supplier was the leading factor in consumer purchasing decisions. As the utility companies expand their retailing opportunities through branding and the development of customer segmentation, in an ever competitive world it may only be a matter of time before branding reaches the cable market.

At present consumers generally know Pirelli through their tyre manufacturing and Pirelli calendars. Would customers buying electricity through a branded utility supplier be more likely to trust them if they knew that their supplies were carried by Pirelli Cables rather than some unknown entity? Would they be keen to understand that their supply is ecologically friendly?

## International Developments

Many countries in the world, besides the UK, are moving towards liberalizing or privatizing the electricity supply industry. The European market is slowly moving towards a free internal market within the EU. There are moves to restructure and introduce competition in generation in parts of the USA. In Latin America, there is wholesale privatization occurring with Chile leading the way. The UK leads the world on deregulation with the following strategies:

- Privatization (change in ownership).
- Vertical de-integration.
- Horizontal de-integration.
- Competition in generation.
- Competition in supply and re-regulation through bodies such as Ofgem.

Many countries have attempted some aspects of deregulation, but only the system in England and Wales has been exposed to the full package of measures and has introduced all the measures simultaneously. Some countries are privatizing (Chile, Argentina, Brazil). Countries such as Norway, Argentina and Brazil, are introducing competition in electricity generation across the whole sector, whereas the USA is introducing this piecemeal. Spain, Portugal and Thailand have introduced new generating companies to supply incremental demand. Only the UK and Norway have contemplated supply competition. South Africa, the USA and the Scandinavian countries are introducing new methods of regulation. However, the UK has tried to combine all these elements.

The World Bank has considerable influence on the power-sector policies in the developing world and it appears to be keen to push the UK model in order to encourage privatization and market discipline wherever possible. In many countries this may be resisted (see Appendix 7.). However, the stark reality is that many countries have no choice but to go to international private investors in order to expand their systems to keep pace with demand. The World Bank influence exposes many countries to far reaching reforms in order to attract foreign investment on a large scale. For this reason the deregulation and privatization process set in motion in the UK is of great interest to many countries. This has direct implications for Pirelli Cables, as it gathers experience in the most deregulated market in the world. Already in the UK some electricity supply comes from France. France also supplies much of Belgium's requirements. Pressures for privatization will grow within the EU as many countries will need to find money for social services and it is likely that the utility sector will offer a 'pot of gold' through privatization.

# Appendices

## Appendix 1

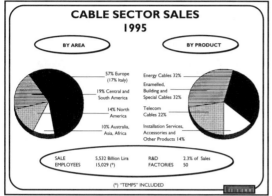

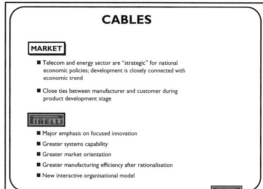

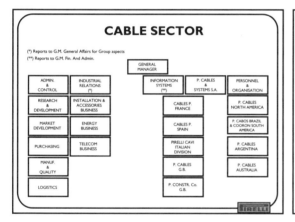

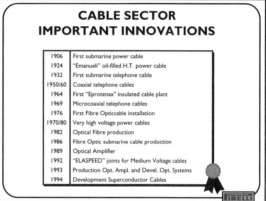

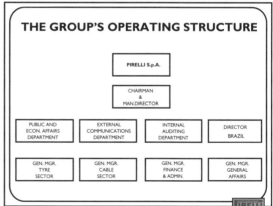

*Figure 9*

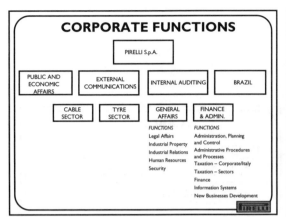

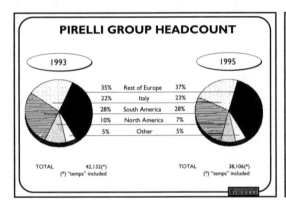

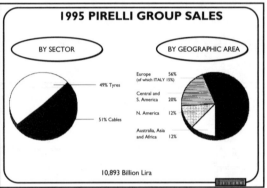

***Figure 9*** *(continued)*

## Appendix 2

**Proposed Demarcations for Contestable and Non-contestable Work**

| Contestable | Non-contestable |
|---|---|
| Connection design including:<br>Design<br>Specification | Determining the point of connection to the existing network/network analysis. |
| Existing connections removal/relocation/ service alterations | Upstream reinforcement. |
| Connections provision – this involves the provision of connection assets. | Using Statutory powers to obtain consents and wayleaves. |
| Connection installation trenching/reinstatement or construction of connection. | |
| Recording assets on site and sending report to distribution business. | |
| Connection to the distribution system including: | |
| Live line working | |
| i) Making final connection to premises. | |
| ii) Making final connection to PES system. | |
| Energization of connection. | |
| Inspection, monitoring and testing of installation. | |

*PES – Public Energy Suppliers*

# Appendix 3

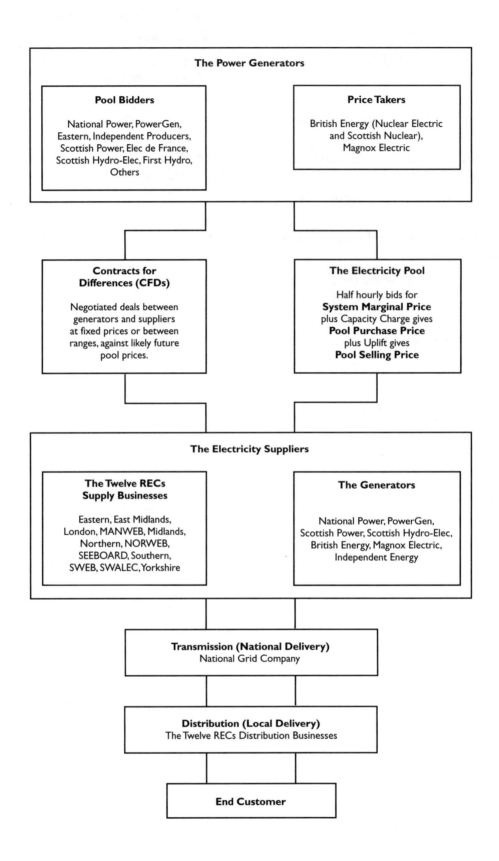

**Figure 10** *The Power Market in England and Wales*

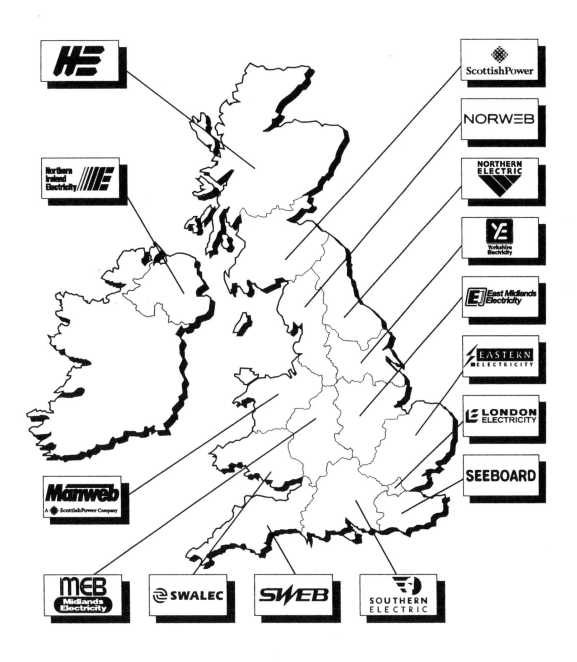

*Figure 11* Buying Electricity and Gas in the Competitive Market (UK). Source: The Electricity Association

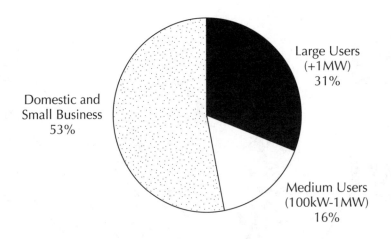

*Figure 12* The Electricity Market in England and Wales by Volume of Power Delivered

**Leaders in the Competitive Power Market in England and Wales**

**The Over 1MW Market**

|  | Sites | Sales Volume |
|---|---|---|
| Eastern | 11% | 8% |
| National Power | 10% | 17% |
| PowerGen | 10% | 23% |
| Southern | 10% | 5% |
| Yorkshire | 9% | 8% |

**The 100kW-1MW Market**

|  | Sites | Sales Volume |
|---|---|---|
| Eastern | 15% | 15% |
| London | 12% | 12% |
| Yorkshire | 10% | 12% |
| Southern | 10% | 9% |
| Northern | 8% | 9% |

*Source: Office of Electricity Regulation*

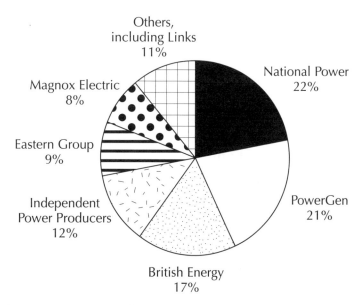

*Figure 13* *Estimated Main Generator Market Share in England and Wales*

## Appendix 4

**Manufacturer UK Market Share by Product Sector**

| | Manufacturer | | | | | | | | | | | |
| | Pirelli | Draka | Alcatel | BICC | AEI | C.E.F. | ABB Wessel | IDH | Thomas Bolton | Others | Total % | Total Market £m |
|---|---|---|---|---|---|---|---|---|---|---|---|---|
| **Product Sector** | | | | | | | | | | | | |
| PVC Building Wires (rigid) | 23% | 23% | 2% | – | 10% | 15% | 10% | 10% | – | 7% | 100 | 76 |
| LSOH Building Wires (rigid) | 12% | 30% | – | – | 20% | – | 20% | 10% | – | 8% | 100 | 13 |
| PVC Building Wires (Flex) | 1% | 5% | – | – | 10% | 10% | 24% | 20% | 20% | 10% | 100 | 16 |
| FP | 36% | 23% | 2% | 10% | 8% | 12% | – | 2% | – | 7% | 100 | 33 |
| 1kV PVC | 20% | 24% | 25% | – | 15% | 5% | 5% | – | – | 6% | 100 | 73 |
| 1kV LSOH | 26% | 25% | 24% | 5% | 10% | – | 5% | – | – | 5% | 100 | 34 |
| 11kv | 23% | – | 20% | 15% | 10% | – | – | – | – | 32% | 100 | 8 |

*Supplied by Pirelli Cables UK.*

### *Energy Utilities Case Studies*

### Case Study 1: National Grid Company

**Assisting the National Grid Company to supply reliable, efficient power to homes and industry throughout the UK.** The National Grid Company is at the heart of the UK electricity supply business, providing reliable efficient power to homes and industry. Pirelli Cables supplies technology to the National Grid Company, for the benefit of the United Kingdom.

**Major benefits of Pirelli Cables' Systems:**

- Completed systems design.
- Reliable technology.
- Extensive in-service experience.
- Preserves the aesthetics of the UK countryside.
- Low Electromagnetic field designs.
- Reduced outages due to severe environmental effects.

## Case Study 2: Sizewell Power Station

*Figure 14*

**Pirelli have designed and developed cables to assist Nuclear Electric in providing a balanced power supply to England and Wales for the next century.**

The UK's first Pressurized Water Reactor (PWR) is now in operation.

This project was one of the UK's largest one site programmes.

This project, eight months ahead of schedule and on budget, achieved full commercial load in 1995.

Where product quality and total reliability were required Pirelli Cables' technology was chosen.

This technology, together with Pirelli manufacturing skill and service philosophy, has helped Nuclear Electric achieve their targets.

## Case Study 3: London Electricity

A 10km cable tunnel linking electricity sub-stations in Wimbledon, Wandsworth and Pimlico. The aim was to upgrade aging cables to maintain reliability and not disrupt the capital's traffic. Pirelli 132kV XLPE cable was chosen as part of this major £52m project. Pirelli technology has been keeping the electricity supply reliable in London for decades. The proven reliability of Pirelli Cables means that it is the chosen technology to distribute London's electricity well into the next century.

*From web site: www.pirelli.co.uk/uk/cables*

# Appendix 5

## *What is Green Energy?*

### Which Company Should I Choose?

So you want to buy green energy. How do you find out how 'green' an electricity company is, or what the other environmentally friendly alternatives are? Friends of the Earth's Green Energy League Table has the answers.

### The Green Energy League Table

We looked at all the companies who we know have plans to sell electricity to the domestic market – not only the Regional Electricity Companies but also Centrica (formerly British Gas) and the new suppliers of green energy Ecotricity and Unit[e].

**Update (October 1999):** Since this table was produced, many more companies have introduced green tariffs, which allow you to support renewable energy schemes through your energy bill. Please see our latest information on available green tariffs.

| | Renewable Energy | Energy Efficiency | Environmental Policy/Reporting | Parent Company Performance | Total Points |
|---|---|---|---|---|---|
| Ecotricity[1] | V. Good | Average | Good | V. Good | 9 |
| Unit[e] | V. Good | Average | Good | V. Good | 9 |
| Eastern | V. Good | Average | Good | Average | 7 |
| Manweb | Average | Good | Good | Average | 6 |
| Scottish Power | Average | Good | Good | Average | 6 |
| Northern | Poor | Good | Average | Good | 5 |
| Scottish Hydro | Average | Average | Average | Good | 5 |
| SEEBOARD | Poor | V. Good | Average | Average | 5 |
| London | Poor | Good | Average | Average | 4 |
| Southern | Poor | Good | Poor | Good | 4 |
| Yorkshire | Average | Average | Good | Poor | 4 |
| Centrica[2] | Poor | Average | Average | Average | 3 |
| NORWEB | Average | Poor | Average | Average | 3 |
| Midlands | Average | Average | Poor | Poor | 2 |
| East Mids[3] | Poor | Average | Poor | Poor | 1 |
| SWEB[4] | Good | Poor | Poor | V. Poor | 1 |
| SWALEC | Poor | Average | Poor | Poor | 1 |

1. Ecotricity is the trading name of the Renewable Energy Co.

2. Formerly British Gas.

3. Since going to print East Midlands Electricity has been taken over by PowerGen and information on parent company performance is therefore no longer applicable. Policies on renewable energy and energy efficiency may change.

4. Southern Western Electricity Board.

**NB.** The 'poor' ratings for NORWEB and SWEB under 'energy efficiency' and for SWEB and Midlands under 'Environmental Policy' were awarded because these companies failed to provide the requested information. Details of their work in these areas can now be obtained from the companies themselves.

### The Ideal Green Energy Company How did the Companies Score

This league table is a summary of FOE's research findings and is accurate at time of printing (August 1998). More detailed information on the judging criteria, league tables for each category (renewable energy, energy efficiency, company policy etc.), methodology and sources, is available.

### Power Points

To produce the table each company was awarded points on the following criteria:
- Whether they offer customers the chance to buy green energy.
- How positive they are towards renewable energy – especially whether they have a target for increased renewables supply.
- Their record on energy efficiency and pollution.
- Their environmental policy in general.
- The environmental performance of the company or parent company.

Some criteria were rated as more important than others, so for example we gave a company more points for having a positive target for increasing renewable energy supplies than for having a green policy for their own offices.

The companies have been ranked according to their overall environmental performance, but you can also see how they scored in different areas such as their commitment to renewables, corporate policy and whether they offer, or plan to offer, a green tariff.

### The Ideal Green Energy Company

In an ideal world, customers would be able to choose a company that offered electricity just from renewable energy and combined heat and power schemes, and provided loans to help you improve the energy efficiency of your home, fit solar panels and reduce your fuel bills. No company we surveyed currently offer this deal. Friends of the Earth is lobbying them to provide these services to the public. You can do your bit to put the pressure on.

### How did the Companies Score?

You will see that the best choice currently for the environment-conscious electricity consumer is either Unit[e] or the Renewable Energy Company, both of which only sell electricity generated from renewable energy projects.

Of the Regional Electricity Companies, Eastern Electricity has come out on top, largely because it has a target of generating 10% of its electricity from renewables, for example from wind and plant (biomass) sources and 10% from Combined Heat and Power. And because it offers a green energy tariff.

Customers choosing this tariff – called 'EcoPower' – will not be buying green energy as such but making a charitable donation to the development of community renewable energy projects. Eastern has not yet announced how it will sell the renewable energy it will generate itself.

*From web site: www.foe.co.uk (information valid as of August 1998).*

Pirelli supplies power cables for one of the biggest
aeolian parks of the world, in Spain

# Blowin' in the Wind

Using the wind to produce electricity: that is the essence
of a power source which does not contaminate and is infinite

*P*irelli Cables y Systemas is
*supplying 250 kms of*
*medium voltage cables to*
*the* Sierra de Hireguela Aeolian
*Park (Spain) project, one of the*
*world's biggest for installed power.*
*An important commitment, because*
*energy generated by the wind is*
*clean, renewable, economi-*
*cal and, as in the case of*
*Spain, renders entire*
*areas of a country elec-*
*trically self-reliant. By*
*the end of 1998, wind*
*was generating 834 MW of*
*power in Spain and now the*
*government has decided to double*
*that figure in the medium term.*

It is no longer an impossible
dream. Aeolian or wind-generated
energy has shown in just 10 years
that it can be a real alternative.

**A reduction of $CO_2$ emission by 1,000 tons**

Using the wind to produce electricity: that is the essence of an
energy source which does not contaminate and is infinite. With pro-
pellers in synthetic resin and high
yield compact generators, the new
windmills produce low-cost electricity.

But the most compelling
reason why the Spanish
government plans to
invest considerable
resources in the develop-
ment of this particular
form of power is that, of
all the renewable forms of
energy, it is the one with the most
viable future, as confirmed by
recent studies carried out by the
*Spanish Institute for the*
*Diversification and Development of*
*Energy.*

Even if yield is normally the final

arbiter in deciding the future of any
energy source, it is environmental
considerations which have indicated the promising future of wind
energy.

Thanks to the aeolian power,
each year more than four million
tons of carbon dioxide and other
harmful substances are not introduced into the atmosphere. By way of
a concrete example, a 500 kW wind
generator reduces the emission of
C02 into the atmosphere by an
annual 1,000 tons.

Even though the development of
wind power has been continuous
since the birth of the aero-generator
in 1888, it was not really taken into
consideration as a serious power
source until the early Eighties -
almost 100 years later. That was the
period of the petroil crisis, the first
nuclear power generating station
problems and when global war-
ming, caused by the emission of
C02 produced by fossil fuels, first
came to light.

*Figure 15*

Today, no-one doubts any more that the wind is a source of energy completely competitive with conventionally produced power. In the Nineties, more than 40,000 aerogenerators or windmills were installed, each able to generate 10,000 MW and producing a total of about 20,000 million kWh a year. In Europe, both at national and European Union level, new wind park projects are planned for Denmark, Germany, Spain, Holland and Italy.

Spain in particular has an extremely high wind power potential. In 1998 alone, 379 MW worth of generators were installed and by the end of the year the total amount of power generated in this way will be equal to that churned out by a modern nuclear power station, producing enough power to satisfy the needs of 575,000 families. The Iberian peninsula is today the world's fifth biggest wind energy producer, after Germany, the USA, Denmark and India.

The technology, in this as in other power sources chosen for the third millennium, is taking giant steps forward. If it is true that in the mid-Nineties we saw the installation of the first 500 kW windmills, the latest generation generator is able to produce 1.5 MW. The new windmills have enormous rotors measuring 60 metres in diameter and can produce electricity at a cost of 0.5 to 0.7 US dollars per kW, the same price as a 500 kW turbine with a carbon core. In addition, a number of locations have already been selected for the construction of marine windmills, which exploit the winds of the high seas. Parks with the advantage of isolating the minimum noise of the generators and reducing the cost of foundations. The latest research includes studies of the dynamics of the structure and the mechanics of fluids, which have permitted the

## The Inside of the Engine Box

1 Tower
2 Paddle
3 Hub
4 Ball bearings
5 Orientation system
6 Main shaft
7 Hydraulic system
8 Multiplier system
9 Brake
10 Generator

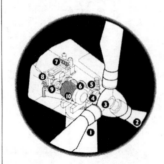

## The Power of the Wind

*Engine box:*
*made of fibreglass*
*Weight: 23 t.*
*Dimensions:*
*6.20 m long*
*2.80 m high*
*2.20 m wide*

*Paddle:*
*made of polyester resin reinforced by fibreglass*
*Length:*
*from 19.5 to 23.5 m*

*Tower:*
*Altitude: 40-55 m*
*Base diameter: 3-3.60 m*
*Weight: 28.5-46 t*

development of original techniques of aerodynamics and loading of the generators. Every time, the result is machines which are more sophisticated, equipped with modern electronic controls which have contribu-

ted much to the exploitation of energy. An example of this tendency is the concept of orientation. To ensure the aero-generators produce a constant yield of electricity, it is necessary that they are oriented in the right direction. That is done by a weathervane placed at the top of the nacelle. This instrument continually measures with precision the direction of the wind and transmits its orders to a control system which turns the nacelle as if it were a sunflower, facing the vanes into the wind. Aero-generators produce maximum power when gusts wind reach 55 km/h.

Pirelli Cables and Systems, which has operated in Spain with its Vilanova y La Geltrù factory since the beginning of the century, has for some time been contributing to the rapid installation of wind energy with the supply of cables and accessories for wind park projects. The most recent example is that of the *Sierra de Hireguela Park* which, with its 169 windmills and 111 MW, represents one of the biggest wind farms in the world for its installed power. The park, which is the property of a Spanish company in which Iberdrola and EHN each have 50%, is under construction and will be fully operational by the end of the year. The area selected for its construction, the Sierra de Hireguela, is a group of small peaks of up to 1,200 metres: continuous wind which they originate makes it an ideal wind farm area.

The electricity the park will generate will be the equivalent to the consumption of almost 25% of the Albacete region's population. And 250 kilometres of medium tension cable and 200 accessories will be supplied by Pirelli so that the wind can do its job.

*by EHN and Josep Maria Abella,*
*Vilanova i La Geltrù, Spain*

**Figure 15** *(continued)*

# Appendix 6

## *Pirelli General plc Report of the Directors*

### For the year ended 31st December 1999

The directors submit their annual report and the audited accounts of the Company and its subsidiary companies ("the Group") for the year ended 31st December 1999.

### Activities

The Group's principal activities are the manufacture, sale and installation of cables for the transmission of power and information.

Particulars of the principal subsidiary companies are shown in note 11 to the accounts.

### Results and Dividends

Group sales in 1999 of £315.2 million produced an operating profit of £0.2 million. After net interest, the loss before taxation was £2.4 million. After taxation, the Group made a loss for the year of £5.2 million.

The directors are recommending the payment of a final dividend for the year of £1.5 million on the Ordinary Shares of £1 each which, with the interim dividend of £1.0 million paid on 4th October 1999, will make a total dividend for the year of £2.5 million. If approved at the Annual General Meeting, the final dividend will be payable on 2 May 2000 pro rata to all shareholders registered at the close of business on 28 April 2000.

### Review of Operations

The Group is responsible for the UK cable making business of Pirelli Cables Limited and the project management and installation business of Pirelli Construction Company Limited.

**Pirelli Cables Limited** manufactures cables in the United Kingdom and is divided into two business areas, Energy Cables and Communication Cables.

**Energy Cables** manufactures and supplies a full range of power cables and accessories ranging from general wiring to 500kV supertension and submarine cables.

Sales of high-voltage cable and accessories returned to normal levels in the year from the high demand seen in 1998. The utilities market remained stable in 1999 and significant long term contracts were secured with Midlands Electricity and Eastern, which consolidated the Company's position. In the general market, domestic sales strengthened, particularly in fire performance products such as FP200®, within a very competitive environment, but exports, especially to Hong Kong, suffered due to the strength of sterling. A major submarine cable contract was secured from a joint venture between Manx Electricity Authority and National Grid Company to link Douglas in the Isle of Man to Bispham in the UK – this cable at 105kms in length will be the longest AC cable in the world.

**Communication Cables** manufactures and supplies optical fibre and optical and copper cables for the transmission of information in the fields of telecommunication, cable television, controls and data networks.

Demand in the domestic market grew during 1999, especially in the second half, and the Company's market position was maintained despite increased competitive pressure. Products and services were enhanced, and a new initiative was undertaken with British Telecommunications plc. Significant new market penetration has been achieved with Pan-European Internet protocol providers and telecom carriers, such as Colt Telecom and Level 3 Communications, culminating in a major order from Worldwide Fibre Inc. for cable incorporating Pirelli high performance fibre, Freelight™.

**Pirelli Construction Company Limited** is the contracting arm of the Pirelli Cable Sector world-wide and performs a wide range of project management and project work associated with the installation of power and communication networks both in the United Kingdom and overseas.

During 1999 Construction personnel were active in 20 countries and turnover increased for the sixth successive year, producing a good level of profit despite the continuing difficult trading environment.

In the Energy installation business in the UK the second major 110kV XLPE contract awarded by Northern Ireland Electricity for installation in Belfast was completed, as was a project for National Grid Company to divert 270kV DC cables connecting the converter station to cross channel cables, in order to clear the route for the new High Speed Rail Link through Kent. Work was completed at Manchester airport, undergrounding a section of 400kV overhead line to make way for the new runway; this project involved the installation of 400kV cables using polypropylene laminate (PPL) construction, giving enhanced performance from smaller cables.

Overseas, the Company operated on 4 continents, undertaking various work ranging from managing major turnkey transmission projects to providing emergency breakdown services. Major turnkey project work progressed throughout the year in Thailand and Lebanon, while significant work was also completed in Kuwait and China. Teams were mobilized at short notice to undertake emergency repair work in a number of locations including Bangladesh, Argentina and Zambia.

In the Communications installation business, work continued on the three year contract for British Telecommunications plc and the Company was successfully assessed under BT's supplier capability programme to qualify for tendering the renewal in 2000. In the export market work was won and executed in Hungary and the Philippines.

## Research and Development

The Group's Research and Development activities have moved towards development and applications engineering support to customers, covering product and system design.

## Future Developments

The strategy towards optimization and integration of resources will continue, especially in the energy cables areas. Notwithstanding an anticipated reduction in research activities in the UK, the Group is bringing new technologies such as 'intelligent system management' and high temperature superconductivity to the market. In the telecommunications field, competition from overseas is very strong, especially in export markets, hence the focus will be on optimization of product offering and reduction of manufacturing cost, to enable the Group to remain competitive in international markets.

## Human Resources

Employee numbers have decreased over the past year as a result of redundancy and restructuring programmes. Overall employment reduced by 8.0%, 16% being in management and staff grades and 6.6% in the blue-collar workforce.

The Board recognises and thanks all employees for their continuing efforts during a difficult year.

## Employment Policies

It is the Group's policy to keep employees informed of the financial, economic and technological factors affecting the Group through a range of consultative and communication procedures. These procedures are kept under review and are supplemented as necessary by special communications exercises.

The Group's policy is to provide equal employment opportunities for disabled persons, where their skills and aptitudes can be used, and to provide disabled employees with the same opportunities for continued employment, promotion, career development and training as other employees.

Close attention is given to the health and safety of employees and to environmental care both within and outside the Group's premises.

## Supplier Payment Policy

It is the Group's policy to agree appropriate terms and conditions with each of its suppliers and then to make payment in accordance with the agreed terms provided the supplier has met its obligations.

At 31st December 1999 the Group had an average of 48 days purchases outstanding in trade creditors.

## Share Capital

There was no change in the authorized or issued share capital during the year.

## Directors

The directors of the Company at the date of this report are shown on page 3. Mr P. J. Margrave was appointed to the Board and as Managing Director – Cables on 1st February 1999, in place of Mr G. Anderson who was a director on 1st January 1998 but who resigned on 31st January 1999. Mr V. Pasturino was appointed to the Board on 1st May 1998 and retired on 31st January 1999. The remaining directors shown on page 3 were directors of the Company throughout the year.

The directors retiring by rotation are Lord Limerick, Mr B. Davies and Mr P. G. Sierra. Mr Davies has decided to retire and not to seek re-election. The Board wishes to thank him for his valuable contribution as Managing Director – Cables from 1993 to 1997 and subsequently as a non-executive director. Lord Limerick and Mr Sierra, both of whom, being eligible, offer themselves for re-election.

There are no directors' interests requiring disclosure under the Companies Act 1985.

## Year 2000 Compliance

Prior to 1st January 2000 the Group reviewed all business critical computer controlled systems and equipment with a view to ensuring that they would function properly in the year 2000 and beyond and new accounting and business information computer systems, designed to be millennium compliant, were installed and are now operational. Other critical items of hardware and software were checked for millennium compliance and were, if necessary, replaced well before the end of 1999. The cost was not significant in relation to the Group's operations.

The Group also considered the impact of failures by key suppliers and customers, and confirmations were sought that they had also taken similar preventive measures.

Up to the date of this report all equipment and business systems have performed normally.

## Pirelli General plc
## Consolidated Profit and Loss Account

For the year ended 31st December 1999

|  | 1999 £000 | 1998 £000 |
|---|---|---|
| **Turnover** | 315,165 | 345,812 |
| Cost of sales | 265,515 | 264,661 |
| **Gross profit** | 49,650 | 81,151 |
| Other operating expenses | 49,437 | 48,989 |
| | | |
| Operating profit before restructuring costs | 3,704 | 32,558 |
| Restructuring costs | (3,492) | (396) |
| | | |
| **Operating profit** | 212 | 32,162 |
| Income from interest in associated company | 40 | 40 |
| **Profit on ordinary activities before interest** | 252 | 32,202 |
| Net interest payable | 2,634 | 3,610 |
| **(Loss) Profit on ordinary activities before taxation** | (2,382) | 28,592 |
| Taxation | 2,843 | 7,648 |
| **(Loss) Profit attributable to members of the parent company** | (5,225) | 20,944 |
| Dividend | 2,500 | 20,900 |
| **Retained (loss) profit for the year** | (7,725) | 44 |

*All items dealt with in the above profit and loss account relate to continuing operations.*

## Pirelli General plc
## Consolidated Balance Sheet

At 31st December 1999

|  | 1999 £000 | 1998 £000 |
|---|---|---|
| **Fixed assets** | | |
| Intangible assets | 3,925 | 6,398 |
| Tangible assets | 135,388 | 141,150 |
| Investments | 3,124 | 3,084 |
|  | 142,438 | 150,632 |

**Current assets**

| | | |
|---|---|---|
| Stocks and long term contracts | **26,550** | 29,790 |
| Debtors | **81,394** | 95,211 |
| Cash at bank and in hand | **12,284** | 8,456 |
| | **120,228** | 133,457 |
| **Creditors: amounts falling due within one year** | | |
| Finance debt | **23,006** | 23,025 |
| Other creditors | **87,261** | 97,824 |
| **Net current assets** | **9,961** | 12,608 |
| **Total assets less current liabilities** | **152,398** | 163,240 |
| **Creditors: amounts falling due after more than one year** | | |
| Finance debt | **–** | 10,000 |
| Other creditors | **4,225** | 3,765 |
| **Provisions for liabilities and charges** | **9,154** | 4,735 |
| **Net assets** | **139,019** | 144,740 |
| **Capital and reserves** | | |
| Called up share capital | **102,100** | 102,100 |
| Revaluation reserve | **29,341** | 27,353 |
| Profit and loss account | **7,578** | 15,287 |
| **Shareholder's funds** | **139,019** | 144,740 |

Approved by the Board of Directors on 13 March 2000

and signed on its behalf by:

**Limerick**

*Chairman*

### Pirelli General plc
### Consolidated Statement of Total Recognized Gains and Losses

For the year ended 31st December 1999

| | 1999 | 1998 |
|---|---|---|
| | *£000* | *£000* |
| **(Loss) Profit attributable to members of the parent company** | (5,225) | 20,944 |
| Unrealized surplus on revaluation of properties | 2,004 | 2,883 |
| **Total recognized gains and losses relating to the year** | (3,221) | 23,827 |

## Note of Historical Cost Profits and Losses

| | 1999 £000 | 1998 £000 |
|---|---|---|
| Reported (loss) profit on ordinary activities before taxation | (2,382) | 28,592 |
| Difference between historical cost depreciation charge and actual charge for the year calculated on the revalued amount | 16 | 21 |
| Historical cost (loss) profit on ordinary activities before taxation | (2,366) | 28,613 |
| Historical cost retained (loss) profit for the year | (7,709) | 65 |

## Pirelli General plc
## Notes to the Accounts

### 1. Turnover

| | 1999 £000 | 1998 £000 |
|---|---|---|
| *Geographical market supplied:* | | |
| United Kingdom | 203,771 | 207,256 |
| Rest of Europe | 69,300 | 64,365 |
| Middle East | 8,072 | 19,305 |
| Africa | 879 | 12,174 |
| Americas | 1,306 | 1,878 |
| Far East including Autralasia | 31,837 | 40,834 |
| | 315,165 | 345,812 |

### 2. Other Operating Expense

| | 1999 £000 | 1998 £000 |
|---|---|---|
| Distribution and selling costs | 27,819 | 28,806 |
| Administrative expenses before restructuring | 18,559 | 20,625 |
| Restructuring costs: | | |
| - Non-redundancy | 902 | 226 |
| - Redundancy | 2,590 | 170 |
| Administrative expenses | 22,051 | 21,021 |
| | 49,870 | 49,827 |
| Other operating income | (432) | (838) |
| | 49,438 | 48,989 |

# Appendix 7

PUBLISHED WEEKLY BY THE NATION GROUP

Aug 28-Sept 3, 2000
UGANDA SH 1000
TANZANIA SH 600
KENYA SH 50
No. 304

# World Bank Pushes Kenya to Privatise Power Companies

■ **Job Cuts:** The move would have seen about two thirds of KPLC's workforce of 6,983 laid off, according to World Bank sources

By KEVIN J. KELLEY
SPECIAL CORRESPONDENT

A WORLD Bank team is expected in Nairobi in about two weeks to urge Kenyan officials to set a specific timetable for the privatisation of the Kenya Power and Lighting Company (KPLC) and the Kenya Electricity Generating Company as part of a new initiative to increase energy-related aid to Kenya.

The privatisation will set up regional power distribution bodies to be responsible for billing customers in their jurisdiction. The entities will tap power from the national grid and supply it to local companies, which will then be obliged to expand the distribution network under an arrangement similar to the current rural electrification programme.

Analysts, however, warn that privatising the two power companies before the World Bank demonstrates its ability to prevail on the government to make the process transparent may lead the country from the frying pan into the fire — as seems to be happening in the telecommunications sector, where the new ownership is said to revolve around politically connected firms and personalities. Few past privatisations have brought tangible benefit to either consumers or the country.

The World Bank's proposal would have seen about two thirds of KPLC's workforce of 6,983 laid off, according to sources, but discussions are still going on.

A World Bank mission that was in Nairobi in June to appraise the proposed $75 million emergency power-supply project recommended that an independent consultant be hired to review KPLC's organisational structure.

Already, donors have established that KPLC can operate more efficiently by contracting out meter reading, billing and collection as well as transport services.

The World Bank team will come soon after an International Monetary Fund mission that arrives in Nairobi this Monday completes its assessment of the amount of new aid Kenya requires as a result of increased government spending to alleviate the effects of drought.

The IMF mission will be listening sympathetically to Kenyan officials' appeals for additional help, because the drought and the consequent threat of famine have significantly strained the national budget.

The IMF senior advisor for Africa, Mr Jose Fajgenbaum, told *The EastAfrican* that there will most likely be a modification of the programme approved by the Fund a month ago. The IMF agreed in late July to provide Kenya with $198 million in poverty-reduction aid over a three-year period.

Soon after that, the World Bank announced its approval of a $150 million loan for Kenya. Mr Fajgenbaum would not be drawn into estimating the amount of new drought-related assistance that might be forthcoming from the Fund.

He said the assessment team would make such a determination following talks with Kenyan officials. The team would then

*Figure 16*

forward a specific recommendation to the IMF's executive board, which would, hopefully, reach a decision in the second half of October.

The Fund will not be the only source of help in counteracting the effects of the drought. A portion of the budgetary assistance needed by Kenya was expected to come from the Paris Club of donors, Mr Fajgenbaum said. He also noted that the World Bank would be financing new power projects soon. The Bank is considering a $75 million loan to Kenya for the expansion of electrical generating capacity.

Mr Fajgenbaum, however, insisted that the IMF would not be setting any conditions for additional aid to Kenya and defended the terms of the $198 million poverty-reduction loan approved by the Fund in late July. Complaints that the loan conditions infringed on Kenya's sovereignty were an exaggeration, Mr Fajgenbaum said, adding that the reporting requirements attached to the aid package were normal. They were the same as had been expected of Kenya as part of previous IMF aid programmes, he added.

The only two new benchmarks in the current package have been added as part of the Kenya government's anti-corruption efforts, Mr Fajgenbaum added. The government agreed to publish the Economic Crimes Bill, an action taken last week and to add certain amendments to the Code of Ethics, an initiative that remains to be completed, mainly because of the legal issues involved.

*Figure 16* (continued)

## Summary

Pirelli is in the unique position of being a truly global company with a strong technological lead in the cable sector. In spite of this it has many difficult issues to face within the sector. The example of the UK section of the market shows the growing infiltration of cheaper imports. The deregulation of the utilities market offers both opportunities and threats, (see Appendix 6 for Financial Statements). The market is truly international, as cables are needed for transmission all over the world and electricity and telecommunications are now taken for granted in most countries. The evolving market structures mean that the company has to be flexible and quick in meeting the demands of its customers. How can the organization transfer its learning across international boundaries? How can it develop a brand leadership in the cable sector? These and many other questions need to be considered as the company bravely enters the new century.

### Additional Information

Pirelli has purchased the power cable business of BICC General in the UK, as part of a worldwide acquisition strategy. This amalgamation helps to create an organization with strong technical skills and manufacturing capacity to satisfy current and future demands in the marketplace. BICC General operates from four sites in the UK, while Pirelli operates from six. The merger means that both organizational structures and marketing strategies will need to be combined and centralized.

**Examination Questions**

As the appointed Marketing Consultant the board have asked you to prepare a report addressing the following questions:

**Question 1.**

Produce a strategic marketing plan for Pirelli in the UK for the next three years, taking recent developments into account.

**(40 marks)**

**Question 2.**

What are the short term and long term marketing implications of Pirelli's development of e-commerce both for the company, its' customers and suppliers?

**(30 marks)**

**Question 3.**

Develop and justify international marketing approaches for Pirelli General.

**(30 marks)**
**(100 marks in total)**

**Note the distribution of marks and allocate your time accordingly.**

# June 2001 – Malaysian Airline System Berhad

## Candidate's Brief

You are Simon Lee, who has recently joined the company as a Senior Marketing Manager. You have worked in various industry sectors, but this is your first post within the airline industry.

You have consulted widely, trying to assess the nature of the industry and MAS's position within it. So far you have gathered together much useful background information on MAS, the industry sector and trends.

At a future meeting to be set on 15th June 2001, you are to present your findings to the marketing team, in order to develop future plans for the company.

### Important Notice

This Case material is based on an actual organization and existing market conditions.

Candidates are strictly instructed NOT TO CONTACT Malaysian Airline System Berhad or any other companies in the industry. Additional information will be provided at the time of the examination. Further copies may be obtained from The Chartered Institute of Marketing, Moor Hall, Cookham, Maidenhead, Berkshire, SL6 9QH, UK.

© The Chartered Institute of Marketing

## Malaysian Airline System Berhad

*'Like Malaysia itself, which is continuing its intensive and high powered transformation into a modern, prosperous nation, Malaysia Airlines is flying proudly into the 21st century.' Quote from the company's annual report.*

Malaysian Airline System Berhad is the national airline of Malaysia. With headquarters in Kuala Lumpur, Malaysia, and using the state-of-art Kuala Lumpur international airport at Sepang as its hub, the airline flies to 111 international destinations in five continents. It also operates a domestic network within Malaysia.

### History

The history of Malaysian Airline System Berhad can be traced back to May 1947, when a charter service was started from Singapore to Kuala Lumpur. Malayan Airways Ltd (MAL), founded by the former British Overseas Airways Corporation (BOAC), Ocean Steamship Co. Ltd and the Straits Steamship Co. Ltd, carried five passengers on the 320 kilometre journey in a twin-engined Airspeed Consul. Within two years, three 21 seater DC3s were added and domestic and regional flights expanded to Jakarta, Medan, Ho Chi Minh City, Bangkok, North Borneo, Sarawak and Yangon.

In 1957, Malaya became an independent country and the airline was then restructured into a public limited company in 1958, owned by the Federation of Malaya and Singapore, Borneo Airways, BOAC and Qantas. It was a period of rapid growth, which saw the addition of the Douglas DC4 Skymaster, followed by the lease of two Vickers Viscounts and the acquisition of a Lockheed Super Constellation.

MAL entered the jet age with the Bristol Britannia in 1962 and five De Havilland Comet 4s in 1963. With the formation of Malaysia in 1963, the airline was renamed Malaysian Airways Ltd. That same year it acquired five F27s. Two years later, Borneo Airways merged with MAL, increasing both the carrier's fleet and network. On the separation of Singapore from the Federation of Malaysia on 9th August 1965, the Governments of Malaysia and Singapore took over majority control of the airline from BOAC and the other shareholders.

Its fleet then consisted of five Comet IVs, six F27s, eight DCs and two Twin Pioneers. It had 2,400 staff.

MAL was renamed Malaysia-Singapore Airlines Limited (MSA) in 1967. That year, MSA expanded its international network to Manila, Perth, Sydney and Taipei.

In April 1971, a split in MSA led to the incorporation of Malaysian Airlines System Berhad (MAS) as Malaysia's national carrier. When the MSA partnership was dissolved in 1971, Malaysia Airlines Berhad was incorporated with an authorized capital of RM100 million. After its incorporation, MAS, as Malaysia's national carrier, took to the skies on 1st October 1972, with a network comprising 34 domestic and 6 international destinations. MAS was installed as a member of Orient Airlines Association (OAA) at the 13th Presidential Assembly of OAA held in Sydney in 1972. In November, the company was renamed Malaysian Airline System Berhad (MAS). The new-look airline took off with a moon-kite logo on 1st October 1972, and MAS began modernizing its fleet with wide-bodied aircraft to meet increased passenger and cargo business. (Singapore Airlines was the other airline that came about from the split of MSA.)

In May 1973, MAS reached the milestone of uplifting 1 million passengers. As development was fast during this period, the 2 million passenger mark was reached in December of that same year. Services to Hat Yai and Taipei were introduced. Five new routes – Tokyo, London, Madras, Manila and Sydney – were soon added to the list, followed by Perth, Jeddah and Amman. *The Wings of Gold* in-flight magazine was introduced in 1975.

MAS was computerized in 1976. That same year, it took delivery of its first wide-body aircraft, a DC10-30. Frankfurt, Seoul, Amsterdam and Paris were added to its destinations. Under the government's privatization plan, MAS became the first government agency to go public. The balloting of 70 million shares for public subscription on 6th November 1985, marked a new era in the national carrier's development. It raised additional funds for the Company's capital expenditure on aircraft fleet expansion.

Although incorporated as a company, MAS was wholly owned by the Malaysian government. The trend amongst international airlines in the 1980s and the Malaysian government's own inclination to privatization of government-owned enterprises, saw the partial privatization of the airline in 1985. The initial public offer to the Malaysian public through a share float was a big success and listed in the Kuala Lumpur Stock Exchange (KLSE). In 1994, a company called Naluri bought 29% of the government's stake in MAS. In order to prepare itself for the future, the company has now developed an e-Enterprise Model structure for the company. (The complex group structure is shown in Appendix 1).

In 1986, MAS moved into its new RM88 million, 36-storey headquarters in Kuala Lumpur. In July, the first direct twice-weekly service to Los Angeles via Tokyo was introduced with the Airlines' brand new B747-300 stretched upper deck Combi aircraft.

Network and fleet expansion continued and by 1987 MAS had a total of 34 domestic and 27 international destinations in its network and a fleet of 37 aircraft. That same year the MAS Esteemed Traveller loyalty programme was launched. Later that year, Malaysian Airline System changed its trade name to Malaysia Airlines to create awareness of the country, in line with the government's efforts to develop the tourism industry. A refined MAS corporate logo, showing a restyled kite, was unveiled, along with the official name change to Malaysia Airlines (see section on Marketing Communications).

In 1989, Malaysia Airlines took delivery of its first two 747-400 aircraft and ordered eight A330 aircraft and equipment at a cost of RM2.4 billion to satisfy the airline's increasing frequency of flights, destinations and passengers. It also ventured into nine new international cities – New Delhi, Karachi, Guangzhou, Zurich, Fukuoka, Pontianak, Istanbul, Brussels and Auckland.

In 1990, the airline spread its wings to more new international destinations, namely Ho Chi Minh City, Vienna, Nagoya, Darwin, Brisbane and Adelaide. This same year, on 9th July, Malaysia Airlines joined the International Air Transport Association (IATA) as an active member.

In 1991, Beijing came online as Malaysia Airlines' 81st destination followed by Kaoshiung in Taiwan, Phnom Penh, Hanoi and Munich via Dubai in 1992. In 1993, the Passages frequent flyer programme was launched.

In 1994, under the leadership of Tan Sri Dato' Tajudin Ramli, Osaka became Malaysia Airlines' 95th global destination. By 30th October, through code-sharing arrangements the following cities came online – Belfast, Glasgow, Edinburgh, Leeds/Bradford and Teeside in the UK; Coolangatta (Gold Coast), Hobart (Tasmania), Canberra and Cairns in Australia on 1st November. The Cargo Division introduced a 24-hour cargo reservations facility to Kuala Lumpur to provide better cargo handling services to customers. A year later, Malaysia Airlines' authorized capital was increased to RM5 billion.

1995 saw Malaysia Airlines entering into code-sharing with Virgin Atlantic to widen its destination reach. Dublin became Malaysia Airlines' 106th online destination on 1st June under another code-sharing arrangement with British Midlands. Dhaka, in Bangladesh was launched on 30th October.

By the end of 1995, Beirut and Lebanon came online.

## Products and Services

Malaysia Airlines flies to over 110 destinations across five continents with a modern fleet of more than 100 aircraft, including the B747-400s and the new B777s. Reflecting a commitment to setting new world standards, South-East Asia's largest passenger carrier continues to break world records and set a number or industry firsts. The first airline in the world to offer a 10.4 inch (26.42 centimetre) in-seat touch screen in the First and Golden Club Class. The world's first airline to offer a Business Centre in the sky, a fully-equipped, state-of-the-art working environment for its' Esteemed Travellers and First and Golden Club Class passengers. It is also the first with a ground-to-air retail transaction service.

While travelling on Malaysia Airlines' new B747-400 and the B777, it is possible to order a bouquet of flowers to be delivered anywhere in the world. Another first came in June 2000, when Malaysia Airlines was chosen as among the world's top five airlines for product development and service delivery. The survey was carried out by international airline qualitative researchers, Inflight Research Services (IRS), in their first global airlines' star rankings on air quality and covered 150 airlines worldwide. (See Appendix 1 for details of service routes and fleet sizes).

## Outstanding In-flight Service

Since the commencement of its services, MAS has strived for the very best in-flight service reputation. Its motto and advertising imagery has been to relate its service, especially its in-flight service, to a golden standard; for 'mas' means gold in the Malay language. The marketing theme has been to portray MAS as having a very high standard in all its service areas... golden smile, golden service and golden lounge.

MAS success in delivering quality in-flight service and reliability has been well recognized. MAS won the first five Boeing awards for Dispatch Reliability in 1974. In 1979, MAS won an Outstanding Performance award for operating Boeing 737s in South-East Asia. It has continued to win numerous awards in in-flight service quality. Last year the American Academy of Hospitality Sciences awarded MAS the 'Five Star Diamond Award'. Inflight Research Services (UK) in its World First Class Survey 2000, voted MAS as having 'The Best Cabin Staff'.

Today, Malaysia Airlines is striving to reach new levels of service and global expansion to elevate it to the status of a truly global airline. The airline's remarkable growth is testament to its commitment to the people of Malaysia and travellers worldwide.

## New Airport

The new Kuala Lumpur International Airport (KLIA) was opened in 1998. The new airport has been rated as one of the best in the world. The ultra-modern complex is located 50 kilometres from the Kuala Lumpur city centre and current access to the airport is by a well planned highway. A fast train to link the airport is expected to be ready in 2002. (Work on the fast train project was delayed due to the Asian economic crisis but work has since restarted; see Appendix 1).

## Global Marketing Issues

### Deregulation and its beginnings

Two key events began the move towards deregulation in the USA. One of these was the advent of widebody aircraft, which significantly boosted airline capacity on many routes. Another was the Middle Eastern oil embargo of 1973, which led to rocketing fuel costs and contributed generally to price inflation. Both coincided with an economic downturn that put severe strain on the airlines. Business was falling at the same time that capacity and fuel prices were rising.

In line with its mandate to ensure a reasonable rate of return for the carriers, the US Civil Aviation Board (CAB) responded to the crisis by allowing carriers to increase fares. It also embarked on a four-year moratorium on authorizing new services, and approved a series of agreements among the carriers to limit capacity on major routes.

None of these moves were popular with the public. It cost more to fly. Furthermore, the CAB action did little to improve the carriers' financial position. Earnings were poor throughout the mid-70s, despite these fare increases and capacity constraints.

In 1974, the Ford Administration began to press for government regulatory reforms, in response to a growing public sentiment that government regulations were overly burdensome to US industry and were contributing significantly to inflation. The Senate Subcommittee on Administrative Practice and Procedure concluded that airline prices in particular would fall automatically if government constraints on competition were lifted.

The staff of the CAB reached the same conclusion in a report issued in 1975. The report said the industry was "naturally competitive, not monopolistic", and that the CAB itself could no longer justify entry controls or public utility-type pricing. Mr Kahn, an economist, was persuasive in arguing that the board should give the airlines greater pricing freedom and easier access to routes.

The same principle of free-market competition was next applied to the passenger side of the business in the Airline Deregulation Act of 1978. Restrictions on domestic routes and schedules were eliminated, along with government controls over domestic rates. Eventually, the CAB itself was disbanded.

The US example of deregulation was followed by British Airways and then many of the European airlines. Deregulation has led to a tighter squeeze on margins for all the airlines and many airlines find it more and more difficult to make profits. In fact even some of the US airlines run at a loss. Many airlines operate strategic alliances such as KLM (Royal Dutch Airlines) and Northwest Airlines. In spite of these moves internationally, many airlines are still owned by state governments.

*Table 1* Shows the ownership characteristics of flag carriers in 1998, with the percentage stake by national government. The government stake in MAS has increased again, as it has bought out Naluri's stake in the Airline, (see the section below on strategic positioning)

| **Americas** | **%** | Air France | 90.1 |
|---|---|---|---|
| Aerolineas Argentinas | 5 | Alitalia | 67 |
| Aeromexico | 0 | Austrian Airlines | 51.9 |
| AeroPeru | 20 | Balkan Bulgarian | 100 |
| Air Canada | 0 | British Airways | 0 |
| Air Jamaica | 25 | CSA Czech Airlines | 83.7 |
| American | 0 | Cyprus Airways | 80.5 |
| Avianca | 0 | Finnair | 59.8 |
| BWIA International | 33.5 | Iberia | 92 |
| CAIL | 0 | JAT Yugoslav Airlines | 100 |
| Continental | 0 | KLM | 25 |
| Delta | 0 | Lot Polish Airlines | 100 |
| Lan-Chile | 0 | Lufthansa | 0 |
| Lloyd Aereo Boliviano | 48.3 | Luxair | 23.1 |
| Mexicanna | 0 | Malev | 63.9 |
| Northwest | 0 | Olympic | 100 |
| Pluna | 49 | Sabena | 33.8 |
| TWA | 0 | SAS | 50 |
| United | 0 | Swissair | 21.5 |
| Varig | 1.2 | Tap Air Portugal | 100 |
| **Asia/Pacific** | **%** | Tarom | 100 |
| Air China | 100 | **Middle East** | **%** |
| Air-India | 100 | El Al | 100 |
| Air Lanka | 74 | Emirates | 100 |
| Air New Zealand | 0 | Gulf Air | 100 |
| Air Niugini | 100 | Iran Air | 100 |
| All Nippon | 0 | Kuwait Airways | 100 |
| Biman Bangladesh | 100 | MEAL Airliban | 0 |
| Cathay Pacific | 0 | Qatar Airways | 0 |
| China Airlines | 0 | Royal Jordanian | 100 |
| China Eastern | 61.1 | Saudia | 100 |
| China Southern | 68.1 | Syrian Arab Airlines | 100 |
| Garuda | 100 | THY Turkish | 98.2 |
| Japan Airline | 0 | Yemenia | 51 |
| Korean Air | 0 | **Africa** | **%** |
| Malaysia Airlines | 25 | Air Afrique | 70.4 |
| PIA | 56 | Air Algerie | 100 |
| Philippine Airlines | 14 | Air Mauritius | 51 |
| Qantas | 0 | Air Zimbabwe | 100 |
| Royal Brunei | 100 | Egyptair | 100 |
| Royal Nepal | 100 | Kenya Airways | 23 |
| SIA | 54 | Nigeria Airways | 100 |
| Thai Airways International | 93 | Royal Air Maroc | 92.7 |
| Vietnam Airlines | 100 | South African Airways | 100 |
| **Europe** | **%** | Sudan Airways | 100 |
| Aer Lingus | 100 | Tunisair | 45.2 |
| Aeroflot RIA | 51 | | |

## What Remains Regulated

### International

Among the CAB functions shifted to other parts of the government was the responsibility for awarding landing rights and other privileges in foreign countries to US carriers. International air services are usually governed by air transport service agreements, referred to as bilaterals, between two nations. These agreements specify such things as the cities each nations' airlines may serve, the number of flights they may operate, and how much regulatory authority the governments will exercise over fares. Bilateral negotiations involving the United States are led by the State Department, with active Department of Transport (DOT) policy input and participation.

Most national airlines are dependent on their revenues from international traffic. In many countries, the geography and demography mitigates against significant domestic networks, (e.g. KLM (Royal Dutch Airlines) and Swissair). The huge number of national carriers attest to the fact that many bilateral agreements exist between countries. These agreements allow many small countries to operate international air travel.

In the 1990s, the United States made a concerted effort to liberalise its international aviation markets, in view of strong airline traffic growth, more liberal trade policies by many partners and the increasing importance of global airline alliances. This effort has been very successful, and as of April 2000, the US had concluded 45 "Open Skies" agreements, which exchange traffic rights without any limitation on routes, the number of carriers or capacity; and provide liberal regimes for pricing, charters, co-operative marketing agreements and other commercial opportunities. In cases where the agreements are less liberal and some restrictions exist, it is the task of the DOT to decide which US airlines get those rights through traditional administrative processes.

### New Carriers

Deregulation has done more than a major reshuffling of service by existing carriers. It has opened the airline business to newcomers, just as US Congress intended. In 1978, there were 43 carriers certified for scheduled service with large aircraft. Today, the number of carriers has doubled.

The number has fluctuated over the years, with changing market conditions. By 1998, however, the number was again on the rise as new airlines offering direct, low cost, no-frills service began to emerge. The new airlines were a result of several factors, most notably low prices for used aircraft and the availability of pilots, mechanics and other airline professionals. This pattern has been repeated in many countries where deregulation has been embraced.

### Increased Competition

The appearance of new airlines, combined with the rapid expansion into new markets by many of the established airlines, resulted in unprecedented competition in the airline industry. Today, 85 per cent of airline passengers have a choice of two or more carriers, compared with only two-thirds in 1978. The airlines compete intensely with one another in virtually all major markets. The growth of hub-and-spoke systems resulted in increasing competition in small markets that would not normally support competitive service with a linear route system. Proportionately, the biggest increase in competition occurred in the small and medium-sized markets.

### Pricing

Pricing within the airline industry is complex. Most individuals purchasing tickets will know that it is possible to pay any one of a large number of different prices to fly a route. Fares vary with time (whether off-peak or peak), class of travel (first, economy, or business class), length of stay at a destination (days, weeks or Saturday night stop over), and where and when the ticket is purchased and paid for. Usually if passengers are willing to book and pay several weeks or months in advance, apex fares apply. Fares also change if passengers want open flexible tickets (more expensive) or fixed flight tickets. Companies utilize a certain amount of price discrimination according to the type of passenger travelling (businessman, student, child, holiday maker). Depending on their image, airlines can also charge a premium for better service, entertainment or landing facilities at airports. In essence most airlines, including MAS, try to get the best yield out of an aircraft and try to maintain a full aircraft within the different classes of seats available. For instance, for Asia Pacific, MAS offers special rates for a flight to Kuala Lumpur, a stop over in Singapore and Perth, before returning to London. Fares range between £550 and £750 on economy class, depending on the time of year. The airline also offers special fares for pilgrims to Mecca.

## Discount Fares

Increased competition has spawned discount fares. From the traveller's perspective, the discounts are the most important result of airline deregulation. Fares have declined more than 35 per cent in real terms since deregulation in 1978. They have become so low, in fact, that interstate bus and rail services have been hard pressed to compete with the airlines, which today provide the primary means of public transportation between cities in the United States. This scenario has not been followed in many countries, including Malaysia, as they are not geographically as vast as the USA.

## Growth in Air Travel

With greater competition on the vast majority of routes, extensive discounting, and more available flights, air travel has grown rapidly since deregulation.

Appendix 2 shows the expected growth in world passenger traffic. According to Boeing, US and Europe are maturing in terms of the numbers of individuals carried, with Asia, the Middle East and Latin America, poised for substantial growth (see Figure 1).

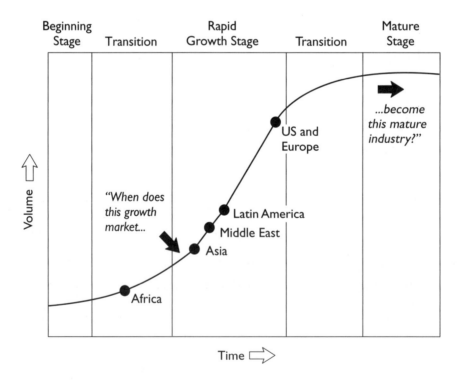

*Figure 1* *Market Life Cycle (Source: Boeing)*

In general it appears that air travel is closely related to the GDP of a country, (see Figure 2).

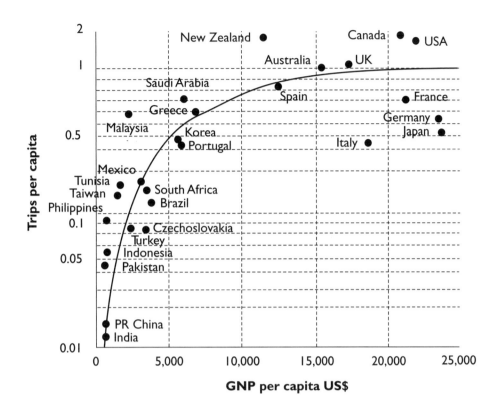

**Figure 2** *International comparisons of air travel related to economic activity, 1990 (Source: Boeing)*

For instance, in North America there are two trips per person per year, whereas in China and India, only one person in a hundred makes an annual air trip. The growth in air travel is also dependent on achieving penetration into the lower income categories in each country in the world. For instance, in the USA 75% of the people in the top income band ($100,000 or more) travel by air each year compared to only 11% in the lowest income band (those on $10,000 or less). The change in family demographics (single parent families, multiple structure families) in the developed world could actually exert an upward increase in air travel. Leisure travel too is growing much faster than business travel. Across the whole world, the leisure/business travel breakdown is now approximately 80/20.

Nonetheless, business travel is very important to airlines as these types of passengers (first class, business class) yield a lot of revenue. For instance, in the case of British Airways, 'Club World' generates 25% of revenue with only 5% of the passengers. The key components of air travel demand are encapsulated in Figure 3. Table 2 shows how the airlines are valued by sales, with Malaysia Airlines ranked 35.

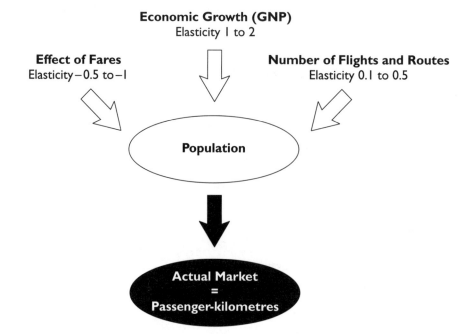

**Figure 3** *Components of air travel demand (Source: Airbus Industrie)*

**Table 2** *The top 40 airlines in 1997 ranked by sales[a]. (Sources: compiled from International Air Transport Association and World Airline Directory,* Flight International, *18th–24th March, 25th–31st March and 1st–7th April 1998)*

|  | Sales (US$ Millions) | Passengers (Millions) | Employees (Number) |
|---|---|---|---|
| 1. American | 18,570 | 81.00 | 111,500 |
| 2. United | 17,378 | 84.20 | 91,779 |
| 3. British Airways[b] | 14,184 | 40.96 | 60,575 |
| 4. Delta | 13,590 | 101.15 | 63,441 |
| 5. Lufthansa | 13,354 | 44.40 | 58,204 |
| 6. Northwest | 10,226 | 54.70 | 50,000 |
| 7. Air France[b] | 10,185 | 33.50 | 46,385 |
| 8. Japan Airlines[b] | 9,936 | 31.36 | 18,127 |
| 9. All Nippon[b] | 8,798 | 40.83 | 15,200 |
| 10. US Airways | 8,514 | 58.70 | 40,246 |
| 11. Swissair | 7,356 | 10.80 | 16,883 |
| 12. Continental | 7,213 | 40.00 | 40,000 |
| 13. KLM[b] | 6,688 | 14.73 | 26,811 |
| 14. Qantas[c] | 6,131 | 18.61 | 30,080 |
| 15. SAS | 5,097 | 20.80 | 20,500 |
| 16. Alitalia | 5,085 | 24.55 | 18,676 |
| 17. SIA[b] | 4,992 | 12.00 | 28,196 |
| 18. Air Canada | 4,024 | 14.00 | 21,215 |

| | | | |
|---|---|---|---|
| 19. Cathay Pacific | 3,958 | 10.02 | 15,747 |
| 20. Southwest | 3,817 | 50.40 | 23,974 |
| 21. Iberia | 3,562 | 16.07 | 20,000 |
| 22. TWA | 3,328 | 23.39 | 25,000 |
| 23. Varig | 3,151 | 10.65 | 18,203 |
| 24. Thai Airways International[d] | 3,120 | 14.38 | 24,186 |
| 25. Korean | 3,029 | 25.58 | 17,139 |
| 26. Japan Air System[b] | 2,651 | 19.13 | 6,094 |
| 27. Ansett Australia[c] | 2,538 | 11.52 | 17,067 |
| 28. LTU International Airways[e] | 2,349 | 7.20 | 5,159 |
| 29. CAIL | 2,221 | 8.60 | 14,233 |
| 30. Air New Zealand | 2,031 | 6.63 | 9,340 |
| 31. Sabena | 2,012 | 6.87 | 9,500 |
| 32. America West | 1,875 | 18.33 | 9,615 |
| 33. Alaska Airlines | 1,863 | 12.25 | 6,477 |
| 34. China Airlines | 1,740 | 7.40 | 8,490 |
| 35. Malaysia Airlines[b] | 1,731 | 15.66 | 2,354* |
| 36. Vasp | 1,667 | 4.57 | 7,156 |
| 37. Austrian | 1,597 | 3.94 | 4,149 |
| 38. Garuda | 1,571 | 6.69 | 13,727 |
| 39. China Southern | 1,541 | 15.24 | 7,820 |
| 40. Finnair[b] | 1,445 | 6.86 | 10,780 |

[a] The list is limited to passenger airlines. Ten cargo airlines that would be included in a top 100 list in terms of sales revenue are: Federal Express, United Parcels Service, Airborne Freight Corp., Asiana, DHL Airways, Nippon Cargo Airways, Cargolux, Permiair, American International Airways, Polar Air Cargo. Federal Express is the largest airline in terms of employees (114,636).

[b] Year to 31st March 1998.

[c] Year to 30th June 1997.

[d] Year to 30th September 1997.

[e] Year to 31st October 1997.

* Number of employees for all MAS operations exceeds 30,000.

## Distribution

### Computer Reservation System (CRS)

Another important development following deregulation was the advent of CRSs. These systems help airlines and travel agents keep track of fare and service changes, which occur very rapidly today. The systems also enable airlines and travel agents to efficiently process the millions of passengers who fly each day.

Several major airlines developed their own systems and later sold partnerships in their systems to other airlines. The systems list not only the schedules and fares of their airline owners, but also those of any other airline willing to pay a fee to have their flights listed. Travel agents using the systems to check schedules and fares for clients, as well as to print tickets, also pay various fees for these conveniences. The key CRSs that are in operation are often based on loose alliances of airlines. CRSs have a powerful impact on travel agents and the travel industry. The big four are Fortworth, Texas based Sabre, which lead the US market share by agency locations and bookings. Atlanta based Worldspan and Chicago based Galileo are in a tight race for the No. 2 spot. Spanish based Amadeus is a distant fourth. Figure 4. shows the key CRSs in the world airline systems. Malyasia Airlines are linked to all CRSs, although they have a stake in Abacus and Worldspan.

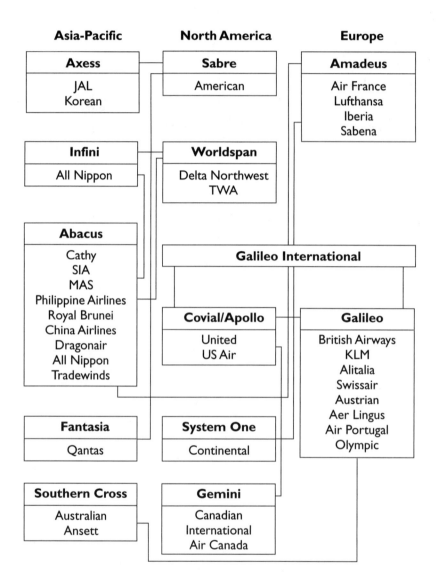

**Figure 4** *Ownership and interrelationships of computer reservations systems, 1992 (Source: International Air Transport Association)*

Recently (January 2001), some of these relationships have been thrown into a turmoil by the proposed takeover of Transworld Airlines (TWA) by American Airlines. Currently TWA own 26.3% of Worldspan. According to non-compete clauses signed by American Airlines with Sabre, it would have to divest TWA's share in Worldspan. Northwest and Delta Airlines have both expressed an interest in purchasing TWA's share in Worldspan.

### Competition and Strategic Alliances

In 1996, Star Alliances was formed with United Airlines, Lufthansa, KLM and three others. In 1998, the oneworld alliance was formed, linking five airlines, led by British Airways and American Airlines and incorporating Canadian Airlines, Qantas and Cathay Pacific. Later Iberia joined the group. Many alliances that are formed between airlines involve no investments in equity. The alliances are limited to marketing and technical co-operation. As Table 3 shows, there has been a tremendous growth in alliances. The number of alliances has increased from 280 in 1994 to 502 in 1998, while the number of airlines involved has risen from 136 to 196. Ohmae the famous Professor of Marketing at Harvard Business School argues that the sheer scale of current global industries and global markets requires collaboration as opposed to developing very large global enterprises. He argues:

*"...globalisation mandates alliances, makes them absolutely essential to strategy. Uncomfortable perhaps – but that's the way it is. Like it or not, the simultaneous developments that go under the name of globalisation make alliances – (business) entente – necessary".*

*Table 3 Growth in airline alliances, 1994–1998 (Source: Airline Business)*

|  | 1994 | 1995 | 1996 | 1997 | 1998 | Percentage Change 1994–1998 |
|---|---|---|---|---|---|---|
| Number of alliances | 280 | 324 | 390 | 363 | 502 | 79.3 |
| Number of airlines involved | 136 | 153 | 159 | 177 | 196 | 44.1 |
| Alliances entailing equity stakes | 58 | 58 | 62 | 54 | 56 | –3.4 |

Ohmae feels that this is necessitated by the convergence of consumer preferences round the world, the need to have collaborators to keep abreast of cutting edge technologies (as no one company can manage to do this by itself). In addition to this, there are the huge fixed costs associated with building information technology, R&D, building brand loyalty, setting up worldwide sales and distribution networks.

Counter to these arguments is the feeling in some quarters that the airline business may be moving from one extreme of regulation and state ownership to another of global consolidation where there is little or no competition. In other words, these alliances could create cartels which can basically charge consumers high prices for tickets.

### Frequent Flyer Programmes (FFP)

Deregulation has sparked various marketing innovations, the most noteworthy being FFPs, which reward repeat customers with free tickets and other benefits. Most major airlines have such programmes, and many small carriers have their own schemes, as well as tie-ins to larger programmes. Whilst they may vary, the essential elements are the same. Once a customer enrolls, he or she is credited with points for every mile flown with the sponsoring carrier or with other airlines tied into the sponsor's programme. The rewards (free tickets and upgrades that convert coach tickets to first class or business class tickets) are pegged to certain points totals.

A more recent development has been the marriage of FFPs with promotions in other industries in general, and the credit card industry in particular. It is now possible to build up frequent flyer points by purchasing things other than airline tickets, and in some cases to exchange miles for other goods and services, (see Table 4 for the influence of FFPs). FFPs may also allow companies to spend less on marketing. However, there may be related problems in the future, if say many individuals suddenly want to redeem their points.

**Table 4** *The influence of frequent flyer programmes*
*(Source: US General Accounting Office)*

| Number of times business travellers choose flights in order to build up Mileage points | Percentage of travel agents reporting % |
|---|---|
| Always or almost always | 57 |
| More than half the time | 24 |
| About half the time | 9 |
| Less than half the time | 4 |
| Rarely if ever | 2 |
| Other | 4 |
| | 100 |

### Code-sharing

Another innovation has been the development of code-sharing agreements. These agreements enable a ticketing airline to issue tickets on the operating airline and to use that operating airline's two-letter code when doing so. Code-sharing agreements can be between a larger airline and a regional airline or between a US airline and a foreign airline. Code-sharing agreements allow two different airlines to offer better co-ordinated services to their customers.

The code-sharing agreements also usually tie each airline's marketing and FFPs, provide for schedule co-ordination for convenient connections between carriers, and in most cases, permit smaller airlines to paint their planes with markings similar to those used by their larger partners.

All the major airlines have code-sharing agreements with regional carriers; in most cases with several regionals, and also with other nationals and majors. Some also own regional carriers outright, giving them greater control over these important services that feed traffic from out-lying areas into the major hubs.

Code-sharing also applies to international routes. Many US and foreign airlines now have code-sharing agreements that essentially enable those airlines to expand their global reach through the services operated by their partners.

Code-sharing differs from interlining, a much older industry practice, in which a carrier simply hands over a passenger to another carrier, to get the passenger to a destination the first carrier does not serve directly. In such situations, the passenger buys a single ticket, and the airline issuing the ticket makes the arrangements for the traveller on the second carrier. However, schedules are not necessarily co-ordinated, there are no frequent flyer tie-ins, and there is no sharing of codes in CRSs. The flights of each carrier appear independently in the CRSs.

### E-distribution

Many airlines, including Malaysia Airlines, are considering the utilization of e-ticketing through electronic distribution (see Appendix 2). For MAS, the key is to participate on other servers and at the same time have its own Asian travel portal where individual systems are all linked up. Currently, 85% of MAS's business comes from travel agents. The company is keen to develop passenger loyalty and already offers a FFP. The e-ticketing will allow individuals to tailor flights to suit their needs. 50% of MAS's bookings come through the CRSs and incur an average of US$3.80 booking fee. The rest of the bookings come through MAS's own network, which is KOMMAS, and covers all local bookings. Eventually airlines such as MAS will be looking to provide airline tickets which are charged through a credit card over the Internet. No tickets have to be issued as all the data will be transferred to the airports and will be easily accessed anywhere. This can be used with both local and international flights through the generation of a unique bar code for each individual booking (see Figure 5).

The customers can also be offered insurance through dedicated Independent Financial Advisors (IFAs).

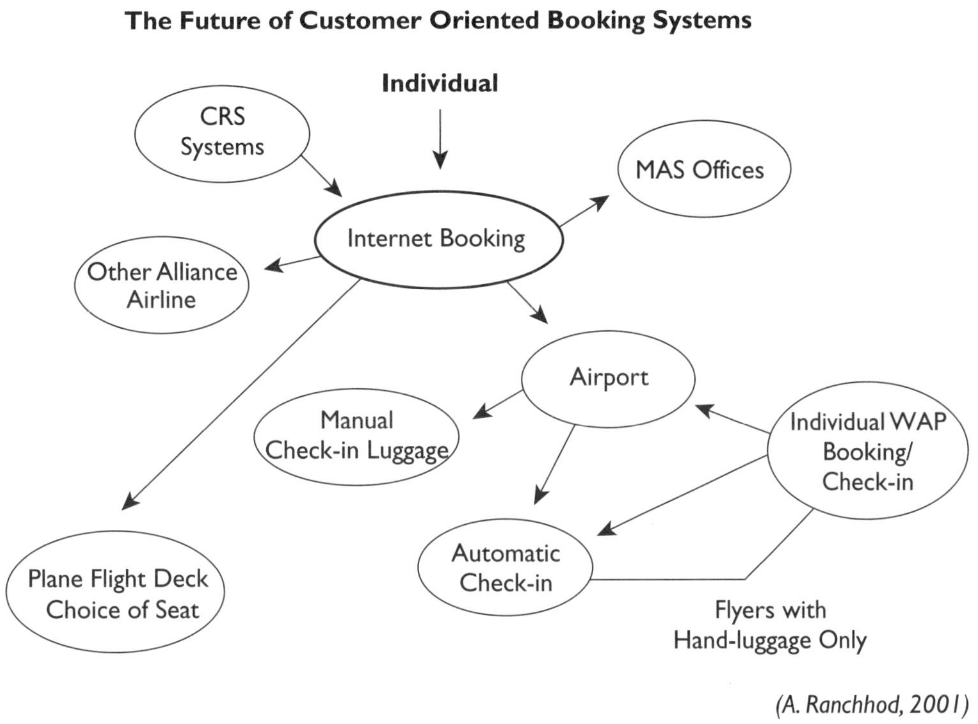

**The Future of Customer Oriented Booking Systems**

(A. Ranchhod, 2001)

*Figure 5* *The future of bookings and check-ins*

Many of the CRSs are also providing e-ticketing services to consumers as they already have excellent information systems. Some are already linked to web portals such as Travelocity. In the longer run, airlines such as MAS will be torn between establishing their own portals and utilising the age old CRSs with a new Internet face.

## Strategic Positioning Issues for MAS

In the middle of 1998, many Asian countries, including Malaysia, faced currency crises, undermining many economies and setting off a downward economic spiral. This affected many airlines. The US economy, apart from late 2000, continued to boom, and consequently the most profitable world airlines were mainly American, interspersed with some European players such as British Airways and Lufthansa. In sharp contrast, five of the ten heaviest loss makers were Asian carriers (see Tables 5 and 6). Even Singapore International Airlines dropped from its number one position as the world's most profitable airline to sixth place. In terms of operating costs, however, the Asian airlines are among the cheapest in terms of stage length and cost per tonne-kilometre (cost per seat mile). This is partly due to lower salary levels in Asia, and also it reflects the relatively lower cost of living in the region. The longer the stages, the lower the cost, reflecting less costs incurred in take-off, landing, climb and descent (see Figure 6).

**Table 5** *Ten most profitable airlines, 1997 (Source: Airline Business, September 1998)*

| | | Net Profit (US$ Millions) | Net Margin (Net Profit as % of Sales) |
|---|---|---|---|
| 1. | US Airways | 1,025.0 | 12.0 |
| 2. | American | 985.0 | 5.3 |
| 3. | United | 949.0 | 5.5 |
| 4. | Delta | 845.0 | 6.2 |
| 5. | British Airways | 755.0 | 5.3 |
| 6. | SIA | 671.2 | 13.4 |
| 7. | Northwest | 596.5 | 5.8 |
| 8. | Lufthansa | 481.7 | 3.6 |
| 9. | Continental | 385.0 | 5.3 |
| 10. | Southwest | 317.8 | 8.3 |

**Table 6** *Ten heaviest loss-making airlines, 1997 (Source: Airline Business, September 1998)*

| | | Net Loss (US$ Millions) | Net Margin (Net Loss as % of Sales) |
|---|---|---|---|
| 1. | Japan Airways | 767.0 | −7.7 |
| 2. | Korean Air | 234.0 | −7.7 |
| 3. | PIA | 119.7 | −14.7 |
| 4. | TWA | 110.8 | −3.3 |
| 5. | Philippine Airlines | 95.2 | −8.1 |
| 6. | Air-India | 82.7 | −8.2 |
| 7. | Malaysia Airlines | 69.8 | −4.0 |
| 8. | Sabena | 67.0 | −3.3 |
| 9. | South African Airways | 60.1 | −4.3 |
| 10. | Aer Lingus | 59.9 | −5.7 |

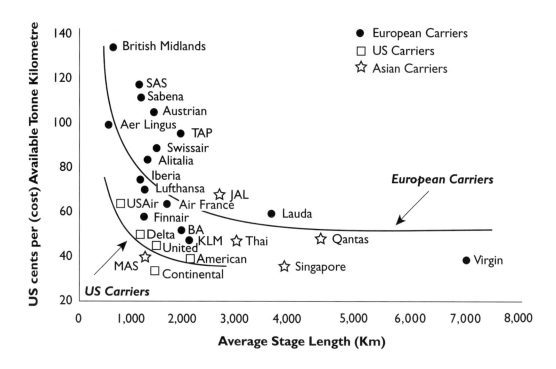

**Figure 6** *Unit operating costs as a function of stage length (Source: Comité des Sages, 1994)*

With regards to the Asia Pacific crisis, Malaysia has made considerable progress towards resolving its debt overhang of M$85 billion (US$22.4 billion). This is approximately 20% of total loans. Malaysia's Corporate Debt Restructuring Committee was set up in 1998 to facilitate talks between corporate debtors and their creditors. As part of this restructuring, the government has bought back Naluri's stake in MAS for M$1.79 billion, at roughly the same price that Naluri paid for it when it was bought from the government in mid-1994. The current market price is probably less than half this amount as reflected by share value. Since the Asian economic crisis and continued losses of the airline, the share price that once plunged to a low of M$1.60 is now trading around M$4.00. A number of other Malaysian government agencies also have sizeable share holdings in the company.

MAS is regarded as a global carrier operating all around the world. It has a relatively young fleet and its revenue breakdown is as follows:

*Table 7*

|  | **Domestic** | **International** |
| --- | --- | --- |
| Revenues | 25% | 75% |
| Passengers carried | 40% | 60% |

The ratio is likely to be tilted further towards international flights as these are on the increase within the region. For instance, there is a large growth in traffic to and from India, especially to Chennai in South India. However, the traffic is restricted somewhat by the difficulty in obtaining landing rights, as the Indian Government appears to be protectionist in its policies. Malaysia is an attractive tourist centre and the traffic is growing between it and Australia, Europe, Japan and China. MAS is keen to promote the new airport as a hub for traffic to and from China, India and Vietnam. Within Malaysia, MAS is viewed as a preferred carrier compared to China Airlines, Thai Airways, Japan and ANA Airlines, Cathay Pacific and Garuda, especially on Asian routes.

Another key factor in traffic growth is related to Malaysia's growing reputation as a centre of education. There is already considerable student traffic from Indonesia. In response to this growth, MAS have introduced GRADCARD, which is a preferential student travel card. According to the International Civil Aviation Organisation (ICAO) total world airline scheduled passenger traffic, in terms of passenger-kilometres, is expected to grow at an average annual rate of 5.5 per cent over the period 1995-2005, compared with 5.0 per cent per annum over the period 1985–1995. Appendix 2 shows the expected growth in air traffic in general and by region. The fastest growing international route groups for passenger traffic are forecast to be the Transpacific and Europe-Asia/Pacific route groups. The airlines of the Asia/Pacific region are expected to show well above average growth in both passenger and freight traffic. MAS's selling strategy has been price driven in order to maximize the volume of passengers. Initially this was done to attract passengers to a relatively unknown destination such as Malaysia, compared to Bangkok and Singapore. Both MAS and Singapore Airlines tend to be very competitive outside their home markets.

## Green Issues

There is growing concern for the environment throughout the world and the growth in air traffic is not always welcomed by many citizens. Many airports are located near major conurbations, with increasing noise and chemical pollution. The chemical pollution affects the air and waterways, as de-icing chemicals are often used in the cold regions of the world. In addition to this, solvents, used for aircraft maintenance, escape into the air. Aircraft are responsible for between 2–3% of total human carbon dioxide ($CO_2$) emissions globally. Aircraft also produce significant quantities of nitrogen oxides (NOx). Air travel in general is inefficient over shorter distances, resulting in greater energy wastage. Newer aircraft now being manufactured by Boeing and Airbus are taking these issues into account and are building quieter, more fuel efficient and aerodynamic aircraft. In Malaysia, the ecological issues seem to have been taken into account, and the new Kuala Lumpur airport has been built approximately 50 kilometres out of town. An efficient high-speed rail link is being built to complement this, thereby reducing car pollution. In the future, such strategies may be the way forward for many international terminals as passenger traffic increases.

## Marketing Communications

As in all things, change is a necessary part of growth. In 1947, the country's first airline, Malayan Airways Limited – with its 'winged tiger' symbol (1947 logo) – took off with just a pilot and a wireless operator as crew, and five passengers. Since then, changes have been both significant and memorable. Malayan Airways Limited, formed by the Straits Steamship Company, Ocean Steamship Company and Imperial Airways, became in time Malaysian Airways Limited, as a result of the formation of Malaysia in 1963. Realizing the potential of the airline, the Governments of Malaysia and Singapore jointly acquired majority control of the airline and formed Malaysia-Singapore Airlines (MSA) in 1967. In keeping with this new company, a new symbol was born (1967 logo). As time went by, new priorities became apparent for Malaysia – that of growing domestic and regional air transportation needs, rather than international destinations. So in 1971, MSA was restructured and Malaysian Airline System Berhad or MAS came into being.

Stylized from the Kelantan kite (1972 logo), a new logo took to the skies to chart the new airline's destiny and to serve first and foremost the country, and gradually the world.

15 years later, Malaysia's national airline again redefined its status and stance. Changing values, increasing international coverage, responding to the national tourism policy emphasis and the need to create Malaysia's presence in the world marketplace, pointed the way to a new direction and growth. In order to reflect the new adventurous approach, the corporate logo was revamped (1987 logo), implementing the new image.

**Logos**

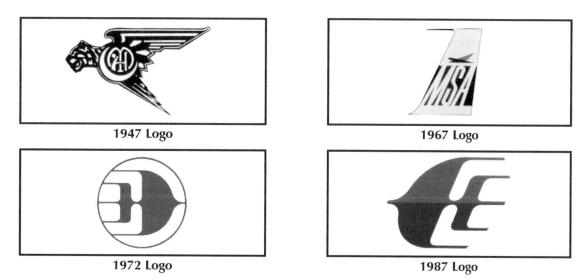

1947 Logo

1967 Logo

1972 Logo

1987 Logo

MAS currently work with one of the major advertising agencies in the world, Leo Burnett. However, the current advertising spend is 3.5–4% below the industry average. The greatest challenge that MAS faces is in building a consistent image for its brand. Currently the thematic nature of advertising concentrates on the *Future of Travel*. There is also a need to improve consumer perceptions of the airline from being a second-tier airline, in terms of service, to a premier airline, such as Cathay Pacific or Singapore Airlines. The problem is that the public perception is variable, whereas in reality the service and the destinations offered by MAS are extremely good (as discussed before). The cabin service is generally excellent. The service culture is inherent within Malaysian society and the staff are open and friendly. Somehow the challenge for MAS is to communicate this to the general global consumer.

Companies are now seeking novel ways of enhancing their brands globally. So in an interesting departure from the norm, Emirates Airlines recently agreed a US$35 million deal with Chelsea Football Club in London. As English football has global appeal, Emirates Airlines obviously feel that any advertising and branding is likely to be mutually beneficial. International interest in the English Premier League is continually increasing. This is reflected in the value of international broadcast rights. This season, matches are broadcast in 127 countries, compared with only 27 when the Premier League was formed. Interestingly, Vodaphone's US$44 million agreement with Manchester United is to capitalize on the club's global following, in order to increase brand awareness of its own products.

Malaysian Airlines sponsors sports tournaments and the Grand Prix in Malaysia. It also has its fair share of billboards at major sporting events in Europe.

## A Footnote about Malaysia

Malaysia is made up of Peninsular Malaysia, and the states of Sabah (formerly called British North Borneo) and Sarawak. It has a population of 22 million people made of Malays (57.5%), Chinese (27.2%) and Indians (8.9%). Other minority groups such as Ibans, Dayaks and Kadazans make a small percentage of the population. Malays were the early inhabitants of the country, whilst the Chinese and Indians arrived as immigrants in the early part of last century under British rule. The Chinese came to work in tin mines and the Indians in rubber plantations. Today, Malaysia is a fine example of a multi-racial and multi-cultural country, with a very stable political environment. The Federal Government is modelled after the Westminster system with elections held every five years.

The airline continues to spread its wings wider and further, with fleet modernization pro-grammmes and new international destinations. This record of tremendous growth and success is closely tied to the values and objectives of economic and tourism growth in Malaysia. The company is building a world-class reputation by fully supporting the government's 'Vision 2020', which calls for Malaysia to be a fully developed and prosperous nation by that year. Thus, as one of the pillars of the nation's future, Malaysia Airlines prides itself on being the ambassador of a new, contemporary Malaysia, flying farther than ever before.

The Malaysian economy is very dynamic and export oriented. Per capita income stands at US$4,370 and Malaysians enjoy one of the highest standards of living in Asia. Malaysia has a very strong and diversified modern economy, based on natural resources and manufacturing.*

It is a world leading manufacturer of a large range of consumer goods, appliances, electronics, micro-chips and computer accessories. Domestic and international tourism have become very significant economic activities in the last decade, with Malaysia Airlines playing a pivotal role in providing international airline connections to Malaysia. This has seen numerous internationally renowned hotels building good quality hotel accommodation both in the capital city and in the resorts. The Asian economic crisis caused a severe, but short, aberration to its record economic growth during the last decade. The measures taken have helped the country quickly recover and double-digit growth has again been re-established.

The Asian crisis increased the cost of the US dollar against the Malaysian ringgit. Malaysia Airlines has been hit by sharply reduced demand, amid rising costs in US dollar terms. 85% of Malaysia Airlines loans are in US dollars. The ringgit depreciated 40% against US currency during the crisis, lowering the value of the ringgit. There is also the fact that world oil prices have increased in the last 12 months to an average of US$30 per barrel.

## Summary

In many ways, in spite of the company's poor financial performance (see Appendix 3 for financial data), the company is poised for growth in a dynamic region and in a dynamic country. MAS is not a small carrier, but it needs to communicate its strengths effectively to the public. It faces extremely strong regional competition from the likes of Singapore Airlines and Thai Airways. There is a growth in leisure and tourism and the company has an off-shoot called Golden Holidays to handle this business. The current trend towards higher fuel prices makes it difficult to turn around losses on regional flights as there is a limit on passing on the charges to the consumer. On the other hand, the economy and business class international travel is growing considerably. Internet distribution and more direct links with the consumer could lower transaction costs considerably. However, currently the company is linked to travel agents for the bulk of its business. The travel to and from India is poised for growth with approximately 200 million Indians now in the high income category and with 1.6 million indigenous Indians in Malaysia.

Many industry experts believe that the global airline industry will become more and more concentrated. Boeing predict that by the year 2010, the top 20 airlines in the world will carry 66% of the world's traffic (see Figure 7 and see Appendix 2 for further details). It is also estimated that by 2010, more than half the world's traffic will start or end in South-East Asia. Air traffic in this region is currently growing at at least twice the rate of Europe or the US. Many airlines that have strategic hubs are expected to continue to do well. In this respect, further development of the airport at Kuala Lumpur must be a priority. MAS faces many difficulties and challenges, but the recent government buyback shows a degree of confidence in the airline and its ability to grow and become profitable in the future.

---

* Natural resources include rubber, tin, palm oil, rice, cocoa, timber, natural gas and high-grade petroleum.

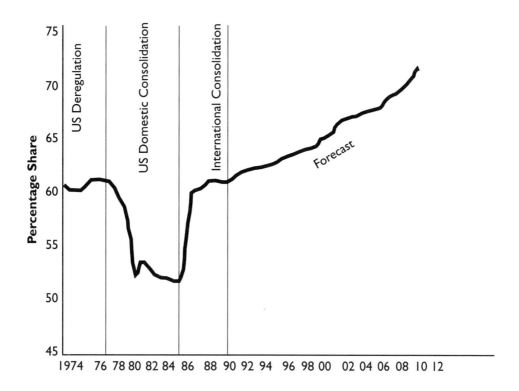

*Figure 7* Top 20 airlines' share of world passenger-kilometres, 1974–2010 (Source: Boeing)

# Appendices

## Appendix 1

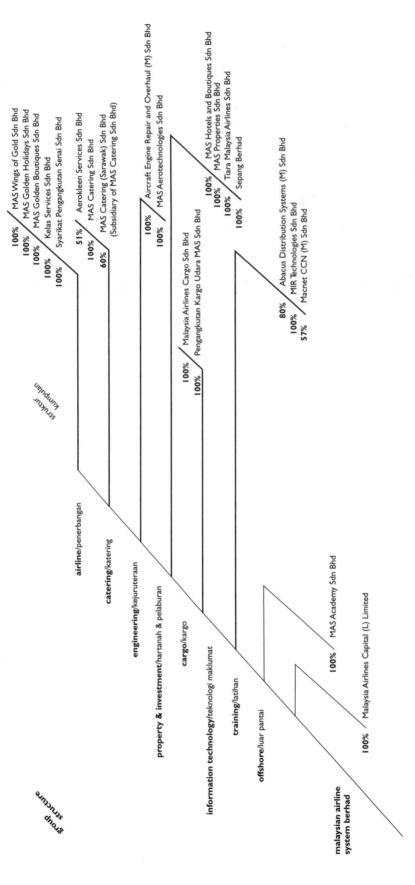

*Figure 8* (*Source: Malaysian Airline System Berhad, 1999 Annual Report*)

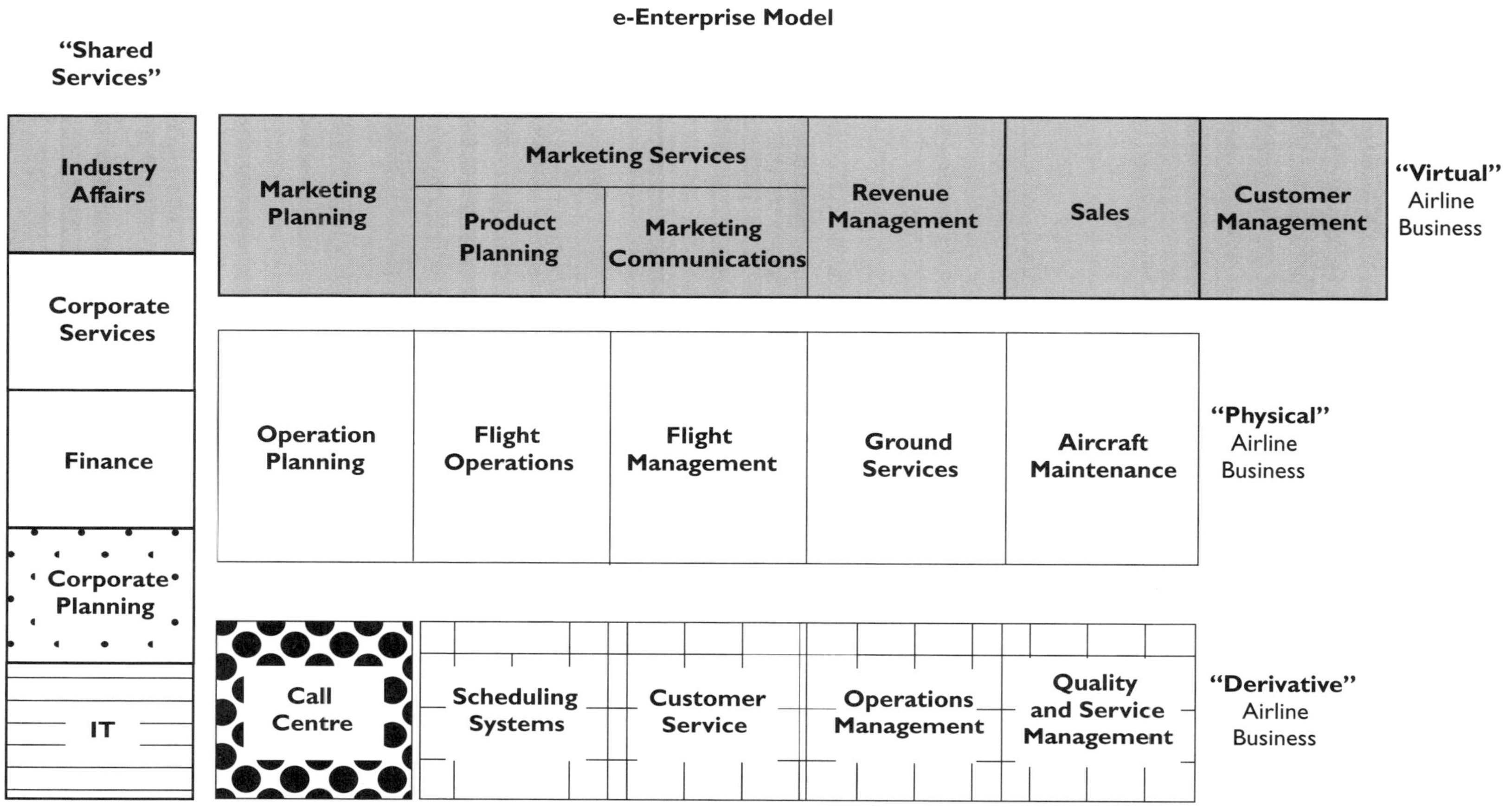

# e-Enterprise Model

| "Shared Services" | Marketing Services | | | | | "Virtual" Airline Business |
|---|---|---|---|---|---|---|
| Industry Affairs | Marketing Planning | Product Planning | Marketing Communications | Revenue Management | Sales | Customer Management |

"Physical" Airline Business

| Corporate Services | | | | |
|---|---|---|---|---|
| Finance | Operation Planning | Flight Operations | Flight Management | Ground Services | Aircraft Maintenance |

"Derivative" Airline Business

| Corporate Planning | | | | |
|---|---|---|---|---|
| Call Centre | Scheduling Systems | Customer Service | Operations Management | Quality and Service Management |

| IT |
|---|

*Figure 9*

*Fleet Status* *Number of aircraft as at 31st March 2000 (Source: Malaysian Airline System Berhad, 1999 Annual Report)*

| MAS Owned Aircraft | In MAS Operation | Leased to Third Parties | Average Age |
|---|---|---|---|
| B747-4H6P | 13 | – | 4.9 |
| B747-4H6C | 2 | – | 10.6 |
| B747-3H6C | 1 | – | 13.7 |
| B777-200 | 3 | – | 2.3 |
| B747-236 Freighter | – | 2 | 18.0 |
| DC10-30 | 2 | – | 22.4 |
| A330 | 10 | – | 4.8 |
| B737-500 | – | – | – |
| B737-400 | 31 | 4 | 6.6 |
| B737-300 Freighter | 1 | 1 | 6.2 |
| F50 | 10 | – | 10.0 |
| DHC6 | 5 | – | 13.9 |
| **Total Owned Aircraft** | **78** | **7** | **7.6** |

| Leased Aircraft | In MAS Operation | Leased to Third Parties | Average Age |
|---|---|---|---|
| B777-200 | 8 | – | – |
| MD11 Freighter | – | – | – |
| A330 | – | – | – |
| B737-400 | 4 | – | – |
| B737-500 | 3 | – | – |
| **Total Leased Aircraft** | **15** | **–** | **–** |
| **Systemwide** | **93** | **7** | **7.6** |

## domestic domestik

**Alor Setar** Bakalalan **Bario** Belag **Bintulu** Ipoh **Johor Bahru** Kota Bahru **Kota Kinabalu** Kuala Lumpur **Kuala Terengganu** Kuantan **Kuching** Kudat **Labuan** Lahad Datu **Langkawi** Lawas **Limbang** Long Banga **Long Lellang** Long Seridan **Marudi** Miri **Mukah** Mulu **Pulau Pinang** Sandakan **Sibu** Tawau **Tomanggong** Semporna

## international antarabangsa

### europe / eropah
**Amsterdam** Belfast **Dublin** Edinburgh **Frankfurt** Glasgow **Leeds Bradford** London **Manchester** Munich **Paris** Rome **Teeside** Vienna **Zurich** Zagreb

### the americas / benua amerika
**Buenos Aires** Los Angeles **New York**

### south pacific / pasifik selatan
**Adelaide** Auckland **Brisbane** Cairs **Canberra** Christchurch **Darwin** Dunedin **Gold Coast** Hobart **Melbourne** Palmerston North **Perth** Sydney **Wellington**

### north asia / asia utara
**Beijing** Fukuoka **Guangzhou** Hong Kong **Kaohsiung** Nagoya **Osaka** Seoul **Shanghai** Taipei **Tokyo** Xiamen

### west asia & africa / asia barat & afrika
**Amman** Beirut **Cairo** Capetown **Colombo** Dhaka **Dubai** Istanbul **Jeddah** Johannesburg **Karachi** Madras **Male** Mauritius **New Delhi** Tashkent **Tehran**

### south east asia / asia tenggara
**Bandar Seri Begawan** Bangkok **Cebu** Chiangmai **Denpasar** Hanoi **Hat Yai** Ho Chi Minh City **Jakarta** Manila **Medan** Phnom Penh **Phuket** Pontianak **Singapore** Surabaya **Tarakan** Yangon

*Figure 10* (Source: Malaysian Airline System Berhad, 1999 Annual Report)

# Kuala Lumpur International Airport

Welcome to Malaysia's newest international airport and the new home of Malaysia Airlines. Kuala Lumpur International Airport (KLIA) is one of the most modern and sophisticated airports in the Asia-Pacific region. As a spectacular feat of architecture and construction, KLIA combines futuristic technology, Malaysian culture and the rich, tropical splendour of its natural resources.

Located within the Multimedia Super Corridor and close to the country's future administrative capital, Putra Jaya, the airport is approximately 75 kilometres south of Kuala Lumpur's city centre. It is accessible via the Kuala Lumpur-Seremban Highway/KLIA Interchange as well as the Shah Alam/North-South Central Link Expressway. Drive time to the city centre is approximately 60 minutes.

**The Terminal Complexes** Passenger flow is contained in three main complexes — the Main Terminal Building, Contact Pier and the Satellite Building. The Main Terminal Building is linked to the Contact Pier while a fully automated Aero train connects the Contact Pier to the Satellite Building.

All pre- and post-flight formalities are situated at the Main Terminal Building and Contact Pier, while boarding and disembarkation take place at the Contact Pier as well as the Satellite Building.

**Arrivals** International flights arrive at the Satellite Building and the Aero train brings passengers to the International Level of the Contact Pier. Other international, domestic and mixed flights arrive on the Domestic Level of the Contact Pier.

**Departures** International flights depart from the Contact Pier as well as from the Satellite Building. Domestic flights depart from the Contact Pier only.

**Food and Beverage** The airport is served by numerous food and beverage outlets and they are situated on the Departure and Arrival Level of the Main Terminal Building as well as within the Satellite Building.

**Shopping, Foreign Exchange and Telecommunications** Shopping outlets, from duty-free to speciality shops, are situated on the Departure and Arrival Level of the Main Terminal Building as well as within the Satellite Building. There are convenient foreign exchange and telecommunications facilities.

**Malaysia Airlines' Lounges**
Malaysia Airlines' International Golden Lounges are available on the Departure Level of the Main Terminal Building as well as within the Satellite Building.

**Transportation** Taxis use a coupon system and taxi booths are available upon exit from the Arrival Hall. There is a choice of an airport limousine service as well as a budget taxi service.

Public bus services to the city are available one floor down from the Arrival Hall.

Private vehicle car parks are connected by the Skybridge on the Station Mezzanine Level.

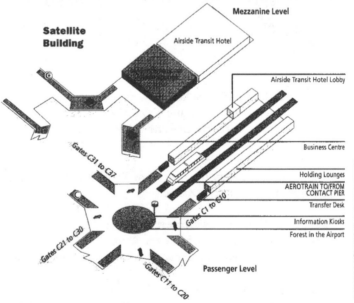

*Figure 11* (*Source: Going Places (Inflight Magazine), January 2001*)

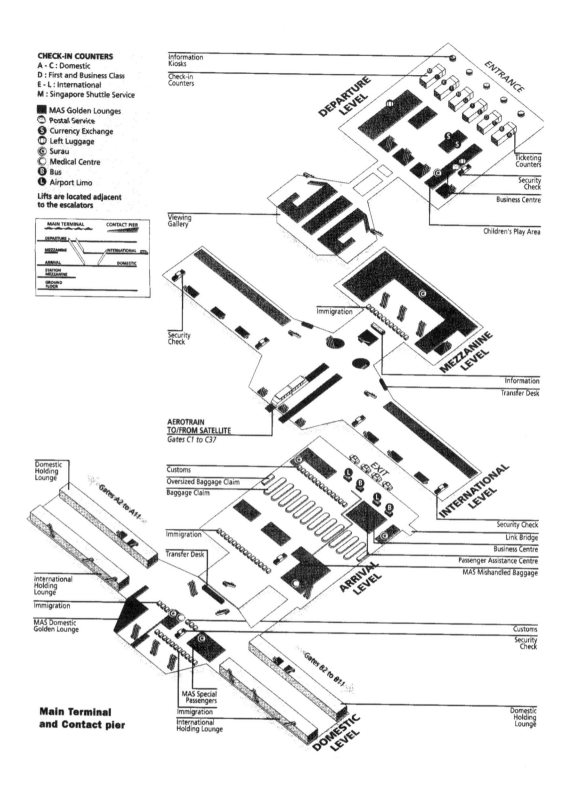

**CHECK-IN COUNTERS**
A - C: Domestic
D : First and Business Class
E - L : International
M : Singapore Shuttle Service

▊ MAS Golden Lounges
⊘ Postal Service
Ⓢ Currency Exchange
Ⓜ Left Luggage
Ⓖ Surau
Ⓒ Medical Centre
Ⓑ Bus
Ⓛ Airport Limo

Lifts are located adjacent
to the escalators

Information Kiosks
Check-in Counters
DEPARTURE LEVEL
ENTRANCE
Ticketing Counters
Security Check
Business Centre
Children's Play Area

Viewing Gallery
Immigration
MEZZANINE LEVEL
Information
Transfer Desk

Security Check
AEROTRAIN
TO/FROM SATELLITE
Gates C1 to C37

Domestic Holding Lounge
Customs
Oversized Baggage Claim
Baggage Claim
Gates A2 to A11
Immigration
Transfer Desk
International Holding Lounge
Immigration
MAS Domestic Golden Lounge
EXIT
INTERNATIONAL LEVEL
ARRIVAL LEVEL
Security Check
Link Bridge
Business Centre
Passenger Assistance Centre
MAS Mishandled Baggage
Customs
Security Check
Gates B2 to B11
Domestic Holding Lounge

**Main Terminal and Contact pier**
MAS Special Passengers
Immigration
International Holding Lounge
DOMESTIC LEVEL

MAIN TERMINAL — CONTACT PIER
DEPARTURE
MEZZANINE — INTERNATIONAL
ARRIVAL — DOMESTIC
STATION MEZZANINE
GROUND FLOOR

*Figure 12* *(Source: Going Places (Inflight Magazine), January 2001)*

## Appendix 2
### Summary of International Civil Aviation Organization Air Traffic Forecasts for the Year 2005
#### I – Worldwide

| | Actual 1985 | Actual 1995 | Estimate 1996 | Forecast 2005 | Average Growth 1985– 1995 | Annual Rate (%) 1995– 2005* |
|---|---|---|---|---|---|---|
| **Total Scheduled Services** | | | | | | |
| Passenger-kilometres (billions) | 1,367 | 2,228 | 2,393 | 3,807 | 5.0 | 5.5 |
| Freight tonne-kilometres (millions) | 39,797 | 83,082 | 87,671 | 163,950 | 7.6 | 7.0 |
| Passengers carried (millions) | 899 | 1,285 | 1,346 | 2,010 | 3.6 | 4.5 |
| Freight tonnes carried (thousands) | 13,742 | 21,488 | 22,169 | 34,600 | 4.6 | 5.0 |
| Aircraft-kilometres (millions) [1] | 10,598 | 18,279 | 19,300 | 28,400 | 5.6 | 4.5 |
| Aircraft departures (thousands) [1] | 11,953 | 16,754 | 17,700 | 21,400 | 3.4 | 2.5 |
| **International Scheduled Services** | | | | | | |
| Passenger-kilometres (billions) | 590 | 1,241 | 1,361 | 2,395 | 7.7 | 7.0 |
| Freight tonne-kilometres (millions) | 29,384 | 70,273 | 74,517 | 145,720 | 9.1 | 7.5 |
| Passengers carried (millions) | 194 | 373 | 404 | 680 | 6.8 | 6.0 |
| Freight tonnes carried (thousands) | 5,884 | 12,982 | 13,619 | 24,400 | 8.2 | 6.5 |

* Rounded to the nearest 0.5 percentage point.

[1] Excludes the Commonwealth of Independent States (CIS).

#### II – By Regional Airline Registration

| | Actual 1985 | Actual 1995 | Estimate 1996 | Forecast 2005 | Average Growth 1985– 1995 | Annual Rate (%) 1995– 2005* |
|---|---|---|---|---|---|---|
| **Total Scheduled Services** | | | | | | |
| Passenger-kilometres (billions) | | | | | | |
| Africa | 36.7 | 51.0 | 55.4 | 77 | 3.3 | 4.0 |
| Asia/Pacific | 222.3 | 549.7 | 600.6 | 1,260 | 9.5 | 8.5 |
| Europe | 428.2 | 549.3 | 586.7 | 870 | 2.5 | 4.5 |
| Middle East | 42.7 | 67.0 | 72.0 | 115 | 4.6 | 5.5 |
| North America | 569.2 | 902.7 | 963.0 | 1,310 | 4.7 | 4.0 |
| Latin America and Caribbean | 68.3 | 107.9 | 114.4 | 175 | 4.7 | 5.0 |
| Freight tonne-kilometres (millions) | | | | | | |
| Africa | 1,163 | 1,418 | 1,523 | 2,050 | 2.0 | 4.0 |
| Asia/Pacific | 9,605 | 28,346 | 30,158 | 71,000 | 11.4 | 9.5 |
| Europe | 14,422 | 24,607 | 25,874 | 40,900 | 5.5 | 5.0 |
| Middle East | 1,880 | 3,775 | 3,995 | 6,800 | 7.2 | 6.0 |

| | | | | | | |
|---|---|---|---|---|---|---|
| North America | 10,622 | 21,253 | 22,111 | 36,200 | 7.2 | 5.5 |
| Latin America and Caribbean | 2,105 | 3,683 | 4,010 | 7,000 | 5.8 | 6.5 |
| **International Scheduled Services** | | | | | | |
| Passenger-kilometres (billions) | | | | | | |
| Africa | 28.6 | 42.1 | 46.1 | 65 | 3.9 | 4.5 |
| Asia/Pacific | 150.2 | 372.9 | 412.7 | 870 | 9.5 | 9.0 |
| Europe | 202.7 | 426.8 | 474.1 | 735 | 7.7 | 5.5 |
| Middle East | 35.2 | 57.1 | 60.4 | 100 | 5.0 | 6.0 |
| North America | 125.3 | 271.7 | 290.7 | 495 | 8.0 | 6.0 |
| Latin America and Caribbean | 36.5 | 70.3 | 77.3 | 130 | 6.8 | 6.5 |
| Freight tonne-kilometres (millions) | | | | | | |
| Africa | 1,070 | 1,320 | 1,425 | 1,920 | 2.1 | 4.0 |
| Asia/Pacific | 8,589 | 26,243 | 27,948 | 66,900 | 11.8 | 10.0 |
| Europe | 11,589 | 23,815 | 25,073 | 40,000 | 7.5 | 5.5 |
| Middle East | 1,807 | 3,694 | 3,900 | 6,700 | 7.4 | 6.0 |
| North America | 4,842 | 12,162 | 12,771 | 24,000 | 9.6 | 7.0 |
| Latin America and Caribbean | 1,487 | 3,039 | 3,400 | 6,200 | 7.4 | 7.5 |

* Rounded to the nearest 0.5 percentage point.

## III – By International Route Group

| | Passengers Carried (Thousands) | | | Average Growth | Annual Rate (%) |
|---|---|---|---|---|---|
| | Actual 1985 | Actual 1995 | Forecast 2005 | 1985–1995 | 1995–2005* |
| **International Scheduled Services** | | | | | |
| North Atlantic | 20,964 | 38,100 | 59,168 | 6.2 | 4.5 |
| Mid Atlantic | 1,471 | 2,570 | 4,186 | 5.7 | 5.0 |
| South Atlantic | 1,244 | 3,260 | 5,838 | 10.1 | 6.0 |
| Trans-Pacific | 8,028 | 19,213 | 37,795 | 9.1 | 7.0 |
| Between Europe and Asia/Pacific | 5,870 | 20,400 | 42,045 | 13.3 | 7.5 |
| Between Europe and Africa | 9,280 | 11,000 | 14,783 | 1.7 | 3.0 |
| Between Europe and Middle East | 3,920 | 7,080 | 9,987 | 6.1 | 3.5 |
| Between North America and South America | 2,622 | 7,445 | 14,100 | 11.0 | 6.5 |
| Between North America and Central America/Caribbean | 15,562 | 24,684 | 38,333 | 4.7 | 4.5 |
| Total above routes | 68,961 | 133,752 | 226,237 | 6.8 | 5.5 |
| Other routes | 124,974 | 239,007 | 453,763 | 6.7 | 6.5 |
| Total world | 193,935 | 372,759 | 680,000 | 6.8 | 6.0 |

* Rounded to the nearest 0.5 percentage point.

# MAS acts as destination marketeers

**By AHMAD ZUBER IBRAHIM**

MALAYSIA Airlines (MAS) is leaving no stone unturned in its quest to make Malaysia a favoured tourist destination.

The national carrier, responsible for ferrying 75% of tourists to the country annually, has recently added another portfolio — that of a destination marketeer.

"MAS is offering state governments and other related bodies our services as tourism consultants. Having been an active player and catalyst for the industry for a long time, MAS is proud to stake a claim as an expert in tourism," said MAS vice-president, (sales) Datuk Rashid Khan.

Rashid said although Malaysia had many attractive tourism products — the country still lagged behind neighbours who seemed to be luring more tourists to their shores.

"It is always difficult to sell Malaysia as a destination, what with more well known destinations just next door. Thailand has been very successful with its *Amazing Thailand* promotion and hopefully our new promotion will do the same.

"Indonesia, for instance, is all about Bali and nothing else. For Malaysia, the focus will be on our many beautiful destinations and cultural mix.

"I do not see destination marketing as an added responsibility but just doing more of what we are doing especially by our subsidiary Golden Holidays."

Rashid said MAS was working closely with other tourism bodies like the Malaysian Tourist Promotion Board and state tourism committees and related agencies to ensure that tourists know of Malaysia's many tourism products.

He said MAS' additional responsibility was the result of an act of god — the haze that blanketed most of the region way back in 1998.

*Datuk Rashid Khan*

Negative media reports on Malaysia, which badly affected the tourism industry leading to faltering tourist arrivals amidst an economic turmoil, woke up many industry players.

"The adverse impact it had on our tourists arrival made MAS take a more active role in developing and promoting the industry," said Rashid.

One of the worst hit destination then was Langkawi, an island resort very much dependent on inbound tourist and MAS was asked to assist in whatever way it could to lure back tourists.

Approached by the Langkawi Development Authority, MAS sat down with the state government and tourism bodies and related sectors and put the tourism industry model in motion.

"We then pooled resources and designed a comprehensive Langkawi tourism brochure distributed at international travel and tourism fairs worldwide.

"The brochures contained all the tourism products that Langkawi has to offer. As such, small time tourism operators like for example the one at Kampung Tok Senik get international exposure through the brochure.

"The Langkawi Travel Mart 1999 was later launched and the island attracted 30,000 visitors between Aug and Dec."

Rashid said for MAS, the main contributor was its *Langkawi Supersavers* packages which proved to be a big hit.

Since then, MAS has been pretty busy and recently helped the Sabah Government package its Sabah 2000 promotion.

"We are ever willing to assist any state government in their tourism marketing and packaging. MAS has also been approached by Malacca to do a similar job and will do the same for others if asked to."

However, Rashid said state governments must from now on try to understand how the tourism mechanism really works.

"Their tourism bodies must take it upon themselves to promote the products available by going to meet the market source. All these while, they have been depending on other agencies to do the job but now it is not enough.

"They will have to do the marketing as there are so many desti-nations to promote and so little time."

On the aviation industry, Rashid said the attractive *Sabah 2000* package recently launched was aimed at getting more tourists to visit Sabah and not a price war as suggested by some quarters.

"It is just a marketing strategy. In a way, the fact that other airlines are coming in with attractive packages is a sign of healthy competition and show there is no such thing as a monopoly."

Rashid added as the national carrier, MAS has had to make many sacrifices like maintaining low domestic fares despite rising fuel costs although it has its advantages too.

*One of the worst hit destination then was Langkawi, an island resort very much dependent on inbound tourist and MAS was asked to assist in whatever way it could to lure back tourists*

*Figure 13* (*Source: The Star, 13th March 2000*)

# The MAS dream can come true

Stories by YONG MIN WEI

THE vision of our national carrier Malaysia Airlines (MAS) to be among the largest, most successful airlines in the world is achievable, but a lot of hard work lies ahead, given the fiercely competitive nature of the business.

The string of awards achieved in the 90s continues with the airline being awarded the prestigious five-star *Diamond* award by the American Academy of Hospitality Sciences in January for outstanding commitment to service and hospitality.

In February, MAS was voted first for its inflight service by the *Luxury Travel* magazine in a survey conducted by 10 of Australia's leading travel writers on the worldwide business class travel experiences.

For MAS to achieve its vision, it will need a consistently high level of service from ground to air, encompassing flight reservations, check-in staff, catering and in-flight service.

MAS currently flies to 114 destina-

| ✈ malaysia | JAPANESE PASSENGERS ON MAS FLIGHTS TO MALAYSIA | | |
|---|---|---|---|
| | Apr99-Mar00 | Apr98-Mar99 | Percentage (%) |
| Tokyo | 74,987 | 72,574 | 3.3 |
| Nagoya | 26,823 | 22,132 | 21.2 |
| Osaka | 48,420 | 28,233 | 71.5 |
| Fukuoka | 15,650 | 19,978 | (21.7) |
| **TOTAL** | **165,880** | **142,917** | **16.1** |

tions across six continents and has a modern fleet of aircraft.which is progressively upgraded.

For passenger comfort, its *B747* and *B777* aircraft are equipped with first class and business class seats.

The *B747* and *B777* have in-flight entertainment with in-seat video screens for all passsengers, equipped with 32 audio channels and 12 video channels.

The video screens informs passen-

gers with the latest news and financial updates via satelite while children would be able to enjoy *Nintendo* and other PC games.

MAS expects its high degree of responsibility, dedication and commitment from its flight stewards and stewardesses.

The airline believes in service as a privilege and that cabin crew should always be attentive and efficient to passengers.

During a MAS media trip last week, some passengers and cabin crew had this to say on board an MAS flight from Kuala Lumpur to Tokyo:

● **Masafumi Asai, executive director (Japanese):** "This is my second flight on board MAS and I am pleased with the service, taking into consideration the long flying hours. The aircraft is clean and the seats are very comfortable. What impresses me most is the kind and friendly service of the crew who are happy to entertain passenger requests."

● **John J. Hoffman, contracts manager (American):** "I am a frequent flyer on MAS and I would say that the service is incredible, irrespective of which class a passenger is travelling. I have travelled on the MAS first, business and economy classes, and find that the cabin crew genuinely enjoy serving passengers. The attitude of the cabin crew seems to be the driving force behind the bagging of MAS awards and worldwide recognition for the airline."

● **Dr Ahmed Tasir Lope Pihie, chief executive (Malaysian):** "Since my first MAS flight in 1976, I have grown with the airline and enjoy flying on it as it suits my lifestyle. The service is better than most airlines although I personally have encountered some unfriendly experiences in my years of travelling. I have to say that MAS has done well but could do better, particularly when the first impression of tourists to Malaysia depends on the attitude of the cabin crew.

● **A. Rajasegaran, MAS chief steward (19-year experience):** "*Service with a smile* is what the cabin crew practises. This is very important. We must be able to maintain the standards of our service by being very attentive to passengers. Passengers have different priorities such as privacy, comfort and entertainment, thus the crew are trained to identify different needs. The perception that MAS often treats foreigners better is incorrect as the crew treat each passenger equally irrespective of race."

*Figure 14 (Source: The Star, 3rd April 2000)*

# MAS making inroads Down Under

MELBOURNE: Malaysia Airlines (MAS), already experiencing unprecedented popularity in Australia, is set to grab a bigger share of the aviation market here with the introduction of additional flights, starting today.

By the end of the week, MAS will have 13 departures a week each from Sydney and Melbourne, and from July 10, the airline will double its number of flights a week from Perth. MAS will have 1,400 more seats on the Australia-Malaysia service.

"This is part of our strategy to increase our Australian market share, which stands at more than 6%," said Azlan Hussain, MAS vice-president for Australia, New Zealand and South West Pacific.

"We have worked together very effectively and we are seeing good results," he said.

He said tourism officials at Penang, Langkawi, Kuala Lumpur and Sabah have been active promoting their attractions.

"I took 10 of Australia's leading tour operators to Sabah recently.

be on the 747 aircraft. Perth will have the 777.

Azlan paid tribute to the co-operation received from major Australian tour operators and his own staff.

"We have achieved a load factor of 79% for all our Australian routes and this is a fantastic achievement. We hope to improve even further with our additional flights."

Azlan, who runs the Australia and New Zealand operations from last July, said Sydney-Melbourne flights would

"They were all most impressed with what Sabah had to offer. The Sabah Government officials and tourism people there gave our Australian friends a very warm welcome and their presentation was first-class," he said.

Azlan would be taking another group of Australian tour operators to Langkawi this month.

He said MAS had received a good hearing from the Australian Civil Aviation Authority in its successful application from more flights.

"They have been most helpful and very good to us. The Australia and New Zealand region is a very important market for MAS. There is excellent potential for growth.

"With the introduction of the new flights, MAS will have 55 departures a week from Australia's main cities. We have seven flights a week to New Zealand.

"We plan to have more flights when demand increases. More Australians are flying MAS on the kangaroo route to Britain and Europe. A

stopover in Kuala Lumpur, Penang or Langkawi is welcomed by Australians who make the long journey to Europe. And then we have a big Malaysian student population here who fly MAS."

Azlan said Malaysian investment in Australia was picking up following the economic recovery in the region.

"So we have a lot of business people flying to and fro now. Also Australian investors are going to the region seeking business opportunities," he added. — Bernama

*Figure 15 (Source: The Star, 3rd July 2000)*

# Three new Indian destinations for Malaysia Airlines

**Besides flights to New Delhi and Chennai, Malaysia Airlines will fly to Mumbai, Bangalore and Hyderabad**

### By ZETY FAZILAH BAHARUDDIN

MALAYSIA Airlines will offer direct flights from Kuala Lumpur to three new destinations in India by next month, which will make the national carrier the international airline with the biggest number of destinations in that country.

Besides the existing services to New Delhi and Chennai (formerly Madras), Malaysia Airlines will fly to Mumbai (formerly Bombay), Bangalore and Hyderabad.

Transport Minister Datuk Seri Dr Ling Liong Sik, who announced this yesterday, said approval has been given by the Indian authorities, despite complaints over the increase of airfares to Chennai recently.

"The approval was granted to Malaysia Airlines by the Indian Civil Aviation Ministry after two meetings.

"The first meeting was held in Kuala Lumpur two weeks ago, while the second was in India," he told newsmen after attending this week's Cabinet meeting in Kuala Lumpur.

Following the approval, Malaysian Airlines will add seven flights to India from the existing two flights a week to New Delhi and daily flights to Chennai.

Under the latest agreement, Malaysia Airlines will fly four times a week to Mumbai, twice to Bangalore and once a week to Hyderabad.

Apart from this, Malaysia Airlines was granted an additional two flights a week to New Delhi.

On the increase in airfares to Chennai, which was brought up by the Indian Chamber of Commerce, Dr Ling said it should not be blown out of proportion as this is a commercial issue.

"Why must they specifically raise the airfare issue on the Kuala Lumpur-Chennai route, when the increase was actually across the board?" he asked.

Dr Ling explained that the airfare increase is not only on specific routes but throughout the region. For instance, he said, the Kuala Lumpur-Los Angeles route saw a 45 per cent increase.

Furthermore, he added, Malaysia Airlines is not the only airline that increased airfares as carriers of other countries in the region — such as Taiwan, Hong Kong, Indonesia and the Philippines — are doing the same.

With the price increase, passengers from Kuala Lumpur to Chennai have to pay an extra RM300 from today.

On domestic airfares, Dr Ling agreed with Malaysia Airlines that the national carrier has not revised its air ticket prices since 1982.

During the period, he said, airfares in the Philippines have been revised upwards nine times, Taiwan three times, South Korea six times, Indonesia five times and Thailand four times.

Malaysia Airlines' fares are the cheapest in the world at 43 sen per nautical mile per passenger, compared with 77 sen in Indonesia, 52 sen in Thailand, 43 sen in the Philippines, A$1.65 (A$1 = RM2.14) in Australia, 52 sen in India and US$3.42 (US$1 = RM3.80) in the US.

*Figure 16* *(Source: Business Times, 14th September 2000)*

# Long-term prospects still look promising

Nervousness set in when the dotcom bubble came under strain, but many feel the best of online trading is yet to come

Speed kills, observed the San Francisco-based internet research company Webmergers.com recently, referring to the past year's rash of dotcom failures. The new medium's early lift-off has inspired "fantasyland assumptions" about the rate at which it would continue to develop.

"The flattened bodies now littering the information highway are victims of a sector that was travelling at an unsafe rate of speed," says Webmergers.

Business travel organisers might argue that, just as timid drivers can be a hazard on motorways, slowness has also been a factor – the time taken to access and navigate web sites and the need for greater acceleration if online booking systems are to catch up with the eager expectations prompted by their launch.

While only a handful of the 100-plus e-commerce companies which went out of business in 2000 were internet travel agencies, general nervousness about the dotcom sector can have done nothing to encourage growth in internet reservations.

Whether it is actually deterring business users is as yet unknown but in any case, believes Ian Hall, chairman of the Institute of Travel Managers in the UK and Ireland, corporate e-booking has reached a plateau. Companies excited by the prospect of saving time and cutting costs by organising everything online are now looking longer and harder at the potential value of the associated IT investments.

"There was clearly more interest two years ago when dotcom companies were coming to the fore, but people have discovered that they were less likely to be able to use the systems as rapidly and effectively as they thought they would," says Mr Hall.

"From the travel manager's point of view, this means there has been a rethink. It was thought e-booking could stand alone, but companies are now looking to integrate it with the whole procurement and payment process. When extranets are developed, with direct access to particular suppliers, they will need to be able to allow communication with other suppliers to enhance the overall flow of information.

"I am sure it will continue to develop, but until it's easier for people to get all the information they want and make all the changes they need online they will still want to pick up the telephone and talk to someone."

David Boni, director of distribution development at Hilton International, accepts that efforts to launch corporate extranets have been slow to take off, but says that, overall, bookings taken via the internet have more than doubled during the past year. "They probably make up about 4 per cent, and while it is hard to say absolutely whether guests are travelling on business, I would say there is a roughly even split between them and leisure travellers."

Patrick Brugger, Sabena's director of e-business development, agrees that "a lot of companies are not too enthusiastic", but says the Belgian airline is working to provide them with individual solu-

## BA has seen a 40% increase in web bookings over the past year

tions. "Rather than going for one size that fits all we are concentrating first on our biggest accounts, looking at ways to ensure compliance with travel policies, for example, and providing reports for finance departments without obliging the customer to change their existing systems substantially or buy new ones. There are cost savings in this for both sides."

British Airways, in contrast, says that while it was encountering reluctance to set up extranets a year or so ago, that has changed. "It seems to have completely flipped now," says Pat Gaffey, head of e-commerce at BA. "We have about 165 and we are getting more every week. There is also a lot of interest from overseas. We are about to implement 10 in the New York area.

"We don't have booking engines in them yet, but we are working with two corporates in the UK to put them in."

Mr Gaffey accepts that the recent travails of the dotcom sector have created "an aura of cynicism", particularly in Europe, but says that, despite this, the airline has seen a 40 per cent rise in online bookings over the past year.

Although such bookings still represent only a small percentage of airline industry business, figures from two leading US carriers also contradict any suggestion that they have tapered off. American Airlines says that, up to last July at least, the number of flights booked by frequent travellers on its web site was still growing rapidly.

Delta, which says revenues from online sales to business and leisure passengers now account for 5 per cent of all its reservations, saw the figure rise 270 per cent last year.

One reason some companies have been slow to embrace the brave new world is the prospect of staff wasting valuable time – and money – booking complex trips on the web. Increasingly, they are compromising by introducing systems which allow employees to check flights and availability but oblige them to channel their requests through a travel manager or agent.

The BBC has just launched such a system. Covering all the broadcaster's travel and transport needs, from flights to taxis, it provides staff with an onscreen form to fill in.

"Suppose they want to go to Hamburg.", says travel manager Alan Waddell. "They can surf the web to see how they want to get there and where they want to stay. Then they enter that on the form which is e-mailed automatically to our travel agent. This gets around the problem that the traveller might want to go out with one airline and back with a different one, for example. The agent looks at the booking and checks that this is the best way to do it, then sends a confirmation back to the booker with a reference and price. The same information also goes back to the relevant budget-holder."

Mr Waddell reflects the prevailing view, however, that the e-booking revolution is one of those great leaps whose short-term impact has been over-estimated but whose long-term effect is being under-estimated.

"In an increasingly ticketless environment, the whole booking process for simple travel will move online," he says.

*(Source: Financial Times, 12th February 2001)*

## Appendix 3
### *Performance Highlights*

| | | 1999/00 | 1998/99 | % Change |
|---|---|---|---|---|
| **GROUP** | | | | |
| **Financial** | | | | |
| Total Revenue | RM Million | **8,288.3** | 7,510.1 | **+10.4** |
| Total Expenditure | RM Million | **9,566.1** | 8,621.5 | **+11.0** |
| Profit/(Loss) After Tax | RM Million | **(255.7)** | (696.7) | **−63.3** |
| Shareholders' Funds | RM Million | **3,222.3** | 3,496.2 | **−7.8** |
| Earnings/(Losses) Per Share | Sen | **(33.6)** | (90.9) | **−63.0** |
| Dividend Per Share | Sen | **2.0** | 2.0 | **+0.0** |
| Cash Flow Per Share | RM | **0.6** | 1.3 | **−53.8** |
| **Operating Statistics** | | | | |
| Available Tonne Kilometres | Million | **7,531.5** | 6,649.1 | **+13.3** |
| Load Tonne Kilometres | Million | **4,853.4** | 4,246.9* | **+14.3** |
| Overall Load Factor | % | **64.5** | 63.9* | **+0.6** |
| Available Seat Kilometres | Million | **48,905.5** | 45,442.3 | **+7.6** |
| Passenger Kilometres Flown | Million | **34,930.1** | 30,592.9 | **+14.2** |
| Passenger Load Factor | % | **71.4** | 67.3 | **+4.1** |
| **Staff and Productivity** | | | | |
| Employee Strength | | **21,587** | 23,076 | **−6.5** |
| Available Tonne Kilometres Per Employee | | **348,890** | 288,141 | **+21.1** |
| Load Tonne Kilometres Per Employee | | **224,829** | 184,039* | **+22.2** |
| **COMPANY** | | | | |
| **Operating Statistics** | | | | |
| Available Tonne Kilometres | Million | **6,344.7** | 5,787.5 | **+9.6** |
| Load Tonne Kilometres | Million | **4,246.0** | 3,719.3* | **+14.2** |
| Overall Load Factor | % | **66.9** | 64.3* | **+2.6** |
| Available Seat Kilometres | Million | **48,906.0** | 45,442.3 | **+7.6** |
| Passenger Kilometres Flown | Million | **34,930.1** | 30,592.9 | **+14.2** |
| Passenger Load Factor | % | **71.4** | 67.3 | **+4.1** |
| Aircraft Utilization (Average) | Hours Per Day | **9.6** | 8.9 | **+7.9** |
| **Staff and Productivity** | | | | |
| Employee Strength | | **16,427** | 17,313 | **−5.1** |
| Available Tonne Kilometres Per Employee | | **386,238** | 334,285 | **+15.5** |
| Load Tonne Kilometres Per Employee | | **258,477** | 214,829* | **+20.3** |

* Revised based on standard free baggage weight.
(*Source*: Malaysian Airline System Berhad, 1999 Annual Report)

### Directors Report

The directors hereby submit their report together with the audited accounts of the Company and of the Group for the financial year ended 31st March 2000.

### Principal Activities

The Company is principally engaged in the business of air transportation and the provision of related services.

The principal activities of the subsidiaries are described in Note 27 to the accounts.

There were no significant changes in these activities during the financial year.

### Results

|  | Group RM'000 | Company RM'000 |
|---|---|---|
| Loss after taxation | (258,574) | (41,301) |
| Transfer from general reserve | 200,000 | 200,000 |
|  | (58,574) | 158,699 |
| Retained profits brought forward | 99,506 | 164,919 |
| Profit available for appropriation | 40,932 | 323,618 |
| Proposed tax exempt dividends of 2% | (15,400) | (15,400) |
| Retained profits carried forward | 25,532 | 308,218 |

### Balance Sheets (as at 31st March 2000)

|  | Note | Group 2000 RM'000 | Group 1999 RM'000 | Company 2000 RM'000 | Company 1999 RM'000 |
|---|---|---|---|---|---|
| **Current Assets** |  |  |  |  |  |
| Cash and cash equivalents | 3 | 965,426 | 543,663 | 926,153 | 525,226 |
| Debtors | 4 | 1,754,612 | 1,452,727 | 1,706,610 | 1,373,476 |
| Stocks | 5 | 336,743 | 312,913 | 327,880 | 296,344 |
|  |  | 3,056,781 | 2,309,303 | 2,960,643 | 2,195,046 |
| **Current Liabilities** |  |  |  |  |  |
| Creditors | 6 | 2,377,190 | 2,077,438 | 2,134,001 | 1,983,985 |
| Borrowings | 7 | 951,318 | 1,565,852 | 951,318 | 1,565,852 |
| Other liabilities | 8 | 1,493,561 | 1,336,229 | 1,493,561 | 1,336,229 |
| Taxation |  | 73,994 | 100,024 | 67,574 | 77,670 |
| Proposed dividend |  | 15,400 | 15,400 | 15,400 | 15,400 |
|  |  | 4,911,463 | 5,094,943 | 4,661,854 | 4,979,136 |
| **Net Current Liabilities** |  | (1,854,682) | (2,785,640) | (1,701,211) | (2,784,090) |
| **Fixed Assets** | 9 | 12,311,144 | 14,231,647 | 11,782,472 | 13,670,565 |
| **Investments** | 10 | 283,807 | 151,031 | 927,620 | 763,581 |

| | | Group | | Company | |
|---|---|---|---|---|---|
| Deferred Charges | 11 | **2,400,693** | 2,813,679 | **2,400,693** | 2,813,679 |
| Due to a Subsidiary | 12 | **–** | – | **(1,795,500)** | (1,581,000) |
| Borrowings | 7 | **(9,388,594)** | (10,295,987) | **(7,593,094)** | (8,714,987) |
| Deferred Income | 13 | **(517,548)** | (607,615) | **(517,548)** | (607,615) |
| Deferred Taxation | 14 | **(1,433)** | (1,656) | **–** | – |
| | | **3,233,387** | 3,505,459 | **3,503,432** | 3,560,133 |
| **Represented by:** | | | | | |
| Share capital | 15 | **770,000** | 770,000 | **770,000** | 770,000 |
| Share premium | | **1,925,214** | 1,925,214 | **1,925,214** | 1,925,214 |
| General reserve | 16 | **501,530** | 701,530 | **500,000** | 700,000 |
| Retained profits | | **25,532** | 99,506 | **308,218** | 164,919 |
| Shareholders' funds | | **3,222,276** | 3,496,250 | **3,503,432** | 3,560,133 |
| Minority interests | | **11,111** | 9,209 | **–** | – |
| | | 3,233,387 | 3,505,459 | 3,503,432 | 3,560,133 |

(*Source:* Malaysian Airline System Berhad, 1999 Annual Report)

### Profit and Loss Accounts (as at 31st March 2000)

| | | Group | | Company | |
|---|---|---|---|---|---|
| | **Note** | **2000** | 1999 | **2000** | 1999 |
| | | **RM'000** | RM'000 | **RM'000** | RM'000 |
| Turnover | 17 | **8,160,737** | 7,471,861 | **7,152,175** | 6,635,930 |
| Loss for the year | 18 | **(1,277,768)** | (1,111,364) | **(1,077,145)** | (1,035,025) |
| Profit on sale of aircraft and spare engines | | **949,965** | 395,518 | **949,965** | 395,518 |
| Share of losses of associated companies | | **(9,509)** | (16,618) | **–** | – |
| Loss before exceptional item | | **(337,312)** | (732,464) | **(127,180)** | (639,507) |
| Exceptional item | 19 | **100,422** | 62,729 | **100,422** | 62,729 |
| Loss after taxation | | **(236,890)** | (669,735) | **(26,758)** | (576,778) |
| Taxation | 20 | **(18,813)** | (26,961) | **(14,543)** | (27,832) |
| Loss after taxation before minority interests | | **(255,703)** | (696,696) | **(41,301)** | (604,610) |
| Minority interests | | **(2,871)** | (3,355) | **–** | – |
| Loss after taxation and minority interests | | **(258,574)** | (700,051) | **(41,301)** | (604,610) |
| Transfer from general reserve | 16 | **200,000** | 500,000 | **200,000** | 500,000 |
| | | **(58,574)** | (200,051) | **158,699** | (104,610) |
| Retained profits brought forward | | **99,506** | 314,957 | **164,919** | 284,929 |

| | | | | |
|---|---|---|---|---|
| Profit available for appropriation | | **40,932** | 114,906 | **323,618** | 180,319 |
| Proposed dividends | 21 | **(15,400)** | (15,400) | **(15,400)** | (15,400) |
| Retained profits carried forward | | **25,532** | 99,506 | **308,218** | 164,919 |
| Retained by: | | | | | |
| The Company | | **308,218** | 164,919 | | |
| Subsidiaries | | **(247,096)** | (38,840) | | |
| Associated companies | | **(35,590)** | (26,573) | | |
| | | **25,532** | 99,506 | | |
| Loss per share | 22 | **(33.6 sen)** | (90.6 sen) | | |

(*Source:* Malaysian Airline System Berhad, 1999 Annual Report)

## Consolidated Cash Flow Statement (for the year ended 31st March 2000)

| | 2000 RM'000 | 1999 RM'000 |
|---|---|---|
| **Cash Flow from Operating Activities** | | |
| Loss before taxation | **(236,890)** | (669,735) |
| Adjustment for: | | |
| Loss retained in associated companies | **9,509** | 17,306 |
| Depreciation of fixed assets | **1,130,442** | 1,151,010 |
| Profit on sales of aircraft and spare engines | **(949,965)** | (395,518) |
| Profit on sale of fixed assets | **(693)** | (19,174) |
| Gain on disposal of investment | **(100,493)** | (62,729) |
| Provision for doubtful debts | **48,883** | 28,857 |
| Provision for Year 2000 program | **–** | 44,836 |
| Amortization of deferred income/charges | **(87,459)** | (113,875) |
| Aircraft spares deleted | **16,540** | 16,871 |
| Provision for aircraft maintenance | **341,825** | 301,211 |
| Writeback of unavailed credit balances on sales in advance of carriage | **(26,112)** | (23,524) |
| Unrealized exchange loss amortised | **605,061** | 578,871 |
| Provision for stock obsolescence | **13,411** | 14,891 |
| Stocks written back | **(5,313)** | 10 |
| Fixed assets written off | **212** | – |
| Deposits written off | **54** | – |
| Interest income | **(67,078)** | (28,914) |
| Dividend income | **(1,870)** | (839) |
| Interest expenses | **563,307** | 659,166 |
| Operating profit before working capital changes | **1,253,371** | 1,498,721 |
| Increase in debtors | **(318,275)** | (252,337) |

| | (31,928) | (59,208) |
|---|---|---|
| Increase in stocks | **(31,928)** | (59,208) |
| Increase in creditors | **450,366** | 422,342 |
| (Increase)/decrease in due from associated companies | **(6,670)** | 12,094 |
| Increase in sales in advance of carriage | **170,479** | 139,248 |
| Decrease in provision for aircraft maintenance | **(328,860)** | (92,381) |
| Cash generated from operations | **1,188,483** | 1,668,479 |
| Interest paid | **(713,921)** | (659,166) |
| Taxes paid | **(45,558)** | (8,755) |
| Net cash generated from operating activities | **429,004** | 1,000,558 |

(*Source:* Malaysian Airline System Berhad, 1999 Annual Report)

## Consolidated Cash Flow Statement (for the year ended 31st March 2000)

| | 2000 RM'000 | 1999 RM'000 |
|---|---|---|
| **Cash Flow from Investing Activities** | | |
| Purchase of investment in associated companies | **(5,124)** | (5,519) |
| Proceeds from sale of other investments | **103,696** | 78,534 |
| Purchase of other investments | **(133,202)** | (8,572) |
| Purchase of fixed assets | **(1,663,689)** | (1,759,666) |
| Proceeds on sale of assets | **3,387,602** | 964,145 |
| Interest received | **34,585** | 28,914 |
| Dividend received | **1,870** | 839 |
| Net cash generated from/(used in) investing activities | **1,725,738** | (701,325) |
| **Cash Flow from Financing Activities** | | |
| Drawdown of term loans | **556,000** | 1,126,082 |
| Repayment of terms loans | **(1,560,090)** | (1,145,664) |
| Lease payments | **(712,520)** | (510,343) |
| Dividends paid | **(15,400)** | (15,400) |
| Dividends paid to minority interest in a subsidiary | **(969)** | (2,146) |
| Net cash used in financing activities | **(1,732,979)** | (547,471) |
| Net increase/(decrease) in cash and cash equivalents | **421,763** | (248,238) |
| Cash and cash equivalents at beginning of year | **543,663** | 791,901 |
| Cash and cash equivalents at end of year | **965,426** | 543,663 |
| Cash and cash equivalents comprise: | | |
| Cash and bank balances | **103,362** | 145,136 |
| Short term deposits | **862,064** | 398,527 |
| | **965,426** | 543,663 |

(*Source:* Malaysian Airline System Berhad, 1999 Annual Report)

### Aircraft and Spare Engines

(*Source*: Malaysian Airline System Berhad, 1999 Annual Report)

Aircraft and spare engines are depreciated over their estimated useful commercial lives having regard to their planned withdrawal from service. Life-years and residual values are as follows:

|                | Life-years | Residual Value as a Percentage of Cost |
|----------------|------------|-----------------------------------------|
| Boeing 777     | 15         | 20                                      |
| Boeing 747     | 7–15       | 20                                      |
| Airbus A330-300| 15         | 20                                      |
| Airbus A300B4  | 15         | 20                                      |
| DC10-30        | 7–15       | 20                                      |
| Boeing 737     | 10         | 20                                      |
| Fokker F50     | 10         | 20                                      |
| Twin Otter     | 7          | 20                                      |
| Spare engines  | 7–15       | Nil                                     |

### Share Capital

(*Source*: Malaysian Airline System Berhad, 1999 Annual Report)

|                                                                     | Group and Company | |
|---------------------------------------------------------------------|-------------------|----------------|
|                                                                     | 2000 RM'000       | 1999 RM'000    |
| **Authorized:**                                                     |                   |                |
| Ordinary shares of RM1.00 each                                      | 5,000,000         | 5,000,000      |
| One special rights redeemable preference share of RM1.00*           | –                 | –              |
|                                                                     | 5,000,000         | 5,000,000      |
| **Issued and fully paid:**                                          |                   |                |
| Ordinary shares of RM1.00 each                                      | 770,000           | 770,000        |
| One special rights redeemable preference share of RM1.00*           | –                 | –              |
|                                                                     | 770,000           | 770,000        |

* The Special Rights Redeemable Preference Share (Special Share) would enable the Government through the Minister of Finance (Incorporated) to ensure that certain major decisions affecting the operations of the Company are consistent with the Government's policy. The Special Share, which may only be held by the Minister of Finance (Incorporated) or its successors or any Minister, representative, or any person acting on behalf of the Government of Malaysia, carries certain special rights as provided by Article 5 of the Company's Articles of Association (as amended at the Extraordinary General Meeting held on 19th April 1995). These special rights include:

i) The right to appoint not more than three persons at any time as directors of the Company.

ii) The right to repayment of the capital paid up on the Special Share in priority to any other member in the event of a winding-up of the Company.

iii) The right to require the Company to redeem the Special Share at par at any time.

Certain matters, in particular the alterations of specified Articles of Association of the Company, require the prior approval of the holder of the Special Share. The Special Share does not carry any right to vote at General Meetings but the holder is entitled to attend and speak at such meetings.

## General Reserve

(*Source*: Malaysian Airline System Berhad, 1999 Annual Report)

| | Group | | Company | |
|---|---|---|---|---|
| | **2000 RM'000** | 1999 RM'000 | **2000 RM'000** | 1999 RM'000 |
| **Distributable:** | | | | |
| At 1st April | **701,530** | 1,201,530 | **700,000** | 1,200,000 |
| Transfer to profit and loss account | **(200,000)** | (500,000) | **(200,000)** | (500,000) |
| At 31st March | **501,530** | 701,530 | **500,000** | 700,000 |

## Turnover

(*Source*: Malaysian Airline System Berhad, 1999 Annual Report)

| | Group | | Company | |
|---|---|---|---|---|
| | **2000 RM'000** | 1999 RM'000 | **2000 RM'000** | 1999 RM'000 |
| **Traffic revenue:** | | | | |
| Scheduled services | | | | |
| – Passenger and baggage | **5,988,716** | 5,310,210 | **5,988,716** | 5,310,210 |
| – Cargo and mail | **865,517** | 1,104,092 | **612,009** | 738,791 |
| | **6,854,233** | 6,414,302 | **6,600,725** | 6,049,001 |
| Non-scheduled services | **102,131** | 58,304 | **102,131** | 58,304 |
| Other revenue | **1,204,373** | 999,255 | **449,319** | 528,625 |
| | **8,160,737** | 7,471,861 | **7,152,175** | 6,635,930 |

Other revenue for the Group comprises aircraft charters and rental, provision of airport handling services, provision of trucking and warehousing services, coach transportation, computerised reservation services, civil aircraft turbine engine, component repair services, laundry services, catering services, retailing of goods, tour wholesaling and related activities.

## Segmental Information

(*Source*: Malaysian Airline System Berhad, 1999 Annual Report)

**Analysis by Business Activity:**

|  | Turnover 2000 RM'000 | 1999 RM'000 | Profit/(Loss) Before Taxation 2000 RM'000 | Profit/(Loss) Before Taxation 1999 RM'000 | Total Assets Employed 2000 RM'000 | Total Assets Employed 1999 RM'000 |
|---|---|---|---|---|---|---|
| Airline operations | 6,682,717 | 6,671,612 | (21,680) | (587,804) | 17,326,079 | 18,729,097 |
| Cargo services | 1,039,724 | 366,174 | (156,583) | (72,223) | 228,739 | 251,758 |
| Engineering services | 153,801 | 160,821 | (6,782) | 18,562 | 82,531 | 107,781 |
| Catering services | 203,916 | 203,204 | (38,169) | (25,873) | 163,018 | 188,511 |
| Others | 80,579 | 70,050 | (4,167) | 14,221 | 252,058 | 228,513 |
|  | 8,160,737 | 7,471,861 | (227,381) | (653,117) | 18,052,425 | 19,505,660 |
| Share of loss of associated companies | – | – | (9,509) | (16,618) | – | – |
|  | 8,160,737 | 7,471,861 | (236,890) | (669,735) | 18,052,425 | 19,505,660 |

## Revenue Composition by Category 1999/2000

(*Source*: Malaysian Airline System Berhad, 1999 Annual Report)

|  | 1999/00 RM Million | 1998/99 RM Million | Change % |
|---|---|---|---|
| **Group** | | | |
| Passenger | 6,053.4 | 5,328.7 | +13.6 |
| Cargo and Mail | 1,244.1 | 1,078.5 | +15.4 |
| Airport Services | 228.0 | 253.7 | −10.4 |
| Charters | 40.4 | 58.6 | −31.1 |
| Others | 722.4 | 785.3 | −8.0 |
|  | 8,288.3 | 7,504.8 | +10.4 |
| **Company** | | | |
| Passenger | 6,053.4 | 5,328.7 | +13.6 |
| Cargo and Mail | 612.0 | 738.8 | −17.2 |
| Airport Services | 100.7 | 122.6 | −17.9 |
| Charters | 28.7 | 51.6 | −44.4 |
| Others | 475.7 | 437.9 | +8.6 |
|  | 7,270.5 | 6,679.6 | +8.8 |

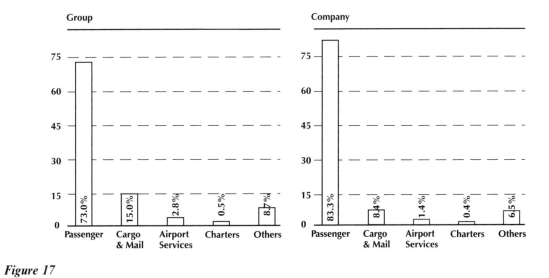

*Figure 17*

## Expenditure 1999/2000

(*Source*: Malaysian Airline System Berhad, 1999 Annual Report)

|  | 1999/00 RM Million | 1998/99 RM Million | Change % |
|---|---|---|---|
| **Group** |  |  |  |
| Staff Costs | 1,529.7 | 1,424.6 | +7.4 |
| Depreciation | 1,130.4 | 1,151.0 | −1.8 |
| Fuel and Oil | 1,569.3 | 1,083.5 | +44.8 |
| Ground Handling | 811.8 | 698.3 | +16.3 |
| Hire of Aircraft | 574.3 | 431.9 | +33.0 |
| Finance Charges | 563.3 | 659.2 | −14.5 |
| Commission | 541.5 | 477.0 | +13.5 |
| Loss on Foreign Exchange | 546.9 | 392.8 | +39.2 |
| Others | 2,298.9 | 2,303.2 | −0.2 |
|  | 9,566.1 | 8,621.5 | +11.0 |
| **Company** |  |  |  |
| Staff Costs | 1,269.8 | 1,192.3 | +6.5 |
| Depreciation | 1,061.8 | 1,111.3 | −4.5 |
| Fuel and Oil | 1,403.5 | 983.8 | +42.7 |
| Ground Handling | 708.7 | 622.4 | +13.9 |
| Hire of Aircraft | 395.6 | 355.4 | +11.3 |
| Finance Charges | 562.9 | 659.2 | −14.6 |
| Commission | 474.4 | 495.0 | −4.2 |
| Loss on Foreign Exchange | 547.5 | 393.4 | +39.2 |
| Others | 1,923.4 | 1,901.8 | +1.1 |
|  | 8,347.6 | 7,714.6 | +8.2 |

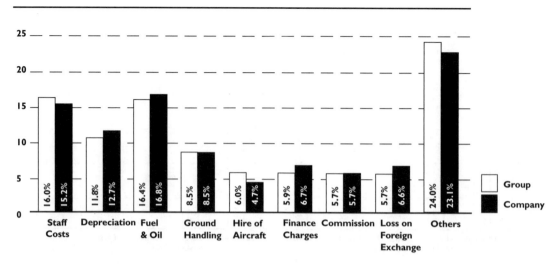

*Figure 18*

## Analysis of Airline Operations (including freighter) by geographical/route region

(*Source*: Malaysian Airline System Berhad, 1999 Annual Report)

| | 1999/00 | 1998/99 | % Change |
|---|---|---|---|
| **Route Revenue (RM Million)** | | | |
| Malaysia | 1,087.7 | 951.9 | +14.3 |
| Asia | 2,455.6 | 2,160.4 | +13.7 |
| Europe, Middle East and Africa | 2,365.6 | 2,111.8 | +12.0 |
| Australia and New Zealand | 1,010.6 | 828.5 | +22.0 |
| United States and Canada | 421.7 | 419.9 | +0.4 |
| | 7,341.2 | 6,472.5 | +13.4 |
| **Passenger Load Factor (%)** | **1999/00** | **1998/99** | **Points** |
| Malaysia | 76.5 | 65.9 | +10.6 |
| Asia | 66.9 | 60.1 | +6.8 |
| Europe, Middle East and Africa | 72.9 | 71.6 | +1.3 |
| Australia and New Zealand | 71.7 | 74.5 | −2.8 |
| United States and Canada | 72.1 | 63.7 | +8.4 |
| | 71.4 | 67.3 | +4.1 |
| **Overall Load Factor (%)** | **1999/00** | **1998/99** | **Points** |
| Malaysia | 68.9 | 59.1 | +9.8 |
| Asia | 65.3 | 60.4 | +4.9 |
| Europe, Middle East and Africa | 65.7 | 68.5 | −2.8 |
| Australia and New Zealand | 58.5 | 65.8 | −7.3 |
| United States and Canada | 66.7 | 65.6 | +1.1 |
| | 64.5 | 63.9 | +0.6 |

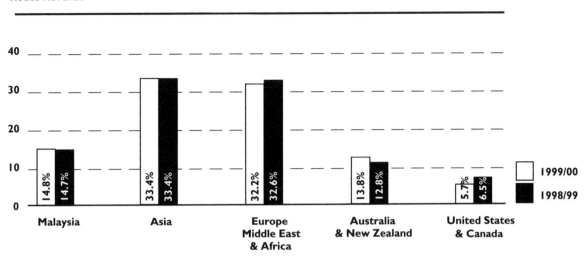

*Figure 19*

# Ten Years Statistical Review of the Company

| | | 1999/00 | 1998/99 | 1997/98 | 1996/97 | 1995/96 | 1994/95 | 1993/94 | 1992/93 | 1991/92 | 1990/91 |
|---|---|---|---|---|---|---|---|---|---|---|---|
| **Financial** | | | | | | | | | | | |
| Total Revenue | (RM'000) | 7,270,477 | 6,679,610 | 6,439,608 | 6,021,017 | 5,684,053 | 4,888,093 | 4,125,855 | 3,791,824 | 3,584,440 | 2,945,339 |
| Total Expenditure | (RM'000) | 8,347,623 | 7,714,635 | 7,285,813 | 5,735,164 | 5,456,639 | 4,746,375 | 4,123,861 | 3,975,421 | 3,546,085 | 3,114,006 |
| Taxation | (RM'000) | 14,543 | 27,832 | 27,922 | 9,340 | 9,304 | 8,394 | 6,696 | 9,932 | 5,112 | 5,776 |
| Profit/(Loss) After Tax and Exceptional Item | (RM'000) | (41,301) | (604,610) | (254,173) | 318,893 | 232,838 | 261,043 | 7,122 | 143,556 | 110,785 | 288,467 |
| Shareholders' Funds | (RM'000) | 3,503,431 | 3,560,133 | 4,180,143 | 4,449,716 | 3,662,261 | 3,485,774 | 3,272,152 | 3,277,036 | 1,452,116 | 1,385,081 |
| Profit/(Loss) as a % of Revenue | (%) | (0.5) | (9.0) | (3.9) | 5.3 | 3.8 | 2.8 | 0.2 | 3.8 | 3.1 | 6.7 |
| Return on Shareholders' Funds | (%) | (1.2) | (17.0) | (6.1) | 7.2 | 6.0 | 3.9 | 0.2 | 6.6 | 7.6 | 14.1 |
| Earnings/(Loss) Per Share | (sen) | (5) | (79) | (33) | 42 | 31 | 19 | 1 | 30 | 32 | 56 |
| **Production\*** | | | | | | | | | | | |
| Network Size | (KM) | 366,578 | 361,203 | 383,453 | 419,494 | 353,443 | 308,878 | 294,228 | 264,482 | 237,889 | 210,983 |
| Time Flown | (Hours) | 330,205 | 306,949 | 319,332 | 309,035 | 279,416 | 242,466 | 224,702 | 210,065 | 187,921 | 156,797 |
| Distance Flown | (000 KM) | 200,223 | 189,754 | 186,522 | 179,664 | 156,795 | 130,441 | 118,925 | 111,328 | 102,160 | 85,958 |
| Available Capacity | (000 TKM) | 7,531,473 | 6,649,146 | 6,411,308 | 6,149,219 | 5,381,925 | 4,184,923 | 3,509,192 | 3,316,091 | 3,083,460 | 2,430,592 |
| Available Passenger Capacity | (000 Seat KM) | 48,905,537 | 45,442,288 | 42,293,932 | 40,096,883 | 35,161,376 | 30,078,472 | 26,337,120 | 23,862,164 | 21,583,437 | 17,257,749 |
| **Traffic\*** | | | | | | | | | | | |
| Passenger Carried | (000) | 15,371 | 13,709 | 15,117 | 15,371 | 14,311 | 13,093 | 12,405 | 11,594 | 10,976 | 9,382 |
| Passenger Carried | (000 Pax KM) | 34,930,136 | 30,592,900 | 28,698,112 | 27,903,706 | 24,565,816 | 21,003,448 | 18,191,572 | 16,053,855 | 14,928,784 | 12,237,417 |
| Passenger Load Factor | (%) | 71.4 | 67.3 | 67.9 | 69.6 | 69.9 | 69.8 | 69.1 | 67.3 | 69.2 | 70.9 |
| Cargo Carried | (000TKM) | 1,664,600 | 1,477,403 | 1,531,709 | 1,419,544 | 1,328,061 | 913,176 | 694,637 | 713,967 | 740,124 | 602,353 |

| | | | | | | | | | | | |
|---|---|---|---|---|---|---|---|---|---|---|---|
| Mail Carried | (000TKM) | **2,828** | 2,006 | 2,726 | 3,832 | 3,299 | 7,224 | 15,669 | 19,037 | 19,392 | 12,741 |
| Overall Load Carried | (000TKM) | **4,853,377** | 4,246,894** | 3,887,652 | 3,706,753 | 3,354,670 | 2,675,755 | 2,242,322 | 2,086,275 | 2,032,207 | 1,675,286 |
| Overall Load Factor | (%) | **64.5** | 63.9** | 60.6 | 60.3 | 62.3 | 64.0 | 63.9 | 62.9 | 65.9 | 68.9 |
| Staff | | | | | | | | | | | |
| Employee Strength | (At 31st March) | **16,427** | 17,313 | 17,688 | 15,230 | 17,766 | 19,381 | 19,509 | 19,783 | 17,869 | 16,149 |
| Revenue Per Employee | (RM'000) | **443** | 387 | 364 | 395 | 320 | 252 | 211 | 192 | 201 | 182 |
| Available Capacity Per Employee | (TKM) | **386,238** | 334,285 | 312,570 | 344,475 | 302,934 | 215,929 | 179,876 | 167,623 | 172,503 | 150,510 |
| Load Carried Per Employee | (TKM) | **258,477** | 214,829** | 190,039 | 210,928 | 188,825 | 138,061 | 114,938 | 105,458 | 113,728 | 103,739 |

* Including Freighter operations

** Revised based on standard free baggage weight

| Malaysia GDP Million in | | | | | | | | | | | |
|---|---|---|---|---|---|---|---|---|---|---|---|
| Current US$ | | 78,735 | 72,489 | 100,203 | 100,850 | 88,832 | 74,482 | 66,895 | 59,151 | 49,134 | 44,025 |
| Exchange Rate Ringgit/US$ | | 3.80 | 3.92 | 2.81 | 2.52 | 2.50 | 2.62 | 2.57 | 2.55 | 2.75 | 2.70 |

## Corporate Charts

**Overall Capacity and Demand**

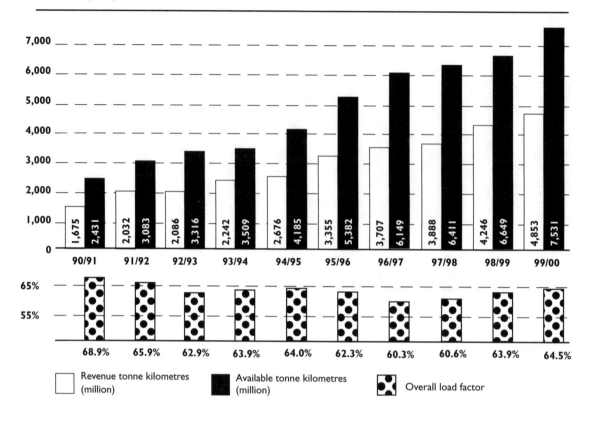

*Figure 20*

**Passenger Capacity and Demand**

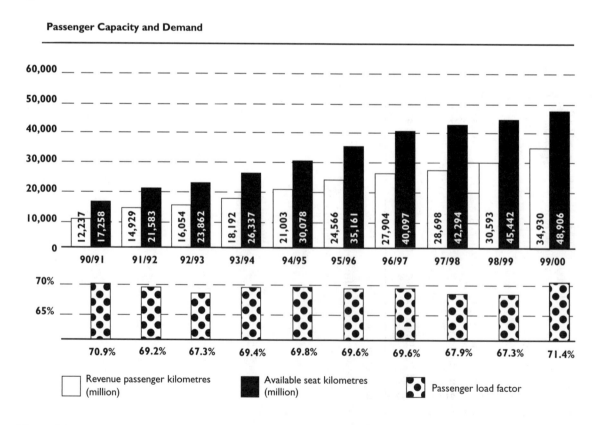

*Figure 21*

142

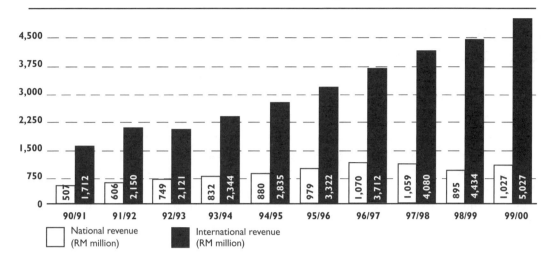

**Passenger Revenue for International and National Routes (excluding charters)**

National revenue (RM million) | International revenue (RM million)

| | 90/91 | 91/92 | 92/93 | 93/94 | 94/95 | 95/96 | 96/97 | 97/98 | 98/99 | 99/00 |
|---|---|---|---|---|---|---|---|---|---|---|
| National | 507 | 606 | 749 | 832 | 880 | 979 | 1,070 | 1,059 | 895 | 1,027 |
| International | 1,712 | 2,150 | 2,121 | 2,344 | 2,835 | 3,322 | 3,712 | 4,080 | 4,434 | 5,027 |

*Figure 22*

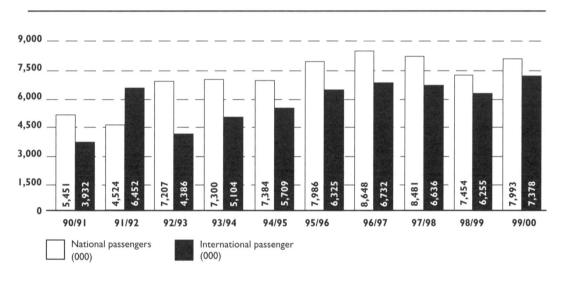

**Passengers Carried for International and National Routes**

National passengers (000) | International passenger (000)

| | 90/91 | 91/92 | 92/93 | 93/94 | 94/95 | 95/96 | 96/97 | 97/98 | 98/99 | 99/00 |
|---|---|---|---|---|---|---|---|---|---|---|
| National | 5,451 | 4,524 | 7,207 | 7,300 | 7,384 | 7,986 | 8,648 | 8,481 | 7,454 | 7,993 |
| International | 3,932 | 6,452 | 4,386 | 5,104 | 5,709 | 6,325 | 6,732 | 6,636 | 6,255 | 7,378 |

*Figure 23*

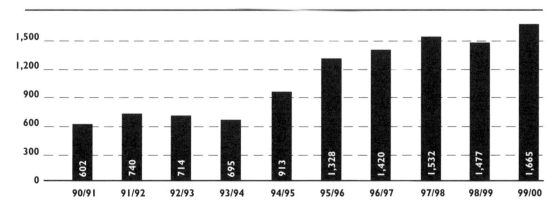

**Cargo Carried (million tonne kilometres)**

| | 90/91 | 91/92 | 92/93 | 93/94 | 94/95 | 95/96 | 96/97 | 97/98 | 98/99 | 99/00 |
|---|---|---|---|---|---|---|---|---|---|---|
| | 602 | 740 | 714 | 695 | 913 | 1,328 | 1,420 | 1,532 | 1,477 | 1,665 |

*Figure 24*

# Malaysian Airline System Berhad
# Examination Paper

## Additional Information

Malaysian Airlines can look forward to a brighter future with newly appointed Managing Director Datuk Mohamed Nor Yusof at the helm. Mohamed Nor is likely to make sure that the national carrier gradually returns to profitability through a series of consistent and painstaking programmes aimed at tackling specific problem areas. Two months prior to his appointment as MAS Managing Director, Mohamed Nor was already looking at the airline's balance sheet. He believes that the 'company deserves a better future and can do better.' The key issues to tackle are the losses and obtaining better yields from the operations. MAS expects to announce its financial results in a few weeks and the numbers are not going to be rosy. An even more challenging task ahead is to rebuild the image of the national carrier. According to Mohamed Nor, 'First and foremost, MAS is the national flag carrier. So there is a lot of prestige built around that, and to restore that prestige is our first imperative.' He said MAS had all the ingredients to achieve a better image, but he was not going to opt for a logo change and throw good money away on big expenses. Instead, Mohamed Nor is talking about re-imaging by ensuring that the public realize the inherently outstanding capabilities of the staff of this global operation.

## Examination Question

In your capacity as the newly appointed Senior Marketing Manager for MAS, you have been asked to present the answers to the following questions as reports to the marketing team:

### Question 1.

Develop a marketing plan for MAS, indicating short term (one year) and long term (three years) strategies for the company, justifying your position.

**(40 marks)**

### Question 2.

Analyse and critically assess the importance of key *factors* related to developing a marketing communications strategy for MAS. (Note this question is not asking for a communications plan).

**(30 marks)**

### Question 3.

Analysing the relevant data and information given in the case, develop a coherent international marketing strategy for MAS.

**(30 marks)**
**(100 marks in total)**

## Candidate's Brief

Daugavpils is Latvia's second city and, in Soviet times, was an industrial powerhouse. Now after ten years of Latvian independence, it is a shadow of its former self.

In March 2001, a new Mayor, Richard Eigims was elected together with a new administration. He is a businessman and self-made millionaire. After a thorough review of the city finances and organization, he created a new department to advise him on business and marketing. Ilya Podkolzins has been appointed to head this new department.

You are a Marketing Consultant funded by the European Union pre-accession funds and have been assigned to Daugavpils to help address the above challenges. At a meeting you will present your findings to Ilya Podkolzins, who will share them with the municipality.

**N.B.** The municipalities in Latvia are similar to the American model where the Mayor, as the leader of an elected majority, runs the town. Most of the facilities are controlled by the municipality.

---

### Important Notice

Additional information will be provided at the time of the examination. Further copies may be obtained from The Chartered Institute of Marketing, Moor Hall, Cookham, Maidenhead, Berkshire, SL6 9QH, UK.

---

© The Chartered Institute of Marketing

# City of Daugavpils

## Introduction

This case is set in the city of Daugavpils in the Latgale region of Latvia. Daugavpils has had a turbulent past and an interesting history. As the result of the momentous changes in Russia and Soviet withdrawal from the city in 1991, it has become a city which is trying to stabilize itself and find a new meaning for its existence. It has a mayoral system which is based on the American model where the Mayor carries a lot of influence and power, and is not just a figurehead for the citizens. The country itself is polarised as Riga has the base of power and wealth with cities such as Daugavpils being regarded as backward and poor. There is little understanding of the region and its potential in Riga, the capital of Latvia. The new Mayor Richard Eigims is determined to create a new future for the city. Part of creating this future lies in marketing the city within and outside Latvia. Riga is the centre of power and prosperity in Latvia.

## The Country, Latvia

Latvia has a long and somewhat chequered history, being controlled at various times by Sweden, Russia, Poland and Germany over the last 800 years. The national identity was established during a brief period of independence between the World Wars. The Nazi holocaust and the Soviet Pogroms resulted in a large percentage of the nation being displaced, killed, or replaced by ethnic Russians and other Soviet peoples. The last phase of Russian control ended in 1991, marking the opening of the 'Iron Curtain'. Latvia's leaders are anxious to seal their country's independence from Soviet rule by forging stronger links with the Western economies.

Latvia is in the centre of the three Baltic States. To the south, Lithuania has strong geographical and historical links with Poland. Together they once formed an empire that reached the doors of Moscow and threatened Russia. Estonia has strong cultural and geographic links with Finland. They share a common language and culture and have many business links. This leaves Latvia with nominal friends across the Baltic Sea, namely Sweden and Denmark, and greatly dependent on Russia.

Latvia now has strong economic links with the west and nearly two-thirds of its exports go to the European Union (EU). The country is preparing for EU entry and is beginning to fulfil many of the requirements for full status. However, in spite of the growing links and business with the EU, the country is still highly dependent on the flow of Russian oil through the country. A large proportion of its income is derived from transit services as up to 15% of Russian oil is exported from the port town of Ventspils. Russia therefore has a great interest in what happens to the country. Another reason is that 30% of the population is Russian. The current government's somewhat contentious policy of only granting citizenship to Latvian speaking individuals has left some of the Russian speaking population stateless. Many of the ethnic Russians are uneasy about Latvian being the main language. The country, as a result of historical events, has been left with a mixed demography and a Soviet economic legacy. As a result, Daugavpils is essentially Russian speaking and presents the country with the challenge of dealing with ethnic and economic variations. Unemployment in the area has been rising steadily, ever since the collapse of the Russian empire, with its large and inefficient factories. Latgale is one of the poorest regions in Europe with a high concentration of small farms and an ageing population. These factors pose a specific challenge for the country, especially as most of its resources are located in Riga. In the long term it will also pose a challenge for the EU, when it extends so far east. Latvia as a country only has a few attractions from an economic point of view, if Porter's competitive advantage of nations is taken into account. Porter considers that the key factors in determining a country's competitive advantage are as shown below (*Figure 1*). Latvia has been pushed towards the west, largely as a result of the economic crisis in Russia in the late 1980s and early 1990s (*for economic details see Appendix 1*).

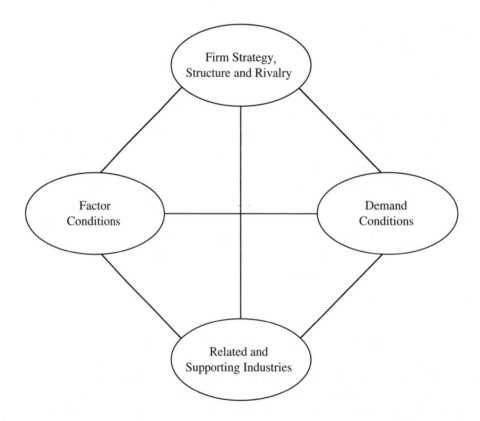

**Figure 1** *Porter, 1998*

A major problem that is holding Latvia back, in common with the other Former Soviet Union (FSU) countries, is the Soviet management system. This has given rise to very hierarchical, authoritarian, military style organizational structures. In the fast moving commercial sector, these structures are extremely inefficient and inflexible. They are not competitive, but they are the current role models. This makes it even more important to attract back former Latvians with knowledge of western methods and culture. Currently there are large numbers of successful Latvians living in the USA and Canada. Without their knowledge of western practices, it will take one or two generations to move from the Soviet model to the western model. The key element in changing the culture of the individuals who were used to a centrally planned and largely inefficient economy is instilling the importance of developing and implementing a market oriented view of business (*see Appendix 2 for country statistics*).

## History

The city was formed in 1275 by Ernest von Raceburg, Master of the Livonian Order. The new town was sacked by Lithuanians twice within the next 100 years. Soon there were occupations by the Poles and the Russian Czars. Instead of rebuilding the old castle, Ivan the Terrible built a new fort. It was later controlled by Poland and became a major trading centre. Jesuit monks settled there in 1620 and peace and prosperity returned. However, this was shattered by a war between Poland and Russia. Following this, the Swedes ruled the area for a short period. The next period saw the city being exchanged several times between the Russians and the Poles. Eventually it was ruled by the Russians. In 1810, a remarkable fortress was being built along the Daugava to keep out the French, under Napoleon's command. However, the French managed to occupy the structure while it was still being built. After the Napoleonic wars construction was resumed with the help of 10,000 Russian soldiers and 30,000 workers. In the 1860s, Dinaburg (as it was known then) grew rapidly and became a major railway junction. World War I stopped the town's development. Upon liberation in 1920 by Polish forces, the town was renamed Daugavpils in Latvian.

During this independent period between World Wars I and II, the town became culturally more Latvian. However, the peace was shattered again by the arrival of Soviet tanks in 1940. During World War II, much of Daugavpils was ruined: 72% of the city's buildings were destroyed by bombing and fire; much of the downtown area was burnt down. Fortunately, the most distinguished monument of history and architecture in Daugavpils – the fortress – survived, but the beautiful baroque style church was destroyed.

After the war, the city was restored under Soviet occupation and several new factories and blocks of houses were built. Daugavpils became a large industrial centre with workers flowing from the regions of Belarus and Russia. The ethnic composition of the population changed. The number of Russians, Belarussians and Ukrainians rose to 69.4% in 1949, whereas the local population decreased because of the arrests and deportations in 1945 and 1949. Latvians constituted only 13% of the local population. The results of these influxes of individuals and ethnic clearances are currently reflected in the ethnic distribution of the town.

**Table 1** *Demographics – Ethnic Distribution*

| Ethnic Origin | Daugavpils City |
| --- | --- |
| Latvians | 14.36% |
| Russians | 58.61% |
| Poles | 13.25% |
| Belarussians | 8.27% |
| Ukrainians | 2.83% |
| Lithuanians | 0.84% |
| Romanians | 0.34% |
| Estonians | 0.03% |
| Other | 1.48% |

## Geography

Daugavpils is the second largest city in the Republic of Latvia, located 232 km from the capital, Riga. Its closest neighbours are the Republic of Lithuania (25 km to the border), Belarus (33 km to the border) and Russia (120 km to the border). This juxtaposition of three countries has been of great benefit to the city over the centuries, enabling it to become an important hub of transport and trade in eastern Latvia. Railroads connect Daugavpils with Riga, St. Petersburg, Moscow, Vilnius, Panavezius and Saulai (*see map of Daugavpils in Appendix 1*).

Daugavpils is located in southeastern Latvia on either side of the Daugava River. This river is 1,020 km long with 367 km lying within Latvia. The river ends its run in Riga and enters the Baltic Sea. The city is located in the southeastern part of Eastern Latvia's low-land, on the Jersika plain (*see Appendix 1*). It is surrounded by the Latgale heights in the north-east, and by the Augzeme heights in the south and south-east. In the east, it borders on the protected Augsdaugava region. The city lies on unusual geological formations, with abundant sandstone slate and clay available within its environs. These deposits have been used for buildings for many centuries. Daugavpils has a continental climate, being about 200 km inland from the sea. The highest temperatures are around 34 °C and the lowest around −25 °C. Precipitation is around 650 mm per annum and the sunlight hours are around 1,809 per annum. The land around the city is well endowed with water, having 15 large lakes (with approximately 350 small ones), 8 rivers, numerous brooks and economically significant water reserves. The area has outstanding natural beauty and is well forested with approximately 10,400 hectares of trees. The forests and lakes support a wide range of mammals and fish.

## Politics

The Mayor of Daugavpils effectively runs the town and is responsible for schools, hospitals, local police, street cleaning, rubbish collection and disposal, sewage, water treatment, heating, etc. and a wide range of property and local businesses.

The local elections in March produced a new Mayor, Richard Eigims. He is the leader of the Latgales Light Party and has 7 of the 15 seats. His party has formed a coalition with the Social Democrats (1 seat) and the Human Rights Party (2 seats) for a total of 10 seats.

The previous Mayor and leader of the Daugavpils City Party, Alexei Vidavskis, had 13 of the 15 seats. This was reduced to 5 seats at the March elections. He now leads the opposition. This is a new development as Daugavpils was effectively a 'one-party state' from independence to March 2001. The City Party has its roots in the former Communist Party.

The Latvian State Government changes about every 12 months and appears to be based on the Italian model. As a result, most local politicians form their own parties. They avoid affiliation with national political parties as this can lead to unpopularity when that particular government goes out of favour. This creates problems for creating a consistent brand image for the city.

## Religion

There are churches for the following religions in Daugavpils: Catholic, Lutheran, Jewish, Baptist, Old Orthodox and Orthodox. This broad range of religions is a demonstration of the multi-cultural society that is Daugavpils. The two with the largest following are the Catholic and Orthodox churches. The former is actively supported by the Polish community. The churches are full most Sundays and during religious festivals, but, with the exception of the Catholic church, the congregations largely comprise older women.

## Regional Development

To date, regional development has been fragmented and unco-ordinated. In order to address this, the Latgale Regional Development Agency (LRDA) was formed. The LRDA has produced the first regional development plan in Latvia. They have pioneered co-operation amongst the region's municipalities and are raising the region's profile in Riga. EU Project Partners are based in the LRDA Daugavpils office, together with two other projects.

## Education

Daugavpils has a University of around 3,000 students. Originally it was dedicated to teacher training, but latterly the demand for teachers has gone down significantly owing to low birth rates. This institution is in the process of changing its mission to support local business and transforming itself into a full University. Now there are 500 students taking business related courses. There is an affiliation with both Salford University in the UK and a Riga-based business school.

There are many good schools in Daugavpils. Unfortunately, they have generally become polarized as 'Russian' or 'Latvian'. English is emerging as a required language, in addition to Latvian and Russian. School number 9 has an excellent academic record and has won many English Speaking contests.

## Health

There is a large local hospital which is being partially modernized with a loan from the World Bank. With a staff of 900, it is the largest single local employer. There is also a small Nurses Training College of about 150 pupils. In Soviet times there were several large, attractive 'sanatoria' in and around Daugavpils. They were very popular with Russians, especially from St. Petersburg. They were somewhere between a convalescent home and a health farm, and served as both. After independence, they all fell into disuse and have been closed. A good example of this is a very grand 19th century building on the banks of the Daugava. There are excellent views and beautiful grounds, but the building has been abandoned and has fallen into disrepair. Interestingly enough, Lithuania has kept some of these sanatoriums going and they are proving to be popular amongst the Latvians! Doctors' salaries are low and vary between 10–150 lats a month. Most are state employed. Many are also very dedicated and return to Latvia after spells abroad. (*For details on healthcare, see Appendix 2*). Currently the city has no plans for developing 'health tourism'. Health tourism is a growing market in countries such as India, where many westerners feel that they can get better care at cheaper costs with excellent doctors.

## Multi-cultural Society

The Daugavpils District is ethnically diverse with over 20 nationalities living in peace and harmony. This is a major achievement that goes largely unrecognized outside the area. The inevitable growth of Latvian nationalism after independence, e.g. through the language laws, has increased local tension and provoked an equal and opposite nationalist backlash amongst the other communities. However, there is still a high rate of inter-marrying and social and cultural activities across ethnic boundaries. There are many flourishing societies that promote social cohesion, e.g. Latvian-Belarus, Latvian-Lithuanian, Latvian-Polish societies. There is also a small Roma community that co-exists with the other ethnic groups. Latvia has a Roma representative in the parliament (Saeima).

The city's Culture Hall was opened in 1937. It includes a theatre and an acting company with an average age of 30. There have been productions of works by Russian writers, Faulkner and Lorca. Plans are being started for the refurbishment of this theatre so it can again take its place as the cultural heart of the city.

## Agriculture

There is a lot of subsistence farming around Daugavpils that will go through the painful transition to medium sized, multi-function farms as part of the EU accession, e.g. the SAPARD programme. There is little local preparation for this. However, the Naujenes Pagast in the Daugavpils District is a good example of Rural Development. The community is based around a disused Soviet airfield, which they are redeveloping as a local business and social centre.

## The Elderly

Approximately 29% of the Daugavpils population are pensioners on very low incomes and with few assets. Families generally care for their elderly, but there are those who have no support and end up in Homes.

## The Unemployed

Unemployment is high in this area – how high is difficult to judge because after 6 months, claimants drop out of the system. It is estimated at 28% or double the 'official' figure. The State Employment Services is legally obliged to document details of training, job vacancies, etc. only in Latvian. This is clearly a disadvantage for those whose native language is not Latvian.

## Education

Education in Latvia begins at seven, with compulsory basic education lasting 9 years.

The number of pupils at basic school level in the year 1998–1999 was 293,385. Education is generally free and accessible. The country places a great importance on education and the literacy rates are higher than many developed countries at around 95% (*for further details on Daugavpils see Appendix 2*).

## Marketing Issues

As a result of the problems that the city faces and the opportunities that exist, the Mayor has created a new structure to help to promote Daugavpils (*see Appendix 3*).

The marketing needs of the city are complex and touch on different sectors in different ways. Initially, the biggest challenge facing the city council is understanding and counteracting the poor perception of Daugavpils in Riga. As Riga is the powerhouse of the Latvian economy, little thought is given to the far off city lying to the east of the country.

## Marketing for Business Growth

The city, as explained before, lies at the crossroads of many different countries. In many ways it looks both to the east and the west. However, it is likely that investment for growth will come more readily from the west and the EU. The Daugavpils District Enterprise Support Centre is a business focal point in the Daugavpils District. They are currently running two US sponsored projects. US Peace Corps volunteers have assisted in the development of this NGO. This is a multi-lingual centre and all training material is available in both Latvian and Russian.

Foreign investment is vital to the regeneration of this industrial area. So far the following foreign companies have taken the plunge: Zieglera, Rhodia, Axon Cable and Swedtex; one German, two French and one Swedish. Rhodia has bought a very large site containing many serviceable buildings. The largest covers 10 hectares! This is the local equivalent to a business park and represents an excellent opportunity for any foreign companies wishing to invest here. Axon Cable has bought two buildings and employs 80 people making cables for computers. Swedtex is a Swedish textile company making ladies' stockings. It employs 70 people and plans to double its workforce. In addition to this, Le Bois Massif of France is starting to build wooden houses for export to the west. It expects to employ 120 people by next year. Others attracted to the site include Falck, a Danish security company which has its local headquarters in an office block, Aga the German-Swedish industrial gases company and Magistr, a local company which buys and recycles waste from Rhodia's operation. Magistr also employs 220 people and supplies high quality ropes and fishing nets to companies around the world. The company was founded and is run by individuals who were cybernetics experts in the former Soviet army.

Then there are the 'dinosaur' companies left over from the Soviet era. Generally they supplied one item for the whole of the Soviet Union. At independence, their main market disappeared overnight. For the few that survived, employment is 10% of the previous number. For example, the Driving Chain Company made bicycle chains for the whole of the Soviet Union. It continues to survive through creative schemes such as supplying a Belarus factory with bicycle chains with payment in finished bicycles which it then sells locally. Much progress has been made and the factory recently gained ISO 9000 certification. The city is a key railroad juncture for the former Soviet empire and as a result of this, railway coaches were built and engineered in the city. This has left a legacy of good engineers and craftsmen. Zieglera, a German company manufacturing heavy-duty grass cutters has taken advantage of this fact.

The city council needs to develop a marketing strategy that will attract new businesses from international sources to the region. Currently, there is a lack of a coherent marketing plan to attract business to the area.

The city has:

a. A plentiful supply of cheap labour with average wages running at $60 a month.
b. A good, skilled labour force left over from the Soviet era.
c. Huge factories which are currently lying empty.
d. An old decaying industrial infrastructure.
e. An educated population.

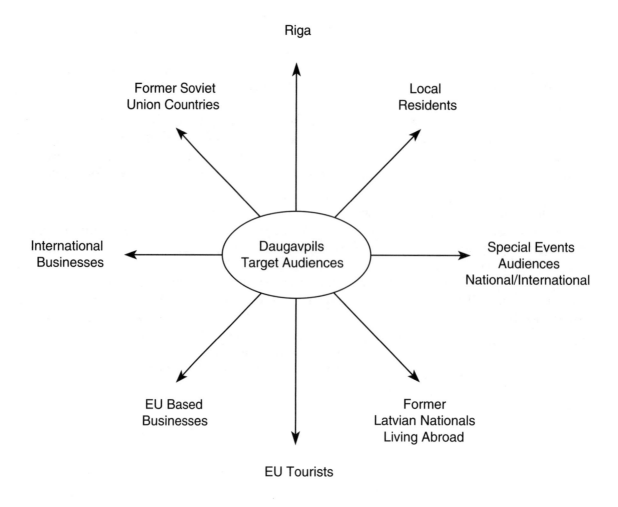

*Figure 2* *Multiple Audiences for Daugavpils*

One of the first studies into assessing cities, took place in the Netherlands. The cities were assessed on the basis of a scale developed by Ashworth and Voogd. They considered the following issues:

- Qualities of the site.
- Transport infrastructure.
- Land cost.
- Possibilities of subsidies.
- Attitude of authority.
- Commercial contacts.
- Residential amenity.
- Labour markets.

These particular areas were then assessed and a general 'potency' score was developed. This allowed a competitive analysis of different cities. Based on this, differential marketing strategies can be developed. In another study the key elements in the promotional image of 16 medium sized Dutch towns were studied.

*Table 2* Information Produced by Towns in the Netherlands

| Types of Information | % of Towns (%) |
|---|---|
| Tourism marketing | 81 |
| Tourist overview | 69 |
| Description of monuments | 56 |
| Historical | 56 |
| Description of museums | 50 |
| Town guide | 50 |
| Town map | 50 |
| Historical account | 44 |
| Water recreation facilities | 31 |
| Description of coat of arms | 31 |
| Sport facilities | 31 |
| Parking facilities | 31 |
| Other public services | 31 |
| Lists of monuments | 25 |
| Lists of cafes/restaurants | 25 |
| Calendar of events | 19 |
| List of commercial firms | 19 |
| Description of public parks | 6 |
| Description of housing | 6 |
| Description of schools | 6 |

Tourism marketing is now becoming an important part of most cities' strategies. However, tourism marketing is probably one of the most difficult areas to develop successfully. Daugavpils generally has a very negative image. For instance, a recent poll of residents showed that 75% would wish to live elsewhere. Most individuals in Riga have a poor image of the city and generally feel that it is backward and too close to the Russian border. The ethnic mix of the population also deters local Latvians from visiting the town. Yet the town has many positive assets. It has:

- Beautiful churches.
- An excellent pedestrianized centre with beautiful architecture.
- Pleasant parks.
- An old historical fort.
- Tree lined avenues.
- A good but old tram service.
- Beautiful unspoilt countryside dotted with lakes.
- Friendly and generally helpful people.
- Safety.
- An excellent ice hockey stadium.

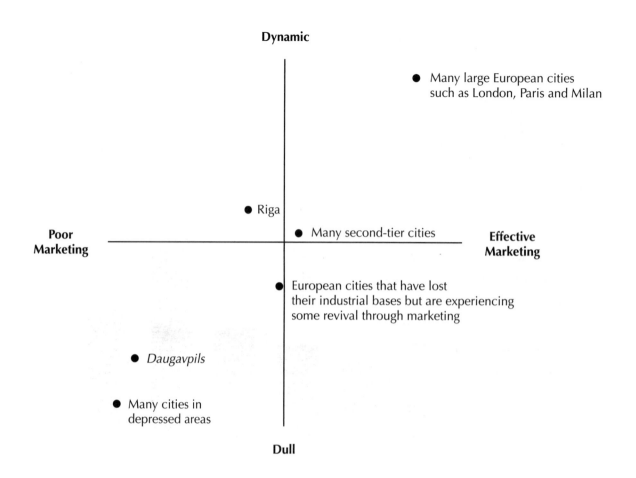

**Dynamic**

● Many large European cities
such as London, Paris and Milan

● Riga

● Many second-tier cities

**Poor Marketing**

**Effective Marketing**

● European cities that have lost
their industrial bases but are experiencing
some revival through marketing

● *Daugavpils*

● Many cities in
depressed areas

**Dull**

*Figure 3  Positioning of Cities (Source: Ranchhod, 2001)*

The figure above shows some of the key ways in which cities are perceived both by locals and the general public.

In many ways the city has to create a positive image out of a negative. Although the history is somewhat chequered, there are many ways in which it could be sold to potential tourists. For instance, the great Soviet writer Pushkin was actually imprisoned in the great fort.

An example of a city that has created a positive image is Bradford in England. For many decades it suffered a poor image coupled with an industrial base which was declining inexorably. The city council recognized this problem and allocated £100,000 to expand and search for tourist markets. They undertook an audit and promoted some of the key sites used for television programmes such as *Wuthering Heights, Emmerdale Farm* and *Last of the Summer Wine*. They also took into consideration its industrial heritage, based on the National Museum of Photography, Film and Television. The city also cleverly promoted its ethnic mix by promoting the city as the 'Curry Capital of the North'. The city was promoted for short breaks in order to entice people from local cities. Package holidays were offered to travel agents. As tourists began to flood into the city a degree of confidence returned to the residents and local businesses.

The surrounding area of Daugavpils offers a different kind of experience for individuals interested in hunting and fishing. The immense history also offers scope for development. The region has plenty of attractive natural landscapes. Several lakes and two significant highland areas – Augszeme and Latgale highlands – are located in the Daugavpils region. A number of historical monuments and religious buildings provide good background for the development of tourism. However, the tourist industry still has a lot of room for development (*see Figure 4 and Appendix 2*), as the popularity of the region is significantly below average in Latvia and cannot be compared with the most prosperous regions in the Baltic States. Some of the most popular spots in the region are the Daugavpils Fortress from the 17th century, Peter-Paul Cathedral, a fortress built in the beginning of the 19th century, the Boris-Gleb Church, Vaclaiciena Palace and other churches built over the centuries. One of the most dramatic edifices is the Duke Jacob's Channel in Asare (500km long), built in 1667–1668 to link the two rivers, Vilkupe and Eglaine, to connect the Daugava and the Lielupe water routes so that traders could reach the sea without going through customs in Riga.

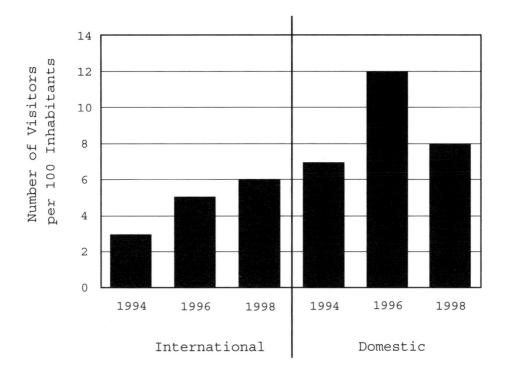

**Figure 4** *Tourism Figures, Daugavpils Region*

## The Airport

Although Daugavpils is the second largest city in Latvia and although some very big companies are located there, it is still regarded as a development area. Owing to the lack of flight connections, the business environment has difficulties in exploiting new markets as well as attracting investors and tourists. The current Daugavpils airport is a former Soviet military airport with a runway of 2,500m. When the Russian army left, all technical installations and equipment were dismantled, including the landing lights. The airport needs updating. During the Soviet period, Daugavpils was a busy airport serving more than 60,000 passengers per year. There were 7 daily flights to Riga, one daily flight to Moscow and one to Minsk. The big factories also used air transportation for cargo in connection with sales and supply. The airport is owned by the municipality and a number of business people. The Daugavpils region and the Daugavpils City Government as the major stakeholders have a great interest in opening the airport for commercial and tourist traffic as it is such an important pivot for developing a marketing strategy for the region. Within a 100km radius of Daugavpils, there are 800,000 people. It is by far the biggest city after Riga in Latvia. A survey carried out by a group of Danish consultants showed the key export markets and the key destinations for passengers, (*see Appendix 1, Table 5*)

## Sport in Daugavpils

There are three major sports facilities in Daugavpils:

- Lokomotiv Stadium.
- Ledus Halle.
- Football Stadium.

### Lokomotiv Stadium

This is the only speedway (motorcycle racing) stadium in the Baltic States and hosted the European Championships on the 14th to 15th September 2001. There has been a very basic facility here for some years, but last spring a new stadium was built and the facilities greatly enhanced for the European Championship. This stadium holds 4,000 spectators. Latvia has a very good speedway team which participated in these championships.

### Ledus Halle

This is the Ice Hockey Stadium and was completed one year ago. It holds 3,000 spectators in a modern building with all the facilities expected in a new arena, including good toilets and an excellent cafeteria. There is a local league of about 8 teams (still growing) that are well supported. Last winter, they had their first 'sell out' when the leading teams played. As well as the local league, there are matches between Latvian towns and the occasional friendly international.

Ice hockey is very popular in Latvia and the World Championships will be held there in 2006. The national team does well at international level and beat the USA at the last World Championships in Germany. Many Latvian fans travelled to Germany to support the national team.

### Football Stadium

The local team is called Dinaburg, the old name for the town. They do very well in the Latvian national league, finishing 2nd or 3rd. They have qualified for the UEFA Cup tournament this season. There is a local league of teams within the town.

### Other Sports

In addition to the above, there are 3 large swimming pools, tennis courts and volleyball courts. Daugavpils is home to an Olympic Gold medallist, a biathlete (skiing and shooting) and Miss Universe (body building).

## Internet Marketing Communications

Internet marketing is set to play an increasingly important part in the marketing of locations. Currently Daugavpils has a site but it is basic and slow and has few hyperlinks to anything of real interest. Fishing for instance is an increasingly important international sport, yet it is difficult to get into the fishing site in Latvia.

The importance of the new technologies is being increasingly recognized by the tourism industry, with the World Tourism Organization Business Council (WTOBC, 1999) describing the Internet as ... 'having a greater impact on the marketing of travel and tourism ... since the invention of television'. They are also being recognized, in particular, by public sector organizations such as local authorities, which commission a range of tourism marketing programmes/services. Increasingly, Government Tourist Offices (GTOs) are playing an important role in the promotion, marketing and management of tourism destinations. This type of service benefits both the industry and tourists. The service can be improved and its efficiency can be increased by the utilization of information technology. In the future it is quite possible that good IT systems will enable individuals to undertake a 'virtual tour' before embarking on a trip. The Internet is driving the changes within the tourist industry with travel and tourism pages taking up a large proportion of the World Wide Web. Hence, for local authority tourism providers, the

Internet and WWW are of critical importance. This can be further confirmed by the rapid changes taking place in the tourism market environment today, including:

- Consumers are increasingly demanding greater, instantaneous access to higher quality, timely visitor information.
- Effective marketing is becoming increasingly important as markets become increasingly competitive, vying for the 'cash rich-time poor' visitor pound.
- Resource pressures within local authorities to provide 'global' tourism marketing/ marketing communications on shoestring budgets, are increasing. Electronic forms of communication can navigate traditional barriers to awareness and can help to reduce value chain costs (of intermediaries and agents, distribution and logistics, etc.).
- The greater usage, acceptance and abundance of new technologies within society generally and specifically within the tourism marketplace today – particularly by consumers in lucrative long haul international markets such as the United States of America. Technologies are impacting upon consumers and travel trade tourism providers in a huge way.

The WTOBC argues... 'the destinations that will win (in the Information Age) will be those that can satisfy this thirst for information, that can convince the tourist online that their destination and the products that can be experienced there are worth the time and expense of visiting', and... 'If you are not online you are not on-sale' (1999).

## Internet Strategy Model Guidance

The WTO argues that the **web-objective setting process** is very important for DMOs such as public sector local authorities. They must clearly define a role for their web sites that the commercial sector does not already fill, setting objectives in the context of wider public/private sector partnerships. Decisions therefore must be taken on the web construct and how it will affect (strategically and practically) value chains and intermediaries, particularly concerning e-commerce development. In addition to setting clear web objectives, the WTOBC argues that best practice **Internet marketing strategy** must also **specify web site functionality**, resourcing the project via appropriate **internal and external (agency) human resources, testing and piloting the site, monitoring and evaluation**, and finally, **promoting** the web site.

The WTO model approach is detailed below (*see Table 3*).

**Table 3** *Model 'Functionality' Criteria*

**Home Page**
Logo/brand
Text description
Photograph/graphic of
  destination
Moving/changing text
List of internal links
Click on graphic to enter site
Language/translation option
List of awards given to site
Number of visitors to site
Email address
Local time
Gateways

**General Information about
  the Site**
Photographs of destination
Climate, geography,
  topography
Clothing
Money
Shopping hours
How to get to destination
Public transport
Telecommunications
Culture and customs
Suggested itineraries
Events and attractions
Destination specific activities
Maps

**Features of the Site**
Language options
List of site contents on
  every page
Link back to home on
  every page
Site map
Information on site design
Statistics on site usage
Virtual, multi-media tours,
  live cams

Visitor comments
Customer forms (to request
  information)
Online registration form

**Search Facility**
Key word search available?
Use of directories to search?

**Online Shop**
Clothes/souvenirs/books/
  maps?
Minimum order value?
Do you have register to
  shop?

**Interactive Trip Planner**
(*can search database to find...*)
How to get to the destination
What to do
Attractions/events
Where to stay
Transport
Tours
Hire
Where to look for further
  information

**What is included in the
results?**
Name, address, phone of
  service provider
Fax number
Photograph of service
  provider
Pricing information
Textual description of
  service offered
Link to email and URL
  of provider

**Virtual Brochures**
Registering compulsory for
  first time users
Information from the site
  included
Can the brochure be edited?

**Accommodation Information
  (Non-interactive)**
One list of accommodation
  options
Listed on the basis of
  location
Listed on basis of style
  (i.e. hotel)
Listed on the basis of price

**Accommodation (Interactive)
(Can search the database to
  find...)**
Style of accommodation
  (hotel, hostel)
Location of accommodation
Price
Facilities of accommodation
  providers
*Information provided on...*
Address/phone/fax details
Photograph of accommoda-
  tion
Text description of
  accommodation
Room rates
Check in/check out times
Child facilities
Quality accreditation rating
Link to email and URL of
  provider
Online booking through the
  web site

*Adapted from WTOBC, 1999: Pages 156–157*

In many ways Daugavpils has to consider these and branding strategies for the area. The current logo is shown below. The entrances to the city also have the monuments as depicted in the photos shown.

**Figure 5** *The Current Logo*

**Figure 6** *The Entrances to the City*

## Summary

The city of Daugavpils is in many ways symptomatic of the plight of many cities in Europe. The situation in Daugavpils is particularly interesting because it finds itself in a situation where it has to market itself both to Russia and the east, and also to the EU. However, one of the biggest challenges facing the Mayor and the council is the perception of the city both in Riga and amongst the residents themselves (*see Appendix 3 for a profile of new Mayor and the organization chart*). The city has an interesting past and some beautiful locations; however, the brand image is poor. The marketing communications are carried out by a Personal Assistant to the Mayor who handles the PR for the city. In fact, the case presented the city with a PR opportunity and this was exploited for the purposes of local television and national TV. The budget spend on marketing is rather fragmented. A high quality book on the region has been produced as well as some leaflets. There is little co-ordination between the departments and little in the way of a comprehensive marketing exercise. Part of the problem lies in the centralist Soviet approach where marketing had little or no meaning. The Mayor has a formidable task ahead of him. He realizes that the city has many strengths and there are many opportunities to further its cause. The general feeling is that marketing is likely to play a major role in rejuvenating the city.

# Appendices

## Appendix 1

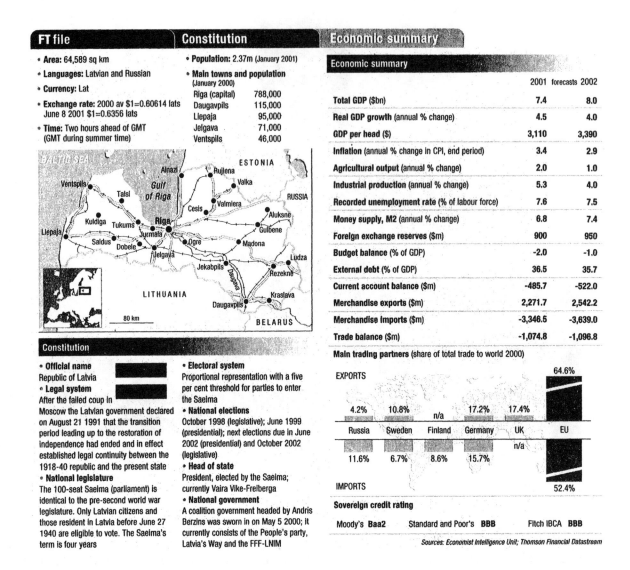

*Article 1* Latvia Facts and Figures  (Source: Financial Times, Friday, 15th June 2001)

## Political Structure

| | |
|---|---|
| **Official name** | Republic of Latvia. |
| **Legal system** | After the failed coup in Moscow the Latvian Government declared on 21st August, 1991 that the transition period leading up to the restoration of independence had ended and in effect established legal continuity between the 1918–1940 republic and the present state. |
| **National legislature** | The 100-seat Saeima (parliament) is identical to the pre-Second World War legislature. Only Latvian citizens and those resident in Latvia before 27th June, 1940 are eligible to vote. The Saeima's term is four years. |

| | | |
|---|---|---|
| **Electoral system** | Proportional representation with 5% threshold for parties to enter the Saeima. | |
| **National elections** | 3rd October, 1998; next elections due June 2002 (presidential) and October 2002 (legislative). | |
| **Head of state** | President, Vaira Vike-Freiberga, elected by the Saeima on 17th June, 1999. | |
| **National government** | A new government, headed by Andris Berzins, was sworn in on 5th May, 2000; it consists of three parties from the previous coalition – People's Party, Latvia's Way and the FFF-LNIM – as well as the small New Party. | |
| **Main political parties** | Ruling coalition: People's Party (24 seats); Latvia's Way (21 seats); For Fatherland and Freedom-Latvian National Independence Movement (FFF-LNIM, 16 seats); New Party (8 seats); | |
| | Opposition: For Human Rights in a United Latvia (FHR, 16 seats); Social Democratic Workers' Party (SDWP, formerly Social Democratic Alliance, 14 seats); Independent (1 seat). | |
| **Council of Ministers** | **Prime minister** | Andris Berzins (Latvia's Way) |
| | **Special tasks minister for co-operation with international financial institutions** | Roberts Zile (FFF-LNIM) |
| | **Special tasks minister for state administration and municipal reform** | Janis Krumins (New Party) |
| **Key ministers** | **Agriculture** | Atis Slakteris (People's Party) |
| | **Culture** | Karina Petersone (Latvia's Way) |
| | **Defence** | Girts Valdis Kristovskis (Latvia's Way) |
| | **Economy** | Aigars Kalvitis (FFF- LNIM) |
| | **Education and science** | Karlis Greiskalns (People's Party) |
| | **Environmental protection and regional development** | Vladimirs Makarovs (FFF-LNIM) |
| | **Finance** | Gundars Berzins (People's Party) |
| | **Foreign affairs** | Indulis Berzins (Latvia's Way) |
| | **Interior** | Mareks Seglins (People's Party) |
| | **Justice** | Ingrida Labucka (New Party) |
| | **Transport and telecommunications** | Anatolijs Gorbunovs (Latvia's Way) |
| | **Welfare** | Andrejs Pozarnovs (FFF-LNIM) |
| **Central bank governor** | Einars Repse | |

*(Source: EIU Country Report, October 2000)*

**161**

## Economic Structure

**Annual Indicators**

|  | 1996 | 1997 | 1998 | 1999 | 2000[a] |
|---|---|---|---|---|---|
| GDP at market prices (LVL bn) | 2.8 | 3.3 | 3.6 | 3.7 | 3.9 |
| GDP (US$ bn) | 5.1 | 5.6 | 6.1 | 6.3 | 6.4 |
| Real GDP growth (%) | 3.3 | 8.6 | 3.9 | 0.1 | 4.0 |
| Consumer price inflation (av; %) | 17.6 | 8.5 | 4.7 | 2.4 | 2.8 |
| Population (m) | 2.5 | 2.5 | 2.5 | 2.4 | 2.4 |
| Exports of goods fob (US$ m) | 1,488.0 | 1,838.0 | 2,011.0 | 1,889.0 | 2,059.0 |
| Imports of goods fob (US$ m) | 2,286.0 | 2,686.0 | 3,141.0 | 2,916.0 | 3,289.4 |
| Current account balance (US$ m) | −280.0 | −345.0 | −651.0 | −642.0 | −570.9 |
| Foreign exchange reserves excl. gold (US$ m) | 654.1 | 704.0 | 728.2 | 840.2 | 940.0 |
| Total external debt (US$ bn) | 0.5 | 0.5 | 0.8 | 0.9 | 1.0 |
| Debt-service ratio, paid (%) | 2.4 | 4.3 | 2.5 | 4.8 | 8.3 |
| Exchange rate (av; LVL: US$) | 0.551 | 0.581 | 0.590 | 0.585 | 0.615 |

29th September, 2000 LVL0.615:US$1; LVL0.542: €1

| Origins of Gross Domestic Product 1999 | % of Total | Components of Gross Domestic Product 1999 | % of Total |
|---|---|---|---|
| Agriculture, hunting and forestry | 4.0 | Private consumption | 65.5 |
| Manufacturing | 14.9 | Public consumption | 19.0 |
| Electricity, gas and water supply | 5.0 | Gross fixed investment | 25.0 |
| Construction | 7.6 | Increase in stocks | 1.4 |
| Services | 68.4 | Exports of goods and services | 46.7 |
| **Total incl. others** | **100.0** | Imports of goods and services | −57.6 |
|  |  | **Total** | **100.0** |

| Principal Exports 1999 | % of Total | Principal Imports 1999 | % of Total |
|---|---|---|---|
| Wood and wood products | 37.3 | Machinery and equipment | 22.0 |
| Textiles | 15.4 | Chemicals | 12.0 |
| Metals | 11.5 | Mineral products | 11.4 |
| Machinery and equipment | 4.9 | Transport equipment | 8.3 |
| Foodstuffs | 3.8 | Metal products | 7.0 |

| Main Destinations of Exports 1999 | % of Total | Main Origins of Imports 1999 | % of Total |
|---|---|---|---|
| Germany | 16.4 | Russia | 15.2 |
| UK | 10.7 | Germany | 10.5 |
| Sweden | 10.7 | Finland | 9.1 |
| Russia | 6.6 | Sweden | 7.2 |
| EU | 62.5 | EU | 54.5 |

[a]EIU estimates

*(Source: EIU Country Report, October 2000)*

## Quarterly Indicators

| | 1998 3 Qtr | 1998 4 Qtr | 1999 1 Qtr | 1999 2 Qtr | 1999 3 Qtr | 1999 4 Qtr | 2000 1 Qtr | 2000 2 Qtr |
|---|---|---|---|---|---|---|---|---|
| **General Government Consolidated Budget (LVL m)** | | | | | | | | |
| Revenue | 414 | 403 | 370 | 393 | 397 | 430 | 394 | 420 |
| Expenditure | 406 | 459 | 375 | 446 | 425 | 488 | 395 | 458 |
| Balance | 7 | −56 | −4 | −53 | −28 | −58 | −1 | −38 |
| **Output** | | | | | | | | |
| GDP at 1995 prices (LVL m) | 699 | 669 | 657 | 697 | 700 | 687 | 693 | 730 |
| % change, year on year | 2.4 | −1.7 | −1.5 | −1.1 | 0.2 | 2.8 | 5.5 | 4.8 |
| Industrial production index[a] | 99.3 | 88.6 | 86.8 | 84.5 | 94.4 | 99.8 | 104.5 | 105.2 |
| % change, year on year | −0.7 | −11.4 | −13.2 | −15.5 | −5.6 | −0.2 | 4.5 | 5.2 |
| **Employment, Wages and Prices** | | | | | | | | |
| Employment ('000) | 1,047 | 1,033 | 1,028 | 1,035 | 1,046 | 1,041 | 1,037 | 1,039 |
| % change, year on year | −0.1 | −1.0 | −1.9 | −2.1 | −1.1 | −0.7 | −0.3 | 0.4 |
| Unemployment rate (% of the labour force) | 7.4 | 8.5 | 9.8 | 10.1 | 9.7 | 9.2 | 9.1 | 8.7 |
| Average monthly wages (LVL) | 136.5 | 140.8 | 132.6 | 141.0 | 142.6 | 147.7 | 141.4 | 149.3 |
| % change, year on year | 11.7 | 8.7 | 7.8 | 6.1 | 4.5 | 4.9 | 6.6 | 5.9 |
| Consumer price index (1995 = 100) | 133.4 | 133.9 | 135.9 | 136.5 | 136.1 | 138.0 | 140.4 | 140.7 |
| % change, year on year | 3.9 | 2.8 | 2.5 | 1.8 | 2.1 | 3.1 | 3.2 | 3.1 |
| Producer price index | 115.7 | 113.3 | 110.5 | 110.0 | 110.4 | 110.6 | 111.4 | 111.2 |
| % change, year on year | 2.3 | −0.5 | −4.0 | −4.9 | −4.6 | −2.3 | 0.8 | 1.1 |
| **Financial Indicators** | | | | | | | | |
| Exchange rate | | | | | | | | |
| LVL: US$ (av) | 0.597 | 0.572 | 0.579 | 0.593 | 0.589 | 0.580 | 0.591 | 0.603 |
| LVL: US$ (end-period) | 0.583 | 0.569 | 0.590 | 0.598 | 0.579 | 0.583 | 0.596 | 0.600 |
| LVL: Ecu/€[b] (av) | 0.666 | 0.671 | 0.648 | 0.625 | 0.617 | 0.602 | 0.582 | 0.562 |
| LVL: Ecu/€[b] (end-period) | 0.683 | 0.666 | 0.634 | 0.618 | 0.618 | 0.586 | 0.569 | 0.573 |

| Interest rates (av; %) | | | | | | | | |
|---|---|---|---|---|---|---|---|---|
| Deposit | 4.7 | 6.0 | 5.5 | 4.9 | 4.9 | 4.9 | 4.0 | 4.8 |
| Lending | 14.9 | 16.2 | 16.9 | 15.7 | 12.1 | 12.1 | 10.1 | 10.9 |
| Money market | 2.9 | 7.1 | 5.2 | 4.4 | 4.5 | 4.7 | 2.5 | 2.6 |
| M1 (end-period; LVL m) | 619 | 601 | 613 | 652 | 624 | 639 | 670 | 707 |
| % change, year on year | 19.7 | 6.0 | 6.5 | 0.8 | 0.8 | 6.3 | 9.4 | 8.5 |
| M2 (end-period; LVL m) | 980 | 959 | 955 | 1,012 | 1,006 | 1,038 | 1,109 | 1,186 |
| % change, year on year | 16.7 | 6.7 | 3.3 | −1.7 | 2.6 | 8.3 | 16.1 | 17.3 |
| Dow Jones RSE index[c] (2nd Apr 1996 = 100) | 113.5 | 98.0 | 81.9 | 83.9 | 70.9 | 87.8 | 116.6 | 108.7 |

**Sectoral Trends**

| | | | | | | | | |
|---|---|---|---|---|---|---|---|---|
| Cargo turnover by rail (m t/km) | 3,243 | 3,266 | 2,744 | 3,237 | 3,104 | 3,125 | 3,480 | 3,127 |
| % change, year on year | −1.8 | −13.2 | −15.0 | 0.3 | −4.3 | −4.3 | 26.8 | −3.4 |
| Cargo handled in ports ('000 tonnes) | 13,027 | 13,498 | 12,438 | 14,014 | 11,905 | 10,676 | 13,327 | 13,199 |
| % change, year on year | 5.9 | 4.5 | −5.6 | 11.3 | −8.6 | −20.9 | 7.1 | −5.8 |

**Foreign Trade (LVL m)**

| | | | | | | | | |
|---|---|---|---|---|---|---|---|---|
| Exports fob | 262 | 247 | 245 | 254 | 255 | 254 | 275 | 291 |
| Imports cif | −476 | −487 | −375 | −422 | −440 | −487 | −416 | −485 |
| Trade balance | −214 | −240 | −130 | −168 | −185 | −233 | −141 | −194 |

**Foreign Payments (US$ m)**

| | | | | | | | | |
|---|---|---|---|---|---|---|---|---|
| Merchandise trade balance | −299 | −372 | −179 | −236 | −264 | −348 | −189 | −262 |
| Services balance | 53 | 45 | 80 | 91 | 89 | 81 | 125 | 124 |
| Income balance | 22 | 8 | −29 | 3 | −5 | −17 | −24 | −11 |
| Current account balance | −195 | −278 | −102 | −127 | −149 | −264 | −64 | −130 |
| Reserves excl. gold (end-period) | 739 | 728 | 746 | 887 | 768 | 840 | 847 | 832 |

[a] Corresponding period of previous year = 100. [b] Ecu before 1999. [c] End-period.

Sources: Central Statistical Bureau of Latvia, *Monthly Bulletin of Latvian Statistics*; IMF, *International Financial Statistics;* Bank of Latvia, *Quarterly Bulletin*; Standard & Poor's, *Emerging Stock Markets Review*
*(Source: EIU Country Report, October 2000)*

**Inflation**

The lat's peg to the IMF's SDR has shielded Latvia from most of the international inflationary pressures caused by oil price rises. The most recent spike in oil prices, the future strength of the euro and growing domestic demand will accelerate inflation slightly in the coming months, but annual average inflation for 2000 will not exceed 3%. Inflationary pressures from producer prices will remain almost non-existent in the short term, but are likely to build up as economic growth increasingly allows producers to pass costs on to consumers.

**Exchange Rates**    The lat is pegged to the IMF's currency basket SDR and at the moment its stability is secure. At the end of August the Bank of Latvia's currency and gold reserves were US$920m, which provides more than 4 months of import cover. The lat is expected to remain constant against the SDR during the forecast period, and given the low level of inflation in Latvia, the real appreciation of the lat will be small.

**External Sector**    The current account deficit widened in the second quarter of 2000 on the back of a deteriorating balance of trade and we expect this trend to continue as economic recovery boosts domestic demand for imports. High oil prices bring higher revenue for the Latvian transit sector, and the economic recovery in Russia will boost transit to Russia as well.

**Forecast Summary**

(% Unless Otherwise Indicated)

| | 1999[a] | 2000[b] | 2001[c] | 2002[c] |
|---|---|---|---|---|
| Real GDP growth | 0.1 | 4.0 | 5.0 | 3.0 |
| Industrial production growth | −4.7 | 4.6 | 6.0 | 6.0 |
| Gross agricultural growth | −7.3 | 1.0 | 2.0 | 1.0 |
| Unemployment rate (av) | 9.1 | 7.4 | 7.0 | 6.8 |
| Consumer price inflation | | | | |
| Average | 2.4 | 2.8 | 3.4 | 4.8 |
| Year end | 3.2 | 1.8 | 5.0 | 4.4 |
| Short term interbank rate | 14.2 | 15.0 | 13.0 | 13.0 |
| Government balance (% of GDP) | −4.2 | −2.5 | −1.5 | −1.0 |
| Exports of goods fob (US$ bn) | 1.9 | 2.1 | 2.3 | 2.6 |
| Imports of goods fob (US$ bn) | 2.9 | 3.3 | 3.6 | 4.0 |
| Current-account balance (US$ bn) | −0.6 | −0.6 | −0.6 | −0.7 |
| % of GDP | −10.3 | −9.0 | −8.8 | −9.6 |
| External debt (year end; US$ bn) | 0.9 | 1.0 | 1.2 | 1.4 |
| Exchange rates | | | | |
| LVL: US$ (av) | 0.585 | 0.615 | 0.620 | 0.591 |
| LVL: ¥100 (av) | 0.514 | 0.576 | 0.597 | 0.597 |
| LVL: € (year end) | 0.586 | 0.569 | 0.607 | 0.607 |

[a] Actual. [b] EIU estimates. [c] EIU forecasts.
*(Source: EIU Country Report, October 2000)*

**Fast Recovery Fuels Trade Deficit as Investment Grows**    As a result of the fast growth in imports, the trade deficit has started to increase again. In January-July 2000 the trade deficit was LVL407m (US$610m), up by 13.9% from the same period in 1999. Latvia – like other emerging markets – has traditionally run large merchandise trade deficits in order to finance its substantial investment needs. Now that the Latvian economy is growing rapidly, the attendant growth in investment is once again exerting pressure on the country's external balances.

The reason behind this dynamic is that Latvia's main exports are relatively low in value added. Timber exports and textiles constitute around 50% of exports – sawn wood alone accounts for some 35% of Latvia's exports to the EU – and Latvia has so far not been able to upgrade its productive capacity in a way that would allow it to compete in EU markets with more advanced products. Conversely, on the import side the most important single category is machinery and mechanical appliances, which make up some 20% of imports, showing Latvia's need to import technology in order to upgrade its productive capacity – a process necessary if the country is to move towards the production of goods with higher value added.

**Trends in Foreign Trade**

(LVL m Unless Otherwise Indicated)

|  | 1999 1 Qtr | 1999 2 Qtr | 1999 3 Qtr | 1999 4 Qtr | 2000 1 Qtr | 2000 2 Qtr |
|---|---|---|---|---|---|---|
| **Exports fob** | **246** | **254** | **255** | **254** | **275** | **291** |
| of which: | | | | | | |
| to the EU (%) | 65 | 63 | 60 | 62 | 68 | 64 |
| to the CIS (%) | 10 | 12 | 14 | 12 | 8 | 8 |
| **Imports cif** | **−375** | **−422** | **−440** | **−487** | **−416** | **−485** |
| of which: | | | | | | |
| from the EU (%) | 56 | 57 | 54 | 52 | 53 | 54 |
| from the CIS (%) | 14 | 13 | 16 | 17 | 15 | 17 |
| **Trade balance** | **−129** | **−168** | **−185** | **−233** | **−141** | **−194** |
| % of GDP | 15 | 17 | 19 | 23 | 15 | 18 |
| Export unit values | | | | | | |
| (% change, year on year) | −1.5 | −0.5 | −5.5 | −4.1 | −1.8 | −2.0 |
| Import unit values | −7.1 | −7.5 | −4.7 | −1.8 | −5.9 | −6.3 |
| (% change, year on year) | | | | | | |

*Source:* Central Statistical Bureau of Latvia, *Monthly Bulletin of Latvian Statistics.*

**Import Bill Drives
Current-account Deficit**

After a substantial quarter-on-quarter fall in January-March 2000, the current-account deficit widened again in the second quarter of the year, reflecting a pick-up in import demand that increased the merchandise trade deficit by 35%. Whereas, according to revised data, the current-account deficit in the first quarter of 2000 amounted to LVL33m (US$56m), in the second quarter of the year it more than doubled, reaching LVL78m. Year-on-year comparisons show that, although in US dollar terms the current-account deficit remained stable, in lat terms the second-quarter deficit also widened in comparison with the same period of 1999. However, in the context of the recovering economy the current-account balance has improved, falling from a deficit of 8.1% of GDP in the second quarter of 1999 to one of 7.4% of GDP.

*(Source: EIU Country Report, October 2000)*

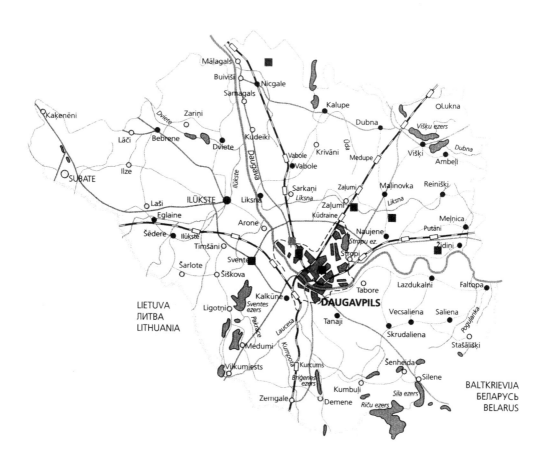

*Article 2* Map of Daugavpils *(Source: Daugavpils A5 Brochure)*

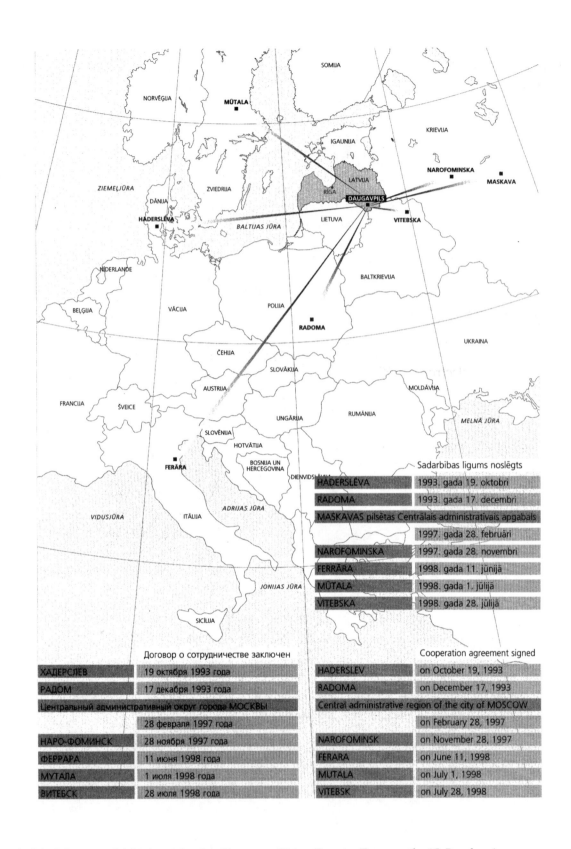

*Article 3* Daugavpils' Links with other European Cities (Source: Daugavpils A5 Brochure)

## Appendix 2
### *Extracts from the Daugavpils Municipality Facts and Figures*
#### Daugavpils

- Second largest city of Latvia.
- First mentioned 1275.
- Developing economy – big crossroads for transport, centre of culture and education.
- Located in SE of country on banks of Daugava, 230km from capital city of Riga.
- In favourable geographical situation because adjacent to Belarus (33–35km from the border) and 120km from the Russian border.
- In 2000 the city population is estimated at 114,000 inhabitants (58.59% Russian, 14.4% Latvian, 13.3% Polish, 8.3% Belarussian, 2.8% Ukrainian).
- Owing to the close proximity of the borders, there are three Consulates in Daugavpils, Russian, Belarussian and Lithuanian.
- Daugavpils is a manufacturing centre and transport junction. Main transport links are with Moscow, St. Petersburg, Vilnius and Panavezius. Good road links with Lithuania, Belarus and Russia are developing. There is also the potential to develop a new airport.
- City industry comprises 30 big enterprises and companies, metalworking companies, Pievadkedes PLC (car and motorbikes, children's bikes, agricultural machinery), Dauer-D PLC (electronics), Zieglera Masinbuve (agricultural mowers), Rhodia Industrial Yards (synthetic threads and yards) and the company Magistr (synthetic cables).
- Light industry companies include: clothes sewing companies Daugavpils suveja, Dinaburg apgerbs, Linko-D and Triad.
- Also general production companies – milk production Kraslava Dairy, Antaris and Daugavpils Bakers; Pallada produces alcoholic beverages; Annas-V and Aviz'D are fish producers.
- Products are of high quality and compete in the external market.
- Dinaz has active co-operation with the Baltic States, some FSU countries and the West, and trades in transit of petroleum products, storage and marketing.
- Besides these companies are another 2,000 businesses. City enterprises generate an income of 52 million lats a year, of which 30% is from export to the West, 40% to FSU. Some 9,000 people work in these companies.
- The city has a bus and tram system. There are more than 1,100 other businesses (shops, kiosks, cafes). Major companies amongst them are Antaris, Gurons and Ditton BC.
- In Daugavpils almost all the major Latvian banks are represented. Investment projects are also being realized related to water supply and sewage purification; they are being funded by the World Bank, Phare, NEFCO and others (US$22.3m).
- Daugavpils is an important cultural centre in the East of Latvia. There are 27 schools for general education, 4 extra-curricular establishments, 29 kindergartens and 9 technical institutions, 'Sun School' Art College and a Music College.
- Each year 1,000 teaching and engineering students graduate from the Daugavpils Pedagogical University and Riga Technical University.
- The city has revived the theatre, working with national and cultural institutions, has a cinema, cultural centre and other cultural organizations. The Daugavpils Ice Hall has also been built.
- The city is also actively working towards an Exhibition Centre.
- Daugavpils has many architectural, historical and cultural monuments. The largest and most important of them is the Daugavpils fort, built in the 18th century.
- The city has an environment of many beautiful lakes. Daugavpils has the potential for development of foreign tourist trade.

## Daugavpils History

Daugavpils has a long history. This began in 1275 when the Livonians built the first stone castle – Dinaburg. During the Livonian war (1558–1583) Daugavpils moved to a new location 19 km down the Daugava. The city has had many different names: Dinaburg (1275–1893), Borisoglebsk (1656–1667), Dvinsk (1893–1920) and Daugavpils (since 1920).

## Twinnings

Daugavpils is twinned with:

- **Hadersleva (Denmark)**
  Legal contract 19.10.93
  District matters
  Cultural exchange programme
  Municipality specialist experience exchange programme
  Lions Club collaboration
  Charity work with orphanages and old peoples' homes

- **Radom (Poland)**
  Legal contract 17.12.93
  Cultural exchange programme
  Teachers and students exchange programme
  Promotion of business contacts

- **Russian Federation Moscow City Central District Administration**
  Legal contract: 28.02.97
  Business, cultural, educational contacts

- **Narofomiks (Russian Federation)**
  Legal contract: 28.11.97
  Students' development programme
  Cultural development programme
  Municipality co-operative programme
  Promotion of business contacts

- **Ferrara (Italy)**
  Legal contract: 11.06.98
  EU integration matters

- **Mutala (Sweden)**
  Legal contract: 01.07.98
  Municipal co-operation programme

- **Vietbsk (Belarus)**
  Legal contract: 28.7.98
  Promotion of business contacts
  Cultural exchange programme
  Municipality specialist experience exchange programme
  Teachers and students exchange programme

- **Tampere (Finland)**
  Co-operation agreement signed between Daugavpils Municipal Enterprise, Daugavpils Udens and Tampere city water supply and sewage company, signed in 1996 and extended in 1999.

## City Development Priorities

Agreed priorities for the city.

Most important objectives of city development:

- To improve economic development.
- To improve employment.
- To improve streets and roads.
- To ensure all have the right to culture and education.
- To improve security in town.
- To give all citizens healthcare.
- To give all citizens safe, healthy, pleasant and motivating environment.
- To save the city centre as an important part of European cultural and historical heritage.
- To create modern architecture and to preserve architectural heritage as an important quality of the city's scenery.

## Projects in Daugavpils

General development of city.

- Project for Daugavpils water supplies and sewage
  Financed by: Bank of International Reconstruction and Development, NEFCO, Sida (Sweden), DEPA (Denmark) EU Phare, Finnish Ministry of Environmental Protection, Latvian Government, Daugavpils Municipality and Municipal PLC, Daugavpils Water
  General costs of project:                $22.3m
  Daugavpils Municipality input :          L1.8m
  Project co-ordinator: Daugavpils Executive Director Richard Draba
  Term of project: 1996–2001
- Research on how dangerous industrial waste is created in a region and management of such waste
  Financed by: VARAM, Finnish Ministry of Environmental Protection and Daugavpils Municipality
  General costs of project:                L94,900
  Daugavpils Municipality contribution:    L5,000
  Project co-ordinator: (Environmental Projects VARAM) Vlads Pjankovskis
  Term of project: 1999–2001
- South Latgale Household Waste Project, implemented in terms of investment programme – '500'
  Project foresees creation of a joint system of waste management for Daugavpils, Kraslava, Preili regions and the creation of one waste tip.
  Financed by: Finnish Ministry of Environmental Protection, B\ip, BSG
  General costs of project:                L7.2m
  Daugavpils Municipality contribution:    L364,000
  Project co-ordinator: (Environmental Projects VARAM) Vlads Pjankovskis
  Term of project: 1999–2003
- 'Daugavpils and Mutala – 2010' – ways to develop Daugavpils city and analysis of the surrounding environment
- Emergency Management
  Financed by: SWEBALTCOP, Mutala Municipality and Daugavpils Municipality
  General costs of project:                SKr2,092,000
  Project co-ordinator: Inga Melnikova, Daugavpils Municipality
  Term of project: 1999–2001
- General management point for crisis situations
  Project finance given by: Swedish Nuclear Safety Institute and Daugavpils Municipality
  General costs of project:                L45,500
  Daugavpils Municipality contribution:    L17,800

Project co-ordinator: Daugavpils Municipality, G. Zvirbulis and others from the Municipality State Emergency Services – professionals for crisis management and City Health Department – R. Margevics and A. Faibusevics

Term of project: 2000

(Further details of improvements to be made and deadlines)

Improvement and development of the management centre: Swedish Safety Institute plans to finance until 2003 the purchase of different equipment and logistics, for the sum of approximately L2,000 Latvian State Emergency Services, Ministry of Internal Affairs provided equipment for modem connections and information/communication systems

- Latgale Region Development Plan
  Project financed by: EU Phare
  General costs of project:                        L500,000
  Project co-ordinator: Inara Stalidzane, Latgale Region Development Agency (LRDA)
  Term of project: 1999–2000
- SPP Pilot Project 'Urban Development'
  Financed by: EU Phare
  General costs of project:                        (L371,000) €700,000
  Project co-ordinator: Maija Muceniece, LRDA
  Term of project: 2000–2001
- LRDA Capacity Improvement for Working with Pre-structural (EU) Funds
  Financed by: Danish Government
  General costs of project:                        (L111,392) DKr1,547,100
  Project co-ordinator: Iveta Puzo
  Term of project: 2000–2001

### *Daugavpils Education Department*

- State Programme for Latvian Language LAT 2
  Financed by: LWAP Latvian State Language Acquisition Programme
  Co-ordinator: Silva Kucina (Latgale Bureau) and Vitalis Cirss
  Term of project: Ongoing in all teaching institutions
- Nord Prison Project – teaching prisoners in Griva jail
- Reconstruction of heating system in educational institutions and control systems for heat consumption
  Financed by: Daugavpils Municipality and Department of Education
- Improving effectiveness of use of revenue and improvement of quality of education in educational institutions (phases 2 and 3)
  Financed by: World Bank
- Latgale Programme
  Financed by: Ministry of Education and Science
- Establishment of examination centre for professional education in South Latgale
  Financed by: Ministry of Education and Science and EU Phare
- LEIS (Latvian Educational Information System)
  Financed by: Ministry of Education and Science
- Socrates Project in city schools, EU Educational Programme
  Financed by: EU
  Co-ordinators: City Educational Institutions and Department of Education, IZM
- State Investment Programme Full Reconstruction of the 1st Gymnasium's Boarding School
  Financed by: Latvian Government and Municipality
  Co-ordinators: Daugavpils Municipality and Department of Education
- Project for rehabilitation of abused children
  Financed by: Ministry of Welfare and Department of Education
  Co-ordinators: Department of Education and Centre of Psychological Support

- Renovation of Polish Secondary School Sports and Culture Complex
  Financed by: Latvian Government and Polish Government
  Co-ordinators: Daugavpils Municipality and Department of Education

## Health and Social Care

State Health Reform pilot project: Optimization of infrastructure system of healthcare in Daugavpils and Kraslava regions.

Daugavpils sub-project should be realized:

- Daugavpils PVA (healthcare system) improvement and transfer of children's hospital.

Objectives:

- To empower the network of healthcare activities.
- To improve PVA services, quality and intensity.

Tasks:

- Former children's hospital wards/rooms – 5 healthcare practice places to be installed which are placed according to traditional microareas of the town.
- Transfer the Daugavpils children's hospital to the available empty space in City Central Hospital.
- Create regional centre for Oral Health in the former children's hospital.
- Create regional rehabilitation centre in facilities of former children's hospital.
  Financed by: Latvian Government and World Bank
  General costs of project: US$1,035,700
  Project co-ordinator: Dr A. Faibvusevics, Director of Daugavpils Municipality Health Department
  Term of project: 1999–2001

## Culture and Recreation

Diary for the year 2000, anniversary of 725 years of establishment of the city, with different events throughout the year.

**January:**

- Sacred Music Festival with Choral Competition.

**March:**

- Festival for Latvian Minority Children's Folk Festival.
- Charity concerts in Kalupe, Kalkune, Auseklitis and Priecite Orphanages.
- Two big concerts in Latvian Cultural Centre and Culture and Sports Centre.

**April:**

- Traditional art days 'Moving with Time'.
- Jazz Festival, 6th International Traditional Jazz Festival (France, Sweden, Belarus and Latvia).

**May:**

- Children's competition 'Sunbeams' – singing, dancing and arts.
- Week of Slavic Culture, concerts, Polish, Russian, Belarussian culture. Also, Scientific Conference 'Dinaburg – Dvinsk – Daugavpils' – scientists from 6 countries.
- Daugavpils 725 celebrations 31st May to 4th June; visit of the President of Latvia; exhibition of candelabra; concerts; first stage of Baltic Water Motorcycle Championships.

**September:**

- Annual Poetry Days.
- 7th Festival of Chamber Music.

**October:**

- Swedish Days in Daugavpils. Mutala's Music School string quartet, Jazz Group, wall hangings and seminars on EU affairs, water protection, medicine.

**December:**

- Traditional Christmas Tree – switching on of lights by Latvian Prime Minister.
- Second day of Christmas activities.
- New Year Celebrations – fireworks.

## City Sports

*Table 4* Children's and Youth's Sports Schools

| Number | Name of School | Number of Pupils | Type of Sport |
|---|---|---|---|
| 1 | School Board | 613 | Football, weight lifting, fencing, shooting, canoeing |
| 2 | School Sports Committee | 574 | Field and track, basketball, swimming, boxing, Greco-Roman wrestling, free wrestling |
| 3 | Specialized Volleyball | 926 | Volleyball, tennis, Hockey |
|  | School Total | 2,113 | 15 sports categories |

### Sports Clubs

Includes:

- 23 social sports clubs (darts, stiga, football club, basketball, boxing clubs, Lokomotiv, VK, tennis clubs, etc.).
- Two education establishment clubs (DP University, Railway Technical School).
- Six different companies' clubs (SC Daugava, Police SK, Dinaburg Football Club, Speedway Centre, etc.).

### Sport Groups

Includes:

- 26 educational based groups.
- Eight company based groups.

### Personnel Working with Sports

Number of employees in sports work – 189.

Including 46 coaches, 100 in schools and educational establishments, and 43 in clubs and sports centres.

## Sports Centres

- Stadia – 3 (Celtnieks, Lokomotiv and football stadium Esplanade).
- Sports grounds – 40 (volleyball, basketball, football, multi-sports, tennis courts).
- Swimming pools – 10 (25m indoor pools, 6; non-standard, 3; 50m outdoor pools 1).
- Shooting galleries – 3.
- Sports halls – 45.
- Track and field centre – 1.
- Rowing centres – 2.
- Karting and moto tracks – 2.
- Sports hotels – 2.
- Ice hall – 1.

Popular sports in the city – speedway, volleyball, football, weight lifting, track and field, basketball, freestyle wrestling and hockey.

## Airport Survey Results:

**Table 5** *Airport Survey Results*

| | |
|---|---|
| Russia | 21% |
| CIS | 14% |
| Belarus | 11% |
| Lithuania | 5% |
| Germany | 16% |
| Others | 33% |
| | 100% |

**Table 6** *Top 5 Destinations*

| | |
|---|---|
| Moscow | 22% |
| St. Petersburg | 20% |
| Minsk | 16% |
| Berlin | 8% |
| Warsaw | 6% |
| Others | 28% |
| | 100% |

**Table 7** *Impact on Business if there are Flight Connections*

| | |
|---|---|
| Significant | 59% |
| Some | 24% |
| None | 17% |
| | 100% |

**Table 8** *Number of Travellers*

| Persons | Year | | Month | Week | Day |
|---|---|---|---|---|---|
| International | 4,162 | | 347 | 83 | 14 |
| To Riga | 6,051 | | 504 | 121 | 27 |
| | 10,213 | | 851 | 204 | 41 |

| Current Train Passengers | Daugavpils–Riga 1996 |
|---|---|
| Fast Train | 63,767 |
| Slow Train | 27,540 |
| | 91,307 |

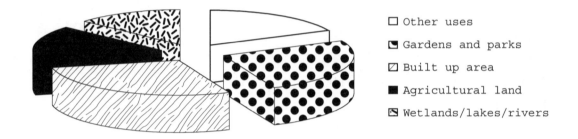

- ☐ Other uses
- ◨ Gardens and parks
- ▨ Built up area
- ■ Agricultural land
- ◩ Wetlands/lakes/rivers

**Figure 10** *Daugavpils: Breakdown of Area*

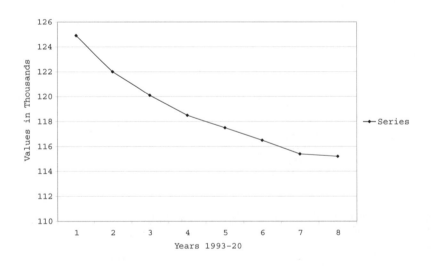

**Figure 11** *Population Changes*

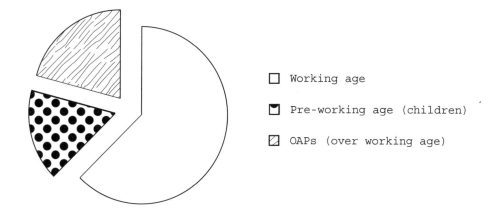

**Figure 12** *Inhabitants by Age Group*

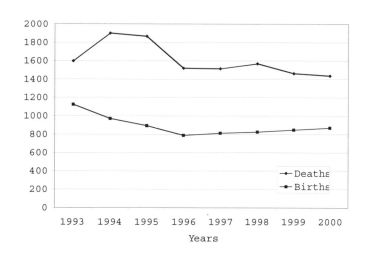

**Figure 13** *Death and Birth Rates*

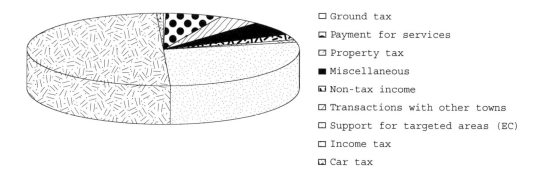

**Figure 14** *City Income Sources*

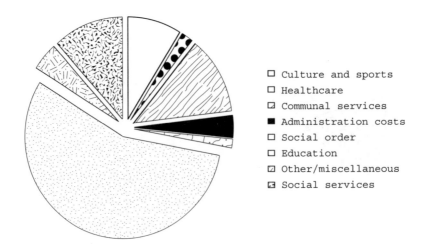

□ Culture and sports
□ Healthcare
□ Communal services
■ Administration costs
□ Social order
□ Education
▨ Other/miscellaneous
▨ Social services

*Figure 15* Daugavpils' Budget Expenditure for 2000

## Analysis of Demands in Rural Tourism

**Latvia**

| | | |
|---|---|---|
| Number of tourists | Year 1996 | 2,468 |
| | 1997 | 3,630 |
| | 1998 | 6,200 |
| | 1999 | 6,621 (for 10 months) |
| Breakdown into countries | Latvian tourists | 89% |
| | Foreign | 11% |
| Foreign tourists | Germany | 15% |
| | Finland | 14% |
| | USA | 10% |
| | India | 10% |
| | Canada | 6% |
| | France | 6% |
| | Netherlands | 5% |
| | Denmark | 4% |
| | UK | 4% |
| | Russia | 3.5% |
| | South Africa | 3.5% |
| | Other | 20% |
| Age breakdown | Up to 30 years old | 45% |
| | 30–40 | 28% |
| | Over 40 | 27% (locals) |
| Trip's objectives | In summer: water, swimming, bath, eating, horses, host-guide, renting of bicycles and sport games. | |
| | In winter: baths, fireplace, celebrations, eating and winter sports. | |

*Source: Compiled by Irina Gorkina, Daugavpils Enterprise Support Centre, Latvia, 31st July 2001*

## Health Statistics

From the Yearbook of Healthcare Statistics in Latvia, 2000 Published by the Ministry of Welfare

Overall trends in Latvia:

- Reform of the health system is decreasing the total number of hospitals and increasing the number of outpatient institutions.
- Lack of money is decreasing the number of outpatient visits and increasing mortality after urgent surgical operations.
- Deaths still exceed births but the gap has narrowed to 12,019 in 2000.
- Population density has declined from 37.8 (1999) to 37.5 (2000) people per sq km compared with a European average of 116.
- Decrease in population in rural areas has been more marked, making provision of healthcare in rural areas even more expensive per capita.
- Females make up 53.7% of the population and this has been constant since 1989.
- 61% of the inhabitants are of working age (15–59).
- 21% are 60 or over; there is a considerable increase in the population over working age in Ventspils, Daugavpils and Rezekne.
- The large gap in life expectancy between males and females (11.1 years) identifies Latvia as a developing country (gap is 5–7 years in developed countries).
- Life expectancy at birth (1999): male 64.7 years, female 75.4 years compared to the UK at 74.9 and 79.9 respectively.
- Poverty increases use of psychoactive substances (alcohol, tobacco, drugs), depression, suicide, deviant social behaviour and criminality, risk of unsafe food.
- Diptheria in Latvia is the highest in Europe; it peaked in 1997 and there were 264 cases in 2000, i.e. 10.9 per 1000 inhabitants; only 54.3% of population are immunized.
- Polio has been eliminated through immunisation.
- In 2000 sexually transmitted diseases increased markedly.
- HIV cases rose from 247 to 467 and deaths from AIDS from 17 to 24 (1999 to 2000) for all of Latvia.

*Table 9* Main Causes of Death by Age in Latvia (2000)

|  | 0–14 Years | 15–59 Years | 60 Years + |
|---|---|---|---|
| Total | 361 | 7,458 | 24,383 |
| Infectious/parasitic diseases | 10 | 229 | 144 |
| of which tuberculosis | 0 | 196 | 92 |
| Neoplasms | 28 | 1,293 | 4,312 |
| Circulatory system diseases | 5 | 2,143 | 15,717 |
| Respiratory system diseases | 5 | 285 | 567 |
| Digestive system diseases | 3 | 327 | 668 |
| External causes of which: | 96 | 2,561 | 1,118 |
| Transport accidents | 22 | 543 | 43 |
| Alcohol poisoning | 0 | 181 | 55 |
| Drowning | 35 | 175 | 69 |
| Suicide | 5 | 540 | 223 |
| Homicide | 9 | 409 | 125 |

**Table 10** *Daugavpils*

|  | Total | 0–14 Years | 15–17 Years | 18 and Over |
|---|---|---|---|---|
| Latvia | 2,424,150 | 432,215 | 103,791 | 1,888,144 |
| Daugavpils | 114,510 | 18,513 | 4,994 | 91,003 |
|  | 4.72% | 4.28% | 4.81% | 4.82% |

|  | Live Births | | Deaths | | Change | |
|---|---|---|---|---|---|---|
|  | Total | Per 1,000 | Total | Per 1,000 | Total | Per 1,000 |
| Latvia | 19,396 | 8.0 | 32,844 | 13.5 | −13,448 | −5.5 |
| Daugavpils | 833 | 7.2 | 1,462 | 12.7 | −629 | −5.5 |
| France |  | 12.6 |  | 9.2 |  | 3.4 |
| Germany |  | 9.6 |  | 10.4 |  | −0.8 |

|  | Lyme Disease | | Tick borne Encephalitis | |
|---|---|---|---|---|
| Per 1,000 | 1999 | 2000 | 1999 | 2000 |
| Latvia | 11.5 | 19.5 | 14.4 | 22.4 |
| Daugavpils | 12.1 | 24.5 | 0.0 | 6.1 |

|  | Syphilis | | Gonorrhea | |
|---|---|---|---|---|
| Per 1,000 | 1999 | 2000 | 1999 | 2000 |
| Latvia | 63.2 | 42.1 | 45.1 | 30.7 |
| Daugavpils | 133.9 | 81.2 | 71.9 | 74.2 |

|  | Registered Mental Patients | | of Which New Patients | |
|---|---|---|---|---|
| Total | 1999 | 2000 | 1999 | 2000 |
| Latvia | 63,323 | 62,108 | 7,629 | 6,577 |
| Daugavpils | 4,740 | 3,577 | 532 | 332 |

| Per 1,000 | Latvia | | Daugavpils | |
|---|---|---|---|---|
| | **1999** | **2000** | **1999** | **2000** |
| Physicians | 33.0 | 33.6 | 34.0 | 36.7 |
| Medical personnel | 62.9 | 61.6 | 94.5 | 92.2 |
| Hospital beds | 90.5 | 85.2 | 142.8 | 141.1 |
| Outpatient visits | | 4,700 | | 5,000 |
| Laboratory tests | 905 | 877 | 980 | 458 |
| Physiotherapy | 102 | 10 | 95 | 78 |
| Diagnostic tests | 52 | 51 | 41 | 34 |
| Radiology | 82 | 87 | 70 | 69 |
| Emergencies | 208.8 | 206.1 | 33.0 | 33.0 |

*Table 11* Ministry of Welfare: Hospital Bed Utilization

| | **Average Bed-days Per Patient** | | **Bed Turnover** | | **Bed Occupancy %** | |
|---|---|---|---|---|---|---|
| | **1999** | **2000** | **1999** | **2000** | **1999** | **2000** |
| Latvia | 12.1 | 11.6 | 24.4 | 25.1 | 81.1 | 79.5 |
| Daugavpils | 11.3 | 11.4 | 23.6 | 21.6 | 73.2 | 67.5 |

*Table 12* Local Authority: Hospital Bed Utilization

| | **Average Bed- days Per Patient** | | **Bed Turnover** | | **Bed Occupancy %** | |
|---|---|---|---|---|---|---|
| | **1999** | **2000** | **1999** | **2000** | **1999** | **2000** |
| Latvia | 8.6 | 8.3 | 32.6 | 34.0 | 76.8 | 77.3 |
| Daugavpils | 8.2 | 7.9 | 37.2 | 38.7 | 83.3 | 83.2 |

# Appendix 3

Латгалия занимает в Латвии особое положение. Смешение народов и культур придаёт этому краю неповторимый колорит. Но в сытой Риге к Латгалии всегда было снисходительно-барское отношение: что взять с этих чангалов? Пьют, бездельничают, в лучшем случае — батрачат. Говорят на ужасном диалекте латышского, а то и вообще на русском или польском... А отсталость региона давно уже многими воспринимается как фатальная неизбежность.

В редакции «Вестей» мало верят в подобные мифы и поэтому решили снарядить первую латгальскую экспедицию, чтобы получить ответ на простой вопрос: камо грядеши, Латгалия? Первым пунктом нашего маршрута стал Даугавпилс — неофициальная столица «озерного края». А первым собеседником — её градоначальник Рихард Эйгим.

**ЛАТГАЛИЯ**

1) Древняя историческая область в Восточной Латвии, населенная латгалами. В X–XIII вв. княжества: Ерсика, Кокнесе, Талава. В XIII веке захвачена немецкими рыцарями.

2) С начала XVII века — название юго-восточной части этой территории южнее реки Айвиексте. Часть Задвинского герцогства, в 1629 году оставшаяся за Речью Посполитой. В 1772–1917 гг. в составе Российской империи (Двинская провинция), затем — западная часть Витебской губернии. С 1918 года — в составе Латвии.

*«История Отечества»*
(издательство «Большая Российская Энциклопедия»)

Рихард ЭЙГИМ.

# Рихард ЭЙГИМ:
# «Здесь будет город-сад!»

**Андрей ПЕТРОВ**

## Новый мэр мечтает превратить ДАУГАВПИЛС в маленькую ВЕНУ

**ИЗ ДОСЬЕ**

Рихард ЭЙГИМ родился 1 мая 1962 года в местечке Вишки (Даугавпилсский район). Закончил сельскую школу, затем юрфак Латвийского университета. С 1993 года — президент АО «Сталкерс», занимающегося торговлей нефтепродуктами. С ним «Сталкерс» вошел в число крупнейших налогоплательщиков Латвии. В 1999-м Рихард Эйгим был признан в Даугавпилсе «Человеком года». В марте этого года стал мэром Даугавпилса, победив на выборах бывшего хозяина города Алексея Видавского. А в мае «засветился» в традиционном латвийском списке миллионеров рижского журнала Klubs (и не в первый раз). Отличный спортсмен — чемпион Латвии по автоспидвею и чемпион Даугавпилса по хоккею с шайбой. Активно занимается благотворительностью: помогает детским домам, школам, малоимущим, церкви. Разведен, имеет двоих детей. 17-летняя Кристина и 16-летний Александр учатся в Русской гимназии.

Рихард Эйгим управляет городским хозяйством всего два месяца. Делать какие-то выводы пока рано, но появление около думы цветочных клумб и небольшого сада настраивает на оптимистический лад. Сразу вспоминается, что еще в бытность «простым» бизнесменом Эйгим построил единственный в Латгалии 4-звездочный мотель в 20 км от Даугавпилса. А к принадлежащему «Сталкерсу» автозаправочному комплексу подъезжают свадебные кортежи: у молодоженов Даугавпилса появилась новая традиция. Дело в том, что такой живописной автозаправки нет не только в Риге, но и, пожалуй, во всей Восточной Европе. Кругом зелень, бьют фонтаны, в пруду плещется рыба.

Но после 11 марта 2001 года для Рихарда Эйгима начался новый отсчет времени — он стал градоначальником. Тут фонтанами не отделаешься...

Итак, мы беседуем с мэром Даугавпилса в его служебном кабинете. Кофе — бодрящий, конфетка — сладкая, разговор — откровенный.

### Что? Где? Почём?

— Скажите, пожалуйста, какой журналистский вопрос вызывает у вас наибольшее раздражение, и я задам какой-нибудь другой.

— Такого вопроса нет. Все вопросы хороши (улыбается)... Журналисты задают «журналистские» вопросы — работа у вас такая. Мы — те, кому их задают, — не можем выбирать: этот вопрос мне нравится, а этот не нравится, не буду отвечать.

Такого просто не должно быть.

— Греет ли вашу душу очередное попадание в миллионерский список журнала Klubs?

— Я к этому отношусь совершенно спокойно. Это, как говорится, не я придумал. Журнал получает где-то информацию, цифры, знакомит с этим читателей. Значит, так оно и есть.

— Но разве это не есть своего рода признание вашей деловой состоятельности?

— Я и до появления своего имени в журнале ощущал себя достаточно обеспеченным человеком...

— И вы можете рассказать нашим читателям о вашей движимости и недвижимости? На чем ездите, где живете?

— У меня все время спрашивают, что у меня есть и почем. И я ничего не скрываю. В одной газете я прочитал о том, чем миллионер Эйгим отличается от других миллионеров. Оказывается, тем, что у него есть трактор МТЗ!

— И почем трактор?

— Он был приобретен в 92-м за... примерно три тысячи латов. Сейчас, конечно, цены значительно выросли.

— А сколько у вас иномарок?

— Одна. Это «Рено Шафран». Я не изменяю этой машине с 93-го года. Она хороша для наших дорог, у нее мощный двигатель, что меня очень устраивает. И стоит она — я предугадываю ваш вопрос — 25 тысяч латов.

— Где находится ваш дом?

— У меня трехкомнатная квартира в Даугавпилсе. Вилл на островах у меня нет, хотя они могли бы быть. Но я считаю, что в доме должен быть хозяин, в нем должны жить люди. Зачем мне вилла, которую я буду «навещать» раз в год?

### Всем отдыхать!

— Все знают, что вы автогонщик и хоккеист. Но чему бы все-таки отдали предпочтение?

— И то, и другое интересно. Я думаю, мужчине не надо долго рассказывать про риск и азарт. Кроме того, это помогает в работе. То есть помогает сохранять работоспособность. В зимний сезон играю в хоккей (с октября по май), а гонки хороши тем, что начинаются в мае и кончаются в октябре. Такой же цикл, как и в работе. Я называю это «спланированным спортом».

— Это можно назвать активным отдыхом. А как вы отдыхаете по-настоящему, расслабляетесь, так сказать? Когда были в отпуске последний раз?

— Я в отпуске каждый год. Те, кто «пропускает» отпуска, поступают, по-моему, в высшей степени неразумно. Все, кто со мной работали, всегда ездили куда-нибудь в отпуск. Ввожу это правило в приказном порядке. Также я против работы по выходным. Чего хоро-

шего можно ждать от измученных, морально и физически измотанных работников?

— Где, кстати, вы любите проводить отпуск?

— Я, как правило, делю его на две части. Зимой две недели посвящаю горным лыжам, летом люблю отдыхать у моря.

— У Красного, Средиземного?

— У любого, у океана... Меня к океану тянет.

— Где катаетесь на лыжах?

— В Швейцарии.

— Наверное, в Давосе?

— Нет, не в Давосе. Хотя я там и бывал пару раз. Но в Давосе слишком шумно и многолюдно. Много мировых звезд и тех, кто за ними наблюдает. А хочется отдохнуть... Я нашел место тихое. Но называть его я не хотел бы.

— Боитесь, что все читатели туда ринутся? А где еще вы чувствуете себя комфортно, где бы могли жить?

— Очень нравится Вена — красивейший город! Какие там парки! Хочется что-то подобное сделать и в Даугавпилсе...

*(Окончание — на 4-й стр.)*

---

**ШТРИХИ К ПОРТРЕТУ**

Когда Рихард Эйгим в прошлом году впервые попал в список 100 миллионеров Латвии, опубликованный в Klubs, он с друзьями долго смеялся. Очевидно, о такой возможности он даже не догадывался. Тем более, что буквально за день до выхода журнала в свет новоиспеченный миллионер купил на городском рынке чудные туфли за 14 латов. Обувь оказалась очень удобной, о чем Эйгим и рассказал в своем офисе. Через год Klubs снова ввел г-на Эйгима в список миллионеров, на этот раз состоящий из 150 имен. И журналисты не упустили случая «реанимировать» историю с туфлями, чтобы лишний раз напомнить читателям о том, что миллионеры — тоже люди.

К примеру, они не лишены милосердия. Тот же Эйгим уже несколько лет подряд делает рождественские подарки детям всей Латвии, «снаряжает» в 1-й класс ребятишек Даугавпилса. Две хоккейные коробки в городе — тоже из списка его добрых дел. А в январе «Вести» писали о том, как Эйгим провел электричество в лютеранскую церковь Даугавпилса — в кирху, где несколько лет не было света. Можно вспомнить и о реконструкции церкви в Дагде.

---

*Article 4* The Mayor of Daugavpils (Source: Magazine: National Geographic, 24th May 2001, Author: Andrew Petrou)

**Daugavpils** (*continued*)

*(Source: Magazine: National Geographic, 24th May 2001, Author: Andrew Petrou)*

## Translation of Magazine Article for CIM Case Study

### Article 4– Main Text

Latgale has a special position in Latvia. The mixture of races and cultures makes this region multi-faceted. But self-satisfied Rigans have always had a lordly, condescending attitude towards Latgale: what can you get from those 'Changals'? (Riga nickname for Latgalians; Latgalians call Riga people 'Chuily' meaning interpreter). They drink, they do nothing. If they are lucky they become hired helps or farm labourers. They speak a terrible dialect of Latvian. There are even Russian and Polish speakers. But the region's backwardness is understood by many people as an historic inevitability.

However, the 'National Geographic' editorial staff do not believe in such myths. That is why they have decided to organize the first Latgalian expedition to get an answer to the question, Quo vadis Latgale? The first place on our journey is Daugavpils – the unofficial capital of the 'Land of the Blue Lakes'. And here is our first interview – with its Mayor, Richard Eigims.

Richard Eigims – 'There will be a Garden-City!'

The new Mayor dreams of turning Daugavpils into a little Vienna.

Richards Eigims has managed the city's economy for only two months. It is too early to draw any conclusions, but the appearance of flower beds near the municipality creates an optimistic mood.

The first thing that impresses is that Eigims, from being a 'simple' businessman, has built the only 4-star hotel in Latgale, 20 kilometres north of Daugavpils. Wedding parties now drive to his 'Stalkers' petrol station for photographs. Daugavpils newlyweds have a new tradition. The thing is, such a picturesque petrol station does not exist in Riga, let alone the whole of eastern Europe! Everything around is green with plants, the fountains work, and there are fish splashing in the pond.

But from 11th March, 2001 there was a new beginning for Richard Eigims – he became the new City Mayor. So life is not only about fountains...

So onto our first interview with the new Mayor in his office – the coffee invigorating, the sweets sweet and the conversation open.

'Please tell me what journalists' questions annoy you the most and I will ask something different.'

RE: 'There are no such questions. All questions are good (smiles). Journalists ask journalistic questions – it is your work. We, those who are asked, cannot choose: I like this question, but don't like that so I am not going to answer it. It simply does not happen like that.'

'Has getting onto the list of millionaires in 'Klubs' magazine made you feel happy?'

RE: 'My attitude to this is very calm. That is to say, it was not invented by me. This magazine got their numbers from somewhere, different numbers, and introduced them to their readers. That's how it happened.'

'But isn't it some kind of recognition of your business success?'

RE: 'I already felt successful enough before my name appeared in this magazine.'

'Could you tell our readers about your car and your home? What do you drive? Where do you live?'

RE: 'I am constantly asked what do I have and how much did it cost. I don't hide anything. In one of the newspapers, I read a funny thing about myself. They were telling how millionaire Eigims differs from other millionaires. It turned out it was because I owned an MT3 tractor!'

'And how much was this tractor?'

RE: 'It was purchased in 1992 for approximately L3,000. Now, of course, it is worth much more.'

'And how many foreign cars have you got?'

RE: 'One. It is a Renault Safrane. I have had this car since 1993. It is good for our roads, it's got a powerful engine and it satisfies me. And it cost – I am anticipating your next question – L25,000.'

'And where is your house?'

RE: 'I have a three room flat in Daugavpils. I don't have villas on islands, although I could have them. But I believe there should be someone living in a house. What is the point of having a villa that you visit once a year?'

'Everybody knows you are a car racer and ice hockey player. But which do you prefer?'

RE: 'Both are interesting. I don't think I need to tell you about enjoying the risk and the excitement. Besides it helps me in my work. It helps me to work efficiently. During the winter, I play ice hockey from October until May. But the racing is good, because it starts in May and finishes in October. The same cycle as in work. I call it 'well planned sport'.'

'That sounds very active. But how do you really relax? When did you have your last holiday?'

RE: 'I have my holidays every year. Those who 'skip' holidays act, to my mind, extremely thoughtlessly. All the people who have worked with me went somewhere for their holidays. I will introduce this approach in the municipality. People who don't plan rest for themselves, will be instructed to take a break. I am also against work at the weekends. What can you expect from morally and physically exhausted workers?'

'By the way, where do you like to spend your holidays?'

RE: 'Usually, I separate my holidays into two parts. For two weeks in the winter, I am dedicated to downhill skiing. In the summer, I like the seaside.'

'The Red Sea, the Mediterranean?'

RE: 'At any... any ocean... summer drives me to the ocean.'

'Where do you ski?'

RE: 'In Switzerland.'
'Probably in Davros?'

RE: 'No. Although I've been there a couple of times. It's too busy and noisy in Davros. Many world famous people and those who follow them. But I want to relax... I've found a quiet place, but I don't want to name it!'

'Are you afraid that all our readers will rush there? But where else do you feel at home, where else could you live?'

RE: 'I like Vienna very much – it's one of the most beautiful cities! What parks there are! I would like to create something similar in Daugavpils...

Is it possible to relax in Latgale? Not everyone can go to Vienna or the Swiss Alps.

RE: 'There are many nice places in Latgale – it is the Land of the Blue Lakes! Near Daugavpils we have the lakes of Sventa and Stropi, near Kraslava there are remarkable places, in Aglona, in Cirishi (where my parents live). There are many places to go. And we have plans for creating new relaxation areas with very comfortable facilities and plans to upgrade the old places.'

'Do you use the help of alcohol or smoking to relax?'

RE: 'I relax with the help of sport and Russian Baths (sauna). In winter, after the Russian Bath, I swim through a hole in the ice. And that is enough!'

'Didn't the elections show that politics is a dirty business?'

RE: 'I don't think politics is a dirty business. Only some people do it with dirty hands.'

'Did you make any unexpected discoveries yourself in your new position of Mayor?'

RE: 'I did . . . a big discovery. Having gone through a very demanding pre-election campaign, I have recognized it is impossible to cheat people. They have their own opinion and believe in deeds not words. They know how to sort out the truth from the nicely packaged lie. They have placed their trust in us and we must justify that trust.'

'Is there any conflict between Eigims the Mayor and Eigims the Businessman?'

RE: 'There is, although business and city management are similar in many ways. But, as Daugavpils Mayor I feel a moral responsibility, the need to put people first. In some situations, Eigims the Businessman would act much tougher than Eigims the Mayor! Or, to put it another way, I am a softer touch as Mayor. That's why now, inside myself, there is a kind of 'rebuilding' going on.'

'Is it difficult to fire people? Aren't you conscience stricken afterwards?'

RE: 'When you fire a manager for work or financial indiscipline, you always remember they have a family and children. But those who suffer from such mismanagement also have families and they are much more numerous. That's why we have to take tough decisions, but always within the limits of the law. I never base such decisions on emotions. And I'm not going to hunt down members of the 'strange' parties. For me the elections finished on the 11th March.'

About the soul . . .

'What does charity mean for you? An impulse of the soul? Or is it a sober decision as some people think?'

RE: 'It is about self-help. When you help, you make your soul free from a heavy weight. You see how hard life is for most people, you look into the eyes of the orphans. How can you not share if, in a manner of speaking, your pockets bulge with money. Those who have money are obliged (and I'm not afraid of that word) to help their neighbours. Even more, people with only 10 lats will give 50 santimes to charity. This is far more significant than my help.'

'Haven't you ever been drawn to Riga?'

RE: 'I would leave for any part of the world not to have the problems that I have here. But I was born in Latgale, my parents live here, the graves of my grandmothers and grandfathers are here. And I want to help my native land.'

'Didn't you notice that many of those that voted for you were women?'

RE: 'So people tell me. Also in our city administration there are many women. To my mind it only indicates that the time for the fair sex has arrived. It is not a coincidence that our President is also a woman. There are many similar examples in other countries as well. Now men can lose their positions when judged on purely professional criteria. For me the gender of a staff member has no importance. Professionalism and integrity – that's what counts.'

'Do you feel your age?'

RE: 'It's difficult to cheat your own body. Now and again it reminds you that you are not 18 any more. If it doesn't remind you in the morning, it will during the day.'

'Or at night . . .'

RE: 'Or at night. The other thing is that you should live so that you don't wear yourself out prematurely. A 40-year person shouldn't have the body of a 60-year old.'

'What is the number one problem for Daugavpils?'

RE: 'It's a problem for the whole of Latgale. Unemployment. It can't be solved at once. There is no magic wand. It can only be solved gradually and together with the other regions of Latgale – it's not only Daugavpils, but Rezekne, Ludza, Livani . . . only with our joint efforts will we overcome unemployment.'

'Is there at least one enterprise left in Daugavpils that works to full capacity?'

RE: 'We have an enterprise that works nearly to full capacity. It is 'Lokomotiv' (makes/repairs trains) – one of the oldest factories in Latvia.'

'Can the problem of unemployment be solved without restoring production capacity?'

RE: 'Hardly. One business can't take up this load. Production needs to be increased and we have made a start. We've started with the canning factory. But two months is too little time in which to restore the many factories and businesses.'

'From your point of view, how does Riga see this area? What are their myths about Latgale?'

RE: 'Myths about Latgale were not born in Riga. We, the Latgalians, allowed them to develop. Everything depends on us. We will be respected if we work more and talk less.'

'What is the Latgalian character? Is there a different Latgalian mentality?'

RE: 'There is. Latgalians have their own distinct features. These are – purposefulness, energy and a capacity for work. These qualities will help us achieve success.'

'Thank you for the interview – goodbye.'

## Boxed Articles

*A Spoon of Tar* – Pre-election fights raised the blood pressure of Richard Eigims. Journalists called him a populist and rivals accused him of many things from smuggling oil products to poor knowledge of the Latvian language. And even if the smuggling accusations had no ground, the second point was successfully used by rivals. The Commission of the State Language found that, as a candidate for Mayor, Richard Eigims did have a weak knowledge of Latvian. Despite this he has managed to become leader of the city. And now the Mayor waits impatiently for June and the chance to demonstrate his linguistic skills in the next examination.

*Personal Impression* – The Daugavpils Mayor is undoubtedly a new type of manager. A manager for the 21st century.

He's not like a Soviet style leader, nor like a 'new Latgalian' as he doesn't like to give long speeches or feed people with promises. He knows how to organize work with crises. Women like him and men respect him. He is a charismatic leader and as the popular expression goes, people follow him with songs, not out of duty. And it seems everything will be successful – we hope so.

---

'Latgale – an ancient, historical area in the east of Latvia inhabited by Latgalians. During the 10th to 13th centuries there were three principalities, Jersika, Koknes and Talava. In the 13th century it was conquered by German knights.

From the beginning of the 17th century, the south-eastern part of this territory, south of the River Aivieksne, became part of the Zadvina Dukedom. In 1629, it became part of Pzech Posplita. From 1772–1917, it was within the borders of Imperial Russia (Dvina Province) and then the western part of Vitebsk Province. Since 1918, it has been part of Latvia.'

*From the History of the Motherland – Great Russian Encyclopaedia*

## About Richard Eigims

Richard Eigims was born on the first of May 1962 in a small village, Vishki (Daugavpils District). After local school he went to the legal faculty of Latvia University. Since 1993 he has been president of Stalkers, a joint stock company, trading in oil products. Under him, Stalkers has been included in Latvia's list of top company tax payers. In 1999, Eigims was acknowledged as Daugavpils Person of the Year. This March he became Mayor of Daugavpils, beating the former Mayor, Alexei Vidavskis. But in May he appeared in the Latvian list of millionaires published by the magazine 'Klubs' (and not for the first time). A great sportsman – a champion of Latvia in car speedway and a champion of Daugavpils in ice hockey. Actively works for charity: helps asylums, schools, poor people and the church. Divorced with two children, 17 year old Christina and 16 year old Alexander, who study in the Russian Gymnasium.

When last year, Richard Eigims got into the list of the 100 millionaires of Latvia, he was laughing about it with his friends. Obviously, such a possibility had not occurred to him. In addition, just the day before the article was published, the newly discovered millionaire had bought a pair of shoes in the local market for only L14. The shoes turned out to be very comfortable, he later reported.

A year later 'Klubs' again included Mr Eigims in their list of millionaires that now comprised 150 names. And journalists resurrected the story about the shoes to show that millionaires were just people.

And they are not without charity. Mr Eigims has for several years made Christmas gifts to children throughout Latgale, and provides equipment to the school's first form. He is also a sponsor of local ice hockey.

In January, this magazine reported that Mr Eigims had installed electricity in Daugavpils Lutheran Church, where there had been no light at all for several years. We also can recall a story about the reconstruction of a church in Dagda.

## ПУТЕШЕСТВИЕ БЕЗ КАРТЫ

# Я видел город

## Там очень красивые женщины, проезд в трамвае стоит 10 сантимов, а обездоленным помогают... безработные

Погода благоприятствовала нашим замыслам. В теплый майский вечер от Рижской автостанции, пару раз фыркнув мотором, «отчалил» автобус, взявший курс на Даугавпилс точно по расписанию. Никаких приключений в дороге не было, за окном мелькали традиционные картинки: леса, поля, луга, водоёмы. А вот латгальский пейзаж приятно разнообразили многочисленные гнёзда аистов, свитые прямо на телеграфных столбах. Поездка длилась немногим более трех с половиной часов. Приехали. Даугавпилс. *

### «Я шлялся по городу...»

→ Андрей ПЕТРОВ

Знакомство с латгальской столицей началось на следующее утро. Брал разбег обычный рабочий день. Сразу бросилось в глаза отсутствие на улицах толп спешащих людей с озабоченными и угрюмыми лицами — непременным атрибутом мегаполисов. Неторопливый ритм жизни города, спокойствие и приветливость его жителей не могли не сказаться самым благотворным образом на моем душевном состоянии. Правда, это состояние длилось всего два дня (срок моего пребывания в Даугавпилсе). Не исключено, что через неделю–другую здесь можно было бы заскучать по привычной рижской суете. Но за два дня этого не произошло.

Понятно, что проблем у даугавпилчан будет поболе, чем у рижан. Одна безработица чего стоит. Но на их уравновешенности и доброжелательности это никак не сказывается. Так же, как и на красоте местных женщин и девушек. Их обилие и разнообразие не может не радовать мужской взор (см. фото). Уже на автовокзале можно было увидеть Афродиту, торгующую мороженым. К сожалению, на предложение сфотографироваться «богиня» реагирует неожиданным образом: делает попытку умчаться с тележкой холодного лакомства подальше от заезжих искусителей. Похвальная скромность, но мы ж не из «Плейбоя»...

В городском парке удалось побеседовать с тремя очаровательными и 11-классницами из польской школы — Оксаной, Леной и Наташей. Девушки очень любят свой родной город, но их дальнейшие планы связаны с учебой за границей или в Риге. К сожалению, в местном пединституте обучение стоит дороговато. Так происходит утечка мозгов и... ну вы понимаете...

Приехать в другой город и не побывать на местном рынке — нонсенс. И вот уже слышится до боли знакомое чревовещание: «Сигаретки, сигаретки...» Но, в отличие от Риги, спиртика ни разу не предложили. А вот цыплят или утят можно было купить запросто, хотя вокруг этого мини-зоопарка собираются, как правило, не покупатели, а зрители. Городской рынок в Даугавпилсе чуть меньше рижского «Матвейчика». Попытался сравнивать цены — быстро надоело (да простят меня домохозяйки). Какие-то товары на 10–15 сантимов дешевле, чем в Риге. Какие-то не отличаются

В Даугавпилсе девчонки красивые очень!

по цене. Но это разница весьма важна для горожан, доходы большинства из которых гораздо скромнее, чем у жителей латвийской столицы.

После знакомства с центром города отправляюсь к необычной достопримечательности Даугавпилса — тюрьме с поэтическим народным именем «Белая лебедь». Когда мы с фотографом начинаем «щелкать» тюрьму с воздушного моста, слышим оттуда глас, усиленный мегафоном: «Это закрытый объект — снимать запрещено!» Кричим в ответ (как понимаем — охране): «Мы снимаем не вас, а железную дорогу!» (Она действительно рядом.) «Они говорят, что снимают железную дорогу!» — продолжаются переговоры охраны по громкой связи. Мы так и не знаем, чем закончилась эта содержательная беседа, так как, закончив съемки, благоразумно удаляемся.

«Белая лебедь» во всей красе.

Городской базар.

* Начало серии публикаций о Латгалии см. в №21 еженедельника «Вести» — интервью с новым мэром Даугавпилса Рихардом ЭЙГИМОМ.

*Article 5* Daugavpils the City (Source: Magazine: National Geographic, 24th May 2001, Author: Andrew Petrou)

## Article 5 – Main Text

Travel without a map – I have seen the city.

There are very beautiful women and a ticket for the tram costs 10 santimes, but the people are generally poor and rely on unemployment benefit.

The weather welcomed our arrival. On this warm May evening from the Riga bus station a bus has cast off towards Daugavpils exactly on time. There were no adventures on the journey and many traditional scenes of forests, fields, farms and meadows passed rapidly by. But the Latgalian scenery was nicely typified by the many storks' nests on the tops of telegraph poles. After a ride of three and a half hours, we arrived in Daugavpils.

I was loafing about the city... by Andrew Petrov.

My acquaintance with the Latgalian capital began the following morning. A normal working day was beginning. What was striking? An absence of crowds of people hurrying about with anxious and gloomy faces – a normal attribute of big cities. The unhurried rhythm of the city life, the calmness and cordiality of its people lifted my heart. True, this feeling only lasted two days – the length of my stay in Daugavpils. Perhaps after a week or two, I would have missed the hustle and bustle of Riga. But certainly not in two days.

It is clear that the inhabitants of Daugavpils have more problems than Riga. Just think of the impact of high unemployment. But it does not reflect in their stoicism and benevolence. The abundance and beauty of the local women and girls cannot help but bring tears to a man's eyes. Already at the bus station, it was possible to see Aphrodite selling ice cream. Unfortunately, at the offer to take her photograph, the goddess responds rather unexpectedly. She makes off with her handcart to get away from the strange tempters. Such modesty, but we are not from Playboy!

In the city park, we had the opportunity to talk with three charming pupils from the 11th grade of the Polish school, Oksana, Lena and Natasha. These girls love the town of their birth very much, but their future plans include studies in Riga or abroad. Unfortunately, in the local Pedagogical Institute studying is quite costly. Thus, 'flow away the brains' ...well you know what I mean.

It's nonsense to come to another town and not visit the local market. And there we hear the all too familiar ventriloquism, 'Cigarettes, cigarettes!'. But unlike Riga, spirits were not offered at all. On the contrary, live chicken and ducklings can easily be bought. Although around this miniature zoo, there are more spectators than buyers. The city market in Daugavpils is a bit smaller than Riga's 'Matveichiks'. I did try to compare prices, but soon got bored. (I hope housewives will forgive me). Some goods were 10–15 santimes cheaper than Riga, some did not differ in price. But these differences are only really important for the city dwellers, whose incomes are much more modest than those in the Latvian capital.

After getting acquainted with the centre of the city, I made my way to an unusual attraction of Daugavpils – a jail with a poetic, national name of 'The White Swan Hotel'. When the photographer starts clicking away standing on a bridge, we suddenly hear a disembodied voice from a loudspeaker saying it is forbidden to photograph this prison! We shout in reply, assuming the voice to be from security, that we do not photograph you but the railway. (It really does run nearby). 'They say they photograph the railway' – negotiations continue via the loudspeaker. But we never knew how this conversation ended as by then we had completed our filming and left.

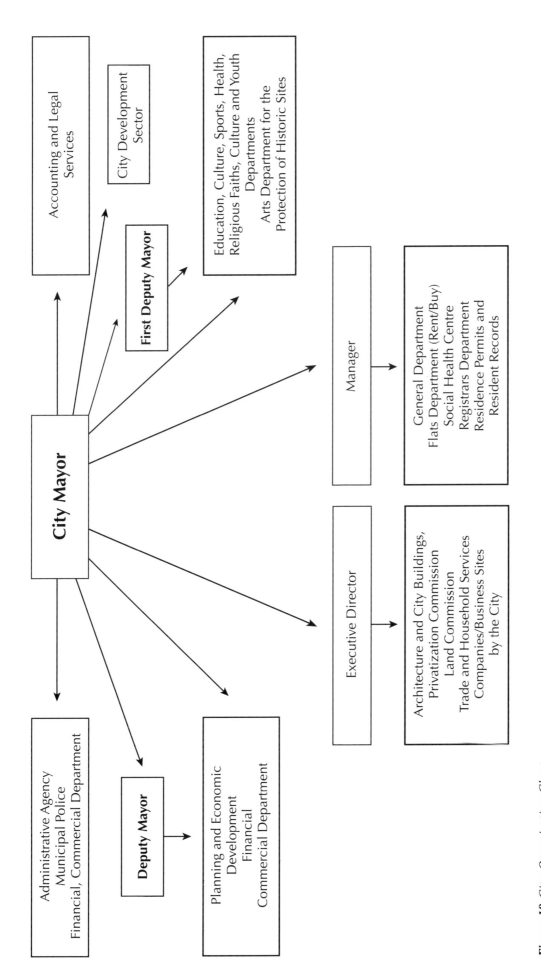

Accounting and Legal Services

City Development Sector

Education, Culture, Sports, Health,
Religious Faiths, Culture and Youth
Departments
Arts Department for the
Protection of Historic Sites

First Deputy Mayor

City Mayor

Manager

General Department
Flats Department (Rent/Buy)
Social Health Centre
Registrars Department
Residence Permits and
Resident Records

Executive Director

Architecture and City Buildings,
Privatization Commission
Land Commission
Trade and Household Services
Companies/Business Sites
by the City

Administrative Agency
Municipal Police
Financial, Commercial Department

Deputy Mayor

Planning and Economic
Development
Financial
Commercial Department

**Figure 18** *City Organisation Chart*

# Part 3: Past examiners' reports and specimen answers

9.54: Strategic Marketing Management: Analysis & Decision – Examiner's Report

Date: December 2000

## General Comments – Pirelli

This paper was an interesting departure from the norm and covered many business to business issues within the cable industry. The pass rate varied according to centres, again showing the importance of centres offering high quality tutoring. Better tutoring would really help to reduce the marginal failures. There is still a marked difference between UK centres and international centres. In some instances, the gap is closing and I feel that my visit to Malaysia and Singapore should be helpful to the tutors who attended the workshops. Some centres in Sri Lanka continue to perform well.

## Question 1

For the first time, I feel that many of the examiners were surprised by the low standard achieved in this question. Many students find it difficult to distinguish strategy from objectives. Often strategies are covered at the end with reams of poor analysis. Justification is still poor and the cover of the marketing mix is skeletal. Marketing budgets and contingency factors were often woefully handled. As usual innovation was lacking. On a positive note, the good centres are performing better than ever and the answers tended to be interesting and well laid out. The pilot centres in general have performed well. However, in some cases students trotted out excellent analyses but performed poorly in the examination, hoping that the analyses would carry them through. More tutor training is required if the pilot studies are to move forward in the future.

## Question 2

This question was generally well handled by most students. A good proportion also considered the short term and long term issues with respect to customers/company/suppliers. Most had a good grasp of e-commerce issues and so even if all the requisite issues were not covered by some candidates, enough valid points were made to enable them to receive a pass mark. This question was handled well globally and this was heartening.

## Question 3

This question was generally handled poorly with students submitting international marketing plans (not asked for) of a very generalized nature. Many of the international candidates used a classic textbook approach with very few links to the actual case. Very few candidates addressed market selection criteria and/or market entry in any specific way.

This is the first time that the marks were distributed 40:30:30. This has now tipped the balance towards Questions 2. and 3., lessening the reliance on well developed standard answers for Question 1. This, I feel is a good move and hopefully addresses many other marketing issues that are generally contained in cases.

# Specimen Answers for Strategic Marketing Management: Analysis & Decision December 2000

## Overview

### The Case

The Case Study has been based on a real organization. The case poses real problems and takes into account the opportunities and difficulties faced by a manufacturing organization that is affected by market deregulation and competition. This case has no personalized comments, is factual and contains no 'red herrings'. Nonetheless, there is the usual problem of an extensive range of detailed information. There is a need to develop clear and concise insights into the key issues involved in developing a strategy.

### Key Issues

i.     The changing market conditions, with the growth of cheap imports.
ii.    The fragmented supply structure.
iii.   Intensely competitive market.
iv.    The differing aspects of deregulation.
v.     The different levels of deregulation in different countries.
vi.    Pirelli's experience of serving the UK market – being the first and most deregulated market in the world.
vii.   Low level of branding in the cable sector.
viii.  The strength of the distributors.
ix.    The potential for direct distribution techniques.
x.     The growth of ecological issues, especially in the UK market.
xi.    Regulatory factors.
xii.   The changing nature of the regional providers.
xiii.  Mergers and acquisitions within the RECs in the UK.
xiv.   The growth of outsourcing within the utilities sector in the UK.
xv.    The potential impact of the Internet B2B strategies adopted by Pirelli on the cables sector.
xvi.   The pressures on cost reduction.
xvii.  The importance of R&D on developing High Tension Superconductor cables.
xviii. The new entrants such as Virgin creating a brand image in a dull sector.
xix.   The potential to work with the World Bank.
xx.    Pirelli's market share per product line is around 20–25%.
xxi.   The structural changes in the industry favour the larger players.
xxii.  Customer service and installation design are important features of the market.
xxiii. International turnkey operations.
xxiv.  Losses sustained by the company in 1999 to the value of £7.7m.
xxv.   The current largest market is the UK, but studies are needed to establish the nature and extent of the growth markets in the rest of the world.
xxvi.  The nature and impact of the merger with BICC.

### The Answers

This case was reasonably straightforward and did not contain many surprises. It was important, therefore, that the following issues were considered:

1.  The application of theory.
2.  The amount of International marketing theory/application to the case as well as the amount of communication theory that can be utilized.
3.  The answers need to be strategic not tactical.
4.  The answers given must be realistic and practical.
5.  A degree of innovation and lateral thinking is important.

6. It is important that the questions are answered within the given context.
7. The additional information is quite important in making a clearer assessment of the company's strategy. The information shows that BICC could improve Pirelli's market share. However, there could be an impact on branding issues.

## Answer – Question 1

### Approach

This question required students to use many of the strategic planning models used by marketers. These are McDonald, Andrews, Doyle etc. Candidates then needed to consider the following:

   a. The objectives that they wished to set for Pirelli for the long and short term.
   b. The rate of technological change and the degree of flexibility allowed by the plan.
   c. The fragmented nature of the products and the markets and mapping out the key growth areas.
   d. The possibility of taking advantage of the changing market structure of the RECs.
   e. The strategic vision should be based on the core values of the company and be reflected in the segments that are targeted.
   f. The strategy should take into account the financial status of the company.
   g. What market positioning strategies should the company adopt vis à vis the different markets? Appendices 4. and 5. and Tables 1. and 2. are quite important.
   h. The company has a good record of product development internationally.
   i. The company needs to rethink its branding stance for the future.
   j. How should the company leverage its BICC merger in the marketplace?
   k. The fragmented market means that the market shares of individual companies are quite small.
   l. The company has to decide how closely it is going to work with the distributors.
   m. Models such as Porter, Ansoff, BCG, GEC, Shell Directional and Gap could be used in the analysis of the case.
   n. What are the constraints on the given strategy? How can the company follow a market led strategy? What would be a realistic marketing budget?
   o. Which markets are the key priorities and why?
   p. As no organization chart is provided, how should the company execute its marketing strategies?
   q. How much of the company's money should be directed towards developing an Internet strategy?
   r. Should the company take a branding stance for the cables based on ecological issues?
   s. The company needs to have a sensible long term B2B strategy for the Internet.
   t. Capitalizing on the key points made in Figure 4.

### Points in a Strategic Plan

   1. Set corporate objectives.
   2. Identify target markets.
   3. Set marketing objectives.
   4. Develop marketing strategy and tactics.
   5. Organize control systems.

Given the points above, the best answers will show a clear grasp of the following:

   1. A good analysis of the current position.
   2. The development of a strategic plan with fully developed implementation strategies.
   3. A good justification of the strategies to be adopted.

For pilot study centres, 15 marks were allocated for the pre-prepared analyses.

## Answer – Question 2

### Approach

Pirelli has fully committed itself to a bold Internet strategy. This is unusual for a large manufacturing company. The implications are great and they encompass the following:

a. A better B2B service.
b. Better customer relationship management.
c. It can leverage its large international network of workstations.
d. Monitoring distribution of goods.
e. Reduction of transaction costs.
f. The potential to cut out the 'middlemen' – the distributors. This has very important implications for pricing and market branding.
g. The need to change a manufacturing culture to a marketing culture.
h. The need to learn from the Italian experience.
i. The need to develop an effective plan with clear goals for the growth of sales through the web.
j. Monitoring effectiveness of the medium.
k. Ensuring that cultural nuances are taken into account.
l. Utilizing the Internet to develop a good branding strategy.
m. Building a supply chain management system.

This was quite an open question and was designed to test candidates' abilities to understand contemporary issues involved in e-commerce business strategies and their impact on marketing.

A good answer will take into the following:

1. Critical analysis of e-commerce issues.
2. Links with the overall strategy, taking into account long and short term issues.

8 marks were allocated for pre-prepared analyses from pilot centres.


## Answer – Question 3

### Approach

The international markets are dependent on the nature and extent of deregulation within each country. An analysis of the accounts shows the following market shares:

|                                   | 1999   | 1998   |
|-----------------------------------|--------|--------|
| UK                                | 64%    | 59.93% |
| Rest of Europe                    | 21%    | 18.6%  |
| Middle East                       | 2%     | 5.6%   |
| Africa                            | 0.28%  | 3.52%  |
| Americas                          | 0.41%  | 0.54%  |
| Asia Pacific including Australia  | 10.1%  | 11.8%  |

There is drop in all the markets, especially in Africa and Asia Pacific. Rest of Europe's share is growing.

As Pirelli gains experience in the deregulated UK market it can utilize this experience in the different markets.

The International Marketing approaches should therefore consider the following:

a. Develop an understanding of the extent of deregulation in each market and the need to monitor this for the potential for future sales.
b. Work closely with the World Bank on development issues.

   c.  Use the Internet for marketing.

   d.  Ascertain the potential for providing the latest technologies in the most developed markets.

   e.  Focus on the European market.

   f.  Brand Pirelli as the cable of choice as there are so many other low cost competitors.

   g.  Monitor large projects in the key markets for the chance to sell turnkey operations and cables.

   h.  Offer a differentiated total package in the different markets, taking a polycentric approach.

Good answers needed to show an understanding of:

- General analysis of International Marketing.
- Developing International Marketing approaches.

For pilot centres, 7 marks were allocated for the pre-prepared analytical material.

## General Observations

As usual I was keen to see coherence, strategic thinking, justification and detail featuring in the answers. The case was quite long and there was a considerable amount of data so that candidates were able to fashion a range of interesting answers. Creativity and innovation were rewarded.

Two specimen answers have been chosen to illustrate how good candidates approached the case. The chosen answers reflect the fact that there are different ways to answer the questions set. Marks are given on the **quality** of the answers and not whether they are deemed to be right or wrong. The answers also demonstrate what is possible to achieve within the given timeframe of three hours.

**Ashok Ranchhod**

**Senior Examiner**

## First Student Answer – Question 1

**Report**

| | |
|---|---|
| **To:** | **Peter J. Margrave, MD Pirelli General** |
| **From:** | **J. Fraser, Marketing Consultant** |
| **Date:** | **8th December, 2000** |
| **Subject:** | **UK Three Year Strategic Marketing Plan: Pirelli Cable** |

### Contents

1. Introduction.
2. Situational Analysis.
3. Mission and Objectives.
4. Strategics.
5. Marketing Mix and Tactics.
6. Organizational Design.
7. Budgets.
8. Implementation.
9. Control, Monitoring and Contingencies.

### 1. Introduction

This report is aimed at establishing a clear marketing strategy and implementation plan for Pirelli Cables (PC) in the UK for the period 2001–2003.

It is the result of analysis of external and internal information, which in some instances is incomplete. It is therefore recommended that further research be undertaken as part of the implementation phase to validate findings and fine-tune plans.

## 2. *Situational Analysis*

### 2.1 The Cables Market

The UK cables market can be segmented into:

a. Telecommunications (including optical fibres – little information held on this market so further research needed).
b. Energy which splits into two sub-segments:
   i. The General Market – the building chain from power generation through to delivery to end consumers.
   ii. The Electricity Market – the supply chain from power generation through to delivery to end consumers.

   Following the purchase of the power cable business in the UK from BICC it is estimated that more than 75% of PC's revenues come from the UK.

### 2.2 Summary of Situational Analysis

Application of PEST and SWOT analyses have led to the following key points:

a. Following purchase of BICC business it is estimated that PC has UK market shares of 22% of the General Market and 70% of the Electricity Market (assumes 75% of BICC share transfers to PC).
b. Competition in the UK is high, particularly through new entrants competing principally on price.
c. Pirelli is a recognizable (global) brand but this does not relate to cables.
d. PC made a loss in 1999. Figures are currently consolidated with construction in Pirelli General's accounts but it appears the loss was due to a fall in revenues and in gross profit margin (23.5% in 1998, 15.7% in 1999).
e. Customers (RECs) are increasingly seeking to outsource both cable installation and project management.
f. Customers are replacing old cables with new technology high efficiency and specialist cables.
g. PC has strength in R&D and competitive advantage in new cable technologies (including environmentally friendly).
h. PC has strength in installation and project management capabilities.
i. E-commerce developments are taking place (in PC and its competitors).
j. Customers are seeking greater efficiencies through just in time (JIT) supply.
k. PC has been product driven rather than market/customer focused.
l. Purchase of BICC provides opportunities to restructure and nationalize into a market bid single company.

### 2.3 Key Issues for Pirelli Cables

a. PC must establish a return for shareholders.
b. PC must establish a competitive strategy vis-à-vis those competing on price as competition will increase (brand is key).
c. E-commerce provides opportunities and threats but is critical in developing relationships.
d. An integrated company with a market focus is critical and points to the importance of Customer Relationship Management (CRM) and Key Account Managers (KAMs).

## 3. Mission and Objectives

### 3.1 UK Mission Statement

Pirelli Cables' mission is to serve the needs of its customers by being the leading provider of innovative, integrated solutions for the transfer of power and information.

### 3.2 Corporate Objectives

For UK:

- To improve return on shareholders' funds to 15% by 2003.

### 3.3 Marketing Objectives

a. To grow market share in UK General Market by 2% p.a. over next three years (currently 22%).
b. To maintain market share in the UK Electricity Market at 70%.
c. To increase awareness of the PC brand (innovative, safe, reliable and environmentally friendly) in end-users in both General and Electricity markets by 10% p.a. over each of the next three years.
d. To achieve marketing oriented culture with quality standard recognition by 2002.
e. To establish a Marketing Information System (MkIS) that can be benchmarked on providing works class information for prioritization of R&D and NPD in relation to key customer segments.

## 4. Strategies

### 4.1 Segmentation and Targeting

a. **General**

   Segments into:

   | **Building** | **DIY** |
   |---|---|
   | Distribution | Warehouses |
   | Wholesalers | DIY Stores |
   | Contractors | |
   | End-users | |

   'Contractors' is the target segment, bypassing wholesalers/distributors to increase margins and market and market share.

b. **Electricity**

   Segments into:

   | **Circulation** | **Transmission** | **Distribution** |
   |---|---|---|
   | Power Companies | National Grid | RECs |

   'RECs' is target market (market share focused here: 88%) competing with contractors for outsourcing business.

### 4.2 Strategic Direction

The two key directions to be set to support the objectives relating to competitive strategy (and consequent importance of brand) and market/product development strategy.

## 4.2.1 Competitive Strategy (Porter)

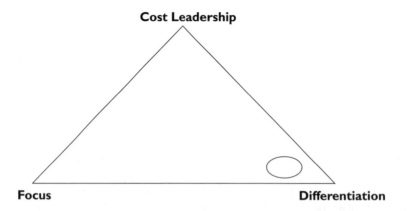

**Focus:** Not recommended. Does not support ambition as market leader.

**Cost Leadership:** Not recommended. Whilst exploitation of market dominance following BICC purchase will enable PC to be competitive on price, following a pure cost (simplification) strategy would ignore core strengths from PC in R&D and cable technology.

**Differentiation:** Recommended to exploit the following:

- Technological advantage.
- Brand awareness.

**Consequent Brand Positioning**

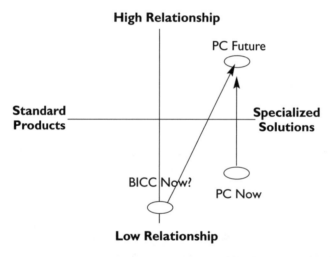

**Note:** Could use BICC to develop a 'fighting brand'. Not recommended at present as it would stretch company too much and this could also create a lack of marketing orientation.

## 4.2.2 Market/Product Development (Ansoff)

|  | **Current Products** | **New Products** |
|---|---|---|
| **Current Markets** | **Market Penetration** <br><br> • Replacement of old cables. <br> • Brand awareness. <br> • CRM and KAMs. <br> • Web marketing. | **Product Development** <br><br> • Consulting capability. <br> • Packaging into integrated solution. <br> • Tailor e-commerce/JIT. |
| **New Markets** | **Market Development** <br> Key market segments already covered in UK. | **Diversification** <br> Too risky. |

### 4.3 Consequent Strategies

#### 4.3.1 Market Penetration/Defence

- Defend Electricity Market share and grow General Market share through **brand awareness** with end users.
- Establish CRM and e-CRM to allow relationship marketing.
- Establish KAMs.
- Focus on RECs and contractors (Electricity and General respectively).
- Web marketing.

#### 4.3.2 Product Development

a. Development of Modular Product offering to include the following package:

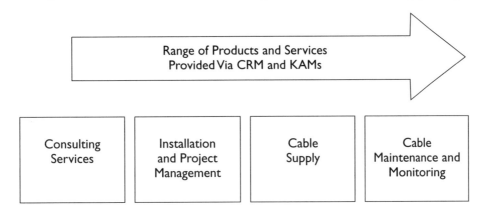

b. E-commerce/e-Pirelli
   - Web-based marketing.
   - JIT systems with dedicated secure access.

## 5. Marketing Mix and Tactics

### 5.1 Product

Develop products/services with following key features:

| | | |
|---|---|---|
| a. | Consulting Services: | Systems Design.<br>Benchmarking.<br>Cost Efficiencies Identification.<br>Technological Advice. |
| b. | Installation and Project Management: | Systems Implementation.<br>Cable Installation.<br>Complete Project Management. |
| c. | Cable Supply: | Standard Cables.<br>Specialist Cables.<br>Link to E-commerce (JIT). |
| d. | Cable Management and Monitoring: | Management Contracts.<br>Upgrade Options.<br>Service Level Agreements. |

### 5.2 Pricing

- Must be **competitive** for core components as the customers are price sensitive.
- **Premium** for value added services e.g. consultancy.

### 5.3  Distribution

a.  Focus on RECs in Electricity Market:

- Distribute complete package of services through KAMs.

b.  Focus on Contractors in General Market:
- Withdraw from distributors/wholesalers.
- Utilize CRM and e-commerce (JIT).

### 5.4  Promotion and Communication

- Pirelli as umbrella brand.
- Individual product brands.
- Push strategy – contractors and RECs through CRM and KAMs.
- Pull strategy – raise awareness with end users.
- Profile strategy – Electricity: Expert in deregulated market.
  - General: Leading industry knowledge in cables.

### 5.5  People

- Train sales managers to become KAMs.
- Recruit Marketing Director.
- Recruit/appoint e-CRM Project Director.
- Recruit consultants.

### 5.6  Process

- Establish service standards.
- Implement e-CRM.

### 5.7  Physical Evidence

- Quality professional literature.
- Help desk for e-commerce.
- Accreditation process for consultants.

## 6.  *Organizational Design*

Establish single company functional design:

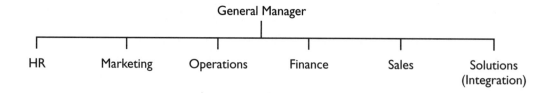

- **Organizational Development**    (See below)
- Training
- Personnel/Recruitment

- **Logistics**
- Solutions Management
- Quality
- Purchasing
- Manufacturing
- R&D

**Marketing Department**

- Market Intelligence and Research.
- Information Systems.

- Product Management.
- Business Planning.
- Marketing Communications.

Internal marketing of changes to be achieved by:

a. Communication to all employees on strategy.
b. Cascade key brand values.
c. Train KAMs.
d. Indicate course for new recruits.

## 7. Budgets

Estimated marketing budget for UK of £5m:

CRM/e-CRM and MkIS                    £2m.

Communications/brand awareness        £3m.

(Below-the-line including web).

## 8. Implementation and Monitoring

| Product Development | 2001 | 2002 | 2003 |
|---|---|---|---|
| R&D. | | | ⟶ |
| MR and MKIS. | | | ⟶ |
| Consulting Recruitment and Implementation. | ⟶ | | |
| E-commerce. | ⟶ | | |
| **Market Penetration** | | | |
| Communications (including web). | | | ⟶ |
| CRM/e-CRM. | ⟶ | | |
| KAM Implementation. | ⟶ | | |

## 9. Control, Monitoring and Contingencies

- Sales and marketing objectives to be defined and broken down into **sales targets** for each KAM.
- Sales MI system (linked to CRM) to provide information on **key performance indicators**:
- Sales versus targets.
- Cross-sales.
- Customer persistency.

**Monitor Response to Marketing Campaigns**

- Sales.
- Responses.
- Web site hits.

**Monitor Key Trades through MkIS**

- Competitor activities.

**Contingency Plans**

- For launch of fighting brand (BICC) if under pressure on price from cheap imports.
- For failure to achieve targets.

---

### Senior Examiner's Comments

This is a good, comprehensive and sensible answer to the question with good analyses of market positioning and current situation. The answer could have been improved by providing more justifications and underpinning detail from the balance sheet. Also the contingency plan is not really a contingency plan. It should be there to provide a realistic fall back position for the company.

---

## First Student Answer – Question 2.

Report

| | |
|---|---|
| To: | Peter J. Margrave, MD Pirelli General |
| From: | J. Fraser, Marketing Consultant |
| Date: | 8th December, 2000 |
| Subject: | Marketing Implications of E-commerce: Pirelli Cables (PC) |

### Contents

1. Background.
2. Key Strategic Issues.
3. Generic Considerations.
4. Strategies:
   - Company (staff).
   - Customers.
   - Suppliers.
   - Other Stakeholders.
5. Summary.

### 1. Background

a. PC has invested considerable amounts in e-Pirelli (and Cable @ Pirelli specifically) delivering both Intranet and Extranet.
b. Analysis of BICC e-commerce capabilities needs to be undertaken – likely they will have invented. May be synergies through UK purchase.
c. Projected e-commerce share of General Market in Italy by 2000 is 65%. European sector sales projected to 40% each (400m Euros).
d. In addition to web site (marketing), the Extranet allows business to business (B2B) relationship.
e. Cable @ Pirelli is currently exclusive to Pirelli distributors.

### 2. Key Strategic Issues

a. Global strategy – issues on pricing strategy and transparency and on consistency of product supply versus country by country adaptation.
b. Cable @ Pirelli must reinforce brand values (innovative, safe, reliable, environmentally friendly).

c. Cable @ Pirelli is a key relationship marketing tool and is also critical in meeting customer needs for JIT delivery.
d. Market research and modelling is needed to identify demand (and hence roll out schedules). Information to hand suggests a large proportion of global market (say 40% within 3 years).
e. Technological integration into e-CRM (and other processing etc.) is critical. WAP compatibility is also important.

## 3. Generic Considerations

a. Products and services provided (and packaging) – provide modular product offering.
b. Pricing – price via sign-up/KAMs (to allow country by country pricing for RECs).
c. Distribution – focused initially at RECs (Electricity Market) and contractors (General Market).
d. Integration of Marketing Communications – Ensure fit with CRM and below-the-line campaigns.

## 4. Strategies

Overall, strategies must be rolled out consistently globally.

### 4.1 Short Term Considerations/Strategies

- Project team to deliver common brand, technology and service levels (send people from PC and BICC).
- Integration into marketing plans.
- Appropriate investments committed to the project.

### 4.2 Overall Strategies for Each Shareholder Group

a. **Company/Staff**
**Short Term Priorities**
- Communication of key managers, brand values, news, executive Q&A via Intranet enables consistent culture.
- Integration of Cable @ Pirelli information into CRM to allow marketing staff to monitor and plan campaigns.

**Longer Term**

- Communication of product knowledge to sales and relationship staff.
- Communication of consistent policies and procedures globally, aiding provision of common service levels to customers.
- Staff ordering goods from suppliers (see below).

b. **Customers**
**Short Term Priorities**

- Secure sign-in targeted at RECs (Electricity) and contractors (General) to use JIT order systems.
- Web marketing allowing customers to view products, specifications and for PC to reinforce its brand values.
- Cable @ Pirelli sold alongside package of products/services by KAMs.
- Features should enable customers to integrate Cable @ Pirelli into office procedures easily (e.g. stock level checking, re-ordering facility, guaranteed delivery options).
- Efficient email and helpdesk facilities.
- Reinforce brand values (see below re other stakeholders).

**Longer Term**

- Roll out to new markets and new segments (e.g. DIY), adapting language and product availability for international markets.

c. **Suppliers**

Lower priority than customer developments but need to:

- Integrate e-commerce to allow ordering of goods by PC staff via Extranet.
- Pull JIT down supply chain to ensure JIT offering to customers does not decrease margins through PC having to hold stock.
- Enable automatic re-ordering from suppliers as to result of sales to own customers (IT systems link).

d. **Other Stakeholders**

Web site will be critical in establishing long term brand values with end-users.

- Web site should include information/PR to reinforce brand values:
    i. Reliability and safety – information on PC cable specifications and users in critical areas.
    ii. Environmentally friendly – information on efficiency/environmentally friendly cables and use in, for example, wind power.
    iii. Innovation – information on R&D and new products.
        - Include web links **to** other sites e.g. environmental groups and key users (reference sites).
        - Web links **from** other sites to attract end-users to the site.

## 5. Summary

- Cable @ Pirelli provides a critical part of the marketing strategy both in the UK and globally.
- Web marketing and dedicated JIT sign-in, targeted at RECs (and contractors) at the critical moments.
- Cable @ Pirelli is critical in establishing brand values and awareness in end-users.

---

### Senior Examiner's Comments

This is a very good, comprehensive answer to the question and addresses the key issues surrounding the development of E-commerce. Further issues that could have been considered were the shortening of the distribution channel in the short term and the problems of changing a manufacturing based organization into a modern E-commerce organization. Some of the short term problems will surely be to improve and develop internal communication.

---

## First Student Answer – Question 3.

Report

To:         Peter J. Margrave, MD Pirelli General

From:       J. Fraser, Marketing Consultant

Date:       8th December, 2000

Subject:    International Marketing Approaches for Pirelli General (PG)

## Contents

1. Situational Analysis.
2. International Marketing Objectives.
3. International Marketing Strategies:
    - Selection of Markets.
    - Entry Methods.
4. Product Mix/Tactics.

5. Budgets.
6. Control and Contingencies.

Approaches are developed and justified within this plan format for ease of reference and translation into implementation plans.

## 1. *Situational Analysis*

- Little information on construction arm of Pirelli General. Assumed that international opportunities focus on cables as a growing market.
- Following BICC purchase, estimated more than 75% of revenues from UK market.
- Factories in 13 countries (cables) and sales presence in most European countries, USA, South America, Africa and Australia.
- Many markets in Electricity are deregulating, privatizing and consolidating (following UK model), providing opportunities.
- Market research is needed on a country by country basis in order to validate plans.
- Worldwide acquisition strategy.

It is critical to Pirelli General to expand internationally in order to achieve its corporate (and marketing) objectives. Changes in Electricity Market justify focusing on this market and targeting of RECs or equivalent (per UK model).

## 2. *International Marketing Objectives*

- To triple Cables' international turnover by 2005 through a focus on key international markets (current estimate £57m).
  (**N.B.**: 5 years needed for international plan to yield returns).
- To strengthen the global position by entering new international markets through focused strategic alliances.

A marketing plan will need to be developed for each country to support these objectives based on the subsequent strategies.

## 3. *International Marketing Strategies*

### 3.1 Selection of Markets

This strategic approach has been determined through GE Matrix analysis, plotting business strength against country attractiveness.

Business strength is determined by scoring strength in:

- Manufacturing plant presence/proximity.
- Sales presence/proximity.
- Knowledge of market/ability to exploit alliances (see market entry strategies).
- Pirelli tyre presence (to leverage brand).

Country attractiveness is determined by scoring:

- Geographical size.
- Population size.
- State of regulation (privatization).
- Strength of competition. (Note: may review this if decide to purchase main competitor, as per BICC model in UK.)

Target market, following UK model, is RECs or their equivalent.

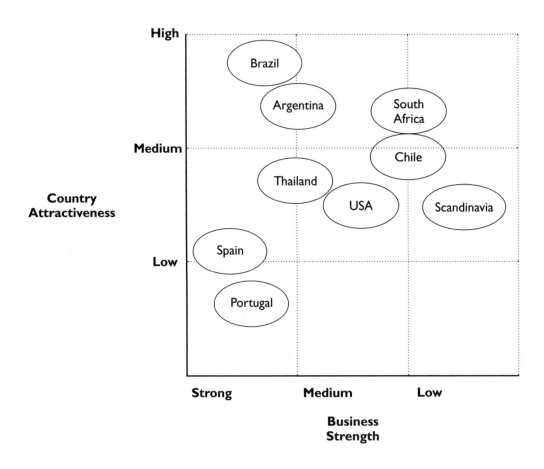

Phase 1 (Priority):      Chile, Brazil, Argentina (South American group – Chile included as key reference country).

Phase 2:                 USA*, South Africa, Thailand.

*N.B.: Critical market in long term may need to accelerate.

## 3.2 Entry Methods

In focusing on the Electricity Market and RECs, capabilities exist to establish/argument own production, sales, distribution and marketing. However, given other players in the deregulation/privatization trend, market entry can be facilitated through:

   a. Establishing alliances with international parent companies of UK RECs to:

- Target electricity market together.
- Share market research.
- Agree global contracts (when power company buys 'REC' in new country. PC Project Managers and Cable Manager to create efficiency).

   b. Establishing alliances with IMF and World Bank to:

- Provide specialist advice to them on deregulation/privatization.
- Position PG as a global expert.
- Position PG to be appointed as supplier to privatized companies.

   c. Consideration of acquisitions (as per BICC in UK) as part of global acquisition strategy to gain market share rapidly.

## 4. Product Mix/Tactics

### 4.1 Product

The modular product offering should be rolled out in phases:

- Consultancy is high priority to provide advice to alliance partners/governments and supra-governmental organizations.
- Cable supply itself is also critical in the initial phase.
- Installation and project management services and cable maintenance and monitoring can be rolled out subsequently.

|  | Consultancy | Installation and Project Management | Monitoring and Maintenance | Cables | New Cable Innovations |
|---|---|---|---|---|---|
| **PHASE 1 Chile** | 1 | 2 | 3 | 1 | 3 |
| **Argentina** | 1 | 2 | 3 | 1 | 3 |
| **Brazil** | 1 | 2 | 3 | 1 | 3 |
| **PHASE 2 USA** | ½ | ½ | 3 | ½ | ½ |
| **Thailand** | 2 | 2 | 3 | 2 | 2 |
| **South Africa** | 2 | 2 | 3 | 2 | 2 |

### 4.2 Tactics

| | |
|---|---|
| **Products** | Standardize globally (in support of global brand). |
| **Price** | Locally to allow for market variation and competitive positioning. |
| **CRM/KAM** | Utilize to grow markets. |
| **Distribution** | RECs/equivalent (research needed). |
| **Promotion** | PR and lobbying, supported by face to face sales, below-the-line marketing and linked to CRM. |
| **People** | Organizational reorganization with country Sales Directors. |
| **Process** | Establish global service standards and roll out of e-Pirelli. |
| **Physical Evidence** | Quality professional literature – **global brand**. |

## 5. Scheduling and Budgets

Income Budgets (incremental)

| €m | 2001 | 2002 | 2003 | 2004 | 2005 |
|---|---|---|---|---|---|
| Phase 1 | – | 24 | 36 | 48 | 60 |
| Phase 2 | – | – | 24 | 36 | 48 |
| Organic Growth (GDP increase from existing revenues) | 2 | 4 | 6 | 6 | 12 |
| | 2 | 26 | 66 | 93 | 120 |

Achieves tripling of revenues per objective.

**Expenditure Budgets**

Require detailed analysis, country by country, to support both marketing and sales. High level estimates for both PR and below-the-line marketing are:

## 6. Controls and Contingencies

Monitoring should take place on:

- Pace of deregulation and privatization, notably in USA where size of market makes it critical to PG's long term success.
- Performance against sales targets (an agreed key performance indicator).
- Cross sales of additional products and services launched.

**Contingency Plans**

- If more rapid change in US market, then will need to accelerate entry.
- Failure to agree alliance partners.
- Changes in governments/political environments for each country.

---

### Senior Examiner's Comments

This answer has been answered well but the candidate was a little hampered by choosing an international marketing plan. Some of the ideas could have been expanded and elaborated more effectively by concentrating on key approaches, as asked for in the question. Although in this instance the answer was good, it is important that candidates do not fall into the trap of answering questions in a pre-formatted manner. Better results can be obtained by answering the question flexibly and innovatively.

# Second Student Answer – Question 1.

Report

To: **Pirelli General Plc Board Members**

From: **Marketing Consultant**

Date: **8th December, 2000**

Subject: **The Future for Pirelli in the UK – a Strategic Marketing Plan**

## 1. Introduction

I am pleased to submit to the Board my report on Pirelli, following my discussions with the Managing Director and Marketing Director and detailed analysis of the information supplied.

Although I have presented my findings of the situation analysis fully in person at an earlier meeting, I shall summarize them here. I shall then outline my recommendations, and the reasons behind them, for the strategic direction of Pirelli over the next three years.

## 2. Background

The environment in which Pirelli operates is undergoing dramatic change:

- Deregulation in the UK utilities market has led to Pirelli's customers, RECs, needing to be more efficient and effective in their own operations; end-users (consumers) are increasingly realizing that they have a choice of supplier.
- This same trend is following across the world, albeit at a slower pace.

Pirelli has an excellent reputation and dominant market position. This position of strength has been increased by the recently announced news of the successful acquisition of the facilities formerly owned by BICC.

Pirelli's reputation is based on supplying quality products and network services. However, this lead is threatened by:

- a. Cheap international imports.
- b. Erosion of previously good business relationships in the DMU as the RECs have changed. This change, however, also offers Pirelli the opportunity to develop new relationships based on customer needs.

Within the general cables market, Pirelli has a lower involvement with the end-users, as the networks of distributors with another agenda are in between them. However, this also implies an opportunity to manage the supply chain more effectively in future to the mutual benefit of all.

Financially, Pirelli has seen turnover decline, and profit margins erode from 23% to 16%. Pirelli needs to reverse this trend in the short term. However, with its fairly low gearing, Pirelli can be bold in the longer term.

To conclude:

Pirelli has pockets of excellence around the world with its products, e.g. Pireflex, its network solutions and its R&D capabilities. However, its weakness is in poor knowledge management on a worldwide basis and insufficient strategic planning.

### 3. Critical Success Factors

My analysis has highlighted the following areas that Pirelli needs to address in its strategic marketing planning:

a.  Adopt a marketing rather than a product oriented approach, looking at:

- Customer focus.
- Customer relationship management.
- Segmentation by customer not product.

Result: More responsive to market changes and customer needs.

b.  Take an integrated planning approach:

- Planning and control systems introduced.
- Avoid tactical reaction.
- Establish a marketing information system.
- Improved innovation management.

Result: Strategic Marketing Plan.

c.  Improve internal/external communications:
- Strategic knowledge management.
- Cohesive E-strategy.
- Integrated marketing plan.

Result: Stronger corporate direction and communication with stakeholders.

### 4. Corporate Vision and Mission

In order fully to involve the whole company in its aim to drive towards a common aim, it is essential to have a mission and vision statement against which all activities can be checked.

The Board needs to finalize this but I submit the following for consideration:

**Vision**

To put Pirelli at the heart of power and communications transmission.

**Mission**

Pirelli aims to provide its customers with quality innovative solutions for transmitting power and telecommunications. It supports the development of environmentally friendly energy production and delivery, and aims to provide its employees worldwide with a stimulating and supportive working environment.

### 5. Corporate Objective

To produce a strategic marketing plan, Pirelli needs to establish its corporate objective. I would suggest that it should aim to build the Pirelli brand around its customer requirements to be a leading supplier of quality solutions.

In light of the amalgamation of BICC's UK cable operations, I believe Pirelli should aim to increase its sales from £315m to £450m.

I have identified the following planning gap:

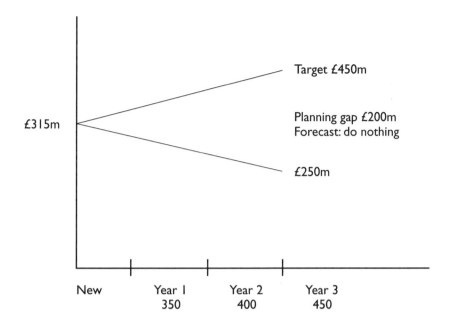

**Justification for Decline if Do Nothing:**
1. Heavy dependence on mature general cables market in UK.
2. Increased international competition.
3. Lack of strategic planning.
4. Poor customer focus.

**Justification for Target**
1. New opportunities in UK utilities market, bundling services etc.
2. International deregulation following UK model.
3. Increased facilities with BICC plant.
4. Pirelli's expertise in network solutions.
5. Opportunities to expand e-commerce developments.

**Strategic Options**

Having identified all of Pirelli's strategic options using the Ansoff model, I have used a GE matrix to evaluate them. I have used the following criteria:

**Strategic Attractiveness**
1. Match with Pirelli's strengths.
2. Degree of risk.
3. Speed to market and payback.
4. Degree of competition.
5. Profitability.

**Competitive Advantage**
1. Matching customer requirements.
2. Technical support.
3. Will improve customer efficiency.
4. Reputation and experience.
5. Quality.

The results are as follows:

|  | **High** | **Medium** | **Low** |
|---|---|---|---|
|  | X Network Services UK | | |
| **High** | X Pireflex UK | X Photonics | **Network Services Internationally** (X) |
|  | e-Pirelli X | X Eco-cables | |
| **Medium** | **Other Branded Cables** X | **X Supply Chain Management** | X Conventional Cables |
| **Low** | | | |

*Competitive Advantage* (vertical axis)

**Strategy Attractiveness**

Pirelli needs to plan for short, medium and long term. Therefore I would recommend:

1. Short term – penetration strategy of total network service to UK.
2. Medium term – new market development of Pireflex in UK.
3. Long term – new product development of eco-cables.

My justification for selecting total network service is that it:

1. Plays to Pirelli's proven strengths.
2. Is low risk.
3. Provides an opportunity to differentiate.

If we assess Pirelli against Porter's Generic Strategic, this gives the company a chance to move from following an undefined strategy to a clear position of a differentiated strategy.

## 7.  Marketing Objectives

   a.  To achieve incremental sales of £40m by Year 3.
   b.  To retain 90% of existing customers (RECs), of LT contract with Midlands and Eastern.
   c.  To become total network service supplier for new bundled energy suppliers (PES); 2 per annum.

### How do we do this?

By offering a total network solution: design, cable manufacture, installation, project management and ongoing maintenance, based on Pirelli's quality products and network expertise.

## 8. Segmentation

The UK market can be segmented as follows:

|  | High | Medium | Low |
|---|---|---|---|
| **High** | RECs UK PES | International Utilities | |
| **Medium** | Large Contractors | Wholesalers | Small Contractors |
| **Low** | | | |

*Competitive advantage* (vertical axis) — *Customer attractiveness* (horizontal axis)

I would recommend that Pirelli focuses on the 12 UK RECs, particularly with whom it has recently signed a long term contract. As secondary targets, London Electricity (42% sales volume in supply sector), Yorkshire (12%) and Southern (9%).

It is important to bear in mind the DMU structure and I would recommend as follows:

| Role | Position | Need |
|---|---|---|
| Influences. | Procurement. | Improved efficiency, quality, reliability. |
| Finances | FD. | Cost effectiveness. |
| User. | Engineer. | User friendly, quality, reliability. |
| Decider. | Procurement. | Seeking the 'IBM' decision. |

## 9. Positioning

To meet the customer requirements identified above, Pirelli needs to position itself as premium supplier of proven quality network system solutions, and all elements of the marketing mix should reflect this.

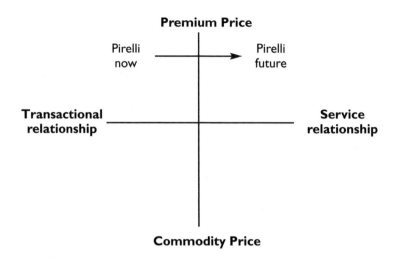

## 10. Targeting

A differentiated strategy is required.

## 11. Marketing Mix

| | Objective | Action |
|---|---|---|
| **Product** | Total network system solution. | Research to identify service and what can be standardized/ tailored. |
| **Price Sensitivity** | To provide realistic price. | Research price. |
| **Place** | Build strong relationships with DMU. | Identify key contacts. |
| **Promotion Profile** | Establish Pirelli as network partner of choice. | Internal marketing to staff etc. PR activities to raise profile. |
| **Pull** | Raise REC awareness of benefits to them. | Personal visits to DMU; leaflets, trade fairs etc. |
| **People** | To motivate and empower staff. | Training schemes Personal objectives and incentives. |
| **Process** | Cross-reference experience. | Maximize use of Extranet and expertise. |
| **Physical Evidence** | Reinforce Pirelli's brand. | Corporate ID etc. |

## 12. Budget

| | Year 1 | Year 2 | Year 3 |
|---|---|---|---|
| Sales £m | 12 | 28 | 40 |
| Profit % | 5% | 8% | 10% |
| Profit £m | 0.6 | 2.2 | 4 |

### 13. Controls

I would recommend using a Gantt chart to schedule and control activities. Other controls could be:

1. Feedback of sales and profit with MIS.
2. Customer satisfaction survey, visits to trade fair etc. with MkIS.

### 14. Implications

Pirelli needs to appoint a 'change manager' to oversee the adaptation to a customer focus. A learning culture must be encouraged.

---

**Senior Examiner's Comments**

This answer concentrates on creating a market oriented company. It is good on the internal issues and has clearly mapped out the way in which the company could increase its profile in the marketplace. There is, however, very little on the new information provided, i.e. BICC. The answer also suffers (as many do) from an overly optimistic view of how quickly the company can grow within three years. More detail regarding the financial commitments would have helped considerably.

---

## Second Student Answer – Question 2.

**Developing E-commerce for Pirelli – Internal and External Implications**

### 1. Background

E-Pirelli has already been introduced and tested in some countries, particularly Italy. The management at Pirelli General has allocated a budget of £619m over two years to the development of e-Pirelli so they have acknowledged its significance. However, Pirelli needs to make sure its use is strategic rather than tactical.

The use of e-commerce will have an implication for:

a. Pirelli – value chain management and knowledge management.
b. Its customers – CRM.
c. Its suppliers – supply chain management.

I will firstly address the implications for Pirelli.

### 2. Pirelli

a. **Objectives**
   Using e-business could help Pirelli to improve its own value chain management by adding value at all stages and making its interactions with stakeholders more effective.

b. **Tools**
   It could be used in four ways:
   i. **Communication Tool**
      Internal/external marketing tool to improve customer relations and build the brand.
   ii. **Indirect Distribution**
      Extranet link with customers to allow Pirelli to provide total solution.
   iii. **Transactions**
      Online technology incorporated into all Pirelli's core businesses to streamline the flow of transactions.

iv. **Information Sharing/Education**

Extranet structure to promote best practice. Using e-business in this way would play to Pirelli's corporate strengths. I would recommend that Pirelli introduces this system in full in UK and then roll out across other markets once it is developed.

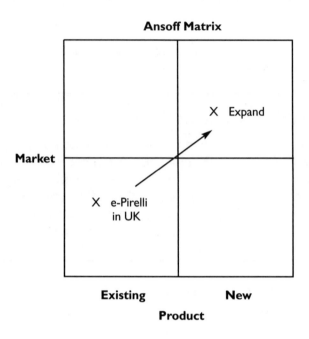

**Ansoff Matrix**

c. **Segmentation**

In the short term Pirelli should focus on approaching innovators and early adopters to use this system.

Evidence has shown that even in the US, only one third of B2B operations are conducted online.

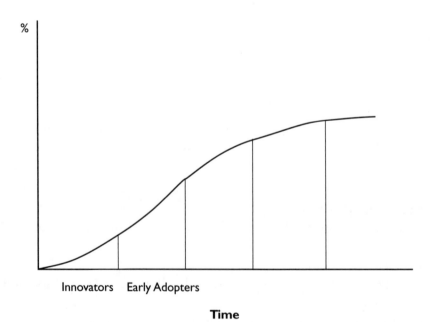

For example, externally it would be appropriate to target RECs and early leaders in bundling energy suppliers and telecommunications (PESs). Internally, e-commerce champions should be identified.

220

d.  **Internal Implications (Short Term)**
    It is necessary to take the following steps to facilitate the use of e-commerce.

    i.   Conduct an audit of internal culture and identify areas for attention.
    ii.  Segment the internal market and identify training needs.
    iii. Make e-commerce part of the corporate paradigm by linking objectives and incentives in its use.
    iv.  Establish a simple mechanic for inputting data, orders etc.
    v.   Establish an effective method of diffusing information, passing on orders, sharing best practice, etc.
    vi.  Set up controls to ensure a continuous learning loop.

e.  **Long Term**
    Having put the short term measures in place to initiate and promote the use of e-business, this will have an implication for Pirelli's long term marketing strategy.

    i.   The increased information available on its customer requirements will enable Pirelli to get closer to its customers in terms of knowing their requirements and offering a tailored solution.
    ii.  The speed of operations on the Internet will allow Pirelli to respond to its customer requirements more rapidly.
    iii. Pirelli will be able to develop a closer relationship to its customers, and develop a partnership rather than transactional relationship with them.
    iv.  The network can be integrated into Pirelli's planning process, to enable more informed strategy development in future.

## 3. Customer Implications

Using e-business as a tool to share information and process order requirements etc. will enable Pirelli's customers to develop a much closer relationship. By incorporating e-Pirelli into their own systems, they may be able to improve their own value chain management. For example, the system can be used to facilitate JIT management of cable supplies, so that Pirelli is requested to supply only the exact amount required on the data specified and at a particular location to avoid the customer holding unnecessary stocks.

If this is added to the general speed of online ordering, it can be seen how this can contribute to the overall efficiency of customers. In light of the current environment, this is particularly important.

E-Pirelli can also be used to share knowledge and best practice across business partners. This enables Pirelli and its customers to enjoy experience curve benefits in terms of time and cost savings.

## 4. Supplier Implications

Not much information is available on Pirelli's suppliers. However, it can be summarized that a certain degree of overlap in activities may exist, e.g. cable stockholding. E-commerce could be used effectively to facilitate the management of this and other stages of the whole supply chain. By adding value to and reducing costs at all possible stages in this supply chain, it is possible to create a powerful performance network to the mutual benefit of all participants. This also provides an effective way to differentiate.

## Conclusion

The widest interpretation of e-commerce should be taken to maximize the potential benefits to Pirelli. It is important at the outset that senior management show their commitment to this, in order to encourage its adoption throughout the division.

### Senior Examiner's Comments

This is a good, well-balanced answer. As far as I can see, all the key issues surrounding e-commerce have been taken into consideration. The candidate has rightly considered the problems of implementation. Also the B2B area is growing, but not hugely and this is the short term problem that the company has.

The candidate could have considered transaction issues, CRM and the potential to bypass the middlemen.

## Second Student Answer – Question 3.

**Report: International Marketing
Approaches for Pirelli**

### 1. Background

Although 65% of Pirelli General's sales in 1999 came from the UK, it still has a considerable interest in other countries, e.g. 22% in Europe and 9% in Asia Pacific. Therefore Pirelli should realistically include International operations in its strategic planning process.

### 2. International Opportunities

The process of plotting all Pirelli's strategic options on an Ansoff chart identified a number of International opportunities. Taking the UK options out of the equation, these International strategies can be rated and weighed on a GE matrix, as follows:

|  |  | High | Medium | Low |
|---|---|---|---|---|
| **Competitive Advantage** | **High** | Network services international utilities e-Pirelli | Pireflex (beyond France, Belgium Germany) |  |
|  | **Medium** | Branded cables | Eco-cables? Photonics? |  |
|  | **Low** |  |  |  |

**Strategy Attractiveness**

There is not enough information currently available to assess the potential of photonics, or the opportunity for eco-friendly cables outside of the UK.

I have already discussed the opportunities for e-commerce in an earlier report and would recommend that the fullest potential of e-business be exploited in the UK, and then expanded internationally.

However, evidence is available to show that utility companies around the world are beginning to go through the same process of privatization and/or deregulation.

Therefore, I would recommend as a primary strategy for international markets that Pirelli offers a similar total network system solution to utility companies in these countries.

## Justification

a. **Experience Curve Benefits**

Pirelli has, and will increasingly have, proven expertise in the area of helping RECs save costs (up to 15%) by being their external supplier of networks and facilities. As international utility suppliers go through the same process, they too will be under increasing demand from their shareholders and customers for improved efficiency and effectiveness. Pirelli will have the competitive advantage of proven expertise in this area and, particularly supported by e-commerce, will be able to offer time and cost savings through experience curve benefits (see below).

b. **Think Global, Act Local**

Taking the information on where around the world Pirelli has its distribution centres, and marketing this information on countries going through the deregulation process, there is a good overlap.

Therefore, Pirelli is well placed to balance the wealth of its global expertise and technical support, with the local operation which would be familiar with the country-specific issues, e.g. culture, technology etc.

c. **Know Your Customer**

While there is not much information currently available, it can be assumed that the DMU in International utility companies would be similar to the UK. While it is necessary to research this issue before proceeding, it is possible to plan on the assumption that the marketing mix, following a differentiated strategy and with the positioning outlined in my first report, would be appropriate.

**Secondary Strategy**

From the GE matrix, I would recommend the secondary strategy of offering branded cables to international markets.

My justification for this approach would be:

i. The opportunity to differentiate Pirelli cables from cheap imports from Poland, India etc.

ii. The opportunity to build a brand leadership strategy for Pirelli. This would enable the company to differentiate itself, and charge a price premium.

iii. If the international markets follow the UK route, end-users of utilities will select their supplier on the basis of known brands. This gives Pirelli the opportunity to create the 'Intel inside' effect with its cable offering.

With the World Bank supporting the move towards a free market for utility companies, there will be opportunities to become involved with LDCs at an early stage before the market becomes too competitive, as well as the more developed markets in Europe and North/South America.

iv. Market Entry Methods

As mentioned before, Pirelli has operations already established in many of the countries identified as going through the deregulation process.

However, there may be opportunities to form a strategic alliance with other similar organizations where Pirelli is not already present. The advantages would be:

    a.   Risk sharing.
    b.   Access to new R&D facilities.
    c.   Access to local customer knowledge.
    d.   Access to other routes to market/channels.
    e.   Access to international suppliers.

## 4. Conclusion

Pirelli should form a strategic plan for its international operations, highlighting the method and country(ies) to be the primary focus.

### Senior Examiner's Comments

The candidate has rightly drawn attention to the fact that there is little data on all the International markets. However, some analysis of the different growth areas from the accounts would have been helpful. The general approaches outlined (as asked for in the question) are well thought through and sensible. The answer could have had better justification of the strategies given and could have discussed deregulation experience much more.

### Overall Comments

These two specimen answers again help to illustrate how different answers can be justified. In both cases there were gaps that could have been filled. However, given the time constraints of the examination, the answers were of good quality. The overall trend on answering questions is getting better and I am encouraged that candidates are taking a more flexible and creative approach. It would be nice to see more detail (usually numerical from the data given) underpinning some of the strategies that are formulated. This case was generally well handled and it was good to see that candidates had a good grasp of e-commerce. For the first time the mark breakdown was 40:30:30 and candidates are beginning to allocate the requisite times to each question, instead of front loading their time on Question 1. I will continue to re-iterate the importance of the diagram below:

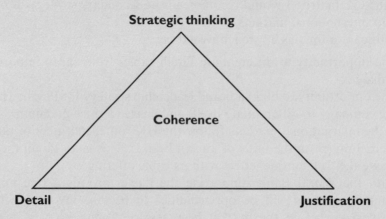

Candidates should always consider these points whenever they are answering their questions.

**9.54:** Strategic Marketing Management: Analysis & Decision – Examiner's Report

**Date:** June 2001

## General Comments

A good range of data for analysis and the development of arguments was presented in the case. The case was also set in a different type of sector. The analysis demanded some financial skills and also some skills with regards to the understanding of global currency fluctuations.

In general, many candidates did not get to grips with the financial figures or the data on productivity and the loading factors on flights. The level of analysis offered by pilot centres was detailed and generally very good. The level of analysis, however, was variable within the pilot centres with some being excellent and others being at best simplistic.

Within the 'normal' centres the following issues cropped up:

    a.   A degree of superficiality in developing strategies.

    b.   An over reliance on pre-prepared answers meant that many candidates were not flexible enough to respond to the needs of the questions asked.

    c.   Many candidates tried to stick to 'plans' for Questions 2. and 3. even though these were not asked for. Although, improving, general flexibility and agility of thinking is still rare.

    d.   As a rule, grasp of theory and the use of models is still patchy and could be better.

    e.   Some International centres were poor and provided generalized scripts with poor reference to the actual case.

    f.   Many candidates possessed a poor grasp of how a case should be handled and analysed.

    g.   When developing strategies, the underpinning detail provided by the case was poor in many instances.

## Question 1

This is often predictable, but many candidates were completely 'thrown' by the short term and long term strategic direction asked for in the question. This is largely a result of pre-prepared answers. Many candidates, instead of preparing good analyses and then utilizing them sensibly in the examination, tend to try and work out full answers. This results in a great lack of flexibility and innovation. General analyses like SWOT, and PEST were reasonably well handled. Porter was used frequently and presented frequently with only a few candidates utilizing the analyses in any meaningful manner. For many candidates, the setting of SMART objectives proved to be difficult. In some instances, even understanding targeting, positioning and segmentation proved to be difficult. These areas need to be further strengthened at centre level. One feels that even though the case is given out a month in advance, real understanding of the issues is weak.

## Question 2

This question asked for a discussion of communication factors. The question specifically prompted the students by saying that a plan was not asked for. In spite of this it was disappointing that the same set formula was used by a large number of candidates. In many cases, the brand image of the company was largely ignored. Even any idea of logo changes was ignored as was the idea of using specific sponsorship. One of the key factors as stated in the additional information was the statement by Nor that the logo would not be changed, and in effect very little money would be available for communications. This information was ignored by many candidates. Again, flexibility, innovation and a clear understanding of the case were necessary ingredients in passing this question.

## Question 3

Although there was enough data in the case on routes and possible growth areas many candidates failed to incorporate good analyses into their answers. Very few candidates used international models. This was a straightforward question which obviously had links to Question 1. The focus on strategy was self evident, yet many candidates got wrapped up in plans.

# Conclusion

Although the above analysis appears to be a litany of woes, there were many very good scripts and answers. The pilot centre pass rates were much higher on average and clearly students seem to benefit from good tutoring. Students are managing their time better and are beginning to understand that Questions 2, and 3, actually carry 60% of the marks. Again, it is important that students actually attend centres and that centres also prepare the students well for the case examination.

# Specimen Answers for Strategic Marketing Management: Analysis & Decision June 2001

## Introduction

In order to be a good and accurate guide to students taking this examination, the following Specimen Answers have not been written by the Senior Examiner but have been reproduced from actual scripts submitted for the June examinations.

Following a standardization exercise, in which all examiners take part, two distinction level scripts were chosen, in full, to illustrate examples of good practice. In real business situations there are no right or wrong decisions, only sensible and realistic ones. By comparing two different high quality answers you will be able to gauge what is realistically possible in a three hour examination.

The complete guideline approach for all the questions, given to all examiners, encapsulates the key points good answers should include. This guideline has also been reproduced in full at the beginning of the Specimen Answers, enabling you to see how a wide variety of approaches can be taken.

The answers have been taken verbatim from complete papers so there is full continuity. At the end of each paper the Senior Examiner makes some comments on why the paper was good and where particular gaps may have arisen.

# Malaysian Airline System Berhad

## Overview

### The Case

This Case Study has created a real landmark by being one of the first CIM cases to be set in Asia Pacific. Malaysian Airlines is a complex organization and all the issues given are based on the problems and opportunities that face the company. The problems of being a quasi-governmental organization are very real within a world market, which is a mixture of deregulation and government intervention. This case has no personalized comments, is factual and contains no 'red herrings'. Nonetheless, as usual, there is the usual problem of an extensive range of detailed information. There is a need to develop clear and concise insights into the key issues involved in developing a strategy.

Key Issues pertaining to the case are:

a. Competing within a deregulated airline market.
b. The intense regional competition.
c. Price competition and discounting.
d. A loss-making company from 1997.
e. Growth opportunities in Asia Pacific with growing GNPs.
f. An excellent airport with the potential to become a hub.
g. Brand image is getting old and shows lack of dynamism.
h. Public perception of the MAS does not match up with the excellence of service.
i. The uncertain impact of the Internet.
j. The possibilities of joining and working with an alliance.
k. Developing the student, Indian and pilgrim markets for flights.
l. Current recessionary climate and increasing oil prices, though Malaysia does produce oil.
m. The cash flow per share has decreased dramatically.
n. An ageing fleet.
o. The government buyback.
p. The domestic market is generally run as a necessity, but is loss-making.
q. Over the ten years the Ringgit has depreciated against the US$, making the revenue stream weaker even though it is growing.
r. The country's GDP has shrunk by some 18% (1997/98 as a base point).
s. Excellent cabin service.
t. Malaysia is an excellent tourist destination.
u. There is a possibility of developing the brand through sports sponsoring.
v. Green issues.

This case is reasonably straightforward and does not contain many surprises. It was important, therefore that the following issues were considered by candidates:

1. The application of theory.
2. The amount of International marketing theory/application that the students can apply to the case. The amount of communication theory that they can also apply.
3. The candidates should be thinking strategically not tactically.
4. The answers given must be realistic and practical.
5. Show a degree of innovation and lateral thinking.
6. The additional information is quite important and shows the stance of the new MD. Candidates could speculate as to which strategies would be accepted or rejected by the new MD.

# Question 1

This question requires students to use many of the strategic planning models used by marketers. Candidates will then need to consider the following:

    a.   Consider the objectives that they wish to set for MAS for one year and three years.
    b.   Take into account the loss-making situation.
    c.   Consider which markets are best addressed in the short term. India/Pilgrim.
    d.   In the longer term consider strategic alliances.
    e.   The strategic vision should be based on the core values of the company and be reflected in the segments that are targeted.
    f.   Special discounting offers should be considered in the short term.
    g.   How can the company penetrate the lucrative Western tourist markets?
    h.   The company has a good record in cabin service. This needs exploiting.
    i.   The company needs to rethink its branding stance for the future.
    j.   Developing a system, which helps to form a hub for the new airport.
    k.   In the very short term, PR and communications are going to be very important.
    l.   Local competition means that brand image will play an important part in repositioning the airline in the longer term.
    m.   Models such as Porter, Ansoff, BCG, GEC, Shell Directional and GAP could be used in the analysis of the case.
    n.   What are the constraints to the given strategy? How can the company follow a market led strategy? What would be a realistic marketing budget?
    o.   Which markets are the key priorities and why?
    p.   As no organization chart is provided, how should the company execute its marketing strategies?
    q.   How much of the company's money should be directed towards developing an Internet strategy?

Points in a strategic plan:

    1.   Set corporate objectives.
    2.   Identify target markets.
    3.   Set marketing objectives.
    4.   Develop marketing strategy and tactics.
    5.   Organize control systems.

Candidates should show what is to be very short term and what is to be a longer three year strategy.

Given the points above, the best answers need to show a clear grasp of the following:

    1.   A good analysis of the current position.
    2.   The development of a strategic plan with fully developed implementation strategies.
    3.   A good justification of the strategies to be adopted.

For pilot study centres, fifteen marks were allocated for the pre-prepared material.

# Question 2

Some key factors that should be analysed and assessed are:

    a.   The company's current brand image and legitimizing the brand. This needs to be through advertising in specific areas such as sports sponsorship. The pros and cons of this possibility could be discussed.
    b.   Creative repositioning of the brand. The brand logo is currently quite old. It does not really capture the dynamism of MAS and Malaysia in general. A key point to consider would be the extent to which the new MD can be convinced that this is necessary and desirable.
    c.   Image building and taking a long term view about building the brand. This needs advertising spend at least up to the current industry levels.

d. Not having excessive promotions on flights so that the image is eroded. High-level impact promotions will expose the airline to more potential customers.

e. The importance of credible communications with the press and having a sustained public relations exercise in the key markets where the company operates in.

f. Utilizing the Internet to build customer relationships and loyalty. The communications need to be personalized and in some ways interactive.

**Specific and Different Messages Sent to Each Segment**

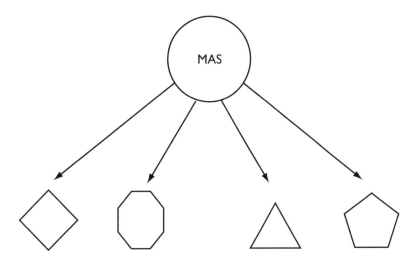

Creating an MAS club. The cost savings through direct booking can be passed onto the customers.

g. The Internet also offers a chance to personalize services, using banner advertising and key offers directly to the key segments.

h. Communicating short-term messages through WAP technology should also be considered.

i. Communicating pricing. The Internet offers a chance to communicate transparently. Again, individualized pricing can be practiced.

j. Communicating a differential advantage compared to other airlines. This is difficult when many airlines practice 'catch up' very quickly. Communication of excellent service, friendliness and good food is highly important.

k. Considering budgets and constraints for communications.

These and any other relevant points should be taken into consideration.

Finally, the students should consider how these factors could be seamlessly linked up with the strategies that the company has developed.

A good answer needs to take the following into account:

- Critical analyses of the key factors.
- Links with the overall strategy.

## Question 3

In considering an international marketing strategy for MAS, students will have to consider the following:

a.   The ratio of national to international revenue is 1:5 (p. 54), even though slightly more national passengers are carried than international ones.

b.   The cargo carried virtually mirrors the growth in carrying international passengers. (Passenger growth on international routes is often accompanied by a growth in exports or imports carried by plane).

c.   Asia, Europe, Middle East and Africa, Australia and New Zealand actually contribute the bulk of the revenue for the airline (p. 51), though the load factor to Australia and New Zealand is low. The company needs to consider how it can improve its revenue stream in Australasia. This could happen if KL becomes a hub airport for the region.

d.   Worryingly, the route revenue to the US and Canada is shrinking.

e.   The company needs to consider the growth in traffic between Malaysia and India and Malaysia and China.

f.   The newspaper articles show how MAS could grow in stature on Indian, Japanese and Australian routes.

g.   The ICAO report shows the growth rates between the different regions. When developing an international strategy this table (p. 33) should be taken into account.

h.   All this should fit in with an international communications strategy.

i.   International marketing growth could be stimulated by sensible use of e-marketing.

j.   The International strategy should consider the image of a friendly and multicultural mix of staff.

k.   Part of the strategy should encompass updating the fleet and raising money from share issues.

Candidates need to take into account the following issues:

- General analysis of International Marketing.
- Developing a International Marketing Strategy.

As usual, it is important to show coherence, strategic thinking, justification and detail in the answers. The case is quite long and there is considerable amount of data so that candidates should have been able to fashion a range of interesting answers.

## First Student Answer – Question 1

Prepared for:   MAS Marketing Team

Prepared by:   Leigh Hindemith – Senior Marketing Manager

Re:   Three Year Marketing Plan – MAS

Date:   15th June, 2001

### 1.0  Introduction

The following plan outlines my marketing plan for MAS covering a three year period following the appointment of Datuk Mohamed Nor Yusof as Marketing Director. The plan places at its centre the key issues of tackling the losses, obtaining better yields from the operations and restoring the prestigious image of MAS.

### 2.0  Overview

MAS is operating in a rapidly growing environment with increasing competition from regional and global players. From the information gathered, there appear to be many opportunities available to exploit if MAS can improve its strategic effectiveness and efficiency.

|  | **Strategic Management** | |
|---|---|---|
|  | *Efficient* | *Inefficient* |
| **Operational** *Efficient* | THRIVE | DIE SLOWLY |
| **Efficiency** *Inefficient* | SURVIVE | DIE QUICKLY |

My initial assessment is that MAS currently occupy the top right quadrant. MAS are recognized as being efficient (stage length and cost per seat rule), however, due to changes in control of the business MAS have become weak in the area of strategic management. MAS's key challenge is to become market led, through increasing knowledge of consumers, changes in the environment and focusing on areas of the business which can drive profitability.

In order for organizations to become profitable, they must be innovative (new products, markets and distribution channels), as this will avoid the downward pressure on prices, which are characteristic of this industry.

## 2.1 External Analysis

The airline industry should be considered to be mature, where the potential for competitive advantage is limited, with competitors often imitating rivals' provisions leading to rapid convergence in product offerings. For instance, any advantages, such as e-ticketing, are quickly copied.

Volume industries where there are few but highly significant advantages, such as airport bases, are often dominated by large players – BA and Heathrow, Cathay Pacific and Hong Kong.

This factor highlights the strategic importance of Kuala Lumpur airport and the need for MAS to capitalize on this valuable asset.

## 2.2 PEST Summary

The global environment has affected MAS and will continue to do so, in the following ways:

- POLITICAL: A 54% government control impacts on MAS strategic direction.
  - Neutrality allows regional co-operation.
  - Region is politically competitive, producing some barriers for MAS.
- ECONOMIC:
  - Elasticity of fares provides scope for price increase, leading to increased revenue.
  - Exchange rate devaluations have had a huge impact on profits – costs for fuel and loans in US$.
  - Economic growth in region will create increased demand.
  - Number of flights has a positive impact but this is marginal; this highlighting the importance of yield management.

## 2.3 Industry Dynamics

Our specific industry demonstrates the following factors. (Summarized – a full version can be obtained upon request).

- THREAT OF NEW ENTRANTS: Deregulation as a driver.
- Europe example has led to the use of the low cost culture. The situation in Asia will need to be monitored carefully.
- SUBSTITUTE PRODUCTS: Main area, which requires continuous analysis, is the increased use of improved telecommunications services, such as videoconferencing, as this will impact on the business level.

- SUPPLIER POWER: Main issue levels to economic factors in that key payments (e.g. fuel) are made in dollars. MAS recorded a 448% increase in costs on fuel between 1999 and 2000.
- BARGAINING POWER OF CUSTOMERS:
    - Travel agents are a key customer – 85% of business.
    - 85% of passengers have a choice of two or more airlines, making loyalty harder to achieve.
    - Classic 80/20 relationship exists between leisure and business customers.
- INDUSTRY RIVALRY: Forecasts that by 2010 more than half the worlds air traffic will start or end in the region, signals that competition will inevitably increase.

The most competitive part of the market is currently the small to medium sized markets as a result of the "hub and spoke" nature of airline logistics. This has led to greater focus on global alliances, which enhance competitive positions.

More specifically our competitors can be identified using the following strategic group analysis:

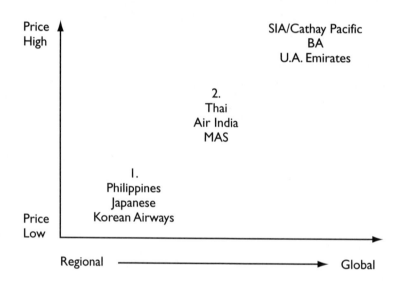

- CONCLUSIONS:
    - Local, regional airways (1.) can be anticipated to have regional goals and are possibly weak financially. Could indicate that there would be relatively weak responses to a challenge from MAS.
    - International airlines are the opposite to this, very strong, financially sound and their response to MAS moves would be aggressive.
    - Competition in this market is fierce as demonstrated by Virgin, who recently announced a fall in profits from £105m to £42.6m.
- PIMS RELATIONSHIPS:
    - It can also be noted from the data supplied that a PIMS relationship exists – meaning that to be profitable, market share is imperative. This again highlights the drive towards global strategic alliances.

## 2.4  Internal Analysis

Following the review of the external market, we can now compare MAS's own position within it. A brief SWOT highlights some further key issues.

- STRENGTHS:      Renewed government confidence in the airline.
  Modern fleet.
  High service standards.

- WEAKNESSES:    Financial positions – losses = 255.7 RM.
  Poor liquidity.
  Poor communication of brand.

- OPPORTUNITIES:  Economic as indicated earlier.
  Kuala Lumpur Airport as a hub.
  Government 2020 vision.

- THREATS:          Economic destabilization.
  Beyond control of MAS.
  Threat of new entrants.
  Competitive pressures mounting.

In summary, despite some immediate problems MAS currently has a number of opportunities which can be capitalized on, to turn around fortunes.

To begin with, looking at possible strategies, I have used the Shell Directional Policy Matrix for its perspective qualities.

**Prospects for Sector Profitability**

| MAS Competitive Capabilities | Unattractive | Average | Attractive |
|---|---|---|---|
| Weak | Disinvest | Phased Withdrawal | Double/Quit CARGO |
| Average | Phased withdrawal | Customer Growth INTERNATIONAL FLIGHTS | Try Harder GOLDEN HOLIDAYS |
| Strong | Cash Generation | Growth Leader | Lender REGIONAL FLIGHTS |

- DOMESTIC FLIGHTS: No room for growth, but MAS is preferred provider and therefore should be used for cash generation. Will play a vital role in CORPORATE IDENTITY.
- CARGO: Despite strong economic growth in region and the exporting nature of Malaysia, MAS has preferred badly – losses = 156,583,000 RM in 2000.
- REGIONAL FLIGHTS: Air traffic in the region is growing at twice the rate of Europe and USA. MAS well positioned to take advantage.
- INTERNATIONAL FLIGHTS: By 2010, 50% of our travel from region. MAS has an opportunity but needs to address resource and capacity issues.

## 2.5  Overview Key Issues:

- CONTROL:    Despite government support MAS needs to develop a strategic focus.

- FINANCE:     Reversing losses is crucial as this will restrain growth activity.

- AIR TRAVEL GROWTH:  Opportunities must be seized upon.
- COMMUNICATION:      To gain support growth, a strong identity is required.

## 3.0  Corporate Mission and Objectives

I propose this mission statement so that the organization has a guide for future operations:

"To grow profitability, through the satisfaction of our customers' transportation requirements and through the continued development of service levels which delight the world and even exceed the expectations of the Malaysian people".

### 3.1  Corporate Objectives

a.  Improve the financial performance of the organization through organic growth, and where appropriate developing networks and alliances to achieve the following targets.

| (RM. 000) | 2000/01 | 2001/02 | 2002/03 | % |
|---|---|---|---|---|
| Total rev. | 8,000,000 | 10,000,000 | 13,000,000 | 61.5 |
| Total exp. | 7,000,000 | 7,000,000 | 8,000,000 | 14.3 |
| Profit (loss) % | 13% | 30% | 39% | |
| Passenger Load factor | 73% | 74% | 75% | |

- JUSTIFICATION:
  - Passenger numbers in region will grow by 8.5%.
  - Expenditure controlled through reducing debt and the cost of servicing this debt – see financial revenues.
  - Increased marketing presence through developing strong brand.

b.  To develop KL airport in partnership with the Government as a key asset.
c.  To become a top 20 airline by association by 2005/6.
d.  Maintain and develop current position as an ambassador for Malaysia, actively developing the economy across all social groups.

## 4.0  Generic Strategy

Drawing from the above analysis, a focused differentiation strategy is recommended for MAS for the period of the plan – broad differentiation will take longer to achieve.

This approach will focus the organization on the key users of our services and will encourage organizational thinking on more than just product and price.

MAS is currently a Market Follower and a strategy of adaptation is suitable.

### Conclusion on Strategy Formulation:

FLANK ATTACK – requiring the targeting of specific segments currently not supplied by competitor products. Initially this takes the form of a regional focus where the number of players are many and disparate. Allows MAS to develop a position of strength, whilst avoiding retaliation from major players.

KL airport should act as our defensive position in the region.

MAS core capabilities will be exploited to develop a competitive advantage based upon:

- Superior product – in the eyes of the customer.
- Advantage of KL airport.
- Strong regional and eventually global alliance partners.

I would also recommend 'guerrilla attacks' to position MAS as the South Asians' people's champion, in a similar manner to that which Virgin Airways operates in the West. This will help increase our brand value and recognition.

## 5.0 Segmentation

| Forms | Primary Requirements |
|---|---|
| • Domestic | Frequency/Low costs |
| • Regional | Accessibility/Frequency |
| • International | Comfort/Integration |
| • Business Travellers | Facilities/Comfort |
| • Tourists | Value/Integration |
| • Students | Cost |

MAS focus will be on:

- Regional travel
- Superior business travel facilities
- Superior tourist travel facilities

## 6.0 Marketing Objectives

- Increase sales to current markets by 30% within 3 years.
- Increase income generation from new markets by 20% in 3 years.
- Reposition brand to achieve positive brand recognition of 70% within 3 years.

## 7.0 Financial Strategies to Fund Growth Programme

a. Divest Cargo Operations: Propose through seeking a franchise agreement. Allows MAS to focus on core competency of passenger travel. Franchise fee expected = 10%.
b. Rights Issue: Requires consultations with Government. To be made available to Malaysian people, further strengthening identity.
c. Debt Restructuring: Due to currency vulnerability against the US$. Establish a financial working party to examine possibility of 'hedging' on currency markets leading to greater predictability.

## 8.0 Marketing Strategies

Market Penetration – Focus for year 1. Aim to increase sales and penetration within the regional sector.

### 8.1 Branding Strategy

Must take initial priority, as much of the good work undertaken by the organization is not recognized. (See Question 2 on key issues relating to this.)

Future brand should comprise the following:

Brand name: Malaysian Airways.
Market Descriptor: Transportation.

Brand Discriminator: The inspiration of South Asia.
Proposition: The future of travel (innovation).
Personality: Proud and courteous.

Activities to support:

Sponsorship – 3 key opportunities:

- Commonwealth Games 2002
- National Games
- World Cup 2001.

### 8.2 Australian and New Zealand Focus

MAS has recently increased capacity on these routes and it is vital that the load factors of 70%+ is achieved. Revenue for these routes are up 22% and growing travel from Australia to Europe via KL airport.

Activities to support:

- Alliance with popular credit card in Australia, for joint promotions.
- Sales promotion in National and Regional Australian press.
- Continued communications work with Australian travel agents to promote Malaysia as a tourist destination.

### 8.3 Distribution

Increased use of PUSH marketing communication strategies to ensure distribution outlets. Recommended detailed research programme regarding service provision and views towards e-commerce developments.

#### 8.3.1 Business Markets

Growing economy represents increased B2B market opportunities. Capitalize through:

- Alliance with regional business travel company (e.g. Hogg Robinson).
- Establish sales key account teams to support corporate clients.
- Support with telesales centre.

### 8.4 Yield Management

Passenger load factor above 70% represents break-even point. Target in Year 1, 73%.

Actions:

- Implementation of 2-class travel, as opposed to current 3. Leisure and business class. Service levels to be increased. See KL airports.
- Discounted airfares for student population.
- Strengthening GRADCARD.

### 8.5 Frequent Flyer Programme

Strengthen and improve benefits. The FFP allows collection of customer data to help establish CRM programme (to be developed over 2–3 years).

### 8.6 Pricing

Domestic prices have not risen since 1984. Negotiation with government to increase with possible bargain tools including increased consultation services with government over tourism.

## 9.0 Years 2 and 3 – Product Development

NPD will ensure MAS remains competitive through innovations, a core brand value. This activity requires considerable investment and can be scheduled for years 2/3 of the plan.

### 9.1 Development of KL Airport

MAS has a fantastic opportunity to develop KL airport as a stronghold, similar to Heathrow. This will be useful as it reinforces brand and provides a bargaining toll for access into new markets.

Recommendation: A dedicated terminal for MAS passengers, reinforcing brand as further quality service control could be escorted before and after flight experience.

Specific developments could include:

- Check-in desks located next to business and leisure lounges.
- Better leisure lounge facilities.
- Train staff to speed up check-in.

### 9.2 Market Developments

This is to focus on a regional approach in order to capture increased travel business. Full details are included in international plan.

Key Targets:

- China and India due to residual population in Malaysia.
- Global presence through alliance building, when profitable in year 3 – become a more attractive partner.

## 10.0 Strategy Implementation

MAS has a good asset base – its staff – to implement this ambitious programme. A communication plan is required to enforce new position.

Key Changes:

- Market led orientation – culture change.
- Review NPD process to ensure effectiveness.
- Development of relationships with stakeholders.

Measurement – will be reflected in achievement of the objectives stated. A control system is vital to regulate the activity of the organization as it progresses towards its goals. Suggest Balanced Scorecard approach.

---

### Senior Examiner's Comments

This answer covers a good range of the strategic directions available to MAS. The question asks for a short term (1 year) and longer term (3 year) plan. The candidate has taken the trouble to answer the question as asked. Some more analyses of the details of financial trouble spots within the organization would have helped. Overall a good answer.

---

## First Student Answer – Question 2

To: Marketing Team

From: Leigh Hindemith

Re: Key Factors in Developing Marcoms Strategy for MAS

Date: 15th June, 2001

## 1.0 Introduction

A key objective for MAS is to revitalize our brand. This is the key communication challenge and factors which will come into play are detailed below.

## 2.0 Brand Strategy

A future brand strategy will need to address the following cultural issues:

- Establish a brand differentiation and personality.
  (How is this achieved in an industry where there is increasing product convergence?)
- Communicate strengths to target audience.
  (Identify stakeholders and their communication needs).
- Develop a favourable image of MAS within the region.

## 2.1  Establishing a Brand Differentiator

With an expanding market size, MAS will need to reposition the brand and provide a stronger point of differentiation for consumers. The distance the brand needs to travel is shown below:

| CURRENT POSITION | GOAL |
| --- | --- |
| PERSONALITY: 2nd Class citizen to Singapore Airlines and Cathay Pacific | Proud and Courteous |
| VALUED: National Symbol | Ambassador of Malaysia |
| EMOTIONAL REWARDS: National Icon | Inspiration of S. Asia |
| RATIONAL BENEFITS: Air travel in modern fleet of aircraft | Regional airline with modern fleet |
| FUNCTIONAL: Low cost base | Low cost base |
| FEATURED: History Product development | Superior NPD |

- Key Factors:   Considerable change is required.
                          Awareness is patchy so a favourable attitude needs to be developed.
                          Time span – needs to be based around a 5 year strategy – consistency.

The repositioning of business activities can be demonstrated graphically below:

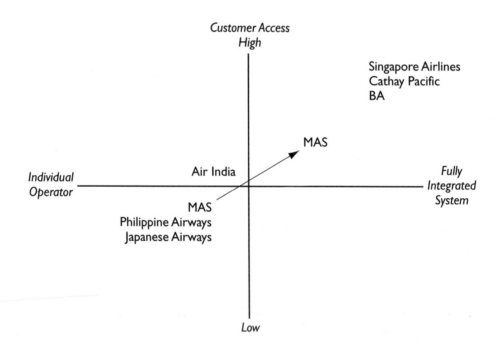

- The MAS brand is a business system and therefore requires complete communication and motivation within the organization.
- Key issue: Development of successful internal marketing programme.

## 2.2  Stakeholder Requirements

MAS has a wide range of stakeholders who all have communication needs. These range from:

- Government
- Finance Institutions

- Future Alliance Partners
- Intermediaries – Travel agents.

Key Issues:

- Consistency of message. They all have differing needs requiring satisfaction, however there must be a consistent theme.

Cultural Issues:

- MAS operate on a global basis and this further complicates communication plans.
- Language – high/low context.
- Aesthetics – design and colour.
- Social institutions.
- Attitudes – e.g. collectivism vs individualism.
- Adaptations vs standardization.

## 2.3 Budgets

MAS currently spends 3–4.5% below industry average. A significant brand shift is required; however a limited budget is available due to financial difficulties.

Key Issues:

- How is budget set?
- Marginal analysis.
- Share of voice vs market.
- Media multiplier.
- How to ensure effectiveness of money spent:
  - % awareness response.
  - Comparison of tool effectiveness.

## 2.4 Selection of Strategy

It is likely that all Push, Pull and Profiles will be utilized; however, a key factor in determining the plan will be to establish what percentage of budget each strategy should be allocated.

- Initial indications are that due to the market the current priority would be to focus more heavily on a push strategy.
- A good profile should be promoted in order to build CORPORATE IDENTITY.
- A pull strategy is also required but needs to use tools other than advertising due to the expense.

## 2.5 Control and Evaluation

In order to ensure delivery of objectives from the input of score resources, an overall control plan needs to be implemented.

- Use of variance analysis.
- Quantitative and qualitative measures.
- Focus groups and teaching studies.

In particular, the objectives set for both marketing and marcoms components will need to be assessed regularly, and should form the main evaluation of the campaign as an integrated marcoms plan.

## 2.6 New Methods

A final key factor will be over the use of internal based communications. This is the latest technology and is rapidly taking hold of the airline industry.

Key issues which result are:

- Degree of functionality required by intermediaries.
- Usage rates in Western and Eastern world.

- Need to acquire/recruit an 'e-specialist'.
- Aware of the lessons of opening up a direct channel – may lead to tensions with intermediaries. Any change needs to be carefully managed.

## 3.0  Summary

The marketing communications strategy for MAS will be complicated to develop, implement and control, due to the global demands and multi-stakeholder requirements. However, a degree of consistency must be achieved if brand repositioning is to be successful.

---

### Senior Examiner's Comments

The key factors have been identified and discussed as asked for in the question. It is surprising that the candidate has failed to consider the actual e-strategy shown in the case and how this will impact on any future strategies. Another key factor is the company's new controller's reluctance to spend more money on advertising. The launch of the new logo has also been put on ice.

---

## First Student Answer – Question 3

To:   Marketing Team

From:   Leigh Hindemith

Re:   International Marketing Strategy

Date:   15th June, 2001

## 1.0  Introduction

As part of the strategic marketing plan, market development has been recommended as a way to achieve the profit targets for years 2 and 3 of the plan. The following plans describe the strategy in order to deliver the income generation target of 20% by year 3.

## 2.0  Stakeholder Expectations

MAS has a number of stakeholders, all of which exert pressure and influence for MAS to develop internationally. These can be summarized as follows:

- GOVERNMENT: MAS is an ambassador for the country and Malaysia's modernization needs representing on a global scale.
- CUSTOMERS: Consumer mobility is rapidly increasing – particularly within South Asia.
- EMPLOYERS: Are motivated by working for an international firm.
- ORGANIZATION: In order to reverse losses, extra revenue is required to be generated through new international market.

## 3.0  Situation Analysis

Global air travel is rapidly increasing (8.5% – 9.5%) as a result, largely, of increased economic prosperity. A number of new opportunities are also arising due to deregulation and increased liberalization of trade, making more landing rights available. There is a strong focus within MAS on regional growth, creating pressures on the organization in terms of cultural adaptation to various standards and values.

### 3.1 Resources and Capabilities

MAS is well placed to focus on increasing new regional business, due to the recently increased capacity of its fleet, demonstrated by the infrequency and new routes opened to Australia and New Zealand.

Financially, initial new market exploration may have to be limited due to losses; however, with revenue expected to grow, progress on this front can be made in years 2 and 3.

## 4.0 Corporate Aims and Objectives

- Income generation from new existing markets by 63.5%.
- Develop alliances to build global position.
- Establish KL airport and MAS as a regional giant.

## 5.0 Marketing Strategies

Market development strategies can be supported by use of the following two models:

i.   Gilligan & Hird
     EXISTING MARKETS: Australia, New Zealand focus. Competitive position is dependent upon MAS enhancing the product to the superior or even breakthrough.
     LATEST MARKETS: India and China. Customer potential here is high and yet this requirement is not being specifically met by a competitor. MAS can achieve success in this market through marketing its current competitive product, making this a high priority target.

ii.  Harrell & Keifer (Segmentation)

**Country Attractiveness**

|                                          |        | High              | Medium            | Low |
|------------------------------------------|--------|-------------------|-------------------|-----|
|                                          | High   | China India       | Regional Dev.     |     |
| **Company's Competitive Position**       | Medium | Regional Dev.     | Int. Flights      |     |
|                                          | Low    |                   |                   |     |

## 6.0 Marketing Strategies and Implementation

### 6.1 China and India

- Both markets have great potential for growth. Malaysia also has a natural link with 27% of population being of Chinese origin and 8.9% of population being of Indian origin.
- Market type suggests current MAS service will prove competitive and successful.
- Government relations should help resolve landing nights issue.

**Suggested Actions:**

- Form an alliance with another hub. MAS should select a few destinations in conjunction with this hub providing the 'spoke' element of the service.
- Work with intermediaries to build good relations.
- Accelerate promotion and PR opportunities though press.

### 6.2 Australia and New Zealand

Aim to increase European traffic via KL airport, supported by the airports development – see answer to Question 1 for fuller details.

### 6.3 Global Ambitions

To become a top 20 airline by association, based on MAS dominance of S. Asia and connecting alliances providing global reach. LT development could include NPD in acquisition of Double Decker Airbus but main strength is seen in joining either STAR or One World Alliance. This represents a further strengthening of Code Sharing work already undertaken.

---

### Senior Examiner's Comments

The candidate has taken a sensible view of the best way of developing an international strategy. The development of a hub and spoke system at KL is an important part of the global strategy. It is good to see that the candidate has utilized some of the international marketing models.

---

## Second Student Answer – Question 1

---

### Senior Examiner's Comments

This answer illustrates the type of generalized answer that examiners often receive. They are good enough for a good pass, but are not outstanding as they miss out the necessary detail from the case. The case is handed out four weeks in advance; examiners expect candidates to analyse the case in some detail and exhibit this within their answers. You should therefore look as to how the answer below could be improved by you.

---

### *Marketing Plan*

### 1 Executive Summary

*1a Synopsis*

Malaysian Airlines System Berhad (MAS) is the loss-making, Malaysian national airline. Fares are the cheapest in the world, passenger numbers are disappointing, and MAS does not benefit financially from its excellent service levels. Despite award-winning, high service levels, its reputation trails that of rivals Singapore Airlines (SIA) and Cathay Pacific (CP). MAS is firmly entrenched as a second-tier national airline, and continuing losses reaffirm this.

MAS's relationship with its customers – despite several frequent flyer programmes – is haphazard and a defined, target market is less apparent. A comprehensive number of international and domestic passenger routes are provided in addition to cargo services. MAS's **international operations** predominantly serve destinations in Asia, Africa, China, India, Australia and New Zealand, with more limited services to North America and Europe. **Domestic operations** serve destinations throughout Malaysia. Internationally, MAS faces strong competition from SIA and CP, but it clearly has somewhat of a monopoly on domestic routes.

MAS is government-owned, and appears to be heavily influenced by the government, particularly in relation to domestic routes. Company operations appear to be extremely insular, and almost backward – a few alliances have been developed, but there is little evidence of links with other airlines, suppliers, major customers and industry bodies to date.

There is complete reliance on just 2 distribution channels – travel agents and an in-house booking system. MAS is linked to all industry computer reservation systems, and has stakes in two. Little has been done to embrace e-business despite its impact on the travel agency business generally.

### 1b  The Future

MAS must now divorce itself from its previously tactical approach, and develop a strategic, marketing-led orientation to achieve profitability within 3 years. Only when it has achieved profitability will it be able to consider setting growth and other business development targets. Different MAS groups must concentrate on their core competencies. Significantly MAS must offer responsibility for its cargo business to the MAS group's cargo division.

#### Stabilizing Finance

MAS must stabilize its financial position in the next year, introducing effective cost controls, and an e-business strategy that encompasses both its distribution and business operations. Effective 'preferred' supplier relationships must also be developed.

#### Repositioning

MAS must reposition itself, and develop its reputation for quality and service. Its positioning must draw on all that is strong in Malaysian culture.

MAS's aim is to be the world-class airline of choice of international air travellers.

MAS must now define its target customers, analyse their needs and shape its marketing mix according to a broader range of needs. Better relationships with these customers are key. MAS must strive to increase customer retention, and derive greater margins from its customers.

It must also attract more customers from its newly defined target market. It must establish more 'business to business' customer relationships to target international business travellers. It must assess and address the needs of all stakeholders.

It is imperative that MAS's cost-leadership pricing strategy is transformed to one that focuses on differentiation. High service levels should be a key differentiator.

MAS must develop alliances with other airlines to enable it to continue to enhance the number of routes, as well as its ability to cater for specialist and multi-stage trips.

MAS is strong in areas such as service delivery, reliability and plane standards, and this plan seeks to build on these strengths.

## 2  Audit – External

### 2a  Political/Legal
- Malaysia is stable politically.
- Domestic and international tourism are important to Malaysia.
- Malaysia is undergoing a government-led transformation.
- MAS is government owned.
- Deregulation of markets.
- Middle East problems.
- Global political instability, especially in Indonesia.
- Global environmental agreements, such as Kyoto.

### 2b  Economic
- Asian financial crisis.
- Exchange rate fluctuations.
- Strong diversified economy in Malaysia.
- Double figure growth.
- High per capita income.

- Growth in air travel.
- Slowing global economy.
- Economic growth in India/China.
- Increasing globalization of business.
- Deregulation increasing competition.
- Oil price hikes.

### 2c  Social/Culture
- Malaysia is a stable multi-racial, multi-cultural country.
- Changing global buyer behaviour.
- Malaysia's strong service culture.
- Changing customers' needs and perception.
- Growing awareness of safety on international flights.
- Changing family structures and demography.
- Growing business/globalization.
- Growing use of technology.

### 2d  Technological
- E-business will change buyer behaviour.
- Growing electronic payments systems.
- Growth in mobile communications.
- Greater support for frequent flyer programme.
- Growth of Internet travel portals.
- Growth in complex travel arrangements.
- In-flight technology developments, e.g. business centre in sky.
- Computer reservation systems (CRS).

## 3  Audit Internal

### 3a  Strengths
- One of largest South East Asian airlines.
- Part of larger group.
- Reputation for service and service innovation.
- Strong work and service ethnic-culture.
- KLIA is well positioned as a hub airport for South East Asia.
- Well established, with good infrastructure.
- Market leader in Malaysia.
- Golden Holidays an asset.
- Government backing.
- Alliances – code sharing.

### 3b  Weaknesses
- Substantial losses.
- Domestic routes and cargo loss-making.
- Confused strategy and an insular company.
- Confused positioning.
- Perception of second tier airline.
- Low advertising spend.
- Cost-leadership pricing.
- Low load factions.
- Heavy reliance on one distribution channel.
- Government links restrict it.
- Unbalanced portfolio.
- No strategy.

### 3c  Opportunities
- Play greater part of 'vision 2020'.
- KLIA becomes South East Asia's hub airport.

- Economic growth in South East Asia, India, China.
- Increased levels of leisure and tourism travel.
- Use of new distribution channels such as e-business.
- Alliances.
- Code sharing.
- Aircraft design.

### 3d Threats
- Global alliances – competition.
- Increasing fuel prices.
- Emergencies of online travel portals such as 'Travel Exchange for Asia Pacific'.
- Increasingly transparent fare structures.
- Increased competition.
- CRS booking system – owned by third parties.
- Global economic situation.
- Stability of Asia economy.
- Currency fluctuations.
- Low cost airlines.
- Global environmental issues.
- Developments in aircraft design.

## 4 Mission
MAS is the world-class airline of choice of international air travellers.

## 5 Corporate Objectives
- To turn MAS into a profitable airline in 4 years.
- To achieve 95% passenger load factors on all flights in 4 years.
- To increase profitability of international and domestic business by 100% in 4 years.
- To increase customers' retention levels by 50% in 4 years.
- To increase profitability of repeat business by 100% in 4 years.

## 6 Corporate Strategies
### 6a Short term
- To implement a financial improvement plan by end of year 1 (2002).
- To develop an e-business strategy by end of year 2002.
- To develop repositioning strategy by end of 2002.

### 6b Long term (3 years – 2002)
- To take 50% of bookings via e-business means by 2004.
- To become a 'passenger airline' by end of 2004.
- To establish an alliance with an airline that increases the number of North American and European routes three-fold by 2004.
- To reposition MAS by end 2004.

## 7 Target Markets
- Domestic air travel within Malaysia. (This plan assumes that government regulations compel MAS to operate domestically).
- International air travel to South East, North and West Asia, Africa, China, India, Australia, New Zealand.
- International air travel to North America and Europe.
- World air travel – multi-segment trips.

## 8 Target Customers
- Domestic business travellers.
- International leisure travellers.
- International business travellers.

## 9 Marketing Objectives

- To reposition MAS as a premier international airline by 2004.
- To increase passenger load factors to 95% by 2004.
- To penetrate the international, leisure travel market, increasing share by 10% by 2004.
- To penetrate market for travel to India and China by 100%.
- To increase customer retention by 50% by 2004.
- To penetrate the international business travel market by 20% by 2004.
- To penetrate market for multi-segment trips by 20% by 2004.

## 10 Positioning

Current perception is poor, and this needs to be improved as illustrated.

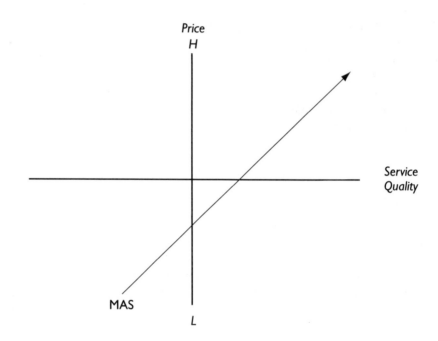

## 11 Development of Business

- MAS must differentiate its service, moving away from cost leadership pricing.
- Its marketing mix must be changed with new services being developed to illustrate the change in position.
- These services can be priced accordingly. Four levels of service are suggested:

    Golden First     Golden Plus
    Golden Club    Gold Standard

- MAS already provide good services and it must promote these to highlight differentiation.

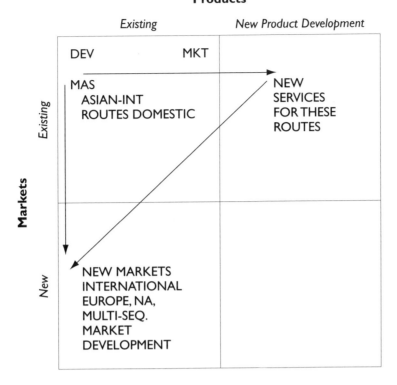

**Products**

|  | Existing | New Product Development |
|---|---|---|
| | DEV　　　　MKT | |

MAS
ASIAN-INT
ROUTES DOMESTIC

NEW
SERVICES
FOR THESE
ROUTES

NEW MARKETS
INTERNATIONAL
EUROPE, NA,
MULTI-SEQ.
MARKET
DEVELOPMENT

**Markets** — Existing / New

## Service Perception Vs Cost of Provision

This model illustrates MAS's current position and where it needs to move to:

**Relative Costs**

|  | High | Low |
|---|---|---|
| **High** | Niche Focus | Outstanding Service |
| | SIA CP | |
| **Low** | Disaster | Cost Leadership |

**Degree of Differentiation**

MAS needs to reposition its service so that it can transport fewer passengers, but with increased revenues.

Currently MAS is 'over-servicing' its customers.

MAS must define appropriate service levels for each of the four services provided.

## 12  Marketing Communications

- MAS must reposition itself as a world-class airline, and target communications at its target market.
- Repositioning – first stage.
- Completed by end of 2004.

### Objectives

- To raise awareness amongst its target customers by 50% by 2004.

### Strategy

- A pull strategy will be implemented to increase demand communicating to all audiences, external and internal.
- An initial burst will be followed/supported by communications to develop the reputation, and generate demand.

## 13  Distribution

- To increase online bookings by 50% by end 2004.
- To increase repeat business by 50% by end 2004.
- To increase business bookings by 50% by 2004.

### Strategy

- Create an e-business strategy in Year 1, enabling MAS to undertake e-ticketing.
- Implement a **customer relationship management** programme by end of 2004, consolidating existing programmes and focusing on target customers.
- Implement a travel portal/MAS web site.
- Participate in various other travel portals by end 2004.
- Establish preferred supplier relationships with 20 major businesses by end 2004.
- A preferred customer development programme will help to establish preferred relationships with preferred business customers. Personal selling will be a key issue.
- MAS is a preferred provider of business travel for these customers.
- Rationalize involvement with travel agents.

## 14  Marketing Research

### Objectives

- Define an MkIS system by end Year 1.
- Establish MkIS by 2004 (phased results).

### Strategy

- New marketing information in repositioning efforts during the period of the plan.

## 15  Budgets

A budget of RM715, 217,500 is requested. Split as follows:

- Marketing research                           5%
- Marketing communication
- (internal and external)                      35%
- Customer relationship management             15%
- Distribution                                 25%
- Alliance development                         15%

## 16 Conclusions/Justification

- MAS needs to **reposition** itself to achieve profitability.
- **Higher profitability** can be **achieved by differentiating services.** (25% of BA's profits come from 5% Club World Customers).
- A **customer relationship management approach** is recommended. Customer retention is easier to achieve than gaining new customer business.
- **E-business** is crucial, as the consumers will determine its use – MAS can benefit and must not be left behind.
- **Alliances** will help MAS increase the services it can provide whilst incurring minimal costs.

## 17 Phasing

| | |
|---|---|
| Year 1 | Achieve financial stability<br>Marketing research<br>'Repositioning' stance<br>E-business plan |
| Year 2, 3, 4 | Reposition<br>Raise awareness<br>Develop distribution channels<br>Develop alliance |

---

### Senior Examiner's Comments

This question has been well answered and shows a great deal of coherence and understanding of the key issues in the case. However, the answer does not pick out the detail within the case. In this sense it is not very strong on analysis. The candidate should have tried to assess the extent of the losses and also assess the liquidity available to the company for further investment. There is enough data in the case on different routes and the yields from these routes. Although the answer is strong on strategy, coherence and justification, the lack of detail on the analysis makes this an average answer.

## Second Student Answer – Question 2

### Key Factors Related to Developing a Marketing Communications Strategy for MAS

### 1 MAS's Current Position

- MAS's current positioning is confused – it is innovative and provides high service levels, yet charges low prices, and its passenger numbers are low.
- MAS is firmly entrenched as a second-tier national airline.
- MAS has no strong reputation.
- MAS has all the right ingredients to be a world-class airline, yet it still remains in the doldrums.

### 2 Key Factors Affecting MAS

i. MAS's poor positioning.
ii. MAS pricing strategy.
iii. Target audiences.
iv. Budgets.
v. Worldwide reach.

### 2a MAS's Poor Positioning

- MAS does not have the strong reputation that competitors such as SIA and CP have, and this is the most significant issue for MAS.
- Where customers are purchasing a service, the brand/reputation is crucial. A brand is key to identifying competitive advantage in customers' eyes. Once customers trust the combination of factors that comprises the reputation/brand, than this contributes significantly to the customers' propensity to buy them a company.
- MAS needs to improve its poor reputation/brand so that it can build profitable business from the service it already provides.
- Building its reputation will be key, and is not simply a communication issue, but an issue that pervades the whole organization and its operations: staff, service, standards, standards of airline, quality, attitudes, corporate communications.
- An integrated marketing communications plan based on strong objectives will need to be achieved. For instance, customers are willing to pay higher prices at Waitrose than at Tesco's because of the service mix provided, as was indicated in the recent 'Which' survey. BA also derives 25% of its revenues from 5% of its club world passengers.

### 2b MAS's Pricing Strategy

- Pricing is key to developments of reputation, in that price must back up the reputation/brand perception. The price paradox theory demonstrates that customers are willing to pay more for the right quality levels of service.
- Currently MAS's pricing strategy is one of cost leadership, this means that the airline may be losing money on each seat or at best breaking even.
- MAS will need to reposition itself quite cleverly in order to create appropriate levels of differentiation. MAS's aim must be to win and retain customers, and this will be difficult without repositioning itself. It will need to overcome current customer perceptions, as well as those industry bodies, and competitors.

### 2c Target Audiences

- MAS must realize that its customers are not its only target audience; rather, it must communicate with all target audiences as well, such as staff, suppliers, journalists, etc.
- MAS must take this into account with its marketing communications strategy.
- All targets have different needs, and key messages need to be modified appropriately to ensure that they are understood. For instance, communication is not necessarily straightforward.

Communicator ——→ Message ——————→ Noise ——————→ Receiver
transmitter

All communications are subject to interference, which may modify the message in a way that MAS had neither intended, nor is positive in its effect on MAS.

- MAS will need to tailor its **marketing communications mix** carefully. Different targets will be receptive to different media. Additionally, there will be benefits to MAS from tailoring its communications mix to the needs of its new **customer relationship management** strategy.
- Better understanding of customers' needs will enable MAS to tailor its marketing communications mix/strategy, involving personal/tailored marketing communications rather than poorly targeting direct mail. For instance, a recent basket analysis trial at Marks and Spencer enabled the retailer to understand buyers' baskets, and target new products and services accordingly.
- An effective marketing communications strategy involving targeted communications will be key in enabling MAS to improve customer retention and levels of repeat business achieved.

### 2d   Budgets

- MAS currently spends below market norms on marketing communication.
- MAS must rectify this situation. Marketing communications strategy will be key to MAS's future profitability.
- MAS will, however, be able to benefit from its customer relationship management strategy in optimizing its budgets. 70% of profits are generated by 30% of customers according to Garth Halburg, of Ogilvy Mather, so more targeted communications will enable MAS to encourage these customers to spend even more with MAS.

### 2e   Worldwide Reach

- MAS communications will need to be worldwide.
- They will need to influence MAS customers, journalists, staff, suppliers, partners, and so on. The company has to communicate the fact that it has 111 flight routes.
- It will be important for MAS messages to be tailored to meet the needs of all these target audiences.
- Communications will need to overcome prejudices, misunderstanding, poor communications.
- MAS's marketing communication campaign cannot possibly satisfy all these diverse needs. MAS will need to ensure that the campaign involves third parties, partners, etc. in order to achieve appropriate awareness levels. Public relations will help here, as will joint publicity with industry bodies when MAS wins awards, etc.
- In all of this, coherence and strong management will be essential.

## 3   Conclusions

MAS has a mammoth task, communicating to many target audiences throughout the world. Coherence and cogency of message will be the key.

MAS will need to be innovative in its approach to maximize its budgets, making much of alliances and opportunities to undertake joint publicity/promotion.

- The use of **appropriate** elements of the marketing mix will be significant e.g.:
  - PR to generate editorial to influence business customers.
  - Personal selling to influence the buyer behaviour of business customers, achieved preferred supplier status.
- There are numerous key factors influencing MAS's communications strategy and this paper highlights the most significant.

## Senior Examiner's Comments

This answer shows a good insight into some of the key factors affecting marketing communications. The candidate has effectively tried to answer the question and has rightly veered away from a communications plan. This is a good answer and could have been made even better by discussing how the company's brand equity could be improved.

## Second Student Answer – Question 3
### International Marketing Strategy for MAS

### 1 Introduction

Malaysian Airlines (MAS) is a loss-making Malaysian national airline. Fares are the cheapest in the world, yet passenger numbers are low. Excellent service levels go unnoticed.

Distribution relies heavily on travel agents (this industry is in turmoil), and whilst MAS has a comprehensive number of routes (111), only 19 of these are European, or North American.

Financially, the business is not strong, with high levels of gearing and poor cost control.

### 2 Mission

MAS is the world-class airline of choice of international air travellers.

### 3 Target Markets
* Domestic air travel within Malaysia.
* International air travel to South East, North and West Asia, Africa, China, India, Australia, New Zealand.
* International air travel to North America and Europe.
* International air travel incorporating multi-segment trips.

### 4 Marketing Strategy

This marketing strategy recommends the following individual strategies:

#### 4a Increased Route Coverage
**Objective**
* Increased business levels and profitability to be achieved by expanding MAS's international routes.

**Route Strategy**
* Increase the number of North American and European routes (to penetrate the North America and European markets).
* Increase load factors of the Asian business, divesting loss-making routes.
* To penetrate Indian and Chinese market, increasing number of routes.

#### 4b Alliances
**Objective**
* To increase international route coverage.

**Strategy**
* To establish an alliance with a major airline/airlines to increase the number of routes that MAS can offer, particularly to North America and Europe.
* To establish a 'domestic' alliance to reduce costs of domestic operations whilst still being able to offer appropriate routes.

## 4c Customer Relationship Management

**Objective**

- To increase customer retention, profitability and repeat business.

**Strategy**

- To implement a customer relationship management system.
- Understand and research target customers and assess their needs.
- Target business to satisfy there needs specifically.
- Specifically understand and develop relationships with business customers, including significant members of target companies' DMUs.
- Understand and respond to the needs of a worldwide audience.

## 4d Electronic Business

**Objectives**

- To increase business levels and reduce transaction costs.

**Strategy**

- Implement e-ticketing.
- Implement or partnerships for travel portals.
- Monitor future developments, and seize new initiatives to develop business.
- Implement associated support services throughout e-business methods.

## 4e Positioning

**Objective**

- To increase MAS's profitability and reputation.

**Strategy**

- To reposition MAS effectively.
- To reposition the services it provides to more closely watch fare structures.
- To position MAS as a **passenger airline**, with appropriate brand values, such as: individual service, friendly personal relationships, high service levels, service innovation seamless efficiency, eagerness to please.
- To grow/develop MAS's reputation.

## 4f Cargo Business

**Objectives**

- To adjust MAS of cargo responsibility.

**Strategy**

- Divest MAS's cargo responsibility to MAS group's cargo division.
- Create coherent business units that concentrate on **core competences**, and who can develop their own value **chains/systems** in a focused manner.

## 5 Phasing

This strategy can only be achieved in a phased manner as reputations and relationships take time to build. It takes time to divest business in a suitable manner.

This strategy proposes commencement of all the strategic activities in this plan during the next 3 years, to achieve specific goals set out in the marketing plan.

Budgets will be as specified in the marketing plan and considerable investment will be necessary.

## 6 Conclusion

A considerable gap was developed in MAS's business, and this strategy will address this:

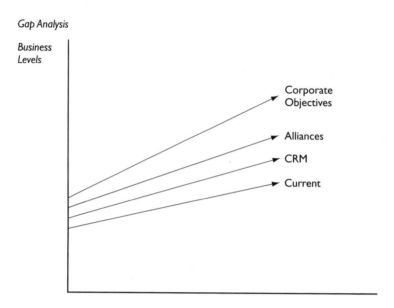

Each individual strategy will help achieve corporate strategies.

The **levels of business** need to be improved, by cost improvement measures as well as the introduction of view routes/generation of new business, and consolidation of domestic business.

**Customer Development and Strategies**

Will improve business levels, and profitability, but will attract less cost than developing new business **and lower costs of sales**.

**Alliances** will help to achieve profitability in a cost-effective manner.

**Electronic business/distribution channels** will **reduce costs of sale**, and will **satisfy customers' needs** in a cost-effective manner.

**Core competence** will be improved by divesting cargo responsibility to a focused cargo division.

---

### Senior Examiner's Comments

This is a good answer. The candidate could have discussed the routes more authoritatively by considering some of the yields obtained on the international routes. Obviously the growth areas represent a good source of revenue. The company needs to consider how much resources it should allocate to these growth areas. The candidate quite rightly refers to customer management systems but then does not capitalize on any clear Internet strategy which would be of great benefit to a company such as MAS.

---

### Summary

Both these answers illustrate different ways of answering the questions set. As usual attention to detail, strategic thinking, coherence and justification are rewarded. Candidates need to spend the four weeks prior to the examination working through the case in order to analyse the figures to utilise them for the required underpinning for developing strategies.

**9.54:** **Strategic Marketing Management: Analysis & Decision–Examiner's Report**

**Date:** **December 2001**

## General Comments

This Case Study was rather unusual as it was based on the marketing of a city in a country which was part of a centrally planned economy during Soviet rule. After several years of freedom, Latvia and the city itself are getting to grips with fundamental issues in marketing. The City of Daugavpils administration is beginning to understand the extent of the problems facing the city and is now working on ways of increasing income through marketing. There are various avenues available for improving the status of the city. These are discussed at length in the case. Students had to be imaginative in terms of the marketing strategies they could develop. The city faces a real problem of identity and of growth. The perception of the city in Latvia itself is poor. This was the first CIM case to be set in an Eastern European country.

Given this scenario, it was good to see candidates demonstrating a good understanding of the international dimensions and the e-commerce issues. Most examiners were pleasantly pleased with the level of answers given. In general, the pass rates were good, but the poorer centres still performed badly.

## Key Points

a. There was less of a tendency to produce 'group' answers, apart from three scripts from Singapore, which contained identical answers.

b. Question 1. was reasonably well answered. However, some students still fail to justify their strategies. Porter's diamond and other models were used appropriately. Some candidates still have a problem with time and sometimes tend to use this question for 'dumping' all their ideas.

c. Question 2. seemed to create problems. Many candidates are still 'locked' into the 'planning' mode. The question asked for issues in branding, allowing students to consider branding theory and settings. However, many students presented superficial and fragmented answers. Communication issues in marketing are still poorly taught at some centres.

d. Question 3. was generally well handled and many students seem to have grasped the relevance of the Internet. In spite of this, it was surprising that many candidates are still unaware of its possibilities. It was even more surprising that the World Travel Organization model described in the case was not used sensibly.

## Summary

This year's pass rate is higher than usual. It appears that the gulf between international centres and UK centres is closing. The gulf is now between good centres and bad centres. As marketing becomes complex and undergoes many changes, it is important that centres are given the right guidance. At the same time, it is important that prospective candidates are urged to attend teaching sessions at the right establishment. Currently the gulf between the poor students and the good ones is getting greater, yet at the same time, the number of better (middle range) students is increasing. The new style of cases and the tutor sessions are helping with standards. Perhaps more candidates are sitting the case as the final Diploma examination. We need to understand these changes so that momentum is not be lost. The key to better success is the ability to apply marketing knowledge to the questions set. It is interesting to note that the pilot centres are still doing well. Finally, Prince Charles was sent a copy of the case and a very favourable letter was received in response.

## Specimen Answers for Strategic Marketing Management: Analysis & Decision December 2001

### Introduction

In order to be a good and accurate guide to students taking this examination, the following Specimen Answers have not been written by the Senior Examiner but have been reproduced from actual scripts submitted for the December examinations.

Following a standardization exercise, in which all examiners take part, two distinction level scripts were chosen, in full, to illustrate examples of good practice. In real business situations there are no right or wrong decisions, only sensible and realistic ones. By comparing two different high quality answers you will be able to gauge what is realistically possible in a three hour examination.

The complete guideline approach for all the questions, given to all examiners, encapsulates the key points good answers should include. This guideline has also been reproduced in full at the beginning of the Specimen Answers, enabling you to see how a wide variety of approaches can be taken.

The answers have been taken verbatim from complete papers so there is full continuity. At the end of each paper the Senior Examiner makes some comments on why the paper was good and where particular gaps may have arisen.

## City of Daugavpils

### Overview

#### The Case

This Case Study is rather unusual as it is based on the marketing of a city in a country which was part of a centrally planned economy during Soviet rule. After several years of freedom the country and the city itself are getting to grips with fundamental issues in marketing. The administration of the City of Daugavpils is beginning to understand the extent of the problems facing the city and is now working on ways of increasing income through marketing. There are various avenues available for improving the status of the city. These are discussed at length in the Case. Students will also have to be imaginative in terms of the marketing strategies they develop. The city faces a real problem of identity and of growth. The perception of the city in Latvia itself is poor. This is the first CIM case to be set in an Eastern European country. This case has no personalized comments, is factual and contains no 'red herrings'. Nonetheless, as usual, there is the problem of an extensive range of detailed information. There is a need to develop clear and concise insights into the key issues involved in developing a strategy.

#### Key Issues

a.  Developing marketing within a population, which does not understand this.
b.  Improving the perception of the city.
c.  Competitively positioning the city within Latvia and Europe/USA.
d.  The city does not have a marketing budget.
e.  Using its position as a transition point between East and the West.

f.  An airport with the potential to become a hub.
g.  Developing a coherent brand image.
h.  Selling the city's tourism and leisure facilities.
i.  Developing aspects of the Internet.
j.  Exploring the possibilities of exploiting the city alliances.
k.  Developing focused and targeted marketing for local/national/international clientele.
l.  Current recessionary climate.
m.  Latvia is regarded as stable and the currency is stable.
n.  No key staff dedicated to marketing.
o.  PR focused on the Mayor Richard Eigims.
p.  The potential for developing medical tourism.
q.  The potential for raising money through the EC for marketing development.
r.  Further marketing of the sporting facilities and fishing as a sport.
s.  Developing the balance in marketing to Latvian and Russian speaking individuals.
t.  Allocating a reasonable (£100,000 approx.) budget to marketing.
u.  There is a possibility of developing the brand through sports sponsoring.

## The Answers

This case is reasonably straightforward and does not contain many surprises. It was important, therefore that the following issues were considered:

1.  The application of theory.
2.  The amount of International marketing theory/application that the students could apply to the case. The amount of communication theory that they could also apply.
3.  The candidates needed to think strategically and not tactically.
4.  The answers given had to be realistic and practical.
5.  A degree of innovation and lateral thinking was rewarded.
6.  It was important that the questions were answered within the given context.
7.  The additional information is quite important and shows the possible impact of HRH Prince Charles's visit to Latvia, and Daugavpils itself.

## Question 1

**Assess the current situation in Daugavpils and outline a marketing strategy for three years.**

This question requires students to use many of the strategic planning models used by marketers. Candidates will then need to consider the following:

a.  Consider the objectives that they wish to set for the city for three years.
b.  Take into account a reasonable but small budget to start with.
c.  Consider segmentation of the various areas that need marketing, such as tourism, business, sports and health.
d.  In the longer term consider how the budget could be increased through EC grants.
e.  A strategic vision and mission needs to be developed.
f.  In the short term consideration needs to be given to increasing growth in tourism from national areas such as Riga.
g.  The administration needs to consider how it can entice European nationals from the EC and also Latvians living in America.
h.  The city offers interesting sites and tranquility at a very low cost. This needs exploiting.
i.  How should the airport be developed?
j.  For PR purposes, how can Prince Charles's visit be built on?
k.  In the very short term PR and communications are going to be very important.
l.  The city's brand image is diffuse and each entrance to the city has different symbols. This needs to be unified.

m. Models such as Porter, Ansoff, BCG, GEC, Shell Directional and GAP could be used in the analysis of the case, modified for use in the public sector.

n. What are the constraints to the given strategy? How can the administration follow a market led strategy? What would be a realistic marketing budget?

o. How should the organization chart be redeveloped to create and maintain an emphasis on marketing?

p. Developing the role for the Internet.

Points in a strategic plan:

1. Set corporate objectives.
2. Identify target markets.
3. Set marketing objectives.
4. Develop marketing strategy and tactics.
5. Organize control systems.

**Given the points above, the best answers showed a clear grasp of the following:**

1. A good analysis of the current position.
2. The development of a strategic plan with fully developed implementation strategies.
3. A good justification of the strategies to be adopted.

## Question 2

**Critically analyse the key issues involved in creating a distinctive brand image for Daugavpils.**

Some key factors that should be analysed and assessed are:

a. The city has a logo, but does not have a distinctive brand image.

b. The entrances to the city do not have a single identity. The statues are all disparate.

c. The city image has to be gradually built up with a distinctive offering and strap line.

d. Developing the need for branding within the city administrators and the city itself.

e. The importance of credible communications with the press and having a sustained public relations exercise with the national press.

f. Making effective utilization of the Internet.

g. Developing a major poster campaign to push the brand in Riga.

h. Working closely with locally based companies to understand the key selling points of the city and using these in the brand offering to outside investors.

i. Developing the brand within the context of marketing the country as a whole.

j. Consideration of repositioning the brand: Psychological repositioning. The peoples' beliefs about the city need to be changed and discussed.

k. Reweighing values and understanding the key values of the city... offering history, tourism and business possibilities.

l. Considering budgets and constraints for communications.

*These and any other relevant points should be taken into consideration.*

Finally the students should consider how these factors could be seamlessly linked up with the strategies that the company has developed.

**A good answer will take into the following:**

- Critical analyses of the key issues.
- Links with the overall strategy.

## Question 3

**Discuss how the Internet could be used as part of a strategy to attract international investment and tourism to the region of Daugavpils.**

This question offers a range of interesting options to students. The key issues to consider are actual Internet possibilities and the links with an international audience.

In essence, the Web will be used for publishing and database marketing. Such a site only offers information and promotional material. The site can be made interesting by having site, sound, video and pictures. It is essential that the administration has a well-developed map of Daugavpils, with an illustration of its tourist features and also its business potential.

Candidates should be able to use ideas developed in the case:

    a. The logo for the site should be better developed.
    b. Photographs of the key sites need to shown.
    c. The site should have key language options.
    d. The site should have good hyperlinks to sister sites of the twinned cities.
    e. There should be interactive trip planners.
    f. The cities brochure should be put online.
    g. The key accommodation outlets both in the city and the outskirts need to be shown.
    h. Key routes to the city need to shown.
    i. For potential investors, there should be a section showing the key benefits for investing in the city.
    j. The site should be linked to potential investors, such as banks etc.
    k. Develop hyperlinks to key business sites, especially where companies are looking for investment possibilities.
    l. Hyperlinks with business sections of the Financial Times.

These and other ideas for Internet development should be considered. At the same time, the team should be ensuring that International development continues through the normal diplomatic channels in each of the countries where Latvia is represented. Key to success are links within EC sites.

As usual, coherence, strategic thinking, justification and detail featured in the answers were duly rewarded. The case is quite long and there is considerable amount of data so that candidates had the chance to fashion a range of interesting answers. The case elicited some interesting answers, two which are featured in this document. Creativity and innovation were rewarded.

## First Student Answer – Question 1

**Report**

| | |
|---|---|
| **To:** | **Mayor of Daugavpils** |
| **From:** | **Marketing Consultant** |
| **Date:** | **7/12/01** |
| **Re:** | **3 Year Marketing Strategy for Daugavpils** |

### Index:

1. Executive Summary
2. Key Issues facing Daugavpils
3. Mission Statement
4. Corporate Objectives
5. Critical Success Factors
6. Marketing Objectives
7. Segmentation of the Market
8. Targeting the Segments
9. Positioning Daugavpils
10. Marketing Mix
11. 3 Year Budget
12. Monitor and Control

## 1 Executive Summary

Daugavpils is in a situation of change but one that brings with it many opportunities. A number of key activities have recently occurred within the city – your election, working towards EU membership and the economy is growing. However, the current multi-cultural residents of the city are not happy with their standard of living, the city is poorly perceived by others and the infrastructure needs urgent attention. To instigate the changes needed to turn this situation around, a marketing strategy that is achievable, sustainable and achieves the city's objectives must be implemented and controlled.

Due to the impending visit of His Royal Highness, Prince Charles, it is imperative that this strategy is agreed and initiated to be able to answer the business and cultural questions that the Prince will have.

## 2 Key Issues

The key issues surrounding Daugavpils are:

1. A poor perception outside the city – it is regarded as 'backwards' and 'poor' by other Latvians.
2. The population of Daugavpils is not content. There is high unemployment (28%) and 75% of the population would leave if they had the option. Additionally, the ageing population is putting a strain on the working population and the economy.
3. The infrastructure is old and decaying. Airports, roads and rail services all need updating to facilitate the business trade and potential visitors.
4. There is no coherent integrated marketing communications strategy.

Yet the situation is not so bleak:

1. Daugavpils has a number of resources which could make it an attractive location to establish a business in. This includes:

    * A cheap, skilled workforce.
    * Big factories currently empty.
    * Area attracts EU funding.
    * Location at the centre of 3 Baltic states.

2. Daugavpils has a natural environment which lends itself well to the tourism market.

    * A unique and interesting heritage.
    * Ornate architecture and historical sites.
    * Beautiful countryside and lakes.

    These features can be enhanced and developed to optimize the growing health tourism market an area in which the city used to have a strong competency.

## 3 Mission Statement

For Daugavpils to be recognized as a multi-cultural thriving environment, in which people are encouraged to live, work, visit and invest in, so that they want to stay or return.

**Daugavpils – the gateway city to opportunities.**

## 4 Corporate Objectives

1. To reduce unemployment from 28% to 14% by 2005.
2. To increase the income from city enterprises from 52m lats a year to 75m lats a year by 2005.
3. To reduce the death rate from 1.3% to 1.0% by 2004.

## 5  Critical Success Factors

## 6  Marketing Objectives

1. Increase the number of international visitors from 6% to 14% and the number of domestic visitors from 8% to 22% by 2004.
2. Increase the satisfaction rate of the population from 25% to 40% by 2004.
3. To increase the number of foreign companies from 30 to 40 by 2004.
4. Develop the Internet site to meet 70% of the criteria set by the World Tourism Organization by 2003.

## 7  Segmentation of the Market

There is a diverse range of audiences that Daugavpils needs to market itself to. These can be segmented by usage and leads to 3 main groups:

1. Visitors.
2. Businesses.
3. Investment.

### 1  Visitors

People will visit Daugavpils for some of the following reasons:

- Visit friends/family (other Latvians, Russians, Poles).
- Tourists to enjoy the environment (external or internal).
- Meetings at existing businesses in the city (business visitors).

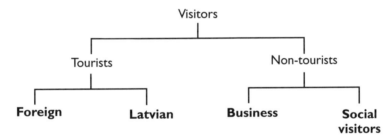

There will be some common market needs, e.g. restaurants, hotels, yet there will be some services specific to the type of visitor (e.g. business visitors and car hire).

Reasons why people may not currently visit Daugavpils include:

- Tourists are unaware of the city and what it offers.
- Other Latvians are unaware of what changes have taken place.

### 2  Businesses

The current businesses are primarily manufacturing. Reasons why they are attractive to invest in Daugavpils include:

- A skilled, cheap labour force.
- Potential EU funding.
- Daugavpils is located near other countries including Russia.

Reasons why businesses are not currently attracted to Daugavpils include:

- Lack of a supporting infrastructure to export products out of the country.

## 3 Investment

Sources of investment include the following:

    a.   Internal e.g. Latvian government.
    b.   External e.g. EU funding, IMF.

Reasons for investing include:

- The city meets the qualifying requirements for funds.
- The city is developing and can demonstrate the potential for repaying loans.
- As Latvia is currently in the process of joining the EU, various standards must be met within the country so funding is necessary for this.

Reasons why funding may not be given include:

- The city already receives 25% of its income from EC support so may have reached its maximum quota.

## 8 Targeting

To prioritize the diverse market segments, the GE matrix can be used to evaluate the alternatives.

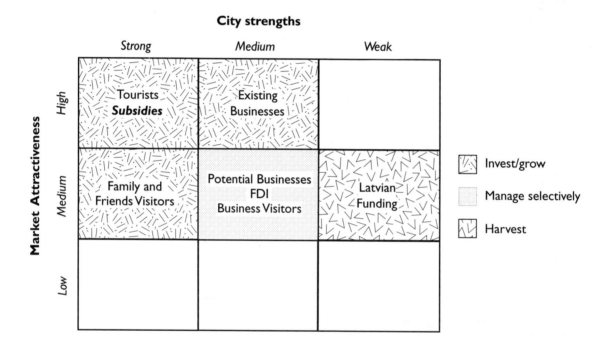

*FDI: Foreign direct investment*

This analysis suggests that the groups to focus on are:

- Tourists.
- Subsidies.

Consider the tourist market – the city already has a number of assets to support this industry (e.g. beautiful landscape, cultural heritage). The market is potentially a large one, yet little is currently being done to capitalize on this.

The analysis suggests that Latvian funding is last on the list of priorities. It should not be ignored since it may be a way to get funding for relatively little effort. Yet it should be recognized that the potential rewards are small in comparison to, for example, external funding.

## 9 Positioning

Having identified which segments to target, Daugavpils must decide upon a positioning strategy which will be an underlying tenet of its marketing plan.

Current and Future Perception

Ranchhod's perception map positions Daugavpils as a dull city with poor marketing. The brand needs to repositioned – e.g. as dynamic, not dull.

**Perceptual Map**

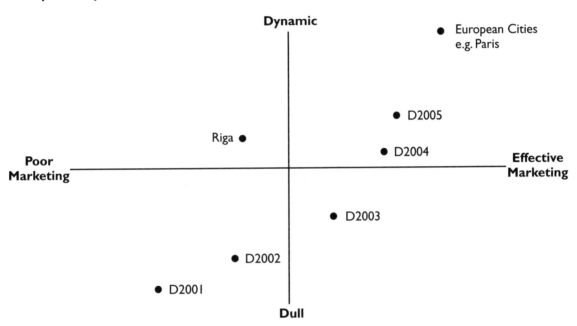

These will be covered further in the accompanying report on brand strategy.

### Porter's Generic Strategies for Competitive Advantage

Porter suggests that an organization should adopt one of three (or a combination of two) generic strategies.

- Cost leadership.
- Differentiation.
- Focus.

Currently the city does not have a clear concentration on any of these three.

I would suggest that Daugavpils can implement and successfully sustain a differentiated strategy with an element of cost leadership.

Differentiation is achievable because:

1. The environment is unique to the locality and there is a strong heritage to the city.
2. The multi-cultural society is a unique one and allows Daugavpils to position itself differently from other cities e.g. Riga.
3. The city has a number of established manufacturing industries which will act as a clustering point for other industries.

Cost leadership should not be the underlying strategy because:

- It is hard to sustain in the long term as the focus is on driving costs down in the future which can lead to economic problems.

However, elements of cost leadership can be adopted because:

- There is a supply of cheap, skilled labour.
- There is a supply of natural resources e.g. water and wood.
- Capital investment is relatively low due to empty factories and EU funding.

A focus strategy would not be considered because:

- This would result in a heavy dependence on one market and therefore susceptible to any downturns in the market.

## Market Position

Daugavpils can be a market niche – in this way it will gain competitive advantage by focusing on a selected group of market segments. This complements the differentiation strategy.

I have ruled out the other positions for the following reasons.

**Market leader:** this seeks to attain market dominance. It is usual for the organization to have a well-established position and attracting the market aggressively – Daugavpils is not currently in this position.

**Market challenger:** this position seeks confrontation with the market leader. To do this, there must be a great deal of resources available – the city does not have this.

**Market follower:** in this position, the city would follow the market leader. This would be suitable for a cost leadership strategy, not a differentiation one.

## Offensive/Defensive strategies

The ability to gain or retain market share leads to the adoption of offensive or defensive strategies. The following can be used by Daugavpils.

## Defensive – Position

The city must strengthen its current position to build on existing assets and retain a happy population – clearly not being achieved currently.

## Offensive – Bypass

This strategy is one in which organizations move into areas where competitors are not active. Daugavpils with its unique qualities is well placed to follow this.

## 10  Marketing Mix
### Product

To develop consistent and coherent brand strategy that is utilized in all marketing communications.

This is achieved by:

- Conducting a brand audit.
- Compiling a repositioning brand.
- Considering areas where the brand can be extended.

### Price

To be perceived as a destination in which residents, visitors and businesses gain value for money through a differentiated and unique proposition.

- Monitor economic indicators e.g. wage cost.
- Ensure value for money – not shoddy nor overpriced via liaison with businesses and shops.

## Place

To ensure all target markets have access to accurate information through a variety of media.

- Visitor guide books.
- Internet site.

## Promotion

To raise awareness and address the poor perception of Daugavpils amongst selected markets by promoting the brand through an integrated marketing plan.

- Use the TV press, particularly for Prince Charles' visit, to communicate the changes in the city and its current position.
- Sales holiday promotional campaigns with foreign travel operators.

## People

To have a marketing team and agency that is equipped with sills and resources to effectively deliver the marketing strategy to the target markets.

- Recruit and train a marketing team.
- Select a full service agency to give integration to all communication.

## Physical Evidence

To develop the city into an attractive location for its residents, visitors and other target markets.

- Co-ordinate resources within the city (enlisting local help) to prepare the city for Prince Charles' visit.

## Process

To be co-ordinated, effective and efficient in the management and delivery of the marketing plans to the city of Daugavpils and its target markets.

- Appoint a Marketing Director and supporting team with clear responsibilities and objectives.

## 11  Budget

Using Bradford's £100,000 spend on the tourist market as a benchmark, the 3 markets for Daugavpils will require c. £300,000. Since the business and investment markets will require considerable personal selling, add on £200,000. Finally, the Internet work will require at least £100,000.

|  | 2003 | 2004 |  | 2002 |
| --- | --- | --- | --- | --- |
|  | % | £k | £k | £k |
| Brand development | 10 | 60 | 60 | 40 |
| Internet marketing | 17 | 100 | 60 | 60 |
| Recruitment and training | 5 | 30 | 10 | 10 |
| Marketing research | 5 | 30 | 10 | 10 |
| PR | 10 | 60 | 80 | 100 |
| Promotions | 9 | 60 | 80 | 100 |
| Relationship marketing | 34 | 200 | 300 | 400 |
| Contingency | 10 | 60 | 70 | 80 |
|  |  | 600 | 670 | 800 |

## 12  Monitor and Control

- Allocate responsibility (e.g. via a new marketing team).
- Regularly report to board on progress vis. objectives.

---

### Senior Examiner's Comments

This is a well-answered question and it covers all the key aspects of the case. One could argue that the recommended budget is quite high given the poverty of the city council. The positioning of the city and the use of the GE matrix are very good, offering valuable insights for further segmentation strategies. Some aspects of the strategy development lack the underpinning detail that has been given in the case vis-à-vis sports, health and industrial make-up of the city.

---

## First Student Answer – Question 2.

**Report**

| | |
|---|---|
| **To:** | **Mayor of Daugavpils** |
| **From:** | **Marketing Consultant** |
| **Date:** | **7/12/01** |
| **Re:** | **Creating a Distinctive Brand Image** |

### Index:

1. Brand Definition
2. Brand Name
3. Brand Iceberg
4. Brand Audit
5. Brand Positioning statement
6. Brand Circle
7. Brand Communication

### 1  Brand Definition

"A successful brand is an identifiable product, service, person or place augmented in such a way that the buyer or user perceives relevant unique added values which match their needs most closely" (de Chernatony).

This suggests that a brand, as applied to Daugavpils, offers 2 beneficial features:

1. Differentiation.
2. Added values.

The markets of the city must be able to suggest features of Daugavpils which allow their minds to differentiate the city, and for it to offer services in such a way that is not possible in other cities.

### 2  Brand Name

The brand name is important because it confers attributes – e.g. consider Diet Coke, which relates the benefits that the Coke name supports. Other qualities that can be communicated via a brand name are:

- Action.
- Acceptability in all markets.

- Distinctive.
- Meaningful.

With a city, there is a limited choice in the name. The city could be renamed, e.g. back to an earlier name such as Dinaburg, like the name of the local football team. This would be an expensive and immense undertaking and one which would encounter much resistance from the local population.

However, to enable some of these attributes to be suggested, the brand logo could use the slogan:

'Daugavpils – the gateway City to Opportunities'

This would relate certain distinctive attributes of Daugavpils:

### Gateway

- Location at centre of 3 Baltic states and linking the East and the West.
- This also links to the visual representation of a city gate on the current logo.

### Opportunities

- For businesses – resources available.
- For visitors – many features to explore.
- For investment groups – potentially a good return for the initial investment.
- For local people – facilities and employment (although achievement of particularly this last point is dependent upon the other 3 markets, e.g. businesses).

## 3 Branding Iceberg

The attributes of a brand can be divided into those features that are visible to the external eye and those that are not immediately obvious. This has led to the concept of a Branding Iceberg. For Daugavpils, this takes the following form.

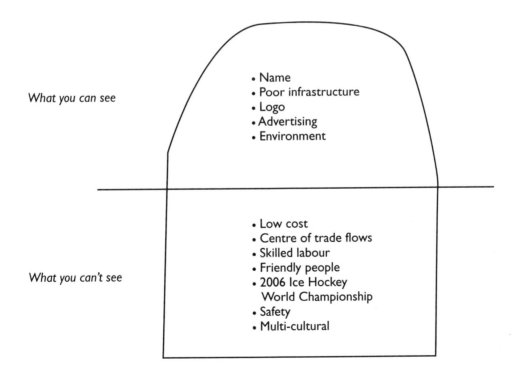

Currently, what our customers see is:

- A poor infrastructure.
- Minimal advertising.
- Unco-ordinated marketing activity.

This partly underpins the negative image which many people hold of Daugavpils.

Our brand communication plan must inform our target markets of those elements that are not so readily visible, e.g. cheap labour, multi-cultural population. These are assets we already have in Daugavpils and can and should be promoted as differentiating features which add value to our offer.

## 4 Brand Audit

To understand what changes need to be effected we need to understand the following:

1. What is the current brand image with stakeholders?
2. How do we want the brand to be positioned in the minds of our stakeholders?
3. How will we change the brand image to close the gap between 1. and 2.?

The current brand image is demonstrated in Ranchhod's positioning map. On to this we can overlay the position where we want the brand to be:

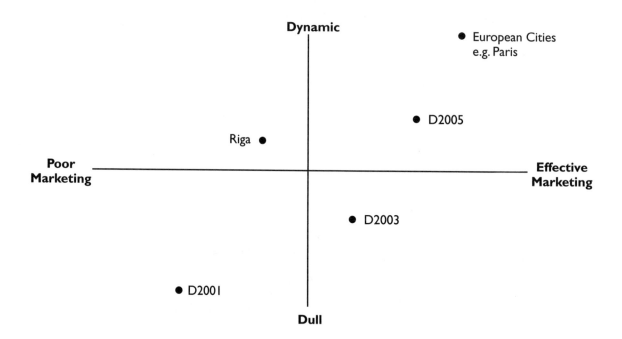

Reposition as:

### Dynamic not Dull

- The City will not be in the same class as Paris or Milan because our economy is currently too small to support this.
- We can be at least as dynamic as Riga because we have many similar features to Riga, but our own unique offering overlaying that.

### Effective Marketing

- Effective marketing is achieved when our target consumer perceives us to be the city we want them to believe us to be. The main barrier to this is our own internal processes and marketing communication strategy.

**Repositioning the Daugavpils brand**

The Daugavpils brand must be repositioned. This can be achieved by 1 or more of the following:

- Real.
- Perceived.
- Competitive.
- Change emphasis of attributes.

For Daugavpils, the emphasis should be on a. and b.:

**Real**

The unemployment of the area is high as is the dissatisfaction level of the population. Real changes need to be made (e.g. new businesses bringing employment) to change this.

**Perceived**

People outside the city believe it to be backward and poor. Whilst this may hold some truth, there is also evidence to suggest that this is not completely so – e.g. GDP per capita is growing, businesses are locating to the area and there are new modern facilities, such as the Ice Hockey Stadium. The marketing plan must emphasize these points so that others hold a truly reflective image of the city.

## 5  Brand Positioning Statement

Core qualities of what the Daugavpils brand means.

| | |
|---|---|
| Brand name: | Daugavpils |
| Target audience: | Internal population |
| | Visitors |
| | Businesses |
| | Investment groups |
| Brand discriminator: | Opportunities for increased prosperity/ returns in a growing economy |
| Core consumer proposition: | Businesses: good quality resources (labour and buildings) at affordable costs |
| Brand differentiators: | Skilled, cheap labour, multi-lingual and multi-cultural, unique location, heritage |
| Brand personality: | Aspirational, dynamic, improving, healthy, safe, opportunities |

## 6 Brand Circle

```
┌─────────────────────────────────────────────────────────────┐
│                      No-go Areas                            │
│                                                             │
│                    Extension Areas                          │
│         ┌───────────────────────────────────────┐           │
│         │                          Natural       │           │
│         │                          cosmetic      │           │
│         │          Outer Core      industry      │           │
│ Nightclub│                                       │           │
│ resort  │                                        │           │
│   Organic│                                       │           │
│   family │  Health      Inner Core     Sports    │ Big theme │
│         │  Tourism     Heritage               │  parks     │
│         │              Resources              │           │
│         │              Multi-cultural         │           │
│         │                        Leisure      │           │
│         │                                     │           │
│         │    Countryside                      │           │
│   Golf  │                                     │           │
│         │         EU investment               │           │
│         └───────────────────────────────────────┘           │
│  Skyscrapers                              Low Cost          │
└─────────────────────────────────────────────────────────────┘
```

| Inner core : | Critical elements in brand identity |
| Outer core : | Optional attributes |
| Extension areas: | Areas to which brand can be widened without damage |
| No-go areas : | Involvement would seriously damage and compromise clarity of brand proposition |

## 7 Brand Communication

- Managed by brand manager
- Communicated : coherent of co-ordinated
  made up of
  functional       : real benefits of attributes
  expressive
- Integrated with overall marketing strategy.

**Senior Examiner's Comments**

This a really well answered question where the candidate has spent a sensible amount of time in understanding the communication issues. It is clear that instead of considering communication issues in general, the candidate has just focused on branding. However, he/she has kept the scope wide enough to absorb the general communication factors. PR factors also need to be considered.

## First Student Answer – Question 3.

**Report**

To:        **Mayor of Daugavpils**

From:    **Marketing Consultant**

Date:     **7/12/01**

Re:       **Internet Strategy for Daugavpils**

### Contents:

1. Executive Summary
2. Situational Analysis
3. Internet Objectives
4. Internet Strategy
5. Web Site Functionality
6. Benefits
7. Concerns

## 1  Executive Summary

The Internet will act as an essential strategic tool for the implementation of the marketing strategy. It is a medium which not acts as an advertising medium, but offers the possibility of promotions, direct marketing (through data collected) and personal selling (through the establishment of a Customer Relationship Management database).

The following Internet strategy will show how this will be of benefit to all stakeholders of Daugavpils, including foreign investment and tourists.

## 2  Situational Analysis

The key issues surrounding the development of an Internet marketing strategy for Daugavpils are:

1. There is a current site but it is slow and basic thus failing to promote (even demotes) the features of Daugavpils in an optimum manner.
2. Travel and tourism (key markets for Daugavpils) take up a large proportion of Internet space and are expected to continue to grow.
3. An Internet site will benefit all stakeholders of Daugavpils, i.e. visitors, industries within Daugavpils and other Latvians, as it will act as a central reference point.
4. Consumer trends indicate that the Internet will play a major role within their cash rich/ time poor lifestyles. This media vehicle will continue to gain acceptance amongst consumers of all ages in many nations.

## 3 Internet Objectives

Overall marketing objectives.

Develop the current Daugavpils Internet site to meet 70% of the criteria set by the WTO by 2003.

### Web Objectives:

1.  To achieve 15,000 hits from our target markets in 2003 and 150,000 hits by 2005.
2.  The average length of the target market's visit to the web site to be 4 mins 30 sec in each year.
3.  70% of respondents to tick 'Good' or 'Very Good' in the 'Your feedback' section of the web page each year.
4.  To have a conversion hit rate amongst the target audience of 3% in 2003 and 10% by 2005.
5.  For the site to achieve breakeven point by 2004 and to make a profit in 2005.

These objectives have been formulated using Chaffey's 'Framework for Measuring Internet Marketing Success'.

1.  *Channel promotion*
2.  *Channel behaviour*
3.  *Channel satisfaction*
4.  *Channel outcomes*
5.  *Channel profitability*

(The no: of the objective links directly to the number within this framework).

## 4 Internet Strategy

The web site can be used to aid customers, whether they be tourists or investors, through the different stages of the buying process.

1.  Generate awareness of Daugavpils and its benefits.
2.  Position the brand of Daugavpils as unique and differentiate to complement and support the overall mission statement.
3.  The site can be used as a vehicle for providing information to individuals, and as a contact point for further information requests.
4.  Facilitate and support an individual's choice of coming to Daugavpils.

## 5 Web Site Functionality

### Target Market

The site will primarily be aimed at international visitors, particularly tourists.

*   The Internet tourism market is a growing one.
*   The Internet is a global media and therefore effective in reaching overseas customers.
*   Overseas visitors often search the web for possible places to visit, or package deals, thus it is important for Daugavpils to be on this map.

Businesses and investment groups would not be the primary target of the web site because these customers generally require specific information which is best communicated on a one-to-one basis. However, the general information on the site will be of use to them, e.g. business visitors looking for somewhere to stay, investment groups gaining an overall picture of the city before actually visiting.

**The Internet Brand**

The Internet site must complement the overall Daugavpils brand strategy. Thus it must support our differentiated positioning and our overall mission statement. The following model from Chaffey is useful to consider.

**Identity**

```
                    Product
                    Quality

          Customer    Brand    Service
          Affinity             Quality
```

**Credibility**

Therefore:

- Our target market should be able to relate to the brand characteristics encompassed within the web site (e.g. pictures used).
- The quality of the site and its associated services must support our differentiated and added value positioning.
- The web site should give Daugavpils a unique position in the customer's mind which is credible and sustainable.

**Key aspects of the web site:**

- High quality content
  Text and visuals are up-to-date and accurate.

- Easy to use
  Easy to understand where you are, what's available and how to get there.

- Ability to download
  All pages should be in formats that are easy and quick to print or download.

- Consistency
  Brand logo and menu options to be available on each page enabling ease of navigation and enhancing brand values.

## 6  Benefits

1. Common source of information for all to relate to.
2. Enhances the brand value and perception of Daugavpils – counters 'backward' title.
3. Individual and businesses within Daugavpils can be involved in setting up the site and will be proud of the result.

## 7 Concerns

1. Cost.
   Developing the site will be costly because it will involve external assistance and support.
2. Resources.
   Will require individuals to co-ordinate the project and manage the inputs and outputs.
3. Value chain links.
   Ideally an online shop and booking facilities would be on the site. Thus would involve complex integration with other businesses (some of which would not have Internet sites).

---

### Senior Examiner's Comments

This is a well reasoned answer taking into account all aspects of Internet promotion. It is also good that the candidate has used one of the models for Internet development. The answer could have been better developed by concentrating more on aspects of internationalization through the encouragement of business links. The city has good twinning arrangements. These portals could be used for better dissemination of Daugavpils' unique offering as a business centre with low wages and a skilled labour force.

---

## Second Student Answer – Question 1.

**Report**

| | |
|---|---|
| **To:** | **Uya Podekins** |
| **From:** | **Marketing Consultant** |
| **Date:** | **7th December 2001** |
| **Re:** | **Daugavpils** |

1. The current situation and outline marketing strategy
2. Key issues in creating a distinctive brand
3. Use of the Internet to attract investment and tourism

### Content:

a. Introduction
b. Current Situation and Strategic Marketing Plan
c. Distinctive Brand
d. Use of Internet
e. Conclusions

### A  Introduction

This report highlights the findings of my recent investigations. The recommendations are based on what I believe is the most appropriate course of action. I would be happy to provide any further detail upon request, as this report is a summary of the detailed work.

### B1  Current Situation – Internal

#### B1.1.1  Strengths

- Mayor – a skilled businessman, good for PR.
- Business-related facilities available.

- Skilled and cheap workforce.
- Transport hub.
- Many and varied tourist attractions.
- Sporting assets.
- Existing international relationships.
- Ethnic diversity.
- Forthcoming visit by Prince Charles.

### B1.1.2 Weaknesses
- Marketing – a lack of a co-ordinated approach.
- Infrastructure – needs improving.
- Perception – a poor brand image.
- Declining population and poor health provision.
- Inheritance – the Soviet Way.
- Ethnic make-up and language barriers.

### B1.1.3 Opportunities
- Political
  Joining the EU.
  Support from World Bank/EU.
- Economic
  Joining the EU.
  Western business investment.
  Projected growth in world economy from end 2002 despite current slowdown.
  LRDA, DDEC movements.
  Recognition of value of area by western economies.
- Social
  Moving to an open capitalist economy.
  Western knowledge (expatriates)
  Health and sport.
- Technological
  Enables global coverage.
  Globalization of markets.

### B1.1.4 Threats
- Political
  Co-ordination very difficult.
  Unstable system.
  Language laws restrictive.
  Riga perception.
- Economic
  World recession/low growth.
  Most of resources in Riga.
  Dependent on Russian oil.
  Inflation pressures.
- Social
  Soviet influence.
  Russian speaking – cultural pressures.
  Latvian culture.
  Citizenship rule.

- Technological
  Reduced barriers to entry.
- Competition
  Relative attractiveness.
  Other Eastern bloc cities provide alternative investment options.

## B1.2 Current Situation – External

### B1.2.1 Political
- Unstable political environment and frequent local elections makes consistency difficult.
- Soviet inheritance – military management approach.
- Limited voting rights.
- Preparing for EU entry.
- Many diverse parties.
- Language laws – have cultural implications, especially for Daugavpils (58% Russian).

### B1.2.2 Economic
- Government – preparing for EU membership, new market.
- Latvia – steady GDP growth, steady economic environment.
- Inflationary pressures likely to increase with growth.
- World Bank/EU are potential sources of investment income.

### B1.2.3 Social
- Government policies are restrictive for culturally diverse Daugavpils.
- Soviet management approach is what people are used to – not Western.
- Russian speaking dominates Daugavpils.
- Good education levels (98% literacy).

### B1.2.4 Technological
- WWW/IT/Telecoms advances – increasingly open up markets and gives access to more consumers.
- Productivity advances.
- Increasing media opportunities.

## B1.3 Current Situation – Competitors

A detailed audit of competitors is recommended. The following competitors and sources of competition have been identified:

Competitors:

1. Riga.
2. Other Latvian cities.
3. Other Eastern bloc locations.
4. Other worldwide cities.

Reasons for competitiveness:

1. Alternative location for business production and manufacturing.
2. Alternative tourist destinations.
3. Better brand/image awareness.

Daugavpils has to outperform these competitive forces in chosen markets.

## B1.4 Conclusion of Current Situation and Key Issues

Daugavpils has a number of products to offer potential tourists and business investors. These are strengths, which can be exploited – especially as the world is becoming a smaller place and the globalization of markets brings opportunities (Levitt).

However, a number of key issues need to be addressed over the next 3 years, and are addressed in the proposed Strategic Marketing Plan.

**Key Issues:**

1. Marketing Strategy
   *Needs to be formulated and adopted.*
2. Branding and Promotional Strategy
   *Positive image is crucial for success.*
3. Regeneration of area
   *Business and tourist investment, maximizing use of technology to drive.*
4. Improved infrastructure
   *To support objectives.*
5. Internal Management Strategy
   *A process of almost radical change is potentially about to commence. Internal support will be crucial.*

## B2 Marketing Strategy – Mission

I recommend that the following corporate mission be adopted:

"To be an attractive city in Eastern Europe for business and tourism, and to provide for the people of Daugavpils a good quality of life through local amenities, services and working opportunities".

This mission balances the economic regeneration priorities of the city with its social responsibilities.

## B3 Marketing Strategy – Corporate Objectives

The City Development Priorities are taken to be the corporate objectives for Daugavpils. In addition, I would recommend:

- To increase municipality revenue from 35m lats to 45.5m lats in 3 years.

## B4 Strategic Direction

Porter offers four strategic corporate directions. I would recommend that Daugavpils would benefit from a focused Differentiation Strategy.

This strategy is supported by:

- Excellent and unique cultural, historical, natural beauty and sporting assets which can be exploited.
- The availability of business resources, plant and personnel.
- The existence of current exploitable markets, but a brand that needs building.
- The variety of target markets to be reached.

Justification, as opposed to other strategic option is:

- Whilst Daugavpils has a cost leadership advantage, this will be difficult to sustain over the long term and doesn't support relationship building for long growth.
- Combining focus differentiation will enable Daugavpils to market all its strengths to a variety of chosen markets.

### B5 Marketing Strategy – Target Audiences and Positioning

Daugavpils will be operating in two distinct markets:

1. Business investment.
2. Tourism.

### B5.1 Business Investment

Bonona and Shapiro present a model for segmenting business markets. This applied to Daugavpils would suggest the following characteristics make up the target market:

1. Industry – Companies in production, manufacturing or engineering.
2. Location – Companies who accept and are actively seeking international operations.
3. Company – Probably small to medium size enterprises.
4. Situation – Companies in countries which Daugavpils already has a relationship plus the UK, due to the forthcoming visit by Prince Charles which will raise awareness.

### B5.2 Tourism

I would recommend a geographic and behavioural segmentation approach.

**Geographic**

- Target domestic tourists through brand improvement
- Target countries with tourists already visiting

**Behavioural**

- Target tourists where demand for services equates with Daugavpils' product portfolio e.g. sports.

### B5.3 Positioning

Daugavpils should be positioned as a dynamic city, with opportunities for all who wish to visit/ invest.

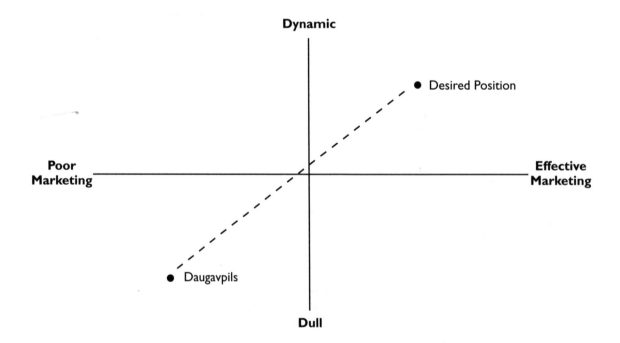

*(Source: Ranchhod)*

## B6 Marketing Strategies and Objectives

Using Ansoff's growth matrix I would recommend a market penetration approach in both business and tourism (see next diagram).

Daugavpils has already established itself with some international markets and business and some tourist markets, it also has a portfolio of products to sell.

|  | Current Product | New Product |
|---|---|---|
| Current Market | Business investment<br>Tourism<br>Brand image improvement | |
| New Market | | |

Market penetration is the lowest cost and least money returned, which suits the current internal and external circumstances.

**Marketing Objectives**

1.  To increase the number of businesses (international) from 4 to 12 in the next 3 years.
2.  To increase the number of local enterprises from 2000 to 2200 in the next 3 years.
3.  To increase the number of international and domestic tourists from 15,960 in 2000 to 19,276 in 3 years.
4.  To improve the brand image of Daugavpils such that 75% of the population want to live here in 3 years.

## B7 Marketing Strategy – Detailed Marketing Plan

| Category | Business | Tourism |
|---|---|---|
| Product | Business Park; Factories; Road/Rail infrastructure; Skilled/cheap labour; Location – transport hub. | Sports; History; Culture; Beauty; Health (all sites and facilities in each category). |
| Place | Which countries:<br>1. Twinned Countries<br>2. UK<br>3. Consulate relationships<br>Through government trade departments, use Internet, Foreign Office, Chambers of Commerce. Use expertise of Nigel Seymour-Dale. | Which countries:<br>1. Domestic<br>2. International and UK<br>Through: Tourist information centres, international tour operators. Specialist media, Internet. |
| Price | Low to medium cost. | Low to medium cost but expensive for Daugavpils. |
| Promotion | **BRAND**<br>Re-brand to Dinaburg – ... success of football team. Internal and External programme. (See section C for more detail).<br>**INTERNAL**<br>Encourage marketing orientation, Newsletters quarterly. Briefings and Training. | |

| Category | Business | Tourism |
|---|---|---|
| Promotion | **External**<br>• Internet (see section D for further details)<br>• Prospect packs<br>• PR – national and internal – Prince Charles's visit<br>• Leaflets<br>• Posters<br>• Direct marketing to prospective companies<br>• New logo | **External**<br>• Internet (see section D for further details)<br>• Prospect packs<br>• Posters<br>• Leaflets<br>• Specialist media<br>• New logo<br>• Tourism – Tour operator visits |
| People | Structure – Marketing Orientation:<br>Recruit Marketing Managers to oversee implementation of plan.<br>Recruit expatriates for training and expertise. | |
| Physical Evidence | Brand, logo, re-positioning products and attributes. | |
| Process | To be agreed in new structure. | |

## B8 Financial Projections

| Income | 2002 | 2003 | 2004 |
|---|---|---|---|
| | **44m lats** | **51.9m lats** | **45.5m lats** |
| **From:** | | | |
| Income Tax | 19m | 21m | 23.7m |
| Support | 15m | 20m | 10m |
| Other – (Car Tax, Property Tax, etc.) | 10m | 10.9m | 11.8m |

Please note, these income projections to be confirmed in the municipality.

Costs, provided below are for marketing promotional costs alone. The percentages show the percentage of income recommended for marketing.

| Item | 2002 | 2003 | 2004 |
|---|---|---|---|
| Daugavpils people Marketing Activity | 60k | 54k | 54k |
| Riga/Latvia – brand building (press) | 100k | 200k | 200k |
| International Business | 110k | 300k | 420k |
| International Tourism | | 395k | 365k |
| Specialist Tourism | | 35k | 35k |
| Other (contingency) | 20k | 40k | 40k |
| | 290k | 1,024k | 1,114k |
| | (0.65%) | (1.97%) | (2.44%) |

## B9   Marketing Strategy – Implementation and Control

Monthly meetings between Mayor and Head of Business and Marketing should be used to evaluate:

1. Performance against target on project plans.
2. Budget spend, actual against planned.
3. Sales against marketing objectives.
4. Image against objectives.
5. Tactical campaign success.
6. Market research feedback, key environmental changes that may require a response.
7. Annual Review (at least) of Strategic Marketing Plan. More frequent if key environmental changes occur.

---

### Senior Examiner's Comments

This not a bad answer and it has all the main elements required for a strategic plan. However, there are many generalities and the good ideas as shown in the Ansoff matrix are not developed further. For instance a more detailed analysis of the data would have shown that there is plenty of scope for developing a varied range of products/services within the city. The first year marketing budget is reasonable, but is a trifle optimistic. Overall an answer which could have been considerably improved by better analysis of the case.

---

## C   The Key Issues Involved in Creating a Distinctive Brand Image for Daugavpils

### C1

One of the key foundations to the success of this plan is the reversal of the brand image. At the moment 75% of the population would rather live somewhere else and clearly Latvia's perception of Daugavpils (especially Riga's) is very negative.

Bringing about a change to a brand image is not an easy task. To illustrate why and to show the key issues involved, I would like to refer to Dowling's model of how the image is created.

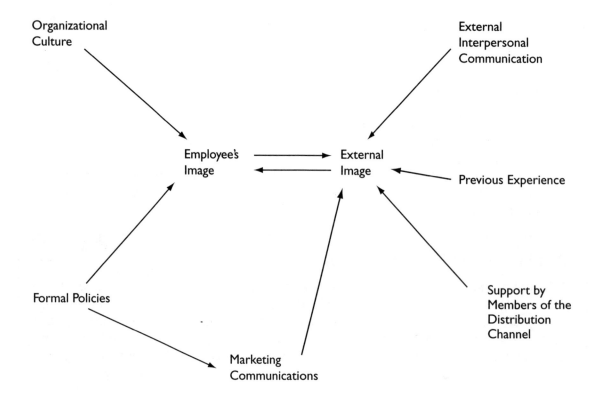

## C2 Uncontrollable Factors

The first key issue to note is that the brand image is not something which Daugavpils has 100% control over. External factors of previous experiences and other external interpersonal communication will still have a part to play.

However, this does not mean that the creation of a distinctive brand is a completely formidable task. Marketing Communications are the controllable messages that an organization portrays about itself. The key issues in this area are which messages to distribute and through which media. The following messages are proposed.

## C3 Key Messages

**Brand Name** – The name Daugavpils is derived from history and of Latvian origin. However, it has poor brand awareness outside Latvia and a poor perception inside Latvia. I would recommend changing the brand name to Dinaburg. Not only would this mean a step change in policy and mean a new era for a new brand, it would also maximize the exposure of the brand internationally through the football team.

**Brand Logo** – I would also recommend developing a brand logo, which is used consistently through all external communications. It could also replace the current inconsistent images, which appear at the various entrances to the city.

Advertising and Public Relations activity should always support the brand logo and image. However, these two attributes alone don't make up a brand. **Brand personality** is the values, beliefs and characteristics the city wants to stand for. Mayor Eigims has already identified that Latgalians have their own distinct features of "purposiveness, energy and a capacity for work". These can combine to be the descriptors of the brand personality. I would recommend adding to it "Opportunity", as I believe this is one of the key features of Daugavpils today.

With the radical changes proposed come additional issues associated with Dowling's **'Organizational Culture'.** The brand is also much about the culture of the organization, how it works. The level of innovation and manoeuvring centric features within the organization; it is this area which probably poses the greatest risk and concern for Daugavpils. The current culture stems back to the Soviet way, there is little in the way of a marketing orientation (yet) and little innovation. The step change in culture will require investment in internal communications and will need to be championed by the Mayor and the Business and Marketing department.

An **internal marketing** plan is recommended for supporting this cultural change. Its components to include:

- Briefings – from Mayor and Head of Business and Marketing sharing strategic direction, rationale and successes.
- Quarterly newsletters – sharing performance and good news stories.
- Training – a programme of training in marketing values theories and implementation. Where possible, the use of expatriates with experience to share.

### C4 The International Dimension

As well as the generic issues facing Daugavpils when creating a distinctive brand image, there is the added difficulty of international differences.

Daugavpils currently operates its brand in a number of international markets whose language, culture, values and beliefs all differ.

The question is over standardization or adaptation of the brand across international waters. In the case of a city, which is marketing its services internationally, the brand name is likely to be standardized although translations may occur. Other forms of adaptation to literature, advertising etc. will need to be included; this will increase the cost but go towards the success of the campaigns.

This will be particularly true of the Internet site, which is becoming an increasingly popular channel for international marketing – this is dealt with in more detail in section D.

### C5 Distinctive Brand – Conclusions

Creating a distinctive brand is not easy and it includes many dimensions, but it forms the important foundations of a strategic marketing plan. Buzzell showed that in the USA, branded companies frequently out-performed unbranded companies in good and bad times and a good brand gives consumer confidence which aids the buying decision process. A good brand is worth investing in, and two final practical considerations need to be considered:

1. Timing – Creating a strong brand, visually and internally takes time it will be a long process.
2. Longevity – It will need constant investment to ensure it remains a good brand for consumers.

---

### Senior Examiner's Comments

This answer has been well fashioned by the use of a model to underpin the discussion. This model is then used to tease out the many factors pertaining to communications. It is interesting that the candidate has not taken into account the disparate images portrayed on the different city entrances. The internal marketing aspects are covered well. Nonetheless the answer would have benefited from understanding and enhancing the role of PR in general. Overall, this is an interesting and useful answer.

---

# Question 3

## D How could the Internet be Used to Attract International Investment and Tourism to the Region

### D1 Background

The Internet has been acknowledged as the fastest growing medium of all time – figures from the British Department of Trade and Industry suggest that 75,000 new pages are added each minute. The World Tourism Organization has also recognized the increasing importance of this medium to the marketing of cities.

In this section I will be showing how the Internet can help Daugavpils achieve its corporate and marketing objectives as laid out in section B of this plan.

I will make use of Kotler's model of marketing distinction (see below) as a framework for my proposals.

Kotler's Model

- Awareness
- Interest
- Evaluation
- Trial
- Adaptation

### D2 Awareness and Interest

In attracting international business and tourism, Daugavpils (Dinaburg) needs to ensure potential investors and visitors are aware of the city and what it has to offer. Over the Internet this can be achieved in the following ways:

1. Links from other relevant Internet sites
   Strategic partners such as government trade operations, international tour operators etc. should be encouraged to provide a link with the Daugavpils web site. Also, look to identify specialist sites, which have links to the facilities Daugavpils offers, e.g. ice hockey, fishing, football.
2. Banner Advertisements
   These might be considered on relevant sites. e.g. specialist or tour operators.
3. Off-line support
   All off-line media advertising can generate by encouraging visits to the Daugavpils web site.

### D3 Evaluation

The content of the web site should be sufficient to enable a business investor and/or tourist to evaluated the suitability of Daugavpils for their purpose.

Examples of relevant content would include:

- Business
  Map, transport links, currency, trade services, import and export regulations, tax support etc.
- Tourism
  Map, facilities, amenities, cost, pictures, climate, transport regularity.

Of critical importance here will be three factors, language, speed of navigation and relevance.

The Internet site will have to accommodate a variety of relevant languages. The structure of the site should be carefully considered and aimed at enabling the user to quickly access relevant information, which should always be up to date.

## D4  Trial and Adoption

Whilst it is difficult to try this sort of offering before adoption, virtual tours are now available via the Internet and could be usefully adopted here – especially for the tourism market.

Adoption is about ensuring that either online purchasing or off-line contacts for purchasing are available.

## D5  Detailed Internet Marketing Plan

### D5.1  The Role the Internet Will Play In The Overall Strategy Plan

The Internet can play a supportive but critical role in the achievement of the Strategic Marketing objectives. I would recommend it be structured with two major parts to the site – business and tourism.

The business section is largely supportive via information provision. Most businesses will want personal relationship in deciding to purchase.

The tourism section can play a role of awareness and 'order winner'.

Both sites should maximize the profile of key events such as the forthcoming visit by Prince Charles.

### D5.2  Proposed Objectives for the Internet

Supporting its role in the plan, the following objectives are proposed:

- To generate relationships with target international business markets.
- To drive 10% of tourism demand on-line by 2003.

### D5.3 Issues and limitations – Items

D5.3.1  Building an Appropriate Site   This takes time. I would recommend the use of an Internet agency, preferably with international experience.

The current web site does not provide the necessary functionality for it to play a role in the achievement of marketing objectives.

Allow six months for development of a core site, but another year to eighteen months for full functionality.

D5.3.2  Cost
- As well as set-up costs there will be ongoing maintenance costs.
- The proposed marketing communications budget in section B incorporated internal development.

D5.3.3  Human Resource   Two types of human resource will be required:
1. Agency development and technical assistance.
2. In-house resource, to maintain and update the site and field any queries. The impact on resource requirements should be considered and will require approval for the successful implementation of any Internet strategy.

## D6  Conclusion

With the right approach, resource and commitment the Internet will become a pivotal part of Daugavpils' strategy and I would predict it could become a major delivery channel, especially for tourism in a very quick time.

## E  Overall Conclusions

I would like to thank Mayor Eigims and Uya Podekins for their help and support in providing information to pull together this plan and its recommendations.

I hope that the recommendations are useful in your plans for the forthcoming year or so, and would be happy to provide any additional information or support if required.

### Senior Examiner's Comments

This is a well developed answer which links back to the previous answers and actually considers the practical aspects of developing an international marketing strategy via the Internet. The answer, however, concentrates only on the tourism potential rather than the business potential. The candidate could have explored the international business dimension more, especially in the light of the twinning arrangements.

## Summary

The specimen answers again show the range of answers that are possible. This time I have tried to show a very good answer and another that is good, but lacking in some areas. This particular case elicited a wide range of interesting answers and the pass rate was good. It is again, important to reiterate the need to be coherent, think strategically, utilize the detail given with justification for given choices of strategy.

## Additional Information

The new Mayor Richard Eigims has recently been on visits to major cities in Europe. He has been on a fact-finding mission to help to improve the city's image in Europe and in Latvia. As part of this exercise, the case study writer was invited onto a prime time television broadcast in the country. Also working with the Mayor's office is Nigel Seymour-Dale, an experienced Consultant with the Voluntary Service Organization of the United Kingdom. Nigel has worked with many multinationals in the past. He is currently helping the council with an impending visit from His Royal Highness the Prince of Wales from the UK. This visit is of vital importance to the city in its quest for greater international recognition. The United Kingdom Embassy in Latvia is arranging this visit from Prince Charles.

## *Examination Questions*

As a Marketing Consultant appointed by the Mayor of Daugavpils you have been asked to address the following:

### Question 1.

Assess the current situation in Daugavpils and outline a marketing strategy for three years.

**(40 marks)**

### Question 2.

Critically analyse the key issues involved in creating a distinctive brand image for Daugavpils. (*Note: This question does not ask for a marketing communications plan*).

**(30 marks)**

### Question 3.

Discuss how the Internet could be used as part of a strategy to attract international investment and tourism to the region of Daugavpils.

**(30 marks)**
**(100 marks in total)**

## Syllabus

This Analysis and Decision paper tests a potential candidate's ability to demonstrate knowledge from different areas of marketing in order to develop appropriate strategies, plans and innovative solutions for organizations. Many of the cases presented will draw from all areas of marketing from the CIM syllabi up to and including Diploma level. As each case is different, candidates should possess the capability to draw upon some of the key topic areas from across the CIM syllabus that will need to be refreshed in order to tackle case studies effectively. There will be a heavier emphasis on the syllabi for Integrated Marketing Communications, Planning and Control and International Marketing Strategy.

Strategic thinking ability, coherence of argument, absorption of detail and clear justification of any solutions offered will be measured outcomes of the effective understanding of the case studies.

Objectives of the Analysis and Decision module are outlined below and students will be expected:

### Aims and objectives

- To utilize the practical and marketing skills which are pre-requisites for analysis of the case and engage students in justifying their strategic recommendations.
- To analyse the case within given constraints and understand possible barriers to implementation.
- To apply the marketing processes within a wide variety of market sectors.
- Develop the ability to cross reference knowledge from other Diploma subjects.
- To develop creative and innovative applications of knowledge of strategic marketing.
- To be able to apply relevant marketing planning models and display critical analytical and decision making skills within the case study examination.
- Comprehend and resolve a wide variety of marketing problems and provide realistic and innovative solutions.

### Learning outcomes

Students will be able to:

- Demonstrate an in-depth understanding of the strategic marketing planning process and to develop a creative and innovative strategic marketing plan.
- Critically evaluate case studies using a wide variety of marketing techniques, concepts and models and an understanding of contemporary markcting issues.
- Understand and apply competitive positioning strategies within a given case study.
- Critically evaluate various options available within given constraints and justify any decisions taken.
- Demonstrate the ability to analyse numerical data and management information and utilize it to make decisions about key underlying issues within the Case Study.
- Synthesise various strands of knowledge from the different Diploma subjects effectively in the context of the Case Study examination.
- Apply both practical and academic marketing knowledge within a given Case Study.
- Comprehend and resolve a wide variety of marketing problems.
- Develop appropriate control aspects and contingency plans.

# Reading list

## Core texts

Doyle, P. (2001) *Marketing Management and Strategy*. 3rd revised edition. Harlow, FT/Prentice-Hall.

Fifield, P. (1998) *Marketing Strategy*. Oxford, CIM/Butterworth-Heinemann.

Hooley, G., Saunders, J. and Pierce, N. (1998) *Marketing Strategy and Competitive Positioning*. 2nd revised edition. Hemel Hempstead, Prentice-Hall.

## Syllabus guides

CIM (2002) *CIM Companion: Analysis and Decision*. Cookham, Chartered Institute of Marketing.

BPP (2002) *Strategic Marketing Management: Analysis and Decision*. London, BPP Publishing.

Ranchhod, A. (2002) *Strategic Marketing Management: Analysis and Decision Coursebook*. Oxford, Butterworth-Heinemann.

## Supplementary reading

Chaffey, D., Mayer, R., Johnston, K. and Ellis-Chadwick, F. (2000) *Internet Marketing*. London, Pitman.

Chaffey, D. and Smith, P. (2002) *E-marketing Excellence*. Oxford, Butterworth-Heinemann.

Chaston, I. (2000) *E-marketing Strategy*. Maidenhead, McGraw-Hill.

Doyle, P. and Bridgewater, S. (1998) *Innovation in Marketing*. Oxford, CIM/Butterworth-Heinemann.

Doyle, P. (2000) *Value-based Marketing: Marketing Strategies for Corporate Growth and Shareholder Value*. Chichester, John Wiley.

Kunde, J. and Cunningham, B. J. (2002) *Corporate Religion*. 2nd edition. Harlow, FT/Prentice-Hall.

Langford, D. (2000) *Internet Ethics*. London, Palgrave.

McDonald, M. and Rogers, B. (1998) *Key Account Management*. Oxford, Butterworth-Heinemann.

McDonald, M. and Wilson, H. (1999*)* *Improving Marketing Effectiveness in a Digital World*. London, Pitman.

Piercy, N. (2002) *Market-led Strategic Change*. 3rd edition. Oxford, CIM/Butterworth-Heinemann.

Quinn, J. *et al.* (1998) *Innovation Explosion*. US, Free Press.

Ranchhod, A., Tinson, J. and Gauzente C. (2002) *21$^{st}$ Century Marketing Strategies*. Harlow, Pearson. (Publication Autumn 2002)

Wilson, R. and Gilligan, C. (1997) *Strategic Marketing Management: Planning, Implementation and Control*. 2nd revised edition. Oxford, CIM/Butterworth-Heinemann.